9/02

FIFTY MODERN THINKERS ON EDUCATION

Fifty Modern Thinkers on Education looks at fifty of the most significant contributors of modern times to the debate on education. Among those included are:

- Pierre Bourdieu
- Elliot Eisner
- Hans J. Eysenck
- Michel Foucault
- Henry Giroux

- Jürgen Habermas
- Susan Isaacs
- A.S. Neill
- Jean Piaget
- Simone Weil

Together with *Fifty Major Thinkers on Education* this books provides a unique history of educational thinking. Each essay gives key biographical information, an outline of the individual's principal achievements and activities, an assessment of their impact and influence, a list of their major writings and suggested further reading.

Joy A. Palmer is Professor of Education and Pro-Vice-Chancellor at the University of Durham, England. She is Vice-President of the National Association for Environmental Education and a member of the IUCN Commission on Education and Communication.

Advisory Editors: **Liora Bresler** is Professor of Curriculum and Instruction at the University of Illinois, Urbana-Champaign. **David E. Cooper** is Professor of Philosophy at the University of Durham.

D0167409

ROUTLEDGE KEY GUIDES

Routledge Key Guides are accessible, informative and lucid handbooks, which define and discuss the central concepts, thinkers and debates in a broad range of academic disciplines. All are written by noted experts in their respective subjects. Clear, concise exposition of complex and stimulating issues and ideas make *Routledge Key Guides* the ultimate reference resources for students, teachers, researchers and the interested lay person.

Ancient History: Key Themes and Approaches
Neville Morley

Cinema Studies: The Key Concepts (second edition)
Susan Hayward

Eastern Philosophy: Key Readings
Oliver Leaman

Fifty Eastern Thinkers
Diané Collinson, Kathryn Plant and Robert Wilkinson

Fifty Contemporary Choreographers
Edited by Martha Bremser

Fifty Key Contemporary Thinkers
John Lechte

Fifty Key Jewish Thinkers
Dan Cohn-Sherbok

Fifty Key Thinkers on the Environment
Edited by Joy Palmer with Peter Blaze Corcoran and David E. Cooper

Fifty Key Thinkers on History
Marnie Hughes-Warrington

Fifty Key Thinkers in International Relations
Martin Griffiths

Fifty Major Economists
Steven Pressman

Fifty Major Philosophers
Diané Collinson

Fifty Major Thinkers on Education
Joy A. Palmer

Key Concepts in Communication and Cultural Studies (second edition)
Tim O'Sullivan, John Hartley, Danny Saunders, Martin Montgomery and John Fiske

Key Concepts in Cultural Theory
Andrew Edgar and Peter Sedgwick

Key Concepts in Eastern Philosophy
Oliver Leaman

Key Concepts in Language and Linguistics
R.L. Trask

Key Concepts in the Philosophy of Education
John Gingell and Christopher Winch

Key Concepts in Popular Music
Roy Shuker

Post-Colonial Studies: The Key Concepts
Bill Ashcroft, Gareth Griffiths and Helen Tiffin

Social and Cultural Anthropology: The Key Concepts
Nigel Rapport and Joanna Overing

FIFTY MODERN THINKERS ON EDUCATION

From Piaget to the Present

Edited by Joy A. Palmer
Advisory Editors: Liora Bresler and David E. Cooper

London and New York

First published 2001
by Routledge
11 New Fetter Lane, London EC4P 4EE

Simultaneously published in the USA and Canada
by Routledge
29 West 35th Street, New York, NY 10001

Routledge is an imprint of the Taylor & Francis Group

Typeset in Times by Taylor & Francis Books Ltd
Printed and bound in Great Britain by TJ International Ltd, Padstow, Cornwall

British Library Cataloguing in Publication Data
A catalogue record for this book is available from the British Library

Library of Congress Cataloging in Publication Data
Fifty modern thinkers on education : from Piaget to the present day / edited by
Joy A. Palmer ; advisory editors, Liora Bresler and David E. Cooper.
p. cm. – (Routledge key guides)
Includes bibliographical references.
1. Education–History–20th century. I. Palmer, Joy. II. Bresler, Liora. III. Cooper,
David Edward. IV. Series.
LB17 .F57 2001
370′.92′2–dc21
[B]2001019308

ISBN 0–415–22408–X (hbk)
ISBN 0–415–22409–8 (pbk)

CHRONOLOGICAL LIST OF CONTENTS

Alphabetical list of contents	viii
Notes on contributors	x
Preface	xiv
A.S. Neill, 1883–1973 *Peter Hobson*	1
Susan Isaacs, 1885–1948 *Robert Hinshelwood*	6
Harold Rugg, 1886–1960 *Stephen J. Thornton*	10
Ludwig Wittgenstein, 1889–1951 *Nicholas C. Burbules and Michael Peters*	15
Martin Heidegger, 1889–1976 *Michael Bonnett*	23
Herbert Edward Read, 1893–1968 *Stephen Mark Dobbs*	28
Lev Semyonovich Vygotsky, 1896–1934 *Alexander Ardichvili*	33
Jean Piaget, 1896–1980 *Leslie Smith*	37
Michael Oakeshott, 1901–92 *Anthony O'Hear*	44
Carl Rogers, 1902–87 *Eleanor Feinberg and Walter Feinberg*	49
Ralph Winifred Tyler, 1902–94 *Elliot W. Eisner*	54
Burrhus Frederic Skinner, 1904–90 *Torsten Husén*	58

Harry Broudy, 1905–98   64
Liora Bresler

Simone Weil, 1909–43   69
Richard Smith

Joseph J. Schwab, 1910–88   73
Ian Westbury and Margery D. Osborne

Clark Kerr, 1911–   79
Debra D. Bragg and Frankie S. Laanan

Benjamin S. Bloom, 1913–99   86
Torsten Husén

Jerome S. Bruner, 1915–   90
Howard Gardner

Torsten Husén, 1916–   96
T. Neville Postlethwaite

Lee J. Cronbach, 1916–   102
Torsten Husén

Donald Thomas Campbell, 1916–96   105
Carol Taylor Fitz-Gibbon

Maxine Greene, 1917–   112
Christine Thompson

R.S. Peters, 1919–   118
John White

John I. Goodlad, 1920–   122
Jianping Shen

Paulo Freire, 1921–97   128
Michael W. Apple, Luís Armando Gandin and Álvaro Moreira Hypolito

Seymour B. Sarason, 1919–   133
Andrew Hargreaves

Israel Scheffler, 1923–   142
Harvey Siegel

Jean-François Lyotard, 1924–98   148
Michalinos Zembylas

Lawrence A. Cremin, 1925–90   154
James D. Anderson

Basil Bernstein F., 1925–2000   161
Ivor F. Goodson

Michel Foucault, 1926–84   170
Michael Peters

Margaret Donaldson, 1926–   175
Martin Hughes

Ivan Illich, 1926–   181
David A. Gabbard and Dana L. Stuchul

Lawrence Kohlberg, 1927–87   188
K. Peter Kuchinke

Paul H. Hirst, 1927–   193
Terence H. McLaughlin

Philip Wesley Jackson, 1928–   199
Elliot W. Eisner

Jane Roland Martin, 1929–   203
Susan Laird

Nel Noddings, 1929–   210
David J. Flinders

Jürgen Habermas, 1929–   215
Keith Morrison

Carl Bereiter, 1930–   224
David R. Olson

Pierre Bourdieu, 1930–   229
Ingólfur Ásgeir Jóhannesson and Thomas S. Popkewitz

Neil Postman, 1931–   234
Dan Inbar

Theodore R. Sizer, 1932–   241
Tamar Levin

Elliot Eisner, 1933–   247
P. Bruce Uhrmacher

John White, 1934–   252
Eamonn Callan

Lee S. Shulman, 1938–   257
Pam Grossman and Sam Wineburg

Michael W. Apple, 1942–   263
Carlos Antonio Torre

Howard Gardner, 1943–   272
Mindy L. Kornhaber

Henry Giroux, 1943–   280
Keith Morrison

Linda Darling-Hammond, 1951–   285
Ann Lieberman

ALPHABETICAL LIST
OF CONTENTS

Michael W. Apple, 1942–	263
Carl Bereiter, 1930–	224
Basil Bernstein, 1925–2000	161
Benjamin S. Bloom, 1913–99	86
Pierre Bourdieu, 1930–	229
Harry Broudy, 1905–98	64
Jerome S. Bruner, 1915–	90
Donald Thomas Campbell, 1916–96	105
Lawrence A. Cremin, 1925–90	154
Lee J. Cronbach, 1916–	102
Linda Darling-Hammond, 1951–	285
Margaret Donaldson, 1926–	175
Elliot Eisner, 1933–	247
Michel Foucault, 1926–84	170
Paulo Freire, 1921–97	128
Howard Gardner, 1943–	272
Henry Giroux, 1943–	280
John I. Goodlad, 1920–	122
Maxine Greene, 1917–	112
Jürgen Habermas, 1929–	215
Martin Heidegger, 1889–1976	23
Paul H. Hirst, 1927–	193
Torsten Husén, 1916–	96
Ivan Illich, 1926–	181
Susan Isaacs, 1885–1948	6
Philip Wesley Jackson, 1928–	199
Clark Kerr, 1911–	79
Lawrence Kohlberg, 1927–87	188
Jean-François Lyotard, 1924–98	148
Jane Roland Martin, 1929–	203
A.S. Neill, 1883–1973	1
Nel Noddings, 1929–	210
Michael Oakeshott, 1901–92	44
R.S. Peters, 1919–	118
Jean Piaget, 1896–1980	37
Neil Postman, 1931–	234
Herbert Edward Read, 1893–1968	28
Carl Rogers, 1902–87	49
Harold Rugg, 1886–1960	10
Seymour B. Sarason, 1919–	133
Israel Scheffler, 1923–	142
Joseph J. Schwab, 1910–88	73
Lee S. Shulman, 1938–	257
Theodore R. Sizer, 1932–	241

Burrhus Frederic Skinner, 1904–90	58
Ralph Winifred Tyler, 1902–94	54
Lev Semyonovich Vygotsky, 1896–1934	33
Simone Weil, 1909–43	69
John White, 1934–	252
Ludwig Wittgenstein, 1889–1951	15

CONTRIBUTORS

Anderson, James D. is Professor and Head of the Department of Educational Policy Studies, College of Education, University of Illinois at Urbana-Champaign, USA.

Apple, Michael W. is John Bascom Professor of Curriculum and Instruction and Educational Policy Studies, University of Wisconsin-Madison, USA.

Ardichvili, Alexander is Assistant Professor in the Department of Human Resource Education, the College of Education, University of Illinois at Urbana-Champaign, USA.

Bonnett, Michael is Senior Lecturer in Education at Homerton College, Cambridge, England.

Bragg, Debra D. is Associate Professor at the College of Education, University of Illinois at Urbana-Champaign, USA.

Bresler, Liora is Professor of Curriculum and Instruction, University of Illinois at Urbana-Champaign, Illinois, USA.

Burbules, Nicholas C. is Professor in the Department of Educational Policy Studies, University of Illinois at Urbana-Champaign, USA.

Callan, Eamonn is Professor of Education at Stanford University, California, USA.

Cooper, David E. is Professor of Philosophy at the University of Durham, England.

Dobbs, Stephen Mark is Executive Vice-President of the Bernard Osher Foundation and Adjunct Professor of Humanities at San Francisco State University, California, USA.

Eisner, Elliot W. is Lee Jacks Professor of Education and Professor of Art, Stanford University, California, USA.

Feinberg, Eleanor is a registered psychologist in private practice, with special interest in Self Psychology, based in Illinois, USA.

Feinberg, Walter is Professor of Education Policy Studies at the College of Education, University of Illinois at Urbana-Champaign, USA.

Fitz-Gibbon, Carol Taylor is Professor of Education and Director of the Curriculum, Evaluation and Management Centre at the University of Durham, England.

Flinders, David J. is Associate Professor in The School of Education, Indiana University, Bloomington, IN, USA.

Gabbard, David A. is Associate Professor in the School of Education at East Carolina University, Greenville, North Carolina, USA.

Gandin, Luís Armando is Professor of Sociology of Education, Federal University of Rio Grande do Sul, Porto Alegre, Brazil.

Gardner, Howard is Professor in the Graduate School of Education, Harvard University, Cambridge, MA, USA.

Goodson, Ivor F. is Professor at the Centre for Applied Research in Education, University of East Anglia, Norwich, England.

Grossman, Pam is Professor of English at Stanford University, California, USA.

Hargreaves, Andrew is Co-Director and Professor at the International Centre for Educational Change, University of Toronto, Canada

Hobson, Peter is Associate Professor in the School of Education Studies, University of New England, Armidale, NSW, Australia.

Hinshelwood, Robert is a psychoanalyst in London and a part-time Professor in the Centre for Psychoanalytic Studies at the University of Essex, England.

Hughes, Martin is Professor in the Graduate School of Education, University of Bristol, England.

Husén, Torsten is Emeritus Professor in the Institute of International Education, Stockholm, Sweden.

Hypolito, Álvaro Moreira is Professor of Education, Federal University of Pelotas, Pelotas, Brazil.

Inbar, Dan is Professor in the School of Education at the Hebrew University of Jerusalem, Israel.

Jóhannesson, Ingólfur Ásgeir is Associate Professor of Education at the University of Akureyri, Iceland.

Kornhaber, Mindy L. is Assistant Professor at Pennsylvania State University, USA and a non-resident Fellow with the Civil Rights Project at Harvard University.

Kuchinke, K. Peter is Assistant Professor in Human Resource Education in the College of Education, University of Illinois at Urbana-Champaign, USA.

Laanan, Frankie S. is Assistant Professor at the College of Education, University of Illinois at Urbana-Champaign, USA.

Laird, Susan is Associate Professor in the Department of Educational Leadership and Policy Studies, University of Oklahoma, USA.

Levin, Tamar is Professor of Education at Tel Aviv University, Israel.

Lieberman, Ann is Senior Scholar at the Carnegie Foundation for the Advancement of Teaching and Visiting Professor at Stanford University, California, USA.

McLaughlin, Terence H. is University Senior Lecturer in Education and Fellow of St. Edmund's College, University of Cambridge, England.

Morrison, Keith is Professor of Education at the Inter-University Institute of Macau.

O'Hear, Anthony is Professor of Philosophy at the University of Bradford, England.

Olson, David R. is Professor and Head of the Centre for Applied Cognitive Science, cross-appointed to the Department of Linguistics and to University College at the University of Toronto, Ontario, Canada.

Osborne, Margery D. is Associate Professor in the Department of Curriculum and Instruction, College of Education, University of Illinois at Urbana-Champaign, USA.

Palmer, Joy A. is Professor of Education and Pro-Vice Chancellor of the University of Durham, England.

Peters, Michael is Professor of Education in the Faculty of Education, University of Glasgow, Scotland and in the School of Education, University of Auckland, New Zealand.

Popkewitz, Thomas S. is Professor in the Department of Curriculum and Instruction, University of Wisconsin, Madison, USA.

Postlethwaite, T. Neville is Emeritus Professor of Education at the University of Hamburg, Germany.

Shen, Jianping is Assistant Professor in the Department of Teaching, Learning and Leadership, College of Education, Western Michigan University, Kalamazoo, MI, USA.

Siegel, Harvey is Professor of Philosophy at the University of Miami, Coral Gables, Florida, USA.

Smith, Leslie is Professor of Psychology and Epistemology of Development, Department of Educational Research, Lancaster University, England.

Smith, Richard is Professor of Education at the University of Durham, England.

Stuchul, Dana L. is Assistant Professor in the Department of Education Studies, Berea College, Kentucky, USA.

Thompson, Christine is Associate Professor of Art Education at Pennsylvania State University, USA.

Thornton, Stephen J. is Associate Professor of Social Studies and Education at Teachers College, Columbia University, New York, USA.

Torre, Carlos Antonio is Professor of Education at the Southern Connecticut State University, and Fellow, Yale University, USA.

Uhrmacher, P. Bruce is Associate Professor of Education, College of Education, University of Denver, Colorado, USA.

Westbury, Ian is Professor, Department of Curriculum and Instruction, University of Illinois at Urbana-Champaign, USA.

White, John is Professor of Philosophy of Education at the Institute of Education, University of London, England.

Wineburg, Sam is Professor of Educational Psychology and Adjunct Professor, Department of History, University of Washington, Seattle, USA.

Zembylas, Michalinos is Assistant Professor of Science Education in the Department of Teacher Education, Michigan State University, USA.

PREFACE

The twin volumes *Fifty Major Thinkers on Education: From Confucius to Dewey* and *Fifty Modern Thinkers on Education: From Piaget to the Present*, are together intended to provide a valuable and fascinating resource for readers with an interest in 'influential lives' relating to critical thinking, action and, in more recent times, research, which has influenced policy and practice in the field of education. As a pair, the two volumes cover consideration of influences upon educational thought and practice from the very earliest times through to the present day. In the first volume we examine the lives and influence of fifty individuals from the time of Confucius to the era of Dewey. The second volume continues where the first ceases, examining the contribution of a further fifty individuals from the time of Piaget to the present.

Each volume and each essay within it follows a common format. An opening quotation sets the scene at the start of each essay. Then, readers are provided with an overview of the subject's work and basic biographical information. Each author then engages in critical reflection which aims to illuminate the influence, importance and perhaps innovative character of the subject's thinking and, where appropriate, research and actions. In other words, authors have moved beyond the purely descriptive and have provided a discussion of the nature of the intellectual or practical impact that the life, thinking and works of each figure made or is making upon our understanding or practice of education.

At the end of each essay, we have provided information that will lead interested readers into further and more detailed study. First, there are the references for the notes to which the numbers in the text refer; second, there is a cross-referencing with other subjects in the two books whose thought or influence relates in some obvious way to that of the subject of the essay; third, there is a list of the subject's major writings (where applicable); and finally, there is a list of references for those who wish to pursue more in-depth reading on the subject.

By far the hardest task in assembling these volumes was deciding on the final list of 100 thinkers on education to be included. How can one begin, in a field so extensive as education, to select 100 individuals from over 2000 years of thought? Inevitably, my advisory editors and I were inundated with suggestions and ideas for influential people who, for the obvious reason of lack of space, had to be left out. The 100 subjects finally decided upon include some very obvious 'great names' such as Plato, John Dewey and

Jean-Jacques Rousseau, alongside some less well-known, yet clearly influential, people. In making our choice we also aimed to provide coverage of a range of fields within the vast and complex arena of teaching and learning – philosophy, psychology, thinking on the early years, on testing, evaluation and so on. Most importantly, we emphasize that this pair of volumes is certainly not exhaustive. As already mentioned our choice of subjects proved to be extremely difficult. Furthermore, the combined work certainly does not pretend to be an overview of the lives of the 100 greatest educational thinkers the world has ever known. We believe that it includes some people who would fall into this category of those who have had arguably the greatest global influence on educational thought and practice, but most importantly, *all* the people in the books have made very substantial contributions to educational thinking in some form or another. It is hoped that some readers will derive great benefit and pleasure from the books because they introduce them to previously unknown lives. As a whole, I hope that the books will be of interest to all who would like to find out more about the lives of individuals past and present who have influenced thinking about knowledge and the education of the people of our world.

Joy A. Palmer

A.S. NEILL 1883–1973

> I believe that to impose anything by authority is wrong. The child
> should not do anything until he comes to the opinion – his own
> opinion – that it should be done.[1]

Alexander Sutherland Neill was born in the small Scottish town of Forfar, fifteen miles north of Dundee in 1883. His father, George Neill, was a schoolmaster who taught in the neighbouring village of Kingsmuir, where Neill received his own schooling. After leaving school at the age of fourteen and taking various jobs for two years, Neill became an apprentice schoolmaster in 1899. He remained an uncertified teacher for four years and was then successful in gaining matriculation to Edinburgh University. He studied Arts and although exhibiting little enthusiasm for university work graduated in 1905 with a major in English literature. He then taught for twelve years in Scottish government schools.

Neill enlisted in the British Army in 1917 and after the war his life began to take on a more positive direction. He first taught in a new experimental school (King Alfred School) and then in 1921 became assistant editor to Mrs Ensor, the founder of the New Education Fellowship. Although this association did not last long, Neill was by now confirmed in his commitment to a new type of education, very different from the traditional form in which he had been raised.

The chance to put his ideas into practice came in 1921 when he was invited to join the staff of a progressive school in Dresden, Germany. He remained there until 1923 when the school moved to an abandoned monastery near Vienna. However, difficulties arose with the local population, prompting Neill to return to England in 1924. He then opened his own school in Lyme Regis in conjunction with Frau Neustatter with whom he had worked in Germany and Austria, and whom he married in 1927. The school was named Summerhill after the name of the property.

There Neill began to implement systematically his revolutionary ideas of pupil freedom and lack of teacher authority. The school became well known and relatively successful although the enrolment in this period averaged only about forty. In 1927 it was moved to Leiston in Suffolk about 100 miles north of London, where it remains to this day as probably the best-known progressive school in the English-speaking world. On Neill's death in 1973 it was run by his second wife, Ena, until her retirement in 1985 and since then by their daughter, Zoe.

The widespread influence of Neill's Summerhill is attributable in no small measure to the twenty books Neill wrote between 1915 and 1972 in which he expounds clearly and forthrightly his educational ideas. The most influential of these (with sales of over two million), was *Summerhill*, a compilation of his writings, which was originally published in America in 1960 and then in England in 1962 with a Penguin paperback edition in 1968. In the very first chapter he states clearly his commitment to the freedom of the child: 'we set out to make a school in which we should allow children to be themselves. In order to do this we had to renounce all discipline, all direction, all suggestion, all moral training, all religious instruction.'[2] The child should never be forced to learn, indeed a cardinal principle of Summerhill is that attendance at lessons is voluntary whatever the age of the child. Only learning that is voluntarily undertaken has any value, said Neill, and children will know themselves when they are ready to learn.

Children will only achieve happiness if they are free because most unhappiness is due to inner hostility created in the child by external repression. Neill was influenced by Freudian theory here and believed that because this inner hostility cannot be effectively expressed towards parents or others in authority, it is turned inwards and becomes self-hate. This then becomes expressed in anti-social behaviour and in the worst cases leads to so-called 'problem children'. Many such children were sent to Summerhill and were cured, Neill maintains, by the application for the first time in their lives of freedom.

Happiness for Neill thus meant the state of having minimal repression. In positive terms it consists of 'an inner feeling of well-being, a sense of balance, a feeling of being contented with life. These can only exist when one feels free.'[3] Conventional education makes the mistake of exalting the intellect over the emotions with the result that children may know a lot of facts but lack inner contentment and fulfilment. Neill accordingly advocated 'Hearts not Heads in the Schools', the title of one of his books.[4] 'If the emotions are permitted to be really free, the intellect will look after itself,'[5] he maintained.

Traditional academic subjects were generally available at Summerhill but were not stressed. One area of this curriculum that was given more weight however was the aesthetic domain (arts, crafts, dancing, drama, etc.) which Neill saw as promoting creativity, imagination and emotional wellbeing. In particular these subjects have a therapeutic function for children with psychological problems and also give the less academically talented children the chance to excel at something.

Neill's strong belief in freedom was linked to another cherished conviction, the innate goodness of children. 'For over 40 years [says Neill] this belief in the goodness of the child has never wavered; it rather has become a final faith.'[6] He also believed that the 'child is innately wise and realistic. If left to himself without adult suggestion of any kind, he will develop as far as he is capable of developing.'[7]

These convictions were a strong factor in Neill's rejection of both moral and religious education. If a child is allowed to develop naturally he will not need the promptings and sanctions of moral or religious lessons, because his natural goodness will be allowed to manifest itself in its own way. Neill even went so far as to assert, 'I believe that it is moral instruction that makes the child bad. I find that when I smash the moral instruction a bad boy has received, he becomes a good boy.'[8] Religion he found totally unnecessary: 'free children who face life eagerly and bravely have no need to make any God at all'.[9]

Naturally there was no place for authority-based punishment in Summerhill. 'Punishment is always an act of hate'[10] thought Neill and the self-regulated child never requires it. How then was social control achieved in Summerhill? The school was run as far as possible as a democracy and most important decisions about the running of the school were voted on at the weekly general meeting where everyone (including Neill) had one vote and the majority wish prevailed. Where a child was found guilty of anti-social behaviour such as bullying, an appropriate punishment was decided by the group and it often took the form of a fine or penalty, for example handing over pocket money or missing the cinema.[11] This approach gave the children valuable experience in running their own lives and has generally been regarded by most observers as a successful aspect of Summerhill.

How did Neill come to hold the beliefs he did and be so committed to them that he devoted his whole life to putting them into practice despite continual struggle and criticism? There is no doubt that his own unhappy schooling and university experiences were a major factor and Summerhill can be seen as a total rejection of such a traditional authoritarian approach to education. In terms of other educational theorists who may have influenced him, one thinks first of Rousseau with whom he shared so much: the belief in the natural goodness of the child, in maximum pupil freedom and in the importance of the emotions, among other things. However, Neill did not read *Emile* until fifty years after opening Summerhill.[12] He also notes that he was somewhat disappointed in reading Rousseau's *Emile* and remarks perceptively that 'Emile was free but only in the set environment prescribed by his tutor. Summerhill is a set environment but it is the community that decides, not the individual tutor.'[13]

Neill was however strongly influenced by more contemporary figures such as Freud in relation to the importance of avoiding sexual repression and guilt, Wilhelm Reich in relation to sexual freedom and the importance of self-regulation, Homer Lane in relation to self government and his idea of rewarding instead of punishing the child for anti-social behaviour (i.e. responding with love instead of hate).[14] Neill knew both Reich and Lane well and devotes a chapter to them and their influence on him in his autobiography '*Neill, Neill Orange Peel*'.[15]

Over the years, Neill has attracted an enormous amount of criticism and praise, some of it quite extreme. For example, in the book *Summerhill: For and Against* we find one writer saying that he would rather send his children to a brothel than to Summerhill, while another refers to it as a 'holy place'.[16] Some of the attacks Neill has received may be written off as conservative overreactions to what is admittedly a radical new educational experiment, but there are some areas where Neill does seem to be vulnerable to criticism.

In the first place, he lacks a systematic, considered philosophy of education, especially a coherent theory of knowledge. His ideas are based primarily on his own experiences and observations, supplemented with some study of psychological (especially psychoanalytic) theory. Certainly one's own experiences are an important part of any educational theory but they need to be supplemented by some more systematic philosophical position on topics such as the nature of knowledge, learning, morality, human nature, society etc. Neill's writing is very readable because of its practical focus but it consists of many unsupported assertions, exaggerations and a common tendency to generalize from individual cases (e.g. anecdotes about particular pupils) to universal educational principles. He also tends to oversimplify complex philosophical issues such as the crucial distinction between freedom and licence, where he thinks it sufficient to merely distinguish the two conceptually and give some random examples of acts he calls either freedom or licence. What is lacking is a clear principle to decide why these cases belong to one category or the other and to help decide between conflicts of interests in such situations.

Similarly it could be argued that Neill had a rather simplistic and outdated view of moral and religious education as necessarily authoritarian and didactic. Modern educational notions of moral and religious autonomy in which children are introduced to such areas through open-ended discussion seem not to have been part of his understanding. Admittedly most of what he experienced and observed in this area would have conformed to the traditional model about which he wrote.

Another significant problem with Summerhill is the anti-intellectual bias that Neill brought to it. Is learning as unimportant as he maintains?[17] Are books really 'the least important apparatus in a school?'[18] Do children always know what is in their best educational interest? Can one fully utilize one's freedom without a solid core of knowledge and understanding on the basis of which to make meaningful choices? Why does educational relevance have to be always of an immediate and practical nature? These are the sorts of questions that begin to bother one when reading Neill's work and for all his conviction and sincerity, they suggest a major dimension of education that he fails to adequately acknowledge.

One good test of an educational theory is to ascertain the views of those who have actually experienced it in practice. Two surveys of ex-Summerhill pupils found very similar reactions.[19] On the whole most appreciated having been to Summerhill saying that it made them more independent, better able to deal with those in authority and more tolerant. Some said it had really helped them through a difficult stage in their life and that they would not have coped nearly as well in a traditional school. However a minority said that Summerhill had not really helped them – these were generally more introverted types who said that Summerhill suited extroverts more. Interestingly, it was found that those who criticized Summerhill tended to come from the pupils who stayed there for a longer period. If there was a generally shared complaint it was to do with the down-playing of the academic side of education and the frequent lack of inspiring teachers.

It seems that Summerhill is not necessarily the answer to all our educational problems and it would not be of benefit to all types of children. However, it does have something valuable to offer for some and is useful in providing a radical alternative to the conventional educational system, which indicates what an education based on freedom of the child really means in practice. One thing that made it work as successfully as it did for so long was Neill's charismatic personality and his genuine love and understanding of children. (This was something that was also commented upon by ex-Summerhillians.)

What then of the future of Summerhill? An OFSTED (Office for Standards in Education) inspection in March 1999 was critical of certain aspects of the school and recommended a number of significant alterations. The school appealed against the inspection arguing that if the recommendations had to be adopted the school's basic philosophy would be compromised. In March 2000 the school won its battle in the courts and can for the time being, at least, keep its basic principles intact.[20]

Notes

1 *Summerhill*, Harmondsworth: Penguin Books, p.111, 1968.
2 Ibid., p.20.
3 Ibid., p.308.
4 *Hearts not Heads in the Schools*, London: Herbert Jenkins, 1944.
5 Ibid., p.99.
6 Ibid., p.20.
7 Ibid.
8 Ibid., p.221.
9 Ibid., pp.216–17.
10 Ibid., p.151.
11 Ibid., p.58.
12 *Neill! Neill! Orange Peel: A Personal View of Ninety Years*, London: Quartet Books, p.238, 1977.
13 Ibid., pp.238–9.
14 See for instance, S. Freud, *Two Short Accounts of Psychoanalysis*, Harmondsworth: Penguin Books, 1962; H. Lane, *Talks to Parents and Teachers*, London: Allen and Unwin, 1928; W. Reich, *Selected Writings: An Introduction to Orgonomy*, New York: Farrar, Straus and Giroux, 1973.
15 *Neill! Neill! Orange Peel*, op cit., Part Two.
16 H. Hart (ed.), *Summerhill: For and Against – Assessments of A.S. Neill*, New York: Hart, 1978; and Sydney: Angus and Robertson, pp.17 and 28, 1973.
17 *Summerhill*, p.37.
18 Ibid., p.38.
19 E. Bernstein, 'Summerhill: A Follow-up Study of its Students', *Journal of Humanistic Psychology*, VIII, 2, Fall 1968, pp.123–36; J. Croall, *Neill of Summerhill: The Permanent Rebel*, London: Ark Paperbacks, chap. 23, 1984.
20 Details of the OFSTED report and consequent court proceedings can be found on the Summerhill website: http://www.s-hill.demon.co.uk.

See also

In *Fifty Major Thinkers on Education*: Rousseau

Neill's major writings

Of Neill's output of twenty books, the five most recent and most influential are:

The Free Child, London: Herbert Jenkins, 1953.
Summerhill, New York: Hart, 1960; London: Gollancz, 1962; Harmondsworth: Penguin, 1968. A new edition appeared as *The New Summerhill*, Albert Lamb (ed.), Harmondsworth: Penguin, 1992.
Freedom Not License!, New York: Hart, 1966.
Talking of Summerhill, London: Gollancz, 1967.
Neill! Neill! Orange Peel! A Personal View of Ninety Years, London: Weidenfeld & Nicolson, 1973; London: Quartet Books, 1977.

Further reading

Croall, J. *Neill, of Summerhill: The Permanent Rebel*, London: Ark Paperbacks, 1984.
Hart, H. (ed.), *Summerhill: For and Against – Assessments of A.S. Neill*, New York: Hart, 1970; Sydney: Angus and Robertson, 1973.

Hemmings, R., *Fifty Years of Freedom: A Study of the Development of the Ideas of A.S. Neill*, London: Allen and Unwin, 1972.

Purdy, B., *A.S. Neill: 'Bringing Happiness to Some Few Children'*, The Educational Heretics Series, Nottingham: Educational Heretics Press, 1997.

PETER HOBSON

SUSAN ISAACS 1885–1948

> The ultimate basis for the sensible practice of the trained educator ... provides a settled framework of control and routine, and definite help along social paths yet with ample personal freedoms. ... This, too, is the corrective for the idea that the child will never learn unless he is scolded or smacked, no less than for the notion that he need not learn, but need only bring out the good in him.
>
> (Susan Isaacs 1933, p.421)

Susan Isaacs brought psychoanalytic ideas to progressive education in Britain; also, she contributed to psychoanalytic theory with her work on 'unconscious phantasy' life which was rooted in her understanding of children.

She was brought up in Bolton in Lancashire, an energetic, blunt-speaking northerner.[1] Her father, a journalist, was a Methodist lay preacher and opposed to a career for his daughter (his ninth child) – especially opposed to educating her when she announced she had become an agnostic. However she managed to find employment tutoring, and then as a governess abroad. She eventually got to Manchester University and did brilliantly going on to further study of psychology at Cambridge in 1912, where she may well have first developed her interest in Freud.

During the First World War she began to attend courses at the training arm of the Brunswick Square Clinic, which provided treatment for returning shell-shock victims, and also offered the first training programmes in psychotherapy and psychoanalysis in Britain. There she met James Glover who, after the war, influenced her to go to Otto Rank in Berlin for some psychoanalysis.

The Brunswick Square Clinic closed in 1924, and Susan Isaacs joined the British Psychoanalytical Society, beginning a new analysis with J.C. Flügel. In 1924 she responded to an advertisement in the *New Statesman* for a graduate to run a school along unconventional lines. This advertisement was placed by Geoffrey Pike, a maverick inventor during the war effort,[2] and his wife Margaret, a pioneer founder of the International Planned Parenthood Federation.

Geoffrey Pike was himself unhappy at school, and wanted to provide his own children with a different experience. He had the use of a house outside Cambridge, and appointed Susan Isaacs to run the Malting House School.

Because of the concern for a new social order after the First World War, the 'new education' movement had come together in 1920 as the New Education Fellowship.[3] The Malting House School contributed to this progressive education movement. The schools in this movement often had founders whose aim was to improve on their own educational experiences. Usually the basis was a freedom for children in their learning.[4] The New Education Fellowship published *New Era* until the 1940s; and spawned a number of parallel experiments including the Elmhirst's Dartington Hall (1925), Dora Russell's Beacon Hill School (1927) and A.S. Neill's Summerhill (1927). These were heavily influenced by Froebel in Germany and Dewey in the United States. Susan Isaacs experiment in teaching lasted two and a half years, and is reported in two books: *The Intellectual Growth in Young Children* (London: Routledge, 1930); and *Social Development in Young Children* (London: Routledge, 1933).

Isaacs educational work at the Malting House School finished in 1927. Pike's business had begun to fail then, and Isaacs may have left partly because of the increasing pinch in the resources. There was also some disagreement with Pike over the importance of words and language in the life of the young child,[5] which contributed to her leaving. The school closed soon after. At that time Flügel was then professor of psychology at University College, London (UCL). In 1927, on the basis of her work at the Malting House School he appointed her to teach child development at UCL. Flügel also had contacts with Sir Percy Nunn, an early associate of the British Psychoanalytical Society and professor at the Institute of Education in London. In 1932, Nunn appointed Isaacs to start up a department of Child Development at the Institute of Education.

Susan Isaacs started from the position that the intellectual development of the child was intimately connected with emotional development, and she disagreed somewhat with Piaget. Though she brought psychoanalytic ideas to the educational setting, she was not the first to do so. In Britain, Homer Lane established the Little Commonwealth (1913–17) where he offered psychoanalytic treatment to individual adolescent delinquents, mixed boys and girls; at the same time he attempted to understand those political processes advocated by Dewey, as group processes in psychoanalytic terms.[6] On the Continent, Freud's daughter, Anna who had been a teacher, developed a pedagogic form of psychoanalysis for children. And with others in Vienna, Hermine Hug-Hellmuth,[7] August Aichorn[8] and Sigmund Bernfeld, applied the theory of instinctual development to education. They stressed the importance of sublimation in childhood, and its role in learning. Anna Freud's lectures for teachers, in 1930,[9] summarized this research. The key factor, they decided, was the super-ego. The super-ego inhibits the child's libido and requires it to be turned to the task of intellectual learning and the acquisition of skills. The role of education is a process by which the repressed instincts could learn to be channelled into socially acceptable activities. The latter is called sublimation.

Isaacs, like others in progressive education in Britain, started with the view that freedom in the classroom will dispel learning inhibition or distortions of character development. She established a culture of freedom and encouraged play as a method of expressing the instinctual life, and of discovery about mastering the world and developing sublimated skills. Because psychoanalysis expounds the theory that neurosis is caused by repression, it was used in arguments to support permissive approaches in progressive schools. However Isaacs soon modified her approach. Simply to

7

provide freedom of expression resulted in extreme rivalry and aggression between children, once liberated. Although education is the sublimation of instincts, freed instincts could also inhibit the natural development of sublimation in learning and self-expression. If instinctual wishes become too powerful then children seem to be overcome and then inhibited, restricted in their formation and use of symbols and words and severely incapacitated in learning. Thus she differed from the way psychoanalysis was used in Vienna to support the super-ego of the child. She turned to Melanie Klein's ideas to understand this.

As soon as Melanie Klein moved to London and joined the British Psychoanalytical Society, in 1926, Isaacs took an increasing interest in the form of child analysis which Klein developed which was somewhat different from Anna Freud's. Klein had pioneered a method for young children in 1918 in Budapest with Sandor Ferenczi and subsequently in Berlin with Karl Abraham. Klein's method[10] gained access to the unconscious life of young children – as young as two years and nine months – by using the child's natural form of self-expression, play. Klein displayed aspects of the super-ego, not known to the Vienna group. She noticed that very young children demonstrated in their play a torturing concern about their own aggression. So, children don't necessarily play more freely just from encouragement – though many do. Too much freedom can lead to the worrying freedom of aggressive urges. The super-ego appeared to be active within the earliest years of life, and in those early forms it is particularly harsh. Klein showed that guilt arising from a harsh super-ego, leads to the child becoming very fearful and then retaliatory against others. Aggression could feed on itself. And the intensity of such a cycle of guilt, fear and retaliation could lead to severe inhibition in learning.[11]

Klein and Isaacs agreed that a regime of tolerance can go some way to mitigating the harshness of the super-ego strictures within. However too much tolerance leads to the child feeling guilt (a comment Klein made after visiting the Malting House School soon after her move to London). Isaacs found the need for a balance between freedom of expression and the curtailment of it.

Under Klein's influence, Isaacs showed that the role of play was not just about mastery of the world and learning sublimated skills. It was also an actual expression of those agonized fantasies which can hold up development. The central role of fantasy, not just in play, but as an expression of the child's difficulties in learning led to her sophisticated view of intellectual development and social relations. The emphasis on free play turned the attention from biological instincts to the expressive capacities. This was the field of research in which Isaacs made her most significant contribution to psychoanalysis and gave her greatest support for Melanie Klein.

Klein pursued a line of practice and thinking relatively independent from Freud and from classical psychoanalysis as it had developed in Vienna. This dispute was quite vituperative,[12] but was significantly heightened when, in 1938, Freud and his family fled as refugees to London. Particularly after Freud's death in 1939, those loyal to Klein and those loyal to Anna Freud began to form separate organized groups, which culminated in the so-called 'controversial discussion', in 1943–44, centring around 18 months of formal meetings of the Society to discuss Klein's innovations.[13] During this time,

Isaacs served as Klein's most trusted lieutenant. She took the lead as the defender of Klein's ideas, and with her sharp mind bore the brunt of the debate. She gave the paper that started off the formal discussions, 'The Nature and Function of Phantasy' (Isaacs 1948) – and this has remained a classic founding text of Kleinian psychoanalysis in which she asserted that fantasy is 'the primary content of unconscious mental processes'.[14] In the debates, Isaacs' much more subtle style out-manoeuvred the arguments of Anna Freud and her group on many occasions. She did not convert the Viennese analysts, but she established the rigour of Kleinian psychoanalytic thinking.

The blending of psychoanalysis with education is one of the most important developments in education in the twentieth century. At UCL, and then at the Institute of Education in London, Isaacs taught and researched the importance of early emotional development for the intellectual and social life of the young child. She was very active in writing short pieces (sometimes under the name 'Ursula Wise') on child development and education for young children for popular magazines.[15] As a psychologist turned educationalist, Isaacs contributed the most up-to-date ideas on child development to teachers; and during the 1930s, she was chair of the Education Section of the British Psychological Society. During the Second World War years, while she was evacuated from London with her Department to Cambridge,[16] she headed a group of Cambridge psychologists who produced the 'Cambridge Evacuation Survey' of evacuated children and families. The emphasis of this work was on the child's point of view.

Isaacs' educational work derived its inspiration from psychoanalysis and the particular notions of repression, sublimation, the importance of play, and the evolving idea of unconscious phantasy; her classic paper on the last of these has become, in turn, her lasting contribution to psychoanalysis.

Notes

1 Dorothy Gardner, *Susan Isaacs: The First Biography*, London: Methuen, 1969.
2 David Lampe, *Pyke, the Unknown Genius*, London: Evans Brothers, 1959.
3 See W. Boyd and W. Rawson, *The Story of the New Education*, London: Heinemann, 1965; and Maurice Bridgeland, *Pioneer Work with Maladjusted Children*, London: Staples, 1971.
4 T. Percy Nunn, *Education: Its Data and First Principles*, London: Edward Arnold, 1920.
5 Gardner (op. cit., p. 67) states:

> Pike was concerned that children should be taught to realize that language was a convention and that words were not objects, but Susan became convinced that young children could not be given that idea in this way and probably not at all till a later stage in their development.

6 David Wills, *Homer Lane: A Biography*, London: George Allen and Unwin, 1964.
7 George MacLean and Ulrich Rappen, *Hermine Hug-Hellmuth, her Life and Work*, New York: Routledge, 1991.
8 August Aichorn, *Wayward Youth*, New York: Viking, 1925.

9 Anna Freud, *Einfürung in die Psychoanalyse für Pädagogen: Vier Vorträge*, Stuttgart: Hippokrates, 1930.
10 Melanie Klein, *The Psychoanalysis of Children: The Writings of Melanie Klein*, Volume 2, London: Hogarth, 1932.
11 Melanie Klein, 'The Importance of Symbol-Formation in the Development of the Ego', *The Writings of Melanie Klein*, Volume 1, London: Hogarth, 1930.
12 Riccardo Steiner, 'Some Thoughts about Tradition and Change from an Examination of the British Psychoanalytical Society's Controversial Discussions (1943–1944)', *International Review of Psychoanalysis*, 12, 1985, pp.12–71.
13 Pearl King and Riccardo Steiner, *The Freud–Klein Controversies 1941–1945*, London: Routledge, 1991.
14 Isaacs, 'The Nature and Function of Phantasy', p.81.
15 Isaacs, *Childhood and After*; and *Troubles with Children and Parents*.
16 She briefly shared a flat there with Melanie Klein.

See also

In this book: Neill

Isaacs major writings

The Intellectual Growth in Young Children, 1930, London: Routledge.
Social Development in Young Children, London: Routledge, 1933.
Psychological Aspects of Child Development, London: Evans, 1935.
Childhood and After, London: Routledge & Kegan Paul, 1948.
'The Nature and Function of Phantasy', *International Journal of Psycho-Analysis*, 29, 1948, pp.73–97; republished in Melanie Klein, Paula Heimann, Susan Isaacs and Joan Riviere, *Developments in Psycho-Analysis*, London: Hogarth, 1952.
Troubles with Children and Parents, London: Methuen, 1948.

Further reading

Gardner, Dorothy, *Susan Isaacs: The First Biography*, London: Methuen, 1969.
Smith, Lydia, *To Help and to Understand: The Life and Work of Susan Isaacs*, London: Associated Universities Press, 1985.

ROBERT HINSHELWOOD

HAROLD RUGG 1886–1960

There is no royal road into the new epoch, at the crossroads before which we now stand; there is only the hard way of education and especially of the building of consent among the people. In this process the school can and must provide leadership. Through the study of society and its problems the school must devote itself to the development of sensitive, clearheaded, fearless and confident young men and women who understand American life as it is actually lived and determined to make it a magnificent civilization for themselves and their children. To this end the life and program of the school must be designed directly from the culture of the people, not from a

classics-intrenched curriculum. Now is the time to build not a
subject-centered school but a truly society-centered as well as
a child-centered one.[1]

Harold Ordway Rugg was a leader of the progressive education movement in
the United States. Progressive educators shared, in John Dewey's words,
belief in 'the school as the primary and most effective interest of social
progress'.[2] Although Rugg's educational thought fails to fit readily into
any one strain of progressivism, he is chiefly remembered for his social
reconstruction perspective and the controversy it engendered.

Rugg's early life gave scant indication that he would become a world-
renowned educator. Born in Massachusetts, Rugg studied civil engineering
in college and briefly practised and taught it. Teaching awakened his
curiosity about how people learn and he enrolled in the University of Illinois
doctoral programme in education. In 1915 he received his Ph.D. and
accepted a teaching position at the University of Chicago. At Chicago, Rugg
worked with a faculty, most notably Charles Judd, who epitomized the
'scientific' strain of progressive education. Both Chicago and wartime testing
work for the government in Washington, DC, meshed comfortably with
Rugg's methodical engineering ways.

During his time in Washington, however, Rugg became acquainted with
artists and cultural critics who strongly influenced him. After a brief return
to Chicago, in 1920 he moved to Teachers College, Columbia University in
New York City. He became a professor and director of research for the
Lincoln School, an experimental school affiliated with Teachers College. In
New York he reinvigorated his wartime ties to creative thinkers in the
bohemian neighbourhood of Greenwich Village. As Lawrence Cremin later
put it, Rugg joined 'the group of artists and literati that clustered around
Alfred Stieglitz ... drinking the heady wine against puritanism, Babbitry,
and machine culture'.[3]

Thus, without ever surrendering scientific method in education, Rugg
added to it a profound commitment to individual creativity. His admiration
for creative self-expression contrasted with the amplified commercialism –
'The chief business of the American people is business,' President Coolidge
pronounced – of America in the 1920s. In progressive education,
commitment to individual creativity manifested itself as child-centred
education. Rugg found much to admire in 'activity' aimed at developing
each child's creativity and intuition rather than marching the whole class
through a prearranged standard curriculum. But he also questioned if child
activity was too limited an educational goal. In the name of self-expression,
Rugg wrote in 1928, child-centred educators 'have tended to minimize the
other, equally important goal of education: Tolerant understanding of
themselves and of the outstanding characteristics of modern civilization.'[4]

Rugg's ambivalence about child-centred education is emblematic of why
his brand of progressive education is not easily classified. A comparison of
Rugg and Dewey is instructive on the idiosyncrasy of Rugg's position. While
Rugg and Dewey, for instance, shared misgivings about the neglect of
substantive subject matter in child-centred methods, Rugg believed Dewey's
experimentalism 'as the sole method of knowing' was restrictive,[5] devaluing
the intuitive and imaginative modes utilized by artists. While Dewey and

Rugg agreed that the school should be an agency of social reform, Dewey had reservations about social reconstruction. Dewey doubted the school by itself could, as Rugg's fellow social reconstructionist George Counts famously put it, 'build a new social order'.[6] Moreover, the overtones of indoctrination in social reconstruction offended Dewey's sense of intellectual freedom. Nonetheless, when censors attacked Rugg, the characteristically principled Dewey sprang to Rugg's defence.[7]

Like many other progressive educators, Rugg evinced great concern for the relevance of popular schooling in an industrial society. Unlike many other progressive educators, we do not have to guess what Rugg's educational theory might look like in practice. During the interwar decades, Rugg developed his ideas into an instructional programme. Rugg saw an urgent need for a programme centred on the rise and consequences of industrial society: that is, a programme based on the demands of modern living.

Rugg declared existing school programmes hopelessly ill-equipped for the task before them: 'nothing short of genius on the part of a student could create an ordered understanding of modern life from such a compartmentalized arrangement of materials'.[8] Rugg's ideal school programme incorporated the breadth of his educational vision including special attention to 'body education' and 'creative work'. Mathematics 'and other techniques' (what, today, would be called 'skills') were the only parts of the curriculum not organized in the form of projects or units-of-study.[9]

The true test of Rugg's ideas, however, is his experimentation and programme development in the social studies (i.e., history, geography, civics, economics, and related subjects). Here Rugg's scientific approach to curriculum development and belief in 'the new social science' coincided, resulting in his most remarkable achievement: an integrated educational programme focused on the problems of modern living. Rugg's impatience with 'armchair' (versus 'scientific') curriculum making convinced him that the otherwise healthy reaction against a dusty, prespecified curriculum had led progressive educators to unrealistic expectations of what could be accomplished by spontaneous curriculum making in the classroom. 'The inevitable result of trying to carry out these precepts with a broad curriculum and thirty to fifty young people', Rugg lamented, 'has been educational chaos.'[10] Rugg was convinced that a defensible programme which would actually be implemented must be planned in advanced (with, of course, due regard for adaptation to special circumstances by users). Developing, field-testing, and refining such a programme in the social studies constituted his major activity in the 1920s and 1930s.

Both friends and foes have recognized that Rugg's carefully crafted programme is an uncommon instantiation of what a progressive conception of curriculum can look like in practice. Rather than traditional subjects such as history and geography, Rugg's materials were built on 'understanding units' that dealt with current problems such as the corporate economy, agricultural depression, unequal distribution of wealth, the need for economic planning, intercultural relations and international cooperation. Full attention was given the resources needed to implement the programme's goals and the sequencing, planned repetition and variety of learning activities necessary for optimal learning. Rugg wished youngsters to learn concepts and generalizations rather than the disconnected factual information he saw as the outcome of traditional methods and materials. For example, in the study of civilizations outside the United States he selected nations representative of particular salient features of the modern world rather than become consumed in a superficial, fact-dominated coverage of more nations than youngsters could make sense of.

Arguably Rugg's very success was, eventually, his downfall. His first materials were for the junior high school, where no other nationally available materials existed for this new set of courses.[11] From 1929 to 1939 over 1.3 million copies of Rugg's textbooks were sold to over four thousand school districts across the United States.[12] Although more liberal than radical in tone, Rugg's materials fitted comfortably with the ideological upheavals of Depression America, especially the spirit of the New Deal. Moreover, evaluations suggested that learning outcomes from Rugg's materials in traditional subjects such as history, geography and civics compared favourably with subject-centred methods.[13]

Even in the early 1930s some of Rugg's books were altered because elements of them were considered too radical. By the late 1930s public attacks began on the books. Business groups and self-appointed 'patriotic' societies charged that Rugg's ideas were anti-capitalist and subversive of American traditions and the existing social order. By the beginning of the 1940s, the attacks increased and within several years Rugg's books were removed from most districts and ceased publication. In retrospect, the demonstrated effectiveness of Rugg's brand of progressive education may have made it all the more threatening to conservatives and reactionaries. Although flexible to how his view of modern living was conveyed, Rugg was convinced it was an accurate distillation of 'frontier' thinking and in time took for granted that educators need to 'boldly ... accept the clear, self-stated truth'[14] derived from these clearly liberal-leaning thinkers.

Rugg responded vigorously to the attacks on his textbooks' focus on modern problems. The problem method, he objected, 'does not imply, as the self-appointed censors say, that we propose a "plan for a new social order," with which to "indoctrinate American youth".' Rugg enjoined that 'young people ... must confront the alternatives set out clearly before them. How else can human beings practice decision making than by confronting issues?'[15] Nonetheless, the attacks proved decisive in the growing conservatism of the 1940s.

Although Rugg was never to be so influential again, he remained an active scholar – even extending his work to explicit treatment of teacher education and imagination – until his death. Moreover, although beyond the scope of this essay on Rugg's educational thought, Rugg continued to contribute to progressive social and political thought, writing during the Second World War, for instance, a spirited brief for a liberal, postwar society.

If effect on educational practice is a valid basis for judgement, then surely Rugg was a giant among progressive educators. Few subsequent progressive educators have exhibited Rugg's enterprise and patience in moving beyond exhortation and distal social critique to construct an educational programme embodying their rationales. Rugg's work should also continue to inspire teacher educators as a model of the distinction between 'subjects' and 'subject matters'. For those of us who admire and approve Rugg's educational thought, what he demonstrated about sound, creative pedagogy and curriculum directed at a more caring and socially responsible society still have much to teach in a time of narrowly instrumental educational policies.

Notes

1 Harold Rugg, *That Men May Understand: An American in the Long Armistice*, New York: Doubleday, Doran, p.xv, 1941.
2 John Dewey, 'My Pedagogic Creed', in D.J. Flinders and S.J. Thornton (eds), *The Curriculum Studies Reader*, New York: Routledge, p.23, 1997.
3 Lawrence A. Cremin, *The Transformation of School: Progressivism in American Education, 1876–1957*, New York: Vintage, p.182, 1964.
4 Rugg and Ann Shumaker, *The Child-centered School*, New York: Arno Press and The New York Times, pp.viii–ix, 1969.
5 Rugg, *Culture and Education in America*, New York: Harcourt, p.4, 1931.
6 George S. Counts, *Dare the School Build a New Social Order?*, Carbondale and Edwardsville, IL: Southern Illinois University Press, 1932.
7 Alan Ryan, *John Dewey and the High Tide of American Liberalism*, New York: Norton, p.340, 1995.
8 Rugg, *American Life and the School Curriculum: Next Steps Toward Schools of Living*, Boston, MA: Ginn, p.332, 1936.
9 Ibid., pp.354–5.
10 Ibid., p.345.
11 Murry R. Nelson, 'The Development of the Rugg Social Studies Materials', *Theory and Research in Social Education*, V, III, p.68, December 1977.
12 Naida Tushnet Bagenstos, 'Social Reconstruction: The Controversy Over the Textbooks of Harold Rugg', *Theory and Research in Social Education*, V, III, p.29, December 1977.
13 B.R. Buckingham, *Rugg Course in the Classroom: The Junior-High-School Program*, Chicago, IL: Ginn, pp.69–72, c.1935.
14 Rugg, *Foundations for American Education*, New York: World Book Company, p.xi, 1947.
15 Rugg, *That Men May Understand*, op cit., pp.244–5.

See also

In *Fifty Major Thinkers on Education*: Dewey

Rugg's major writings

Rugg wrote dozens of volumes and numerous articles, not all on education. Some of his writing is repetitive from one volume to the next. This list is restricted to books representative of his most influential contributions to education. The instructional materials he developed for schools are unlisted but may be accessed through the Department of Special Collections, Milbank Memorial Library, Teachers College, Columbia University.

Rugg, H.O. and Bagley, W.C., *Content of American History*, Chicago, IL: University of Illinois, School of Education, 1916.
Rugg, H.O. and Hockett, J., *Objective Studies in Map Location*, New York: Lincoln School of Teachers College, 1925.

Rugg, H.O. and Shumaker, A., *The Child-centered School*, New York: Arno Press and The New York Times, 1969, c.1928.
Culture and Education in America, New York: Harcourt, 1931.
American Life and the School Curriculum: Next Steps Toward Schools of Living, Boston, MA: Ginn, 1936.
That Men May Understand: An American in the Long Armistice, New York: Doubleday, Doran, 1941.
Foundations for American Education, New York: World Book Company, 1947.

Further reading

Bowers, C.A., *The Progressive Educator and the Great Depression*, New York: Random House, 1969.
Carbone, Peter F., *The Social and Educational Thought of Harold Rugg*, Durham, NC: Duke University Press, 1977.
Kliebard, Herbert M., *The Struggle for the American Curriculum, 1893–1958*, 2nd edn, New York: Routledge, 1995.
Stanley, William B., *Curriculum for Utopia: Social Reconstructionism and Critical Pedagogy in the Postmodern Era*, Albany, NY: State University of New York Press, 1992.

STEPHEN J. THORNTON

LUDWIG WITTGENSTEIN 1889–1951

> In teaching you philosophy I'm like a guide showing you how to
> find your way round London ... a rather bad guide.[1]

Ludwig Wittgenstein was born to an aristocratic family in Vienna, 26 April 1889. He was the youngest of eight very precocious children, and was preoccupied all his life with questions of genius, artistic creativity and suicide (three of his brothers died that way). In 1911, on the advice of Gottlob Frege, he went to meet Bertrand Russell at Cambridge, after which he was admitted to Trinity College. Russell was impressed by Wittgenstein, and urged him to study mathematical logic. They worked as colleagues, even though Wittgenstein was technically an undergraduate. Over time, however, the relations between Wittgenstein and Russell became strained, and in 1913 Wittgenstein left Cambridge. He enrolled in the Austrian army just a few days after the First World War was declared; he was eventually taken prisoner in Italy, but during these years he managed to write the one philosophical book published during his lifetime, the *Tractatus Logico-Philosophicus*. The manuscript was sent to Russell while Wittgenstein was still a prisoner, and with Russell's (somewhat equivocal) support and Introduction it was eventually published in 1922, exerting an enormous philosophical influence, particularly on the positivists of the Vienna Circle, which included Rudolf Carnap, Herbert Feigl, Moritz Schlick and Friedrich Waismann, with whom Wittgenstein became acquainted.

Wittgenstein, on the death of his father in 1913, had inherited a substantial part of his family's fortune. In 1919 he gave it all away and went to work as a teacher in the small Austrian villages of Trattenbach, Hassbach,

Puchberg and Otterthal during the years of 1920–26. Following a series of short stints, he resigned his post in Otterthal under a cloud of suspicion over allegedly striking a female student (not the first student he had struck during his teaching years, apparently). After working as a gardener and helping to design and build a house for one of his sisters, he returned to Cambridge in 1929. His Ph.D. was granted based on the *Tractatus* as his thesis, he was given a five year fellowship, and he taught at Trinity College until 1935, when he left again, spending time in Russia, Norway, Austria and Ireland. By 1935 Wittgenstein was having serious doubts about the value of philosophy, and was actively counselling his students to find a more 'useful' line of work. Yet in 1938 he returned to Cambridge, becoming a professor in 1939.

During the 1930s and 1940s he wrote a great deal in the form of remarks, aphorisms and fragments; but none of this work was published during his lifetime. A large part of what was to become his second major work, the *Philosophical Investigations*, was compiled by 1945, but was not published until 1953, two years after his death. In the *Investigations*, Wittgenstein criticized, and to a large extent rejected, the views developed in the *Tractatus*, specifically in developing a more 'anthropological' and pragmatic view of language – and so we have the remarkable phenomenon of someone giving impetus to two major, and opposed, philosophical movements during his lifetime. Wittgenstein resigned his professorship in 1947, continuing to work on the *Investigations* and other projects until his death from prostate cancer in April 1951. Throughout his career, Wittgenstein struggled with self-doubt about his worth as a philosopher and the value of philosophy itself; about his identity and moral character; and about his sexual and amorous relationships.

Wittgenstein is rarely considered an educational thinker *per se*. Except for a few comments and aphorisms, he wrote very little about the topic. But it is also clear that he thought very seriously about education. It is well known, for example, that he taught in a highly idiosyncratic manner, and that for years after young philosophers at Cambridge mimicked his habits and style. It is less well known that he taught in rural Austria during the 'wilderness years' of the 1920s, during which time he wrote a school textbook. We have been struck by Wittgenstein's frequent use of pedagogical examples and analogies to make philosophical points in his writing. Indeed, we have argued elsewhere that Wittgenstein's style of writing and philosophy is fundamentally pedagogical: that is, premised on *teaching* a way of thinking about philosophical problems or – in certain instances – on *unlearning* certain bad philosophical habits.[2]

There are at least three ways, then, to explore Wittgenstein's educational thought and practice: first, through his university teaching; second, through the accounts of his experiences as a primary- and secondary-school teacher in Austria; third, through his style of writing and composing his philosophical ideas, particularly in his later work.

First, much of what we have from Wittgenstein relies upon recollections or reconstructions of his teaching by his university students. Many of his posthumous 'works' are actually transcriptions, discussions, course notes, or lectures recorded by his students and colleagues. His styles of teaching and thinking in performance, therefore, constitute a significant proportion of his extant works. These accounts of his teaching confirm his intensity of thinking and his honesty as a thinker and teacher. If he was unforgiving in his treatment of his students, it is because he was unforgiving with himself. The long painful silences that interspersed his classes, his disregard for institutional conventions in pedagogy, and his relentless criticism (and self-criticism) were an essential part of his teaching style.

Accounts of Wittgenstein as a teacher of philosophy are legendary. D.A.T. Gasking and A.C. Jackson report the following description Wittgenstein gave of his own teaching:

> In teaching you philosophy I'm like a guide showing you how to find your way round London. I have to take you through the city from north to south, from east to west, from Euston to the embankment and from Piccadilly to the Marble Arch. After I have taken you many journeys through the city, in all sorts of directions, we shall have passed through any given street a number of times – each time traversing the street as part of a different journey. At the end of this you will know London; you will be able to find your way about like a Londoner. Of course, a good guide will take you through the more important streets more often than he takes you down side streets; a bad guide will do the opposite. In philosophy I'm a rather bad guide.[3]

This passage indicates Wittgenstein's penchant for comparing doing philosophy with making a journey.

Gasking and Jackson focus on the 'technique of oral discussion' Wittgenstein used, a technique they describe as, at first, bewildering:

> Example was piled up on example. Sometimes the examples were fantastic, as when one was invited to consider the very odd linguistic or other behavior of an imaginary tribe. ... Sometimes the example was just a reminder of some well-known homely fact. Always the case was given in concrete detail, described in down-to-earth everyday language. Nearly every single thing said was easy to follow and was usually not the sort of thing anyone would wish to dispute.[4]

The difficulty came from seeing where this 'repetitive concrete' talk was leading. Sometimes he 'would break off, saying, "Just a minute, let me think!" ... or he would exclaim, "This is as difficult as hell."'[5] Sometimes the point of the many examples became suddenly clear as though the solution was obvious and simple. Gasking and Jackson report Wittgenstein as saying that he wanted to show his students that they had confusions that they never thought they could have and admonished them by saying, 'You must say what you really think as though no one, not even you, could overhear it.'[6]

Karl Britton reports that Wittgenstein thought there was no test one could apply to discover whether a philosopher was teaching properly: 'He said that many of his pupils merely put forward his own ideas: and that many of them imitated his voice and manner; but that he could easily distinguish those who really understood.'[7] Indeed, this degree of influence made Wittgenstein wonder whether he was a good teacher at all:

> A teacher may get good, even astounding, results from his pupils while he is teaching them and yet not be a good teacher; because it may be that, while his pupils are directly under his influence, he raises them to a height which is not natural to them, without fostering their own capacities for work at this level, so that they immediately decline again as soon as the teacher leaves the classroom. Perhaps this is how it is with me.[8]

G.H. Von Wright, a far from unsympathetic observer, thought that Wittgenstein's concern was well-founded:

> He thought his influence as a teacher was, on the whole, harmful to the development of independent minds in his disciples. ... The magic of his personality and style was most inviting and persuasive. To learn from Wittgenstein without coming to adopt his forms of expression and catchwords and even his tone of voice, his mien and gestures, was almost impossible.[9]

Doing philosophy always took priority for Wittgenstein, whether this was in oral or written form: it was important to show the deep puzzles in our language (and our culture and thinking) as well as dissolving them. Doing philosophy let the fly out of the fly-bottle: it cured our buzzing confusion and allowed us to lead useful and practical lives. Wittgenstein said 'a philosophical problem has the form "I don't know my way about." '[10] His style of teaching philosophy was designed to enable listeners to shift their thinking, to think differently about a problem, which was often in his view the only way to 'solve' it. In this respect, one can teach only as a 'guide'.

Second, Ray Monk, one of Wittgenstein's primary biographers, devotes a chapter ('An Entirely Rural Affair') to Wittgenstein's years as a school teacher during the 1920s.[11] His account of Wittgenstein's teaching service in the village schools of rural Austria paints Wittgenstein as a teacher with exacting standards and little patience, one who was given to violent outbursts against his students.

These are significant biographical details. Indeed, it is suggested by Fania Pascal that it was an episode in Wittgenstein's career as a teacher that involved hitting one of his girl pupils (and which he later denied to the principal), that 'stood out as a crisis of his early manhood' and caused him to give up teaching.[12] Rhees, commenting upon this same episode, quotes from a letter from Wittgenstein to Russell: 'how can I be a logician before I'm a human being! *Far* the most important thing is to settle accounts with myself!'[13]

Monk describes Wittgenstein's misgivings about Glöckel's school reforms and the publication of Wittgenstein's *Wörterbuch für Volksschullen* – a spelling dictionary – in 1925, and yet does not recognize the significance of Wittgenstein's experiences as a school teacher for his later philosophy. William Bartley is one of the few scholars to devote any space to Wittgenstein's development during the 1920s. His major historical claim is that there are 'Certain similarities between some themes of Glöckel's program and Bühler's theories on the one hand, and ideas which infuse the later work of Wittgenstein.'[14] Otto Glöckel was administrative head of the socialist school reform, which had attacked the old 'drill' schools of the Hapsburgs based on passive rote learning and memorization, to argue for the establishment of the *Arbeitsschule* or 'working school' based on the active participation of pupils and a doctrine of learning by doing. Bartley conjectures that the themes of the school-reform movement and, in particular, the views of Karl Bühler, Professor of Philosophy at the University of Vienna and at the Vienna Pedagogical Institute, who was invited to Vienna by Glöckel and his colleagues in 1922, in large measure accounted for the profound change in Wittgenstein's philosophizing in the late 1920s. He bases this claim upon the 'striking similarities' between their ideas and some historical circumstantial evidence. Bartley also provides some textual evidence; he quotes Wittgenstein in Zettel: 'Am I doing child psychology? ... I am making a connection between the concept of teaching and the concept of meaning.'[15] He recounts a story that Wittgenstein used to tell his pupils in Trattenbach from 1921 concerning an experiment to determine whether children who had not yet learned to speak, locked away with a woman who could not speak, could learn a primitive language or invent a new language of their own. Bartley asks us, by way of corroboration, to consider that the *Investigations* begins with a critique of Saint Augustine's account of how a child learns a language.

Yet Bartley's work has also been criticized. Eugene Hargrove, for instance, argues, with Paul Englemann, that it was the direct effect of Wittgenstein's contact with children rather than the school-reform movement or Bühler's ideas that influenced Wittgenstein's views about language:

> I believe we can see the influence of Wittgenstein's time as a teacher on almost every page of the *Investigations*, for there are very few pages in a row that do not make some reference to children. Throughout his later philosophy, Wittgenstein often supported the points he was making by citing personal observations about children. It is these observations, which he made as a school teacher and used as a pool of data later, that, as I see it, are the true influence on Wittgenstein's work, and not principles taught at the teachers college or waved in his face by the school reformers.[16]

C.J.B. Macmillan terms this Wittgenstein's 'pedagogical turn': 'we often find him turning from a consideration of the meanings of a term or concept to ask, "How was this learned?" or "How would you teach it?"'[17]

Third, Wittgenstein's way of 'doing philosophy', as we have noted, differed from traditional attempts to do philosophy: it is aporetic but not Socratic; it is dialogical but not in the traditional philosophical sense. Wittgenstein writes, 'Reading the Socratic dialogues one has the feeling;

what a frightful waste of time! What's the point of these arguments that prove nothing and clarify nothing.'[18] Moreover, Wittgenstein expresses his impatience with the game of eristics:

> Socrates keeps reducing the sophist to silence, – but does he have right on his side when he does this? Well, it is true that the sophist does not know what he thinks he knows; but that is no triumph for Socrates. It can't be a case of 'You see! You don't know it!' – nor yet, triumphantly, of 'So none of us knows anything!'[19]

Hence it should be no surprise that Wittgenstein says that his approach is the *opposite* of Socrates'.[20] Where Socrates, professing his ignorance, sought to disabuse others of their mistaken beliefs, Wittgenstein, through his dialogical forms of teaching and writing, sought to externalize *his own* doubts and questions, showing the nature of certain problems as he tried to work them through in his own mind: 'Nearly all my writings are private conversations with myself. Things that I say to myself *tête-à-tête*.'[21] (Much the same might be said of his teaching, as we have tried to show.)

The *Philosophical Investigations* is Wittgenstein's primary example of a dialogical work; yet clearly it is not dialogical in the sense established by Socrates. And judging by Wittgenstein's comments on Socrates it is evident why the *Investigations* does not follow or try to emulate the Socratic form or method. While the *Investigations* is not written in the form of a dialogue, it draws upon a repertoire of dialogical strategies and gestures. Terry Eagleton recognizes this when he calls the *Investigations*:

> a thoroughly dialogical work, in which the author wonders out loud, imagines an interlocutor, asks us questions which may or may not be on the level ... forcing the reader into the work of self-demystification, genially engaging our participation by his deliberately undaunting style.[22]

The *Investigations* self-reflectively mirrors and models the multiplicity of language-games and gestures it attempts to describe. It functions as an exemplary pedagogical text the aim of which is for Wittgenstein's students to think these problems through for themselves (an aim, it must be said, which he did not feel had always been successful, as we have seen). Wittgenstein's adoption of a dialogical mode of inquiry, along with his innovations with form and composition in writing, were part of his deliberate experimentation designed to shift our thinking. He certainly did not want his readers or audience to imitate him in either the forms or the contents of his thought. Nor did he think that there is only one way to 'do' philosophy.

He agonized over the form of his work and he developed very complex methods of composition: 'Forcing my thoughts into an ordered sequence is a torment for me. ... I squander an unspeakable amount of effort making an arrangement of my thoughts which may have no value at all.'[23] He wrote philosophical *remarks* or fragments, and sometimes referred to his procedure of composition as one of assemblage – philosophy 'consists in assembling reminders for a particular purpose'.[24]

Hence we see that the *Investigations* and later works are interspersed with frequent remarks that begin with asking us to 'imagine', as in 'Let us imagine a language . . .'[25] and elsewhere. At other times he constructs this as 'Suppose . . .' or 'Think . . .' or 'Ask yourself . . .' and so on. These *thought experiments* play a crucial substantive and stylistic role in the *Investigations*, and they are characteristic of a way of writing about philosophy that is more oriented to triggering a shift in thought than in demonstrating a proof; more to showing than to saying; more to pointing than to leading (note the frequent references in Wittgenstein's later work to signposts, wandering through a city, being lost, needing a guide, finding one's way about, and knowing how to go on). This is a conception of teaching, and teaching through writing, far different from the classic Socratic engagement of the *Meno*, which is based on instruction along a specific path of reasoning to a definite conclusion.

Another recurring element in the *Investigations* is a question Wittgenstein asks to himself, posed by an imaginary interlocutor, with multiple possible answers or a hypothetical response, followed by his typical dissatisfied reply, 'But . . .'. Fann notes that Wittgenstein asks on the order of 800 questions in the *Investigations*, yet he only answers 100 of them and of these the majority (some seventy) are answers that he pointedly rejects.[26] Wittgenstein wants to stop us from asking certain kinds of questions: the sort of 'philosophical' questions which require that we provide a theoretical answer abstracted from the context of use and social practice. Instead, his questions and replies serve as *reminders*, bringing us back to familiar aspects of human language and experience; the significance of the fact that we can identify the related members of a family, for example, even when they do not all share the same features in common.

This mode of dialogue, then, is not one of demonstration but of investigation. Wittgenstein's use of imagined interchanges, thought experiments, diagrams, pictures, examples, aphorisms, or parables is meant to engage the reader in a process that was, in Wittgenstein's teaching as well as in his writing, the externalization of his own doubts, his own questions, his own thought processes. His philosophical purpose was manifested, shown, in *how* he pursued a question; his style was his method, and his writings sought to exemplify how it worked. His concern with matters of form and composition were not only about the presentation of an argument, but about the juxtaposition that would best draw the reader into the very state of puzzlement he himself felt. An appreciation of Wittgenstein's philosophical style leads us directly to an understanding of the *fundamentally pedagogical* nature of his endeavour.

Notes

1 D.A.T. Gasking and A.C. Jackson, 'Wittgenstein as a Teacher', in K.T. Fann (ed.), *Ludwig Wittgenstein: The Man and His Philosophy*, New Jersey: Humanities Press; Sussex: Harvester Press, p.52, 1962.
2 Michael Peters and Nicholas C. Burbules, 'Wittgenstein, Styles, and Pedagogy', in Michael Peters and James Marshall, *Wittgenstein: Philosophy, Postmodernism, Pedagogy*, South Hadley, MA: Bergin and Garvey, pp.152–73, 1999. Some of the

material in this essay is adapted from that chapter, and the following chapter, 'Philosophy as Pedagogy: Wittgenstein's Styles of Thinking', pp.174–91.

3 Gasking and Jackson, 'Wittgenstein as a Teacher', p.52.
4 Ibid., p.50.
5 Ibid., p.52.
6 Ibid., p.53.
7 Quoted in M.O'C. Drury, 'A Symposium: Assessments of the Man and the Philosopher', in K.T. Fann (ed.), *Ludwig Wittgenstein: The Man and His Philosophy*, New Jersey: Humanities Press; Sussex: Harvester Press, p.61, 1967.
8 Ludwig Wittgenstein, *Culture and Value*, G.H. Von Wright (ed.) (in collaboration with Heikki Nyman), trans. Peter Winch, Oxford: Basil Blackwell, p. 38, 1980.
9 G.H. Von Wright, *Wittgenstein*, Oxford: Blackwell, p.31, 1982.
10 Ludwig Wittgenstein, *Philosophical Investigations*, trans. G.E.M. Anscombe, Oxford: Basil Blackwell, p.49, 1953, 3rd edn, 1972.
11 Ray Monk, *Ludwig Wittgenstein: The Duty of Genius*, London: Vintage, 1991.
12 Fania Pascal, 'A Personal Memoir', in Rush Rhees (ed.), *Recollections of Wittgenstein*, Oxford and New York: Oxford University Press, pp.37–8, 1984.
13 Rush Rhees, 'Postscript', in R. Rush Rhees (ed.), *Recollections of Wittgenstein*, Oxford and New York: Oxford University Press, p.191, 1984.
14 W.W. Bartley, III, *Wittgenstein*, Philadelphia, PA and New York: J.B. Lippincott, p.20, 1973.
15 Ludwig Wittgenstein, *Zettel*, G.E.M. Anscombe and R. Rhees (eds), Oxford: Blackwell, p.74, 2nd edn, 1981.
16 Eugene Hargrove, 'Wittgenstein, Bartley, and the Glöckel School Reform', *History of Philosophy*, 17, p.461, 1980.
17 C.J.B. Macmillan, 'Love and Logic in 1984', in Emily Robertson (ed.), *Philosophy of Education 1984*, Normal, IL: Philosophy of Education Society, p.7. 1984.
18 Wittgenstein, *Culture and Value*, p.14.
19 Ibid., p.56.
20 Wittgenstein, quoted in J.C. Nyiri, 'Wittgenstein as a Philosopher of Secondary Orality', manuscript, to appear in *Grazer Philosophische Studien*: 'I cannot summarize my standpoint better than saying it is opposed to that which Socrates represents in the Platonic dialogues.'
21 Wittgenstein, *Culture and Value*, p.77.
22 Terry Eagleton, 'Introduction to Wittgenstein', *Wittgenstein: The Terry Eagleton Script, The Derek Jarman Film*, London: British Film Institute, p.9, 1993.
23 Wittgenstein, *Culture and Value*, p.28.
24 Wittgenstein, *Philosophical Investigations*, p.50.
25 Ibid., p.3.
26 Fann, *Ludwig Wittgenstein: The Man and His Philosophy*, p.109.

See also

In *Fifty Major Thinkers on Education*: Russell, Socrates

Wittgenstein's major writings

Philosophical Investigations, trans. G.E.M. Anscombe, Oxford: Blackwell, 1953, 3rd edn, 1972).
Tractatus Logico-Philosophicus, trans. D.F. Pears and B.F. McGuinness, London: Routledge & Kegan Paul, 1961.
The Blue and Brown Books, Oxford: Blackwell, 1969.
On Certainty, G.E.M. Anscombe and G.H. von Wright (eds), trans. Denis Paul and G.E.M. Anscombe, Oxford: Blackwell, 1979.

Culture and Value, G.H. Von Wright (ed.) (in collaboration with Heikki Nyman), trans. Peter Winch, Oxford: Blackwell, 1980.
Zettel, G.E.M. Anscombe and R. Rhees (eds), Oxford: Blackwell, 2nd edn, 1981.

Further reading

Anscombe, G.E.M., *An Introduction to Wittgenstein's Tractatus*, Philadelphia, PA: University of Pennsylvania Press, 1971.
Baker, G.P. and Hacker, P.M.S., *Wittgenstein: Understanding and Meaning*, Oxford: Blackwell, 1980.
—— *Wittgenstein: Rules, Grammar and Necessity*, Oxford: Blackwell, 1985.
Bartley, III, W.W., *Wittgenstein*, Philadelphia, PA and New York: J.B. Lippincott, 1973.
Cavell, Stanley, *The Claim of Reason: Wittgenstein, Skepticism, Morality, and Tragedy*, Oxford and New York: Oxford University Press, 1979.
Engelmann, Paul, *Letters from Wittgenstein with a Memoir*, Oxford: Blackwell, 1967.
Hacker, P.M.S., *Wittgenstein: Meaning and Mind*, Oxford: Blackwell, 1990.
Janik, Allen and Toulmin, Stephen, *Wittgenstein's Vienna*, London: Weidenfield & Nicolson, 1973.
Kenney, Anthony, *Wittgenstein*, Harmondsworth: Penguin Books, 1975.
Kripke, Saul A., *Wittgenstein on Rules and Private Language*, Cambridge, MA: Harvard University Press, 1982.
Malcolm, Norman, *Ludwig Wittgenstein: A Memoir*, Oxford and New York: Oxford University Press, 1984.
McGuiness, Brian, *Wittgenstein: A Young Life, 1889–1921*, London: Duckworth, 1988.
Monk, Ray, *Ludwig Wittgenstein: The Duty of Genius*, London: Vintage, 1991.
Rhees, Rush (ed.), *Recollections of Wittgenstein*, Oxford and New York: Oxford University Press, 1984.
Sluga, H. and Stern, D.G. (eds), *The Cambridge Companion to Wittgenstein*, Cambridge: Cambridge University Press, 1996.
Von Wright, G.H., *Wittgenstein*, Oxford: Blackwell, 1982.

NICHOLAS C. BURBULES AND MICHAEL PETERS

MARTIN HEIDEGGER 1889–1976

> To learn means to make everything we do answer to those essentials that address themselves to us at any given time. ...
> Teaching is more difficult than learning because what teaching calls for is this: to let learn.[1]

It would be difficult to overstate the significance of Martin Heidegger for the thinking of the twentieth century. He was without doubt one of the most influential – and controversial – philosophers of his time and commentators credit him with influencing numerous disciplines in addition to philosophy: theology, psychiatry, literary criticism, historiography, theory of language, philosophy of science, and the analysis of technological society.[2] Over several generations, prominent thinkers such as Jean-Paul Sartre, Maurice Merleau-Ponty, Hans-Georg Gadamer, Hannah Arendt, Michel Foucault, Pierre Bourdieu, Jacques Derrida, Charles Taylor and Richard Rorty have acknowledged their debt to him.[3] In addition to the seminal quality of his writing, there is its sheer mass. It has been estimated that his collected texts, which are in the process of being published, will amount to some hundred volumes. And although he rarely explicitly addressed the topic of education as such, because of the profundity of his insights into the human condition and into the nature of learning, thinking and understanding, the field of education is one in which his ideas have the potential to make a huge impact – which is now beginning to be recognized.

Martin Heidegger was born in Messkirch, Germany on 26 September 1889. He went to the University of Freiburg in 1909 to study theology and philosophy and was appointed to teach philosophy at the University of Marburg in1922. Here he gained a reputation as an inspirational teacher whose passion for thinking shone through in a way that both startled and communicated itself to his listeners.[4] His first major work, the hugely influential *Sein und Zeit* (*Being and Time*), was published in 1927, and this both led him to be appointed to the chair of Philosophy at Freiburg in 1928 and propelled him into international prominence. With some disruption during the Second World War and its aftermath, he continued to give lectures until 1967 and to write until his death on 26 May 1976. He was buried in the place of his birth.

This apparently highly academic life should not deceive one into supposing that his ideas are of merely academic interest. In the context of education, his development of the notions of thinking and of personal authenticity, and his radical critique of the essence of modern technology, have the potential to be taken up in ways that have profound consequences for the development of educational practice. As the quotation that heads this essay suggests, Heidegger saw learning as a highly demanding and participatory affair, which required the full engagement of the learner and was certainly not something that could be instilled from without through a heavily didactic process. Nor, indeed, on his account, could it be conceived of in terms of the achievement of a pre-specified set of detailed learning objectives as set out in some national curriculum. The teacher has to *let* pupils learn, not impose learning upon them. This may make learning sound rather passive in character, but such an interpretation could hardly be farther from the truth. What was crucial for Heidegger was that learners submit themselves to the demands and rigour of thinking – to listen to what *calls* to be thought from out of the unique learning situation in which they are involved. He was against the mechanization of thinking which attempts to enframe it in pre-specified and often highly instrumental structures, thus closing down its possibilities. For Heidegger, genuine thinking is not the assimilation of a series of gobbets of pre-specified information and ideas, but an exciting and demanding journey into the unknown. It is drawn forward by the pull of that which is somehow incipient in our awareness but has yet to reveal itself.

The power of this view of learning is magnified when we consider Heidegger's view of the nature of the authentic life and of authentic understanding. Heidegger's (uncompleted) quest in *Being and Time* is to understand the nature of 'Being' – that through which things exist. In order to pursue this understanding he begins a profound analysis of the place where beings show themselves – human life and understanding ('Dasein').

And while, for Heidegger, this analysis of human existence is only a precursor to investigating the question of Being, it is, in itself, very suggestive for the enterprise of education. Central to Heidegger's characterization of human beings in *Being and Time* is that they are the entities for whom their own being is an issue. We live understandingly, having some conception of ourselves in situations in which there are choices to be made. But for much of the time the personal cogency of this understanding is tranquillized through our submersion in the 'idle talk' and 'hearsay' of what Heidegger refers to as the 'they-self'.[5] This is a frame of mind in which we are carried along by the busyness of immediate practical concern and the 'common sense' of the 'they' – what 'everybody' thinks and says. This is an essentially irresponsible 'averaged off' understanding of life in which we don't think things through in terms of their meaning for our own unique existence – an existence ultimately bounded by, and given urgency by, the fact of our own inevitable death – but understand them only in terms of what is current in the fashion and the gossip, which readily passes on to the next thing rather than test the validity of its assumptions in truly personal terms. To live thus is to live 'inauthentically' – to live in a way which is not true to ourselves.

If we relate these ideas to his view of the nature of genuine thinking previously discussed, we can see that a radical challenge is issued to much that goes on in conventional schools. For example, it raises the following kinds of question. To what extent does the learning that goes on in schools largely have the character of 'hearsay' – pupils having little opportunity, much less encouragement, to truly relate what they learn to their sense of their own existence? To what extent does the conception of education which motivates school learning derive from instrumental conceptions of life and work which eschew underlying questions of personal meaning and the open quality of engagement with issues described earlier? On a Heideggerian account, education proper is no more about acquiring the skills required to feed the demands of global capitalism than it is about the acquisition of knowledge purely for its own sake. It is pre-eminently concerned with the value and meaning that we derive from learning – how we feel it should affect our outlook and our actions, and our conception of ourselves both as responsible individuals and as participants in the human condition.

For this quality of learning to be achieved there is a need for a qualitatively different conception of the teacher–pupil relationship to that which underlies much current practice. Rather than a teacher–pupil relationship envisaged as the vehicle for conveying (or 'delivering') pre-specified knowledge and skills (for which both teacher and pupil can subsequently be held accountable), it becomes an open space which constantly takes its start from the quality of the learner's engagement with the domain in which he or she is operating and arises as a free though not undisciplined response to that engagement. The precise content of learning evolves out of this relationship, not ahead of it, though it is certainly the role of the teacher to stimulate and to provoke further engagement by, for example, helping the learner to identify and to pursue the questions that need to be asked.

In my own development of Heidegger's ideas for teaching, I have described this role as one of 'empathetic challenging' (Bonnett 1994) because it requires the teacher to be both receptive and demanding. The teacher is required to enter sympathetically into the engagement of the learner – but not in such a way as to indulge and thereby stultify this engagement – but rather to provoke and to challenge through a sense of what the subject matter has to offer, what is 'on the move' within it and what might be the issues at stake for this learner in this engagement. Openness and mutual trust become the defining characteristics, with the teacher concerned both to accept and to challenge the pupil's thinking – to listen to what calls to be thought in the engagement and to help the pupil to hear this call for himself or herself. This is clearly far removed from an education driven by a demand to raise generalized predetermined standards, and a form of accountability which requires recurrent public testing for tangible gain in these terms. It is also clearly distinguishable from child-centred views of education, portrayed (often erroneously) as being content to leave everything to what might be the whim of ephemeral and undisciplined interest. A Heideggarian account of education preserves the dignity and the integrity of learner, teacher and content. No doubt it is for this reason he describes the role of the teacher as 'exalted'.[6]

This brings us up against another strand in Heidegger's thinking which is rich in its significance for education: his critiques of technology and rationality. As well as being value laden in all sorts of fairly obvious ways – for example, as expressed in the discipline and moral code of the school, in its rituals, practices, and ethos, its public statement of aims and in the relative status given to various curriculum areas – Heidegger's thinking can sensitize us to the way education conveys values of a more implicit kind which are nonetheless immensely powerful in conditioning our relationship with the world and thus shaping both our view of that world and our view of ourselves. His analysis of modern technology suggests that in its essence it is a way of revealing Being which expresses a drive to mastery and conceives the world as a resource. And, because of its apparent manifest success, this 'calculative' way of thinking, which reckons everything up in terms of its potential to serve human purposes, is in the ascendant and increasingly permeates modern rationality as a whole – firing concerns to classify, to assess, to explain and to predict in order to intellectually possess and to materially utilize. This is a particularly worrying thought in a situation where many of those who resist an overtly instrumental view of education which gears it to economic ends espouse the development of rationality as an alternative educational aim. The intention of such 'liberal educators' is to provide a more generous conception of education which asserts the development and enrichment of the mind as its *raison d'être* and, through the celebration of rationality in education, takes itself to provide a foundation for the full development of the individual as a thinking being. But Heidegger's analysis suggests that this view is itself in danger of importing into education a version of that aggressive instrumentalism to which it ostensibly stands opposed. If even that arbiter of good thinking – 'impartial' rationality – is in fact highly partial and expresses a calculative attitude towards the world, surely educationalists need to be alert to the values that are implicit in the kinds of rationality and knowledge that are used to develop students' thinking and the pictures that they hold up – and legitimize – of ourselves and the world.

This would not simply be a matter of feeling concern that, for example, in the UK ostensibly 'calculative' subjects such as numeracy, science and ICT (information and communications technology) have come to dominate the curriculum in state schools. What is at stake is the character of *all* subjects and of our understanding of the meaning of quality in teaching. Increasingly, it may be that all teaching will be conceived on a very calculative model in which learning objectives are pre-specified independently of individual learners and are systematically pursued in the absence of the kind of full learner engagement previously described. In keeping with this, literature and the arts may be conceived and structured on very rationalist lines which set them up as centring on conventional categories, canons and truths which can be learnt up and objectively applied (and assessed), rather than as opportunities to participate afresh in the non-prespecifiable presencing of things. This contrasts strongly with a curriculum – including maths and science – being taught in a way that celebrates the more open, 'poetic' qualities of its content and the rigour and richness of personal engagement in learning. Among many other things, Heidegger's thinking confronts us with this choice of fundamental orientation and intimates its significance for a conception of education which is truly for 'life'.

Notes

1 *What is Called Thinking?*, trans. J. Gray, London: Harper & Row, pp.14–15, 1968.
2 M. Murray (ed.), *Heidegger and Modern Philosophy*, London: Yale University Press, p.vii, 1978.
3 H. Dreyfus and H. Hall, *Heidegger: A Critical Reader*, Oxford: Blackwell, p.1, 1992.
4 Hans-Georg Gadamer, quoted in *Martin Heidegger: Basic Writings*, D. Krell (ed.), London: Routledge & Kegan Paul, pp.15–16, 1978.
5 *Being and Time*, trans. J. Macquarrie and E. Robinson, Oxford: Blackwell, sections 26–7, 35–7, 1973.
6 *What is Called Thinking?*, p.15.

See also

In this book: Bourdieu, Foucault

Heidegger's major writings

What is Called Thinking?, trans. J. Gray, London: Harper & Row, 1968.
Poetry, Language, Thought, trans. A. Hofstadter, London: Harper & Row, 1971.
Being and Time, trans. J. Macquarrie and E. Robinson, Oxford: Blackwell, 1973.
The Question Concerning Technology and Other Essays, trans. W. Lovitt, London: Harper & Row, 1977.
Martin Heidegger: Basic Writings, D. Krell (ed.), London: Routledge & Kegan Paul, 1978.

Further reading

Bonnett, M., *Children's Thinking*, London: Cassell, 1994.
Cooper, D., *Authenticity and Learning*, London: Routledge & Kegan Paul, 1983.
Dreyfus, H. and Hall, H., *Heidegger: A Critical Reader*, Oxford: Blackwell, 1992.
Mulhall, S., *Heidegger and Being and Time*, London: Routledge, 1996.
Peters, M. (ed.), *Heidegger, Modernity and Education*, Boulder, CO: Rowman and Littlefield, 2001.

MICHAEL BONNETT

HERBERT EDWARD READ 1893–1968

Art should be the basis of education.[1]

Herbert Read was one of the most prolific, cosmopolitan and ambitious English intellectuals and men of letters of the twentieth century. During his lifetime he was practically ubiquitous as a critic, scholar, poet, advocate and educator. He left a singular legacy of academic and popular publications – more than sixty books and 1000 articles and reviews – which include his own considerable literary achievements, and his relentless political and cultural advocacy for interpreting and understanding modern art and literature. He was a man who championed such world-class talents as Karl Jung and Henry Moore, while becoming a public antagonist of others such as T.S. Eliot and W.H. Auden. While his passion for individual liberty has led Read to be widely characterized as a 'philosophical anarchist' (a description which Read would not disavow),[2] the man was personally restrained in speech and at least in public temperament. He was indeed a man of paradox and contradiction.

Herbert Read was born in Yorkshire on 4 December 1893, grew up on a farm, and attended the University of Leeds. During the First World War he served as an infantry officer, an experience which, like others of his generation, found compelling expression in poetry, such as in Read's *Naked Warriors* (1919). After the war Read worked for a few years at the Treasury (1919–22) and then became an assistant keeper at the Victoria and Albert Museum in London (1922–31). He taught briefly at the University of Edinburgh (1931–33) and edited the *Burlington Magazine* (1933–39), a fixture of the British cultural establishment. Throughout the 1930s he championed such modernists as the writers Samuel Beckett and Denton Welch, and such artists as Barbara Hepworth and Ben Nicholson. The magazine editorship provided an open channel to the academic and highbrow community, but Read also proselytized for modernism in a copious series of popular books, magazine and newspaper reviews directed at the general public.

In this ambition Read carried forward the work of John Ruskin and William Morris, nineteenth-century precursors who sought to reduce the distinction between art and life by exploring aesthetic concepts as social value, such as the tradition of craftsmanship, drawn from the visual arts. These might provide remedies for repairing, what they saw as, an increasingly distressed social fabric (imperilled by the Industrial Revolution). Read also emulated Ruskin's affection for the Romantics, and staunchly defended such English authors as Wordsworth, Coleridge and Shelley at a time when the advanced literary criticism led by T.S. Eliot disavowed the older styles.

Read's own creative output struggled for time and attention amidst his editorial and interpretive responsibilities. His poems were well received and appeared in several volumes between 1919 and 1966. In 'Song', published in 1955, Read identified himself with life's continuity, and perhaps that of art and tradition:

> So long my heart
> This little polish'd ball of blood
> Has throbb'd in unison
> With your immortal flood[3]

In fact, Read appears to have considered it his professional mission to simultaneously but selectively defend the traditional – his own preferences were actually oriented towards the classical – while advocating, educating and preparing society for the new. His role as the proponent of modernism was unparalleled in Britain, where the avant-garde often scrimmaged unsuccessfully to bring the nation into the contemporary world. He took up the cause of new forms of industrial design and other visual arts in particular, promoting movements from cubism to surrealism to abstract expressionism.

Read's prominent role as an advocate gave him real cultural power. He was, as his biographer James King has written, 'taste-maker and cultural impresario',[4] taking all of art and culture as his domain. Read's sight and insight was lavished on an impressive array of art forms, including painting, sculpture, architecture, design, ceramics, stained glass, prose and poetry. His audience was often the philistine public, who could find in Read a patient teacher that recognized the bewildering variety and incomprehension with which many modern styles burst upon the scene. In such volumes as *Art Now* (1933), *Icon and Idea* (1955) and *Contemporary British Art* (1964), Read examined the motivation (he was one of the first to apply Jungian psychoanalysis to art) and meaning of artists and their works.

Read the writer was reinforced by Read the 'impresario'. The range of his expertise and scale of his professional contributions was prodigious. In addition to his own literary and critical productivity, Read served as a director of the venerable British publishing house Routledge and Kegan Paul for a quarter of a century; he juried and curated exhibitions, including a major show of the surrealists in 1936 in London and several exhibitions of children's art in the early 1940s which prefigured his own plans for aesthetic education; he created advocacy organizations, including the Design Research Unit in 1943, the Institute of Contemporary Arts in 1948, and the UNESCO-sponsored International Society for Education through Art in 1951; and, he appeared widely in Europe and in the United States, where his Charles Eliot Norton Lectures at Harvard honoured a man who himself had played the role of arts popularizer and cultural entrepreneur while serving as the first professor of fine arts at Harvard in the late nineteenth century.

Ultimately Herbert Read was interested in more than just helping people understand and appreciate innovations in art. He had a fundamental belief in human progress which, like the social aesthetic of Ruskin and Morris, would carry art beyond aesthetics. As Hilton Kramer put it in the *New York Times* obituary of Herbert Read in 1968, Read conceived of art as 'perhaps the most essential constituent of an enlightened social fabric ... a cornerstone of the attempt to effect a wholesale revision of social values'. And in that attempt 'education was to play a major role'.[5]

Read's *Education through Art*, first published in 1943, was thought by its author to be his most influential book. Although now out of print for three decades, a generation of art and other educators (especially in Britain) from the 1940s into the 1960s was nurtured on the social messages of the book. Written at the height of the Second World War, Read hoped to harness the creative and imaginative energies of art to counter the endless cycles of violence. He saw the artist as an 'ideal type' who offers 'awareness of intrinsic value'.[6] In this aspiration Read spoke for art educators and other teachers everywhere who have deeply felt the need to transcend the barriers and encumbrances of nationalism, creed and ethnicity.

The book is instructive without being specific. No programme or curriculum is presented, but the basis for considering art as a framework for general education of the mind and personality is articulated in detailed chapters that examine such topics as 'perception and imagination', 'unconscious modes of integration', and 'the aesthetic basis of discipline and morality'. Read saw himself as a philosopher or critic rather than as a pedagogue. His role was to provide the philosophical foundations for an aesthetic education through which the most urgent problem of human society – the unremitting descent into barbarism (the Holocaust was actually underway when Read wrote the book) – could be addressed and a world order based on humane principles attained.

Education through art, Read contended, is 'education for peace' (the title of a subsequent volume of essays printed in 1949). It may be true that nations that explore, understand and enjoy one another's cultural patrimony will be too busy discovering values in common to go to war. But while the hope was noble, the method was not. Read helped develop the frontier between art and psychology, but he put too much faith in behaviourist agendas for transforming human beings, as likely to lead to indoctrination as to emancipation.

Herbert Read had begun his advocacy educating audiences about the artistic and redemptive power of the new modernism. In *Education through Art* and subsequent writings he turned to 'the total reorientation of the human personality'.[7] The study and practice of art, and the aesthetic education through which it might occur, led inexorably by Read's calculation to ethical virtue. This alone was not a new idea, but Read brought to the argument the capacities of a polymathic scholar, drawing on sources as diverse as theories of education from Plato's *Republic*, principles of gestalt psychology and recent research on children's drawings.

Education through Art is a compendium of contemporary thinking in art education after the progressive 1920s and 1930s, during which psychology and the power of perceptual faculties began to dominate the field, introducing a twenty-year period of hegemony led principally by Viktor

Lowenfeld and Rudolf Arnheim after the Second World War. Read provided philosophical balance.

Herbert Read was unquestionably a productive and sincere scholar. But the contradictions in his character and effort were just as evident. On one hand he was the cosmopolitan who sought to establish Britain's contributions, especially in art and industrial design, to the emerging international modernist order. But at the same time he was more of a traditionalist when it came to British poetry and he famously embraced the Romantics. Read could simultaneously relish the take-no-hostages role of the 'philosophical anarchist' (where, as Kramer put it, 'the dream of uprooting power persists as a romantic aspiration'),[8] while working diligently and comfortably within the establishment as an editor, organizer, or spokesman. Read was, according to his obituary, 'a familiar presence' and 'one of the most celebrated cultural panjandrums of the international cultural bureaucracy', serving endlessly on juries, boards and symposia.[9] But Sir Herbert Read wasn't too much of an anarchist to refuse a knighthood when it was conferred in 1953.

Perhaps the harshest judgement that some critics and biographers have made about Read is that he may have indiscriminately endorsed everything contemporary, with the exception of the so-called 'post-modern' movements whose forms, like pop art, Read despised. He did seem uncritical of modernism's excesses and failures, and acquired the reputation of being especially parochial about British art. In addition, an unsurprising consequence of the packaging and repackaging of content for the general public was a lamentable dearth of original intellectual substance on some occasions, as in Read's best-selling 'concise histories'.[10]

On the plus side, Sir Herbert Read brought a clarifying tendency for explanation and interpretation to the often confused and dynamically changing world of modern art. He enabled thousands of readers and viewers to apprehend what may have been difficult to see and understand, and he considered the awareness for which he was responsible as a social good, leading to an integration of art and life. Perhaps somewhat neglected in some reviews of Read's contributions, given his 'impresario' role in the visual arts, were his literary and autobiographical entries, notably *The Contrary Experience* (1963). At least one of his books was a novel, *The Green Child* (1935). Read also made some significant contributions in literary criticism, as when he elucidated the distinction between organic and abstract form, the former of which Read favoured as more responsive to the needs of the individual artist in a particular context.

In fact, Read's own life was organized to give organic unity to the various parts of his being. As an author, editor and publishing house director, he could help navigate and chart a course through the powerful currents of British literature and criticism. As a lecturer and commentator on modern art, he served the entrepreneurial impulse of drawing people closer to contemporary painting, sculpture and other art forms. Ready with a quip or a philosophical argument, Read laboured to introduce the new to a public that was not always understanding or approving, especially of the avant-garde.

For educators, he left the legacy of 'Education through Art', not just the book but the idealism as well; a humane vision which continues to hold value for animating teachers and others of good will. Students today would look at Read more for historical interest than current citation, but the nobility of that vision and the aspiration for a just society built on principles of individual expression make Read's prose still worth pondering. The spirit of his ideas survive in the social and cultural orientation which draws on works of literature and art as sources for moral encouragement and instruction, and that continues as a priority in the careers of so many writers and artists, teachers, parents and others (an example in American art education would be the 'Caucus on Social Theory' within the National Art Education Association). Read represented the 'English' ideal, perhaps best expressed by those Romantic poets he admired, of a life lived with a sense of one's purpose and fulfilment in the grand scheme of things. Herbert Read knew his purpose and he carried it out with dispatch and fervour.

Notes

1 Read, *Education through Art*, pp.305, 308.
2 Read, *The Cult of Sincerity*, New York: Horizon Press, pp.76–93, 1968.
3 Read, *Moon's Farm & Poems Mostly Elegiac*, London: Faber & Faber, 1955.
4 James King, *The Last Modern: A Life of Herbert Read*, London: Weidenfeld & Nicolson, London, preface, p.xv, 1990.
5 Hilton Kramer, *New York Times*, 30 June 1968, section II, p.23.
6 *Education through Art*, pp.305, 308.
7 Malcolm Ross, 'Herbert Read: Art, Education and the Means of Redemption', in David Goodway (ed.), *Herbert Read Reassessed*, Liverpool: Liverpool University Press, p.199, 1998.
8 Hilton Kramer, op cit.
9 Ibid.
10 Read, *A Concise History of Modern Sculpture*, London: Thames & Hudson, London, 1964.

See also

In *Fifty Major Thinkers on Education*: Plato, Ruskin

Read's major writings

Naked Warriors, London: Arts & Letters, 1919.
Collected Poems, London: Faber & Faber, London, new edn, 1953, *c.*1926.
Reason and Romanticism, New York: Russell & Russell, 1963, *c.*1926.
Art Now: An Introduction to the Theory of Modern Painting and Sculpture, New York: Harcourt, Brace & Company, 1933.
The Innocent Eye, New York: Henry Holt & Company, 1947, *c.*1933.
The Green Child: A Romance, London: Robin Clark, 1989, *c.*1935.
Surrealism, London: Faber & Faber, 1936.
Collected Essays in Literary Criticism, London: Faber & Faber, 2nd edn, 1951 *c.*1938.
To Hell with Culture, London: Kegan Paul, Trench, Trubner, 1941.
Education through Art, London: Faber & Faber, new rev. edn 1958, *c.*1943.
The Grass Roots of Art, New York: Meridian, 1967, *c.*1946.
Art and Industry: The Principles of Industrial Design, London: Faber & Faber, 1947.
Education for Peace, New York: Charles Scribner's Sons, 1949.
Contemporary British Art, Baltimore, MD: Penguin Books, rev. edn 1964, *c.*1951.

Icon and Idea: The Function of Art in the Development of Human Consciousness, Cambridge, MA: Harvard University Press, 1955.
The Contrary Experience: Autobiographies, New York: Horizon Press, 1963.
A Concise History of Modern Sculpture, London: Thames & Hudson, 1964.
The Origins of Form in Art, London: Thames & Hudson, 1965.
The Redemption of the Robot: My Encounter with Education through Art, New York: Trident Press, 1966.
Art and Alienation: The Role of the Artist in Society, New York: Horizon Press, 1967.
Poetry & Experience, New York: Horizon Press, 1967.
The Cult of Sincerity, New York: Horizon Press, 1968.

Further reading

Goodway, David (ed.), *Herbert Read Reassessed,* Liverpool: Liverpool University Press, 1998.
King, James, *The Last Modern: A Life of Herbert Read,* London: Weidenfeld & Nicolson, 1990.
Woodcock, George, *Herbert Read: The Stream and the Source,* London: Faber & Faber, 1972.

STEPHEN MARK DOBBS

LEV SEMYONOVICH VYGOTSKY 1896–1934

Culture is the product of social life and human social activity. That is why just by raising the question of the cultural development of behavior we are directly introducing the social plane of development.[1]

Vygotsky was one of the most important Russian psychologists of the first part of the twentieth century. He is most famous for his research into the development and structure of human consciousness, and his theory of signs, which explains the way in which children internalize language in the course of their cultural development. However, Vygotsky's influence goes far beyond developmental psychology. Special education, adult education, speech-communication, vocational education, information systems research: these are only some examples of areas of research and practice which have been profoundly influenced by Vygotsky and his followers.

Lev Vygotsky was born in 1896 in a small town, Orscha, in Belorussia, to a middle-class Jewish family. His father, a bank manager, was a well-educated man, who endeavoured to provide his son with the best education possible. Lev studied with a private tutor for many years and enrolled in a gymnasium only when he was only at the eighth-grade level (14–15 years of age). During his formative years, Vygotsky was an avid learner, and by the age of eighteen he was already a well-rounded intellectual, conversant in a variety of subjects, including history, philosophy, art and literature. In 1913, at the insistence of his parents, he entered the Moscow University, where he studied first at the Medical School and then at the Law School. However, his real intellectual interest was in the humanities and social sciences, and

Vygotsky enrolled also at the private Shaniavsky University, majoring in history and philosophy.

At that time, Moscow was an exciting place for a young intellectual: new trends were emerging in science and philosophy, Stanislavsky had introduced paradigm-shifting innovations in theatre, a structuralist revolution was being carried out in linguistics and literary theory by the Formalist school (Shklovsky, Jakubinsky and Jakobson), and in poetry symbolists had captivated the minds of Russian intellectuals with their paradigm-shifting innovations in the usage of language structures. Vygotsky had an interest in, and a profound knowledge of, most of these new trends. This became apparent later, when lines from Russian and Western European poets, philosophers and scientists appeared in his works, lending an unusual, Renaissance-style breadth and texture to his writing.

Shortly after graduating from the Moscow University in 1917, Vygotsky moved to Gomel, where his parents lived. He stayed there until 1924, first teaching literature at a provincial school and then lecturing at a local teachers' college. In 1924, after being noticed at an academic conference, where he delivered a powerful presentation on the methodology of psychological studies, he was invited to the Moscow Institute of Psychology to serve as a research fellow. In 1925, he defended his Ph.D. thesis titled 'The Psychology of Art'. In the introduction to this work, Vygotsky argued that psychology cannot limit itself to direct evidence, be it observable behaviour or accounts of introspection. To him, psychological inquiry was an investigation, and like a criminal investigation, it had to take into account indirect evidence and circumstantial clues, which meant that works of art, philosophical arguments and anthropological data were no less important than any direct evidence.

At the Institute of Psychology, the focus of Vygotsky's research programme during 1926–30 was the experimental study of the mechanism of transformation of natural psychological functions into the higher functions of logical memory, selective attention, decision making, learning and comprehension of language. This period was marked by the formulation of principles of Vygotsky's developmental psychology. Although this theory embraced all higher mental functions, his particular interest was in the development of language and speech and their relation to thought. His book on this subject, called *Thought and Language*, first published in 1934, became Vygotsky's most popular work.

The early 1930s – the last period of Vygotsky's research career – proved to be the most difficult and momentous years not only for him, but also for all Soviet academics truly dedicated to their scholarship. The communist regime declared 1929 to be the year of a 'great breakthrough' in all areas of social, political and economic life of the country. In fact, it was the beginning of the tightening of Communist party control over all aspects of intellectual life – a trend that led, in several years, to a complete suppression of all independent thinking and to a physical elimination of a significant part of the intellectual élite of the country. From then on, Soviet psychologists were expected to derive their ideas exclusively from the works of Marx, Engels and Lenin (and, soon, Stalin). Such a turn of events seriously undermined Vygotsky's research programme, which relied upon such 'decadent', and 'anti-Marxist' theories, as psychoanalysis and Gestalt psychology. Vygotsky, who was already seriously ill, continued to work in Moscow until 1934, when he died of tuberculosis. Even before his death, most of his friends and colleagues (among them, Luria and Leont'ev) were forced either to leave the Moscow Institute of Psychology for less visible positions in provincial towns, or to change their research programmes to something less controversial. Contemporary Russian psychologists, in private conversations, express an opinion that, even if Vygotsky did not die of tuberculosis, his chances of surviving the Stalinist purges of 1936–37 were slim.

There are two major reasons for Vygotsky's current appeal in the West. First, he was a rare example of a true encyclopedist in twentieth-century psychology, having profound knowledge of not only his immediate area of research, but also of such diverse subjects as psychology of art, literary theory, neurology, defectology and psychiatry. Vygotsky's theories, therefore, were based on an interdisciplinary synthesis and appeal to scientists from a variety of fields.

A second reason for Vygotsky's popularity with contemporary social scientists is his analysis of the social origins of mental processes. In Vygotsky's view, mental functioning in the individual can be understood only by going outside the individual and examining the social and cultural processes from which it derives. Instead of beginning with the assumption that mental functioning occurs first and foremost within the individual, Vygotsky assumes that one can speak equally appropriately of mental processes occurring between people on the intermental plan. Learning and development occurs when what happens on this intermental plan is internalized by individual participants in intersubjective processes. Vygotsky viewed mental functioning as a kind of action that may be carried out by individuals or by dyads and larger groups. This view is one in which mind, cognition and memory are understood as 'extending beyond the skin', as functions that can be carried out both intermentally or intramentally. Vygotsky referred to his theory as cultural-historical, stressing that the factors determining the individual's life activity were produced by the historical development of culture.

Two concepts, related to the idea of the social origin of mental processes, which have taken on particular importance in contemporary Western developmental psychology, speech-communication research and education are the 'Zone of Proximal Development' (ZPD), and 'inner speech'. According to the ZPD concept, psychological development depends upon outside social forces as much as upon inner resources. The underlying assumption behind this concept is that psychological development and instruction are socially embedded; to understand them one must analyse the surrounding society and its social relations. Vygotsky maintained that the child is able to copy actions which surpass his or her own capacities, but only within limits. When copying, the child is able to perform much better when guided by adults than when working alone. Vygotsky defined ZPD as the distance between a child's 'actual developmental level as determined by independent problem solving and the level of potential development as determined through problem solving under adult guidance or in collaboration with more capable peers'.[2] Therefore, ZPD is an analytic tool necessary to plan instruction, and successful instruction has to create a ZPD that stimulates a series of inner-developmental processes.

Another concept central to Vygotsky's work is that of 'inner speech'. This concept emerged from Vygotsky's quest (which became a central theme of the last period of his work) to find the relation of the invisible act of thought to language as a phenomenon of culture, accessible to an objective analysis. Inner speech, a kind of silent talking to oneself, is a central issue in the problem of the relation between thought and language. Behaviourists maintained that thought is merely subvocal speech – overt speech grown very small. Vygotsky, in opposition to behaviourism, held that the mind evolves to reflect social reality. According to Vygotsky, the process of trying to communicate with others results in the development of word meanings that then form the structure of consciousness. Inner speech cannot exist without social interaction. In a gradual developmental process, symbols, first used in communication, are turned inward to regulate behaviour in the interests of social cooperation.

An analysis of Vygotsky's major works, written during different periods of his life, reveals a striking proof of his theory of the dependence of the creative process on the socio-historical context. If his analysis of Shakespeare's *Hamlet* (Vygotsky's major work started during his student years, and was expanded and completed in 1925) is grounded in symbolism and psychoanalysis, and is preoccupied with the issues of mysticism and religiosity, Vygotsky's later work shows clear signs of the influence of the Marxist 'historical materialism' and Hegelian philosophy of the evolution of the human mind.

Any attempt to describe the influence of Vygotsky on a variety of contemporary social science disciplines can be only partial. This description is even more complicated by the mediated nature of links between successor theories. Thus, in educational psychology, Vygotsky's ideas provided a foundation for Russian developmental psychology,[3] which, in turn, had a profound influence on various branches of Western educational psychology and, later, made possible Davydov's theory of child development.[4]

Probably, one of the most interesting contemporary applications of Vygotsky's ideas is the version of the activity theory by Cole and Engestrom.[5] The broad tradition of the activity theory was first developed out of Vygotsky's social-historical psychological theory by one of his main collaborators, A.N. Leont'ev, beginning in the late 1930s. Cole and Engestrom's version of the activity theory posits the *activity system* as the basic unit of analysis of individual and collective behaviour. An activity system is any ongoing, object-directed, historically conditioned, dialectically structured, tool-mediated human interaction. It could be a family, a religious organization, a study group, a school, a discipline, or a profession. Activity systems are mutually constructed and continuously reconstructed by participants who use certain tools, both physical and cognitive. With the social division of labour, a range of ongoing systems or networks of activity systems arise and proliferate. The use of tools mediates the behaviour of people in activity systems in specific and objective ways that are realized historically, through cooperation and/or competition in the specialized use of tools arising from the social division of labour. Starting in the 1980s, activity theory, still closely associated in the minds of most scholars with its forefather Vygotsky, gained numerous adherents worldwide and now is exercising a tremendous influence on research and practice in such fields as education, linguistics, communication, computer science and computer interface design, studies of work expertise, and many others.

Notes

1 Vygotsky, 'The Genesis of Higher Mental Functions', in J.V. Wertsch (ed.), *The Concept of Activity in Soviet Psychology*, Arnomk, NY: Sharpe, p.164, 1981.
2 Vygotsky, *Mind in Society: The Development of Higher Psychological Processes*, Cambridge, MA: Harvard University Press, pp.85–6, 1978.
3 A.N. Leont'ev, *Activity, Consciousness, and Personality*, Englewood Cliffs, NJ: Prentice Hall, 1978.
4 V.V. Davydov, 'The Influence of L.S. Vygotsky on Education Theory, Research, and Practice', trans. S. Kerr, *Educational Researcher*, 24 (3), pp.12–21, 1995.
5 M. Cole and Y. Engestrom, 'A Cultural-Historical Interpretation of Distributed Cognition', in G. Salomon (ed.), *Distributed Cognition*, Cambridge: Cambridge University Press, 1996.

See also

In this book: Bruner, Hegel, Piaget, Thorndike

Vygotsky's major writings

Thought and Language, Cambridge, MA: The MIT Press, 1999, 1934.
The Psychology of Art, Cambridge: MIT Press, 1971.
Mind in Society: The Development of Higher Psychological Processes, Cambridge, MA: Harvard University Press, 1978.
The Collected Works of L.S. Vygotsky, New York: Plenum Press, 1987.
The Vygotsky Reader, Oxford: Blackwell, 1994.

Further reading

Daniels, H., *An Introduction to Vygotsky*, London: Routledge, 1996.
Kozoulin, A., *Vygotsky's Psychology: A Biography of Ideas*, London: Harvester, 1990.
Wertsch, J. (ed.), *Culture, Communication, and Cognition: Vygotskian Perspectives*, Cambridge: Cambridge University Press, 1985.
Yaroshevsky, M., *Lev Vygotsky*, Moscow: Progress, 1989.

ALEXANDER ARDICHVILI

JEAN PIAGET 1896–1980

BRINGUIER: You formulated principles for restructuring the teaching of mathematics.
PIAGET: *No, no . . .*
BRINGUIER: And didn't it result in a teaching method?
PIAGET: *No.*
BRINGUIER: Oh, I thought it did . . .

PIAGET: *Education, for most people, means trying to lead the child to resemble the typical adult of his society (whereas) for me, education means making creators, even if there aren't many of them, even if one's creations are limited by comparison with those of others.*[1]

Jean Piaget was born on 9 August 1896 in Neuchâtel, Switzerland. He gained his Ph.D. in biology from his local university in 1918, when he also published an intellectual novel, *Recherche*. This seminal text set out Piaget's research programme. Science is factual and religion is value-laden. Their accounts of reality are often incompatible. How can they be combined? But this problem generalizes. Human actions have both causal and normative properties. How, then, does true knowledge develop? This is a fundamental question in epistemology with implications for education. It was central to the prodigious torrent of fifty books and 500 papers published by Piaget and now recognized as a major contribution to human knowledge. Piaget gained his first chair in Neuchâtel in 1925, moving to remain at Geneva University from 1929 onwards. He was appointed Director of the International Bureau of Education in the same year, and was the founding Director of the International Centre for Genetic Epistemology in 1955. He gained his first honorary degree from Harvard University in 1936, followed by more than forty honours which included the Erasmus Prize in 1972. Piaget continued to work after his retirement in 1971 with eleven books on his constructivist epistemology. He died on 16 September 1980 in Geneva with posthumous works and translations continuing to appear.

Piaget's account of education is dependent on his epistemology. The link between them is knowledge and development as normative facts.

Epistemology

Traditionally, epistemology is a normative discipline. When Kant asked 'How is knowledge possible?', he wanted to identify the limits of human rationality in distinguishing science from superstition. His question was normative because knowledge is defined through norms. Norms are values which set out criteria (conditions) about what knowledge is, and so what it is not. One criterion of knowledge is the (objective) truth of what is known. This criterion excludes knowledge of a falsehood, although a falsehood can be believed. Piaget argued that epistemological questions have empirical counter-parts, for example: 'How does knowledge develop?' This question is empirical.[2] One way to gain evidence is through the study of the growth of knowledge during childhood. At issue is not the knower (child) who develops in different cultural contexts, but rather the use of norms in the growth of knowledge. Knowledge does not emerge ready-made in the mind of the child. Norms are not innate. Although some norms are cultural, intellectual norms – such as knowledge entails the truth of what is known – are not cultural. Cultural beliefs can be false (the sun rises every morning, women are devoid of rationality, and so on). Even so, norms are used, better norms are constructed in their use, and true knowledge does develop. This is the 'miracle' of human creativity. Novelty is a fact of life which continues to defy explanation. It is this fundamental problem which was addressed in Piaget's epistemology. Since knowledge develops with the use of norms, these are normative facts.[3] As such, normative facts can be investigated empirically as acts of judgement. These *acts* are due to psycho-social causes. These *judgements* are due to meaningful implications which are normative, not causal. Although 2 does not causally make 4, it does imply that $2 + 2 = 4$.

Here's an example. In replicating one of Piaget's studies of reasoning by mathematical induction, children aged seven years were asked to add 'a great number' to a pair of unequal numbers. Here is an extract from John's reasoning:

INTERVIEWER: How about if you put a great number in that one and a great number in that one. Would there be the same in each, or more there, or more there?

JOHN: *That would be right up to the cover in the sky and that would be right up to God, so then they would still have to be more.*

INTERVIEWER: What's the cover in the sky?

JOHN: *It's on top of where God lives.*[4]

This superb reasoning by analogy exemplifies five intellectual norms (a mnemonic is AEIOU): autonomy, entailment (necessary knowledge), intersubjectivity, objectivity, universality. His reasoning was *autonomous*: it was distinctively his own. It included an *entailment* which is a necessary relation about 'what has to be'. It was *intersubjective* and in line with the Euclidean axiom *equals added to unequals are unequal*, which is a paradigm case of 'common ground' between different thinkers. It was *objective* in being justified as a true response in a valid (truth-preserving) argument. It had a degree (level) of *universality*, whether or not open to transfer under different causal conditions. Each of these norms was used by John in the development of his knowledge.[5] The use made of intellectual norms such as these was central to Piaget's epistemology.

This epistemological shift is important on three counts. One is that action is the basis of knowledge, where *action* covers physical and social actions as well as intellectual operations. Further, there is a logic of action which Piaget characterized in formal models (structures). An 'action logic' is not the same as a 'mental logic'. Metacognition is at issue here in that structures control actions, even if the knower is not conscious of this action-regulation. This control includes a normative element in virtue of its dual function, as an intellectual tool generative of *truth*, and in the construction of *better* tools.[6] Second, an adequate epistemology should identify a mechanism responsible for novel knowledge, i.e. development. According to Piaget, this mechanism is equilibration. Its relation to teaching is taken up below. Third, development of knowledge takes time and is constructed over multiple levels. A couple of centuries separated Newton and Einstein.[7] Yet their theories are now taught at school – a clear case of acceleration, surely! This is education.[8]

Education

Education was defined by Piaget as a two-termed relation linking: 'on the one hand the *growing individual* (and) on the other hand the social, intellectual and moral *values* into which the educator is charged with initiating that individual'.[9] Individuals develop from birth onwards. In part, this development is causal for psycho-social investigation. But there is a normative component as well since educators invoke values. Values are norms which function as directives in identifying what is obligatory, permitted or forbidden. Education is a normative relation between an individual and values. On this view, education covers all types of values and so Piaget's definition does not assign a privileged status to one type over others. Rather, this decision is left to educators who face a common problem. This means that intellectual values during schooling are in the same boat as moral values during life. Teachers in one generation use their (intellectual, moral) values in the education of learners in the next generation. Thereby do they run straight into a fundamental problem. Teaching and learning are actions which have normative – and not merely causal – properties. This means that education is a value-laden exchange the success of which is dependent on both transmission and transformation.

To see what is at stake, imagine a society of exact contemporaries whose members are the same age. For example, *everybody* in this society is a child aged seven years. This society has neither a traditional culture nor generational legacies from the past, still less older or younger members. What would intellectual development be like in such a society?[10] In this thought-experiment, Piaget made clear that the members of such a society would have a major disadvantage. Without transmitted knowledge, development would be very difficult. But it would not be impossible. These contemporaries would have active minds. Transformation is therefore not impossible. Educationally speaking, this distinction is crucial. This causally atypical society generates a normatively typical problem.

Available knowledge is already constructed, and often codified in rule-governed systems through language. Indeed, rules, values and signs are fundamental aspects of human societies. These systems are accessed by teachers who introduce them as new knowledge to learners. This creates the problem of the 'horizon of intentionality'.[11] How do teachers (parents, peers) and learners gain access to the same 'horizon'? And how is it extended? The point is that learning is the action of acquiring knowledge. As such, learning also includes norms. And there are three possibilities here: (1) the norms of the knowledge-to-be-taught and the norms of the knowledge-used-in-learning are the same; or (2) the latter are in advance of the former; or (3) the former are in advance of the latter. Simple learning due to transmission is compatible with (1) and (2). Complex learning in virtue of transformation is required by (3). In Piaget's account, mediation based on norms is always required in learning. Knowledge is transmitted by teachers who are mediators in lowering barriers and augmenting opportunities in (1) and (2). But mediation occurs in a different and more powerful way as complex learning when better norms require construction, as in (3). This requires transformation.

Three instructional issues here concern diagnosis, processes and outcomes. Diagnostic assessment is required in the identification of levels of knowledge, both in teaching and in learning as a check on (mis)matching.[12] Piaget recommended that teachers should be investigative in carrying out their assessments.[13] Even so, his work did not extend to classroom assessment which is recognized to be a harder task. Second, classroom learning occurs in multiple ways, including group learning and 'learning by oneself'. Piaget was explicit in recommending group learning as a standard means of classroom learning.[14] But there was a proviso as well. Learning by oneself was also required. The contradiction here is more apparent than real since this is a normative, not a causal, claim. The claim is not that learning should be solitary, but that it should be autonomous.[15] Autonomy is not anarchy such that learners do what they want; rather, learners should want to do what they do.[16] This subtle distinction bears on the motivation of learning. It rules out heteronomy. Group learning can 'blind' members into accepting its (the group's) view without any regard for the individual's own view. This is also manifest as unthinking conformity or uncritical acceptance of intellectual authority.[17] Autonomy requires the individualization of knowledge, which may occur in group learning. Third, the outcome of learning is important. If the new level is too high, learning is liable to occur as repetition and conformity.

> It is not by knowing the Pythagorean theorem that the free exercise of a person's reason will be assured. Rather, it is assured by having rediscovered that there is such a theorem and how to prove it. The aim of intellectual education is not to know how to repeat or to conserve ready-made truths (a truth that is parroted is only a half-truth). It is in learning to gain the truth by oneself at the risk of losing a lot of time and of going through all the roundabout ways that are inherent in real activity.[18]

This theorem could well be assessed summatively as successful achievement in line with a school's standards. Yet this could occur without regard to real advance in future learning. After all, knowledge develops, and new knowledge has a formation to which present achievement makes a contribution. Correct responses devoid of reasons based on good reasoning are sterile in intellectual formation.

Teaching is no doubt practically necessary. The thought-experiment shows that. But it is not sufficient for good learning. Einstein's teachers did not teach him that $e = mc^2$. Novelty can lead to the recasting of available knowledge in veritable revolutions that go beyond what is taught. Further, good teaching can produce poor learning. Children who are taught to count successfully are often unsuccessful in number reasoning. Teaching children to count 'how many' is not sufficient for reasoning about 'as many'. This normative distinction was due to Frege who pointed out that if equality ('as many') is removed from arithmetic, there is almost nothing left – and this means that there is nothing left to count ('how many'). Piaget was familiar with Frege's work while a student in Neuchâtel.[19] He realized that if teaching is necessary but insufficient, something else is required as well.

This is equilibration, or complex learning.[20] Piaget's account of equilibration was incomplete. Even so, it secured two important principles for education. One is that creativity is important – whether as novel construction by the genius or re-construction by the rest of us – in that every human mind in action has the potential for advance: 'Each individual is led to think and re-think the system of collective notions.[21] A cultural legacy of collective wisdom is a useful starting point. But there is the end-point to reckon with as well. Living minds are minds in action with the capacity to make better judgement. This leads to the second principle that teaching can itself be effective. What is required is the creative design of learning tasks which are normatively empowering rather than causally disabling. This occurs in the triggering of transformations required for novel learning.[22] A criterial question arises here: 'Is reasoning an act of obedience, or is obedience an act of reason?'[23] Transmitting truths to learners who make responses in accordance with (in obedience to) what is taught is all very well. Successful achievement can be put on record. Obedience to reason is another matter. This requires agents to take charge of their learning by converting the reasons for their responses into good reason, even if this amounts to rational disobedience to what is taught.

Notes

1   Piaget, 'Twelfth Conversation', pp.128–32.
2   Ibid., p.18.
3   Normative facts consist in the use made of imperatives which act causally in human interactions. Normative facts themselves evolve (Piaget, *Sociological Studies*, pp.69, 166).
4   See Smith 2002.
5   See Smith 1999, 2001.
6   Piaget, *De la pédagogie*, p.108.
7   'Ideas which have been painfully 'invented' by the greatest geniuses (have) become, not merely accessible, but even easy and obvious, to schoolchildren' (Piaget, *Sociological Studies*, p.37).
8   'All education, in one way or another, is just such an acceleration' (Piaget, *To Understand is to Invent*, p.23).
9   Piaget, *Science of Education and the Psychology of the Child*, p.137.
10 Piaget, *Sociological Studies*, p.57; cf. *The Moral Judgment of the Child*, p.335.
11 This notion is due to G.H. von Wright, *Practical Reason*, Ithaca, NY: Cornell University Press, 1983.
12 Piaget (*Science of Education and the Psychology of the Child*, p.153) contended that actual mismatching in this sense is common. This view was generalized in his exchange model (Piaget, *Sociological Studies*, pp.146–8).
13 Piaget, *The Moral Judgment of the Child*, p.414; *De la pédagogie*, p.191. Following Rousseau, Piaget (*Science of education and the psychology of the child*, p.140; *De la pédagogie*, p.194) agreed that teachers should study – and not merely teach – children due to our collective ignorance of human learning.
14 Piaget, *The Moral Judgment of the Child*, pp.404–12; *De la pédagogie*, pp.45–6.
15 Consider a girl who is counting, and recounting, pebbles 'by herself' on a beach (Piaget, 'Piaget's theory'). This may be a causally atypical setting for normatively typical learning. If she counted ten, and recounted ten, this is one and the same number. This amounts to a truth-preserving inference in logic in line with the norms of objectivity. Nobody can make anyone make this inference.
16 Piaget, *Science of Education and the Psychology of the Child*, p.152.
17 Piaget (*Sociological Studies*, p.25) invoked the difference between learning mathematics and induction into the Hitler Youth.

18 Piaget, *To Understand is to Invent*, p.106; my amended translation. Piaget ('The Significance of John Amos Comenius at the Present Time', p.14) also referred to this as pseudo-knowledge.
19 See G. Frege, *Posthumous Papers*, Oxford: Blackwell, 1979; cf. Smith 1999.
20 Piaget, 'Piaget's Theory', pp.719–22.
21 Piaget, *Sociological Studies*, p.76.
22 Piaget, *De la pédagogie*, p.191; 'Commentary on Vygotsky', p.252.
23 Piaget, *Sociological Studies*, p.60.

Piaget's major writings (on education)

The Moral Judgment of the Child, London: Routledge & Kegan Paul, 1932.
'The Significance of John Amos Comenius at the Present Time', in *John Amos Comenius on Education*, New York: Teachers College Press, 1967.
'Piaget's Theory', in P. Mussen (ed.), *Carmichael's Manual of Child Psychology*, vol. 1. 3rd edn, New York: Wiley, 1970.
Science of Education and the Psychology of the Child, London: Longman, 1971.
'Comments on Mathematical Education', in A. Howson (ed.), *Developments in Mathematical Education*, Cambridge: Cambridge University Press, 1973.
To Understand is to Invent, London: Penguin, 1976.
'Twelfth Conversation', in J.-P. Bringuier (ed.), *Conversations with Jean Piaget*, Chicago, IL: University of Chicago Press, 1980.
Sociological Studies, London: Routledge, 1995.
De la pédagogie, Paris: Odile Jacob, 1998.
'Commentary on Vygotsky', *New Ideas in Psychology*, 18, pp.241–59, 2000.

Further reading

Biography

Barrelet, J.-M. and Perret-Clermont, A.-N., *Jean Piaget et Neuchâtel*, Lausanne: Payot, 1996.
Jean Piaget Archives, *Jean Piaget Bibliography*, Geneva: Jean Piaget Foundation Archives, 1989.
Smith, L., 'Jean Piaget', in N. Sheehy, A. Chapman and W. Conroy (eds), *Biographical Dictionary of Psychology*, London: Routledge, 1997.
Vidal, F., *Piaget before Piaget*, Cambridge, MA: Harvard University Press, 1994.

Child development and education

Adey, P. and Shayer, M., *Really Raising Standards: Cognitive Intervention and academic achievement*, London: Routledge, 1994.
Bickhard, M. (1995) 'World Mirroring versus World Making', in L. Steffe and J. Gale (eds), *Constructivism and Education*, Hillsdale, NJ: Erlbaum.
DeVries, R., 'Piaget's Social Theory', *Educational Researcher*, 26 (2), pp.4–17, 1997.
Ginsburg, H., *Entering the Child's Mind*, Cambridge: Cambridge University Press, 1997.
Lourenço, O. and Machado, A., 'In Defense of Piaget's Theory: A Reply to 10 Common Criticisms'. *Psychological Review*, 103, pp.143–64, 1996.
Moshman, D., 'Cognitive Development Beyond Childhood', in W. Damon (ed.), *Handbook of Child Psychology*, vol. 2, 5th edn, New York: Wiley, 1998.
Müller, U., Sokol, B. and Overton, W., 'Developmental Sequences in Class Reasoning and Propositional Reasoning', *Journal of Experimental Child Psychology*, 74, pp.69–106, 1999.

Smith, L., 'Epistemological Principles for Developmental Psychology in Frege and Piaget', *New Ideas in Psychology*, 17, pp.83–117, 1999.
Smith, L., 'Piaget's Model', in U. Goswami (ed.), *Handbook of Cognitive Development*, Oxford: Blackwell, 2002.

Websites

Jean Piaget Archives, Geneva: www.unige.ch/piaget.
Jean Piaget Society, USA: www.piaget.org.

LESLIE SMITH

MICHAEL OAKESHOTT 1901–92

> Modern governments are not interested in education; they are concerned only to impose 'socialization' of one kind or another upon the surviving fragments of a once considerable educational engagement.[1]

Michael Oakeshott was born in 1901 and died in 1992. He was for many years professor of Politics at the London School of Economics, and it is as a political thinker of a conservative temperament that Oakeshott is best known. However, in an early work, *Experience and Its Modes* of 1933, Oakeshott developed an overall view of human knowledge and experience, from which his conclusions both on politics and on education follow fairly naturally.

Oakeshott's fundamental philosophical stance combines elements of scepticism, idealism and humanism. For him there is no first philosophy, no absolute guarantee that anything we say or do is justified. Reality is mediated to us only in a number of distinct human practices, such as history, morality, politics, science, philosophy and poetry. No particular approach to life or experience should be allowed to assume precedence over the rest. What we have are a number of different practices or modes, which have proved their value over time, and which are appropriate to the particular roles to which they have been honed. Each practice is a specifically human achievement. Each reveals only part of the whole, but it does reveal part. In order to learn what this part might be, we must become apprised of the practice, and this means entering it as something which must be lived. What an Oakeshottian practice is cannot be analysed in terms external to itself, nor can its goals be justified in terms other than its own.

This doctrine has both political and educational consequences. In politics, Oakeshott's great bugbear is what he calls rationalism. Rationalism is when politics is transformed from what should be an evolving mode of living together, against a background of largely unspoken shared understandings of how things should be. Rationalism transforms what should be like a conversation among friends, with no ulterior purpose, into an enterprise or set of enterprises aiming at social engineering and other determinate goals, which can be specified independently of existing traditions of political practice. The upshot will be what Oakeshott calls the enterprise state, in which politics is deformed by ideology, by managerial techniques and abstractions, and by ceaseless legislation and litigation. This indeed is what we find in contemporary politics, with its stress on technique and on seeing problems as always requiring interventionist solutions and soluble through them.

We no longer understand the place in politics of traditional and tacit knowledge, believing that whatever is important can be codified, made articulate and transparent, and set up in sets of 'procedures' and schedules of 'good practice'. We no longer see codes of 'good practice' and the like as, at best, abbreviations of what participants in the practice already tacitly understand. Such codes are in themselves insufficient to bring about that all-important understanding, and vexatiously unnecessary to those who already possess it. We simply fail to understand or even to acknowledge the basic point that a practice depends on unspoken agreement between its participants, agreement which will determine just how any explicit instructions or rules are to be understood or applied.

All this has considerable implications for education, both in its understanding, its purpose and in approaching its methods and Oakeshott wrote several major essays on education, which are also excellent guides to his thinking generally. At the start of the most important of these essays, 'Education, the Engagement and its Frustration', Oakeshott prepares to discuss the point of education by first giving an account of what it is to become a human being:

> Being human is recognising oneself to be related to others, not as parts of an organism are related, nor as members of a single, all-inclusive 'society', but in virtue of participation in multiple understood relationships and in enjoyment of understood, historic languages of feelings, sentiments, imaginings, desires, recognitions, moral and religious beliefs, intellectual and practical exercises, customs, conventions, procedures and practices, canons, maxims and principles of conduct, rules which denote obligations and offices which specify duties.[2]

This variegated and heterogeneous list is typical of Oakeshott's thinking. Against those who would systematize and pigeon hole, Oakeshott will always emphasize the creative untidiness of the human world, what Wittgenstein (with whom Oakeshott had something in common) called the 'motley' of our practices. Oakeshott goes on to stress the way in which to be a human being is to be:

> the inhabitant of a world composed, not of 'things', but of meanings; that is, of occurrences in some manner recognised, identified, understood and responded to in terms of this under-standing. It is a world of sentiments and beliefs, and it includes also human artefacts (such as books, pictures, musical compositions, tools and utensils). ... To be without this understanding is to be, not a human being, but a stranger to the human condition.[3]

In so far as the human condition is defined in terms of historically produced practices or 'conversations' (to use one of Oakeshott's favourite metaphors), the child has to be initiated into these practices and conversations. He or she is not born knowing these things, nor will he or she simply grow into them without instruction, example and encouragement. This is true even of activities like walking: 'for a child to learn to walk is not like a fledgling taking to the air: do I not remember being told to "walk properly" and not shamble along as if I were an ape?'[4] But it goes much further than acquiring a stock of habits or ready-made ideas. What we are after in this 'transaction between the generations' is learning to look, to listen, to think, to feel, to imagine, to believe, to understand, to choose and to wish. So while Oakeshott will obviously emphasize the need for instruction and initiation in education, the ultimate goal is a human being, who by his or her fluency in the various conversations of mankind will be able to carry those conversations on and in the process come to understand both the conversations and himself or herself.

Oakeshott recognizes that not all learning is formal or deliberate. But in view of the nature of many of mankind's conversations, formal instruction becomes vital. This is the point of schooling (and its extension at university level). A school, in Oakeshott's sense, is first a place where learners will be initiated into their intellectual, imaginative, moral and emotional inheritance in a serious and orderly way. Second, the activity of schooling is one which requires effort, specifically the effort of following, understanding and rethinking deliberate expressions of rational consciousness. Third, echoing the Greek *schole* (leisure), school will be a place of detachment from the world, in order for the learner to achieve emancipation through intimations of undreamt of excellence and possibilities. Finally schooling involves a sense of a historic continuity of teachers and learners in which the end of the process for the learner is what that process is, namely the engagement of becoming human. So it aims at no particular skill, it promises no material advantage, it has no ulterior political or social purpose: to see schooling in terms such as these is to misunderstand its nature and to corrupt its performance.

And what of teaching? For Oakeshott, to teach is simply to bring about that the learner understands and remembers something of worth which the teacher intends should be learned. This can be achieved in countless ways, including:

> hinting, suggesting, urging, coaxing, encouraging, guiding, pointing out, conversing, instructing, informing, narrating, lecturing, demonstrating, exercising, testing, examining, criticizing, correcting, tutoring, drilling and so on – everything, indeed, which does not belie the engagement to impart an understanding.[5]

And there, of course, lies the rub. For a great deal of what goes on in the name of education simply does belie that engagement. From Oakeshott's point of view, contemporary education is as deformed by rationalism as is contemporary politics.

In the first place, there are those who, for one reason or another, disparage the notion of education as a transaction between the generations. This may be because they disparage the wisdom and learning of the older generations. Or it may be because they wish to preserve a childish innocence in which the child should confront the world unimpeded by the conceptions of others. Or it may be because they believe that it would be better for a child to work out or 'discover' things for itself. Or it may be because they believe that 'knowledge' is changing so fast that there is little point in learning 'old' knowledge. None of these modern sounding notions is, in fact, new. Oakeshott, indeed, identifies them all in the writings of Francis Bacon in the early seventeenth century. Nonetheless, each is characteristic of modernity, and each needs to be countered by the simple reflection that there can be no understanding except through the understandings our forebears have left us. Far from being a prison, to enter these conversations is our – and our pupils' – only road to liberation from the tyrannies of immediate desire and present fashion.

There are those who would frustrate education by seeing it in terms of socialization, either to produce a workforce or a race of men with the correct political and social attitudes, or a combination of both. While the child-centred themes of the last paragraph are characteristically those of educators, this second type of educational deformation is typically that of politicians, and particularly of those who hold the educational purse strings. From Oakeshott's point of view, seeing education in terms of socialization is to substitute in education an extrinsic purpose for its intrinsic end. The upshot will be as harmful as the first deformation. Both, either wilfully or unintentionally, are depriving children of their inheritance as human beings. Both will produce a race of zombies who, in the full sense of the term, can neither understand nor act. Both are, in Oakeshott's terms, devices for the annihilation of man, for all the high-sounding words and breathless rhetoric with which they are normally surrounded.

Finally, in this brief conspectus of educational deformations, we may take the idea that education is, or should be, primarily about the acquisition of skills (of judgement, of learning, or thinking, or whatever). Obviously Oakeshott will object to any conception of education which removes content from the process, but he has, in addition, a more precise difficulty with the skills conception. It is that learning to think or judge is not a matter of acquiring information. It cannot be pursued in the same way as we add to our stock of information. As he says ' "judgement" can be taught only in conjunction with the transmission of information',[6] and as a by-product of learning geography, Latin, algebra, or whatever. Moreover, there is no general skill of thinking and judging separable from the particular modes and styles of thinking in which previous thinkers have thought. Learning to think is to master these modes and styles for oneself, and that in turn requires the learner to overhear those modes and styles in a mind at work. 'Thinking skills' and the like will give the learner only the copy-book maxims of the second-hand 'thinker', but not 'the connoisseurship which enables him to determine relevance' (for which he will also need the bodies of knowledge disparaged by the skills enthusiasts) and which 'allows him to distinguish between different sorts of questions and the different sorts of answers they call for, which emancipates him from crude absolutes and suffers him to give his assent or dissent in graduate terms'.[7]

It has been said that Oakeshott's educated person is one who possesses a Keatsian negative capability. If this is so, it simply shows how much positive content is required by an apparently negative virtue, and how this negative virtue in fact embodies the whole of human culture and learning. Oakeshott's own ideas on education flow from his general view of human experience, though they are not wholly dependent on them. In fact they represent the twentieth-century's most sophisticated articulation of the traditional conception of liberal learning. On the other hand, those who find the educational views congenial may be led by that route to examine Oakeshott's other philosophical and political views in order to see one way in which a theory of liberal learning can be given a philosophical context.

Notes

Oakeshott's educational writings have been usefully collected in a volume entitled *The Voice of Liberal Learning*, Timothy Fuller (ed.), New Haven, CT: Yale University Press, 1989. All references are to this volume.

1 *The Voice of Liberal Learning*, p.86.
2 Ibid., p.65.
3 Ibid.
4 Ibid., p.66.
5 Ibid., p.70.
6 Ibid., p.60.
7 Ibid., p.70.

See also

In this book: Wittgenstein

Oakeshott's major writings

Experience and Its Modes, Cambridge: Cambridge University Press, 1933.
Rationalism in Politics, rev. and expanded edn, Indianapolis, IN: Liberty Fund, 1991; London: Methuen, 1962.
On Human Conduct, Oxford: Oxford University Press, 1975.
The Voice of Liberal Learning, Timothy Fuller (ed.), New Haven, CT: Yale University Press, 1989.

Further reading

Franco, Paul, *The Political Philosophy of Michael Oakeshott*, New Haven, CT: Yale University Press, 1990.
Grant, Robert, *Oakeshott*, London: Claridge Press, 1990.

ANTHONY O'HEAR

CARL ROGERS 1902–87

> As I began to trust students ... I changed from being a teacher
> and evaluator, to being a facilitator of learning.[1]

Carl Rogers' was an important American psychologist whose name became synonymous with non-directive therapy and education. He developed a subjective, phenomenological approach to counselling that centred on the idea of the self-actualized individual. These ideas offered a significant alternative to the behaviourist and psychoanalytic models of therapy that were available at the time and they were also congruent with certain non-directive approaches to education.

Rogers was born on 8 January 1902 in Oak Park, Illinois. He was the fourth child of a family of five boys and one girl. His parents were fundamentalist Christians who kept to themselves and taught their children strict rules of behaviour and the importance of hard work.[2] By the time he was in his second year at the University of Wisconsin, Rogers had decided to become a minister and later he attended graduate school at the Union Theological Seminary in New York where his interaction with a broad range of people persuaded him that he could not limit himself to a religious vocation and as a result he enrolled in Teachers College, Columbia University where he received his degree in 1931. At Columbia, he was influenced by the ideas of John Dewey, Leta Hollingworth and William Kilpatrick.[3]

Rogers' first position was as a psychologist at a community guidance clinic in Rochester, New York. There he was exposed to the ideas of the renegade psychoanalyst, Otto Rank and Rank's follower Jessica Taft. Rank made a complete break with Freud's ideas about the self-contained mind motivated by unconscious aggressive and sexual drives. Although ostracized by the original Freudian circle because he rejected the idea that Oedipal issues were the psychological bedrock, he was the original object relations theorist. For him, the primary relationship was with the mother and the individual's emotional life stems from this source. It is affect rather than intellectual insight that provides opportunity for learning and understanding. This means that it is not the therapist's authoritarian interpretation that cures but the therapist's empathy. The therapist's understanding and acceptance is essential to the establishment of self-worth. It is through the present therapeutic relationship that thwarted development can become remobilized. He equated growth with change in the self.

Although Rogers' thinking was not as complex or rich as Rank's, his work clearly reflects Rank's ideas about a continually changing self that develops and grows toward individuality within the context of an empathic accepting relationship. Rank's own career, and his expulsion from the Freudian dominated psychoanalytic community is reflected in Rogers' rejection of Freudian psychology and his greater openness to the clients' own interpretive framework. Hence, instead of the client-talk being seen as a means to the revelation that the therapist had in mind all the time, Rogers understands the client as providing the key to the therapeutic process. The function of the therapist thus was more midwife than scientist.

Rogers also had a more traditional scientific side to his work. He pioneered recording and transcribing actual therapeutic cases for research and publication. One of his important contributions was the building up of a base of empirical research that allowed him to examine the patient/client verbal interaction. Later he extended his ideas about individual therapy to educational institutions, as well as to other types of organizations such as businesses and he also applied his ideas to intergroup conflict.

After ten years at Rochester, Rogers became a professor at Ohio State in 1940 and remained there for four years before he was invited to the University of Chicago. While at Ohio State he wrote *Counseling and Psychotherapy*, a book, which laid, out his approach to the therapeutic situation. Here he placed feelings over content as central to the therapeutic endeavour. The therapist's responsiveness and acceptance of feelings became unchanging components of his theory. At Chicago, Rogers was a member of the psychology department and started the University's counselling centre. He remained at the University of Chicago until 1957 and during this time his widely read book, *Client-Centered Therapy* was published. In this book he delineated the necessary conditions for growth within the counselling relationship. He emphasized respect for the client's ability to resolve his or her own problems within the accepting and empathic framework that the counsellor provided. Next Rogers moved to the University of Wisconsin where he hoped to apply his findings to schizophrenics. Although he was unsuccessful in this attempt, while he was at Wisconsin he wrote the book that brought him his greatest fame and influence, *On Becoming a Person*. In this book he further develops his belief about the centrality of personal growth and creativity. He emphasizes the experiential quality of being fully alive, fully a person who lives in the present moment. Although Rogers' writing career was productive, his distinct and insistent opinions made the years spent in academic life divisive. He left academia in 1963 to join the staff at the new Behavioral Sciences Institute at La Jolla, California. He died in 1987.

Rogers first called his method client-centred and then person-centred therapy. However, once he became well known, others simply called it Rogerian therapy. It is to be distinguished from psychoanalytic models and behavioural approaches to therapy. Each of these assumes that the patient is there to be cured by the therapist. Thus in the traditional models the client has the problem and the therapist has the expertise to cure it. As mentioned earlier, Rogers rejected the architecture of Freudian analysis because it left the client's own self-understanding largely out of the picture allowing it credibility only insofar as it served as a way station towards the client's enlightenment, an enlightenment that mirrored the understanding that the therapist had all along. Behaviourism went even further along this route, rejecting as epistemologically relevant, the understanding of the client altogether. Change was to come about by programming behaviour from the outside. In contrast, Rogers' insistence that the therapist listen to patients allowed patients to have reflected back to them their own understandings. In this way the therapist served as a mirror that enabled patients to view their own way of understanding themselves and then to enter into a reflective appraisal of this self-understanding.

Rogers' clinical, phenomenological approach offered a paradigm that was neither psychoanalytic nor behavioural. He placed the self rather than unconscious drives at the centre of personality and gave priority to the desires and self-understanding of the client. He held that a single force motivates the self – the drive for self-actualization, hence implicitly rejecting Freud's unconscious drive theory. When the child or client is provided with the necessary core conditions of unconditional positive regard, empathy and congruence or genuineness, healthy development occurs.

In contrast to Freud who understood the self as inherently aggressive, or the behaviourist who saw the self as simply the resultant of past conditioning, Rogers held a positive view of human nature. He believed that the self can become autonomous and yet maintain a connection to others. As people discover and experience their own thoughts, feelings and impulses and learns to accept them, they become the source of their own independent locus of evaluation. They remain flexible and open to change. The role of the parent, counsellor, or teacher, is to facilitate this process. By making the individual the sole arbiter of its own experience, Rogers de-centres the power relationship and thus promotes a non-directive approach which denies the authority of the expert.

Rogers applied his therapeutic ideas to education, criticizing the uniformity that he believed formal instruction required as well as a prescribed curriculum, teacher evaluation of students and the teacher-as-expert student-as-passive learner model of instruction. He held that true learning in the form of the self-actualized person was impossible without an integration of cognition and emotion.

Rogers' ideas on education were compatible with the more individualistic side of progressive education and paralleled developments such as the value clarification movement, Summerhill-style education, the open classroom and the emphasis on improving self-esteem. All of these movements develop out of a perceived performative contradiction between the goal and the practice of education. Whereas the goal of education is to lead to the independent self-actualized person, the practice of education involved asserting a dependency of the student for the teacher and placing the definition and evaluation of the students' self-actualization in the control of the teacher. Hence the teacher will determine when the student has been self-actualized. Thus the idea behind Rogerian and similar forms of pedagogy was to address this contradiction by placing students in control of their own development.

In recent years this form of education has come under increasing criticism both from educational conservatives, who view it as too child centred, as well as from educational radicals, who view it as too individualistic and forgetful of structural oppression. Because Rogers is associated more with psychology and therapy than he is with classroom instruction, his ideas have been only marginally attacked by educational critics. Nevertheless, attacks on value clarification[4] and on the recent criticism of concern with self-esteem[5] are, by implication, criticism of the Rogerian method. Ironically these criticisms of education arising frequently from conservative critics of progressive education are similar to criticisms of the therapeutic process arising from Marxist critics, such as Christopher Lasch.[6] Both reject the idea that the therapist or teacher should serve only as a passive receptor for the child's values and understandings. Conservatives affirm the idea that right and wrong, good and bad, have an objective status that goes beyond the understanding of the child, and that therapists and teachers have a responsibility to promote the right and the good. The left fears that the exclusive focus on the individual blunts opportunities for more collective action.

As a gloss on Rogers' more extreme statements, such criticisms have obvious merit. The client or the child may not have all of the resources (information, skills, consequential understandings, foresight, historical understandings, alternative frameworks, etc.) to arrive at an adequate resolution of a personal or a moral problem. And individuals alone are inadequate when a collective set of interest need expression. Yet as a criticism of the actual practice of Rogerian therapists or pedagogues it is wanting. The therapist does not just mirror back, as a very clever parrot might do, the expressions of the client. The therapist selects which ones to mirror, alters the tone of expression (say, from exclamatory to interrogative), provides additional context, asks probing questions, etc.

Much the same is true of the teacher involved in value clarification. The teacher exposes some values more than others and probes some harder than others. Moreover, value clarification occurs in an environment in which values, whether good or bad, are reflected everywhere, through the institutionalized norms and practices of teachers, administrators and students. One point of view more sympathetic to the Rogerian, could not fail to see that such forbearance on the part of the teacher or the therapist requires a very strong ethical disposition to help subjects develop the skills to reflect upon and revise their own values. Less disciplined professionals, or professionals working in a different context, might well impose their own values on the situation. The more sympathetic critic might also understand that there is a difference between over-confidence and self-esteem. The former leads subjects to exaggerate their own skill in resolving a problem. The latter allows the subject to develop the confidence needed to learn the skills that would be required to solve the problem. Critics often confuse the two.[7]

Having said this it is important to understand that there are indeed limitations to the Rogerian method. In relying completely on a phenomenological standpoint, Rogers does underestimate the external resources that clients may need to address problems. A well-researched structural hypothesis can add much to the client's ability to recognize and address problems. Similarly, teachers who withhold information or who fail to push a child to a new level of skills and understanding may be exploiting their expert status as much as those who lord it over the child and micro manages every aspect of the learning process. Just as parents may dominate by inappropriately withholding affection, teachers can also dominate by inappropriately withholding information, knowledge or timely challenges.

Educators also need to be concerned about the overly individualistic features of the Rogerian method. Since the method was first articulated within the context of the client–therapist relationship, this orientation is quite understandable. Nevertheless, education is a communal enterprise in which the activities of one are enhanced and constrained by the needs and interests of others. Maintaining an exclusive focus on the individual misses something both important and unique about the educational enterprise where in learning together children also learn how to learn together. This kind of activity requires a more social and a more interactive model of learning than the one that Rogers provides us with.

Notes

1 Rogers, *Freedom to Learn for the 80's*, Columbus, OH: Charles Merrill, p.26, 1983.
2 Rogers, *On Becoming A Person*, Boston, MA: Houghton Mifflin, pp.5–6, 1961.
3 Brian Thorne, *Carl Rogers*, London: Sage Publications, 1992.
4 Warren A. Nord, *Religion and American Education: Rethinking a National Dilemma*, Chapel Hill, NC: The University of North Carolina Press, pp.336–41, 1995.
5 E.D. Hirsch, Jr, *The Schools We Need: Why We Don't Have Them*, New York: Doubleday, pp.100–4, 1996.
6 Christopher Lasch, *Haven in a Heartless World: The Family Beseiged*, New York: Basic Books, 1977.
7 Hirsch, op cit.

See also

In *Fifty Major Thinkers on Education*: Dewey

Rogers' major writings

Counseling and Psychotherapy, Boston, MA: Houghton Mifflin, 1942.
Client-Centered Therapy: Its Current Practice, Implications, and Theory, Boston, MA: Houghton Mifflin, 1951.
On Becoming A Person, Boston, MA: Houghton Mifflin, 1961.
Freedom To Learn: A view Of What Education Might Become, Columbus, OH: Charles E. Merrill, 1969.
Carl Rogers On Encounter Groups, New York: Harper & Row, 1970.

Further reading

Hersher, Leonard, *Four Psychotherapies*, New York: Appleton-Century-Crofts, 1970.
Zimring, F. and Raskin, N., in *History of Psychotherapy: A Century of Change*, Donald Freedheim (ed.), Washington, DC: American Psychological Association, 1992.

ELEANOR FEINBERG AND WALTER FEINBERG

RALPH WINIFRED TYLER 1902–94

> These educational objectives become the criteria by which
> materials are selected, content is outlined, instructional proce-
> dures are developed and tests and examinations are prepared. All
> aspects of the educational program are really means to
> accomplish basic educational purposes. Hence, if we are to study
> an educational program systematically and intelligently we must
> be sure as to the educational objectives aimed at.[1]

Over the course of a century in the context of a field of practice, certain individuals emerge whose work functions as a beacon for others. At times the illuminating quality of the work produced is due to its theoretical power. At other times it is related to its practical utility. At other times still, it is the product of a personal charisma that somehow inspires. Ralph W. Tyler was a scholar, a shaper of policy and an inspiration to many of those concerned with the improvement of education. Tyler was born in Chicago on 22 April 1902, grew up in Nebraska, received his Ph.D. from the University of Chicago in 1927 and served in the Bureau of Educational Research and Service at the Ohio State University between 1929 and 1938. He became Director of the influential Eight Year Study from 1934 to 1942, during which time he returned to the University of Chicago at the invitation of its Chancellor, Robert M. Hutchins. His first appointment at Chicago was as University Examiner and as Chair of the Department of Education from 1938 to 1948 and as Dean of the Division of Social Sciences from 1948 to 1953. In 1953 he moved to Stanford, California to become the Director of the newly established Center for Advanced Study in the Behavioral Sciences, a post he held for fourteen years.

The litany of his accomplishments as an evaluator, a curriculum theorist, a university administrator, the progenitor of the National Assessment of Educational Progress (NEAP), not to mention his seemingly bottomless capacity to serve as consultant in education to nations throughout the world are without precedent. Tyler was not 'merely' a man with great national stature, he was someone who enjoyed the respect of education scholars around the world.

What was it that Tyler brought to the educational conversation? What were the distinctive contributions he made to educational discourse?

Tyler, deep down, was an educational progressive, someone influenced by Dewey's ideas and leavened by the likes of Charles Hubbard Judd and W.W. Charters, scholars with whom he studied. He was fundamentally concerned with both the practical utility of education and the quality of experience students had in schools. Indeed, although he recognized that curriculum planners and teachers could not provide students with experiences – after all, experiences were the result of what an individual student did with what he or she encountered – nevertheless, he insisted on writing about learning *experiences* rather than learning *activities* because he wanted to remind readers that it was the experience that promoted or inhibited the learning, and not merely the activity that a teacher or curriculum developer had planned.

One of Tyler's most important contributions to education is the curriculum syllabus he prepared for his course on the curriculum, which he taught in the Department of Education at the University of Chicago. This syllabus, published initially in 1950, has been published in Dutch, Norwegian, Portuguese and Spanish. It is still in print. It represents a concise distillation of a way of thinking about curriculum planning that has impacted the planning practices of educators not only in the United States, but in other countries as well.

Tyler's commitment to a means-ends model of planning is apparent in the central place that behavioural objectives occupy in what has come to be known as 'the Tyler rationale'. For Tyler, the specification of objectives was the only way in which learning experiences could be meaningfully selected, organized and whose consequences, when the curriculum was implemented, evaluated. But unlike so many others who tenaciously embraced behavioural objectives, he did not fragment them into educational minutiae that swamped the teacher's capacity to use them. Tyler, a model of rationality, underscored the importance of keeping objectives general, but not so general that one couldn't formulate an appropriate form of assessment. He did not fall into the trap of micro-specificity in order to secure test reliability. His vision of objectives was far closer in spirit to the ideas of his mentor, Charles Hubbard Judd, then to the behaviourism of Edward L. Thorndike. There is no question that 'the Tyler rationale', in one form or another, still serves as a major model for a professionally responsible approach to curriculum building and to teaching.

Tyler's interest in objectives in the curriculum field is particularly understandable when one recognizes that his initial educational experience professionally was as an evaluator. Work in evaluation continued throughout his career and influenced his views of curriculum. Evaluation practices almost naturally create the need to specify criteria as a basis for making judgements or for measuring what students have learned. His contributions in the field of evaluation were as seminal as his work in curriculum.

As indicated earlier, Tyler was Director of the Eight Year Study, an effort designed to allow thirty secondary schools the option of pursuing their own progressive practices while providing to the universities to which the students were recommended their own evaluation of the student's performance. The evaluation of students was to be left to the thirty schools. The basic aim of the study was to provide the space needed for schools to function as educational laboratories, a concept first advanced by John Dewey when he established the Laboratory School of the University of Chicago in 1896.

It was Tyler's work with E.R. Smith in *Recording and Appraising Student Progress*[2] published in 1942 that articulates the approach to evaluation that Tyler embraced. Interestingly, many of the evaluation practices in *Recording and Appraising Student Progress* are reminiscent of efforts today to create 'authentic assessments'. The concept of authentic assessment suggests its opposite; '*in*authentic assessments'. The term authentic assessment is a not so tacit critique of testing practices that historically have been much more concerned with ranking students than with determining whether students had achieved the objectives of the curriculum. The whole concept of formative assessment developed by Scriven in the 1960s is not unrelated to the aims of evaluation developed by Tyler and associates in the Eight Year Study.

American testing practices in education were built upon statistical requirements that, for example, made it necessary for test makers to discard test items that did not discriminate between high- and low-testing students. Items that displayed no variance in student performance could not have a place on a test whose reliability depended upon something approximating a normal curve. Tyler argued that the point of testing was not to create a normal distribution among the test students' test scores, but to provide a way of improving the curriculum and for determining if students had reached its aims. Put simply, tests needed, in current terminology, to be criterion referenced rather than norm referenced if the function of the test was to provide information about what students had learned that teachers had intended to teach.

This now obvious insight provided a paradigm shift in our conception of what tests were for and what appropriate test construction criteria needed to be. A test in which all students responded correctly to all items would have no statistical reliability under conventional testing assumptions, but they would be educationally relevant if one were engaged in criterion referenced testing. This shift in perspective is a fundamental one.

Tyler's initiation into the evaluation field found another outlet in the leadership he exercised in the National Assessment of Student Progress. Advanced in the 1960s, Tyler argued that the nation needed some index of its educational health, just as it had an index of its economic health. Education was clearly as important as economics and without a national assessment of educational progress we could not know how, as a nation, we were doing.

Understandably, there was much anxiety about the prospect of a national approach to testing. Educators and school boards were concerned that national testing could function as the thin edge of a wedge in enabling the federal government to secure control of what historically in the United States is a state function. Tyler reassured critics and others anxious about the National Assessment of Student Progress that no comparisons among school districts or even states would be made in NAEP. Indeed, students could not be compared since no student would take the entire battery of tests. Testing would be through a multiple matrix sampling procedure in which only certain items were taken by individual students. By combining the performance of students on these items one could get a rather complete picture of student performance in various parts of the country, by four age levels and by gender. Furthermore, the distinctive feature of the National Assessment of Student Progress as an assessment device is that it provided information about tasks that related not primarily to the academic skills developed in school subjects, but to tasks that citizens of school age were likely to encounter in their daily lives. In other words, the initial assessment exercises were not to be tied tightly to what schools happened to be teaching and, therefore, could not be used to provide leverage to the federal government.

Tyler was a pragmatist. The approach that he took to national assessment as well as to curriculum planning had a practical ring. His most salient intellectual feature was his sense of cool reason. It was a quality that characterized both in his speaking and in his writing. He simply was not obscure or arcane.

Tyler, as statesman, is probably best exemplified in his role as Director of the Center for Advanced Study in the Behavioral Sciences. Located atop a hill near Stanford University, but not a part of it, sits a centre that annually invites forty scholars, largely from the United States, but also from other countries, to come for a year to reflect, to read, to converse and to write with no formal obligations imposed by the Center. This Center has seen the likes of Thomas Kuhn who prepared his draft of *The Structure of Scientific Revolutions*,[3] John Rawls, who worked on *A Theory of Justice*,[4] and a host of others whose seminal work was aided and abetted by their presence at the Center for Advanced Study in the Behavioral Sciences. Tyler was instrumental in providing guidance and was especially sensitive to the creation of an atmosphere that did not try to impose expectations or to monitor performance. The scholars invited, both senior and junior, were on their own in the company of friends. That vision has been critical to its success.

Another example of his statesmanship is the leading role that he played in establishing the prestigious US National Academy of Education. He served as its first President and lent to it the high status he himself possessed. The Academy is constituted of 100 members elected throughout the United States with a limited number of foreign members in various parts of the world.

What one comes to understand in reviewing Tyler's life and educational accomplishments is that he was not a one-eyed specialist. He was a person of broad vision, humane instincts and the energy, clarity and skill to get significant amounts of work done. He shaped the field of educational evaluation, he provided the curriculum field with a model of planning that has not yet been surpassed, he directed the Center for Advanced Study in the Behavioral Sciences, he served as Dean of the Social Sciences at the University of Chicago, and before then as Chairman of the Department of Education, he was instrumental in promoting the acceptance of the National Assessment of Educational Progress, and he travelled the world to share his educational wisdom. There is no one now, nor has been in my view, that has had such visibility, commanded such respect, or addressed as many fields in education.

Two years before he died, I invited him to my course in Curriculum at Stanford to speak to my graduate students. He kindly accepted. He came and he talked about the field of education as he had known it, how it had developed, and what he believed needed attention at that time. During the course of the discussion that ensued his presentation, a student asked him, 'Dr Tyler, what would you say your main accomplishment has been so far?' Tyler paused, looked at the student, and said, 'Living to ninety-two.' This was one of the few occasions I though Ralph Tyler was wrong.

Notes

1 Tyler, *Basic Principles of Curriculum and Instruction*, Chicago, IL: University of Chicago Press, p.2, 1969.
2 E.R. Smith and Ralph W. Tyler, *Appraising and Recording Student Progress*, vol. III, New York: Harper and Bros, 1942.
3 Thomas S. Kuhn, *The Structure of Scientific Revolutions*, Chicago, IL: University of Chicago Press, 1962.
4 John Rawls, *A Theory of Justice*, revised edn, Cambridge, MA: Belknap Press of Harvard University, 1999.

See also

In *Fifty Major Thinkers on Education*: Dewey, Thorndike

Tyler's major writings

Basic Principles of Curriculum and Instruction, Chicago, IL: University of Chicago Press, 1950.

The Challenge of National Assessment, Columbus, OH: Charles E. Merrill Publishing Company, 1968.

Tyler, Ralph W. and Wolf, Richards M. (eds), *Crucial Issues in Testing*, Berkeley, CA: McCutchan, 1974.

'National Assessment: A History and Sociology', in James W. Guthrie and Edward Wynne (eds), *New Models for American Education*, Englewood Cliffs, NJ: Prentice Hall, 1971.

ELLIOT W. EISNER

BURRHUS FREDERIC SKINNER 1904–90

> Teaching is the expediting of learning. Students learn without teaching but the teacher arranges conditions under which they learn more rapidly and effectively.

Burrhus Frederic Skinner, born in 1904, grew up in the little town of Susquehanna in Pennsylvania, not very far from the border to the state of New York. His father was a lawyer who became the General Counsel in a big coal company. The paternal grandfather had emigrated to the United States from England. Skinner's childhood was, according to the first volume of his memoirs, *Particulars of My Life* (1976), a rather harmonious one. During high school he was stimulated by his English teacher to the extent that literature became his major subject in college. His book *The Technology of Teaching* (1968), was dedicated to his former high-school teacher. He went to college at the private Hamilton College close to Uthica. At that time he already displayed a wide repertoire of intellectual and art interests with a strong leaning towards the literary ones. He began to write poems which were submitted to the local newspaper in Susquehanna. Hamilton College offered all the opportunities that culturally interested young people could wish for. He took courses in Greek, and could read the Iliad in its original language. He learnt classic and modern literature, creative writing and drama. He became the editor of the literary student newspaper, wrote many poems, practised music, became a skilful saxophonist and painter. Several of these interests prevailed throughout Skinner's life. In his home in Cambridge, Massachusetts, he had a piano and an organ and gathered friends for drama evenings at home during which the participants read their respective parts.

After college graduation Skinner was strongly determined to become a writer. In his autobiography he reproduces the letter in which his father tries to persuade him to abandon this potential career which would not give any 'butter on the bread'. Yet the young Skinner persisted and spent a year writing fiction in Greenwich Village, the literary quarters in New York City. A letter Skinner received from the poet Robert Frost to whom he sent some short stories, begging Frost not only to pass a judgement about the specimens but also to give advice about his future career, was decisive in his career choice. Frost advised him to think about it for some time before entering upon a writing career. In the meantime, Skinner took the decision to go to Harvard for graduate studies in psychology which he had hardly studied at all in college. Prior to his decisions he had read a major work by the Russian physiologist Ivan Pavlov whose experiments with dogs and conditioned reflexes were published in English in the late 1920s. Pavlov gave a lecture at an international congress at Harvard in 1929. Skinner had also read John B. Watson's work on behaviourism. Watson's writing on behaviourism and elegant style captured Skinner. The same might have been applied to Bertrand Russell whose philosophy Skinner avidly absorbed during this period.

Among the teachers at Harvard were Henry Murray and Edward G. Boring and a few other 'introspective psychologists' who did not fit into the positivistic and behaviouristic patterns that were dominant in Skinner's mind. The philosopher Alfred North Whitehead also had a strong influence and through him Skinner become more familiar with Bertrand Russell. After completing his Ph.D. at Harvard, Skinner became an Associate Professor – first at the University of Indiana and then at the University of Minnesota. He was appointed to a full professorship at Harvard in 1948. At the University of Minnesota he had as graduate students John Carroll and N.L. Gage. Both went on to contribute a great deal to the field of educational research.

During the 1930s and 1940s Skinner developed his theory along with confirming experiments about operant conditioning. His studies were published in *The Behaviour of Organisms*, 1938, *Science and Human Behaviour* 1953, and *Verbal Behaviour*, 1957. These laid the theoretical foundation for his work on a new educational technology known as 'programmed learning', which was fully spelled out in a monograph, *The Technology of Teaching* (1968). The first publication in which Skinner discussed a systematic application of operant conditioning in education was an article in 1954 in the *Harvard Educational Review* (and reprinted in *The Technology of Teaching*). He suggested a model of programmed presentation of the material that had to be learned and the use of so-called 'teaching machines' which could provide reinforcements.

Skinner has himself reported how he got interested in the application of his psychological principles to education. One day when in his capacity as a parent, he visited his daughter's grade 4 class, he listened to a lesson in mathematics. Suddenly the situation appeared quite absurd to him. Here in the class were 'twenty valuable organisms' who were victims of an instruction which, it seemed to him, refuted everything known about the learning process. His main objection against the didactics used was that the technique did not work with genuine reinforcements techniques which have purposeful effect. Frequently the school operates with praise and punishment which generate an artificial motivation. Learning occurs not on the basis of a genuine interest in what has to be learned but for other purposes. A well-known comment by Skinner is the following: 'An American pupil who is good in French can say "Please pass me the salt" gets an A, while a French child simply gets the salt!'

In 1954 Skinner participated in a symposium about modern trends in psychology. He then demonstrated an apparatus, which could be used to guide the process of learning on the basis of the principles governing it. The presentation was published in *Harvard Educational Review* in the same year and made Skinner the 'founder of educational technology'.

The concept of programmed instruction launched by Skinner in the 1950s was based upon the principles of operant conditioning, which Skinner had developed over a period of two decades. The learning material had to be presented to the learner in small steps with regard both to the degree of difficulty and the distance from one item to the other. The learner is activated all the time in dealing with the learning material by having to answer questions and being confronted with the quality of these answers, because the machine is automatically evaluating the reactions. The programming can see to it that the learner is sent on different routines through the material, depending upon his or her answers. Thus the person who gives a wrong answer can be rerouted back to a more elementary level, whereas the person who consistently tends to give right answers is guided to omit some of the material. The programming is such that each element of the learning material is practised by repetition until moving to the next one.

The 'boom' for programmed learning took place around 1960 at a time when schooling and teaching were being intensely debated in the United States. The use of the new educational technology became a major issue at the annual meeting of the American Educational Research Association in 1961 as well as at the International Congress of Applied Psychology in Copenhagen in the same year. The question raised at these and other meetings was to what extent programmed learning facilitated by teaching machines could 'substitute' for teachers in person. The conclusion from these discussions as well as from practice in the schools was that the new technology could serve as a *complement* in practising basic skills, in for instance, arithmetic and communication. At the Copenhagen congress a person in the audience asked Robert Glaser, a leading researcher in didactics, if the main purpose of these new machines was to 'replace' teaching and teachers. The reply has become almost legendary: 'A teacher, who can be replaced by a machine, ought to be!' Seen within the perspective of half a century one can say that programmed teaching with or without special machines has not played the role the enthusiasts once predicted. The last few decades have seen the emergence of personal computers in the classroom, a device which is much more flexible than the machines used shortly after the middle of the twentieth century. But – more importantly – even though programming has contributed to structuring the learning material in a better way than before, one has more and more begun to realize the importance of the personal interaction between teacher and student. Skinner himself in an article in *Teacher's College Record* (1963), where he is looking back on a decade of teaching machines, declares: 'Teaching is the expediting of learning. Students learn without teaching, but the teacher arranges conditions under which they learn more rapidly and effectively.' He did not in this article spell out the consequences of the fact that a machine cannot motivate the student in the same way as the teacher by human interaction. Nor can the machine serve as a role model. Thus, the teacher–student interaction is of crucial importance. Nevertheless, certain technological devices can on a modest scale serve as complements.

The practical aspects of so called 'contingency management' in upbringing at home and in the classroom were dealt with by Skinner who found that he had been misunderstood with regard to the implications of his theory of reinforcement. In the journal *Education* (1969) he underlines that his application of the principles of operant condition in education does not mean that he is preaching a gospel of 'free' education. He emphasizes, however, that punitive sanctions easily lead to behaviours other than those intended. In an article 1973 in *New York University: Educational Quarterly* under the title 'The Free and Happy Student', Skinner points out: 'The natural logical outcome of the struggle for personal freedom in education is that the teacher should impose his control of the student rather than abandon it. The free school is not school at all.'

Perhaps less well known is another of Skinner's inventions which had educational implications in a wide sense. This was his 'Baby in a Box'. Skinner says that in the 'brave new world' in which science and technology influence the woman working at home, something should be done to facilitate child care. Traditionally the baby has been wrapped up in a multitude of clothing in a bed that has not been regulated according to temperature and moisture. This method implies a lot of work for the mother, not least with regard to washing. The 'cage' that Skinner constructed allowed the baby to sit naked within it behind a glass door. The child's reaction regulated the temperature so that it was kept on a pleasant level. Skinner's daughter Deborah spent her first year in the 'box'.

Another application of his psychological principles within a wider social context was spelled out in Skinner's utopian novel *Walden Two* of 1948. Its title refers, of course, to the famous book by Thoreau, *Walden, or Life in the Woods* of 1854, depicting the serene life away from the stress of the city. Skinner acts here as a kind of social inventor, describing a society where the knowledge about how certain human reactions are reinforced and others are suppressed. The founder of the new society, the *alter ego* of the author, says at one place:

> I have only had one idea during my entire life – a really fixed idea. In order to express it straightforwardly – the idea to do it my way. 'Control' is the expression for it. The control of human behaviour. During my early days as an experimenter it was a mad drive to dominate. I remember my anger when a prediction went wrong. I wanted to shout to my subjects: 'Behave, you bastards! Behave as you should!'

When *Walden Two* came out (in the same year as George Orwell's *1984*) it was hardly noticed, at least on the European side of the Atlantic. But in the 1960s when the youth revolt took place in an atmosphere of disenchantment among the young with society, many began to practice the 'Walden-Two' life in so called communes. The sale of the book skyrocketed and it reached a sale of about one million copies.

In introducing Skinner to a Swedish audience in the mid-1970s the present author described Skinner as a 'twentieth-century Rousseau'. Like him, Skinner wrote treatises on how human nature works in the social context. To some extent this might be seen as a compensation for having abandoned early plans to become a writer of fiction.

Beyond Freedom and Dignity was regarded by Skinner himself as his most important book; a kind of testament. In a wider perspective it can be seen as a contribution to educational philosophy and has therefore been called 'Skinner's manifesto'. It is an attempt to spell out a conception of what is basically human and to indicate its relevance in the attempts to establish a better society.

Briefly, the overarching lines of thinking are the following. 'Freedom' and 'free will', as they are usually conceived, are illusions. We have to get rid of the hybris which brings us to reject the thought that human beings are a product of their environment, the reinforcing circumstances. Instead of acknowledging this we persevere in the belief that we have a 'soul' and that somewhere within us there is a centre where decisions are taken about what we should do. But our behaviour is not determined from 'within' but from 'outside'. Behaviour is shaped by its consequences. Each human being is a unique bundle of reactions of which some have been and are genetically transferred from one generation to the next. The conditioning we are subjected to by our social setting determines as 'experience' the behaviour repertoire we have at our disposal.

The notion that the individual is 'responsible' and 'autonomous' is a dangerous myth which is an obstacle to a welfare society where human beings can live in peace and happiness. If humanity is to succeed in surviving, it must employ a social technology built on a scientific and rational basis; in this case the application of operant conditioning.

Skinner points out that in the history of social philosophy it is Rousseau, in particular, who has acknowledged the value of positive reinforcement. Educators in general tend to overestimate the importance of negative reinforcement. Those who write about human freedom tend typically to overemphasize the importance of the alternatives that lead to avoiding discomfort and punishment and tend to overlook the freedom that is embedded in attempts to reach desirable goals. The philosophy that control is something wrong leads in its applications to a system when punishing actions are perpetuated. Skinner underlines strongly that the problem of freedom is not to save people from *all* controls but only from *some* of them.

To attribute the causes behind a person's actions to something outside themselves is, by many, experienced as a threat to self value, to one's dignity. Whereas the negative consequences of a person's actions bring to the fore the issue of individual freedom, the positive ones bring to the fore the question of the value of the individual. If individuals behave badly they are considered to be responsible for it and are punished for having committed a bad action. The more we succeed in classifying the outer situations, the more the 'value' of the individual is reduced.

Strangely enough, those who are most eagerly emphasizing the traditional concepts of freedom and personal value are those who resort to blame and punishment in education. Punishment is based on the assumption that the not-wanted behaviour will diminish by the action taken. But frequently one only achieves a behaviour incompatible with the one wanted, i.e. the punished individual behaves so as to avoid punishment. Skinner interprets many of the Freudian neurotic repressions as avoiding behaviour.

Beyond Freedom and Dignity (1971) ends up with a *credo* that the social sciences, particularly the behavioural sciences, should be able to build a more tolerable society by developing adequate strategies for shaping the human being. In order to succeed in this endeavour behavioural scientists have to stop looking upon human beings as an autonomous entity. They are a product of the interaction between themselves and their environment. In short, this means that the behavioural science should employ the same strategy as biology and physics.

See also

In *Fifty Major Thinkers in Education*: Rousseau, Russell, Whitehead

Skinner's major writings

The Behaviour of Organisms: An Experimental Analysis, Englewood Cliffs, NJ: Prentice Hall, 1938.
Walden Two, New York: Macmillan, 1948.
Science and Human Behaviour, New York: Macmillan, 1953.
'Science and the Art of Teaching', *Harvard Educational Review*, 24, pp.86–97, 1954.
Verbal Behaviour, New York: Appleton-Century-Crofts, 1957.
'Teaching Machines', *Science*, 128, pp.969–77, 1958.
Cumulative Record, New York: Appleton-Century-Crofts, 1959.
'Teaching Machines', *Scientific American*, November, pp.91–102, 1961.
'Teaching Science in High School – What is Wrong?', *Science*, 159, pp.704–10, 1968.
The Technology of Teaching, New York: Appleton-Century-Crofts, 1968.
'Contingency Management in the Classroom', *Education*, Milwaukee, WI, November–December, pp.1–8, 1969.
Contingencies of Reinforcement: A Theoretical Analysis, New York: Appleton-Century-Crofts, 1969.
Beyond Freedom and Dignity, New York: Alfred Knopf, 1971.
'Skinner's Utopia: Panacea, or Path to Hell?', *Time Magazine*, 20 September, pp.47–53, 1971.
'On "Having" A Poem', *Saturday Review*, 15 July, pp.32–5, 1972.
'The Free and Happy Student', *New York University: Educational Quarterly*, Winter, 5, pp.2–6, 1973.
Particulars of My Life, New York: Alfred Knopf, 1976.
Reflections on Behaviourism and Society, Englewood Cliffs, NJ: Prentice Hall, 1978.
The Shaping of A Behaviourist, New York: Alfred Knopf, 1979.
'My Experience with the Baby-Tender', *Psychology Today*, March, pp.29–40, 1979.
A Matter of Consequences, New York: Alfred Knopf, 1983.
'What is Wrong with Daily Life in Western World?', *American Psychologist*, May, 41, 5, pp.568–74, 1986.
Upon Further Reflection, Englewood Cliffs, NJ: Prentice Hall, 1987.

Further reading

Bjork, D.W., *B.F. Skinner – A Life*, New York: Basic Books, 1993.

TORSTEN HUSÉN

HARRY BROUDY 1905–98

> What sort of schooling is needed for enlightened cherishing? Knowledge contributes to enlightenment, but the knowledge that enlightens cherishing includes both scientific knowledge and value knowledge. ... Knowledge for enlightened cherishing is sometimes called wisdom, which combines knowledge of human nature with clear-headedness about what can and cannot be accomplished.
>
> (Broudy 1972, p.53)

Harry Broudy was born in Poland to a well-to-do Jewish family, the oldest of four, and started his education in the traditional Cheder. He emigrated with his family to Massachusetts in 1912, and entered American school without knowledge of any English. He received his BA in German Literature and Philosophy from Boston University (1929), and his Ph.D. in Philosophy from Harvard (1935), focusing on Kirkegaard, Bergson and William James.

Broudy came to education largely because of the anti-Semitism in American universities during times which did not promote Jews for faculty in Ivy leagues. Thus, in spite of a prestigious Harvard degree with Whitehead[1] and Perry, he accepted a position at North Adams State Teachers College (1937), where he taught general psychology and philosophy of education. There, he met and married Dorothy Hogarth (1947). Dorothy, a farmer's daughter and a skilful woman, supported Harry in many ways: protected his time, typed his manuscripts, fixed faucets and did the major driving. Their son, Richard, was born in Massachusetts.

Broudy's recruitment to the College of Education at the University of Illinois in 1957, signalled a productive and gratifying second career. There, Broudy was not interested in having an appointment in the Department of Philosophy but focused on education, addressing the areas of curriculum and pedagogy for secondary and tertiary levels, and developing his ideas on the uses of schooling.[2] He retired in 1974 (continuing to be active in campus committees, teaching, advising, and scholarship for the following fifteen years) and was honoured by a three-day conference on the 'Uses of Knowledge in Personal Life and Professional Service'. Broudy lived in Urbana until his death, and could be seen, in his nineties, walking briskly along the lush (and uninterrupted by cars) lane on Race Street, connecting his house to campus.

I met Broudy in the late 1980s. Inspired by his work which I encountered as a graduate student, I was struck in our conversations by his non-assuming presence, as well as acute and sensitive perception, wit, warmth, compassion and succinct sense of humour. In interviews I conducted with his widow, friends, colleagues and students, they highlighted these, and other aspects of the man. Rupert Evans, Dean of the College in the late 1950s and 1960s, talked about Broudy's amazing command of English (Rupert said he never failed to learn from Harry a new word in each conversation), his popularity and effectiveness as a teacher, the esteem he was held in by colleagues, Provost and University Presidents. Gordon Hoke, an educational evaluator, talked about Broudy's insightful contributions in federal agencies and learned associations, providing vivid examples of how Harry 'did not suffer fools gladly'. Wayne Bowman, a leading music philosopher who worked with Harry on his doctoral dissertation, talked about Broudy's dedication, intellectual excitement, attention to wordings and meaning, and the 'profound and durable effect' Harry had on him. 'It was from Harry that I got my first substantial introduction to philosophical dispositions, tendencies, and propensities.'

Broudy was concerned with the implications of democracy for education, specifically what knowledge belongs in secondary schools' curriculum as they opened to the entire population. He distinguished between two questions: what is good knowledge? and what is knowledge good for?, delegating the first to specialists in the various disciplines, and focusing on the second question (Vandenberg 1992). Unlike Dewey, Broudy did not believe in progressive education, which he regarded as a bold but futile effort to recapture the qualities of small-town life in America. A self-proclaimed classical realist[3] with a strong interest in the problems raised by Existentialism, Broudy held that there is a set of key ideas and learning skills that everyone should possess. This knowledge needs to be translated into a programme that accommodates differences in backgrounds, abilities and interests while maintaining excellence.

Is excellence compatible with democracy? Broudy regarded excellence as situated in the quality of personal and social life, the quality of the society itself, rather than the attainment by the individual of a higher order of cognitive, scientific or artistic achievement. He saw the aim of general education as the realization of selfhood: knowledge can serve as the means to the good life by promoting happiness through enabling self-realization. The arts had an important role in contributing to self-realization. Accordingly, he advocated arts education for *all* students: not just for those identified as gifted or highly interested in art.

Broudy's promise that life will be enhanced if, through education, one's tastes can be altered to approach the tastes of the connoisseur, formed the rationale for aesthetic education, and placed arts appreciation at the centre, as a means to aesthetic literacy. He maintained that the disciplines of arts education consist of a body of knowledge based on expertise and scholarship, beyond exposure and self-expression. The education of the imagination meant that students acquire images of art that function as associative and interpretive resources, supplying contexts that broaden and deepen comprehension. The arts should fill a role similar to the humanities – teaching values, enhancing beauty, reducing ugliness and hate. This implied that the arts adopt goals of general education rather than specific arts education goals.

Like Dewey, Broudy regarded 'the aesthetically satisfying experience … the opposite of the drab, meaningless, formless, pointless passage of time' (1972, p.35). However, unlike Dewey, Broudy's Classical Realism highlighted a curriculum revolving around exemplars, oriented towards the acquisition of knowledge rather than merely problem solving. Broudy, with Joe Burnett and B. Othanel ('Bunny') Smith, and later in his other writings, set the study of exemplars as the major vehicle for the attainment of these teaching values. His proposed secondary-school programme focused on appreciation and the perception of patterns in the 'best' artworks rather than the traditional performance and studio offerings.

The same rationale of values operated in his view of tertiary education. During the Second World War Broudy realized that scientists and engineers did not necessarily develop ethical frames of reference. He saw it as necessary to develop everyone's ethical sensibility so they could control science and technology with wisdom (1943).[4] The development of imagination and the education and perception of emotions were central goals towards ethical education. Serious art creates images of feeling that we may have not yet brought to consciousness: sometimes by making the strange familiar; sometimes by making the familiar strange. Broudy, after Langer, held that 'students should contemplate emotions, not have them' (Broudy 1972b, p.49). Cultivation of aesthetic experience serves to broaden and differentiate the repertoire of feeling and values. Aesthetic experiences then penetrates the educational process, illuminating every other mode of experience.

Rather than leaving these ideas on the abstract level, Broudy applied them consistently to the practical arena of schooling. In a 1943 paper 'History without Hysteria', he responded to publication of results of a test of historical knowledge, claiming their low scores merely showed that the facts were not used in the daily life of the several thousand first-year university students tested. The objective of teaching history, wrote Broudy, was not fact retention but the 'ability to use history for interpreting present problems'. He developed this issue in several of his books, including the last (1988), where he showed the limitations of replication/application aims of the schools, and highlighted interpretation and association. The interpretive and associative uses of schooling were regarded as context building. They function in everyday life but are hidden below the surface of awareness, representing the ability of the generalist to approximate the understanding of the specialist rather than the latter's recall or problem-solving power.

Broudy was considered as the major philosopher of education in the second part of the twentieth century. However, his major impact was in his aesthetics education writing on the fields of visual arts, and less acknowledged, but not less important, on music education (Bresler 2001; Colwell 1992). Starting from 1950, aesthetic education emerged as central to his thinking, even in discussions of general educational issues (e.g., on the uses of schooling, or in discussing how the intellectual disciplines can be transformed into a programme of general education in a democratic society). Broudy's move to the University of Illinois, which had strong music and visual arts programmes, was formative in solidifying his interest and impact in aesthetic education. Charles Leonhard, a charismatic music educator with a deep commitment to aesthetics and its implications to practice, was in the process of building a prominent doctoral programme in music education. He identified Broudy as a major scholar, and sent to his classes his students, including future leader music educators (e.g., Bennett, Reimer and Wayne Bowman) who developed his ideas further in the philosophy of music education. Thus, Broudy's long-term impact was through the students who studied with him in Illinois, as well as through his writings on the philosophy of music education in major music education publications.

The rationale for music education evolved out of Broudy's 1950 publication on the arts in which he examined the formation of the average mind and taste of which popular speech, thought and art are both the cause and expression. Broudy's provision of a philosophical base for using the 'best' music was important to the music education profession. As Richard Colwell put it: 'The 1958 idea that music education should have a philosophy stunned the profession' (1992, p.44). Broudy, wrote Colwell, 'wrote well and few music educators could write'. In the 1970s and 1980s Broudy wrote numerous papers and books advocating the centrality of arts education (cf. 'How Basic is Aesthetic Education? Or is 'Rt the fourth R?', 'Arts Education, Necessary or Just Nice?', 'A Common Curriculum in Aesthetics and Fine Arts') including the seminal *Enlightened Cherishing* (1972) and the Getty publication *The Role of Imagery* (1987). Broudy labelled the struggle of art education to move from the periphery to the core of schooling as a tension between 'nice' and 'necessary'. He claimed that imagination cultivated through arts education provided essential support to other functions of the educated mind.

Broudy added to the skills of perceiving and making a component of knowledge of the principles of criticism, and knowledge about the history of art and its philosophical bases. He regarded aesthetic perception as analogous to 'reading a text where the text is an image or a set of images' (1987, p.49). Communicating with arts requires a language that enables the pupil and teacher to communicate with a work of art and with each other. Broudy advocated a dialogic relationship between production and appreciation, maintaining that production depends on the ability to appreciate works of art more than on explorations for self-expression. He developed the instructional strategy of scanning, focusing on sensory, technical, formal and expressive properties of the artwork. Scanning has been utilized in constructing various arts curricula (e.g. in architecture by Michelle Olson, in music by Carroll Holden, and in visual art education by Nancy Roucher) and formed the foundation of the Getty Center.

His broad philosophical base for music education provided the first articulate philosophy of music education. However, his advocacy of knowledge *about* (rather than *of*) music and his relegation of the traditional band and choruses performances to extracurricular activities did not fit with the customs and cherishing of music educators. His views that students' art is not necessarily good art ('the unspoiled spontaneity of childhood and the uninhibited ignorance of the tyro are more highly regarded than trained maturity', 1972, p.102) and thus cannot be expected to meet the objectives of aesthetic education, neither in studio/performance, nor in composition, were radical for both music and art education. However, these ideas and the arguments about the centrality of the arts to school curriculum resonated with the Getty Center for the Arts[5] mission, aiming to establish arts history, criticism and aesthetics on an equal footing with the studio. In the 1980s, Broudy's writings (with those of Elliot Eisner) signalled a new philosophy of arts education that pointed to the limitations of self-expression as the *raison d'être* of arts education. Broudy was central in the aesthetic education movement with its unifying concern for all of the arts and its attention to the broad spectrum of aesthetic experience. His ideas helped shape the ideal, formal and to some extent the operational curricula of visual arts.

On a more fundamental level, Broudy's work was forecasting in his reconnecting the split, introduced by Kant and dominating aesthetic thinking for 200 years, between ethics and aesthetics. Broudy's ethical rationale of aesthetics deconstructed the independent, and isolated, realm of the arts, the 'art for arts sake', drawing on Plato and Aristoteles' views of the roles of art. This view has significant ramifications for education, shifting the goals of the various disciplines of arts education to general educational goals, affecting arts curriculum and pedagogies. The interdependence between aesthetics and ethics re-emerges in the writing of such people as Wayne Bowman in music, Suzi Gablik in visual arts, and aesthetic environment writers. In the emerging pendulum swing of post post-modernism, this signals a move from deconstruction to a renewed sense of purpose and meaning in aesthetic education.

Notes

I am indebted to Dorothy Broudy, Rupert Evans, Gordon Hoke, Charlie Leonhard, and Bob Stake, who spent with me several sessions each, sharing insightful perspectives on Broudy's work and life. Many thanks go to Eunice Boardman, Wayne Bowman, Dick Colwell, Ralph Page, and Lou Smith for their important communications, and to Sasha Ardichvili, Dorothy Broudy, Rupert Evans, Gordon Hoke, and Bob Stake for their careful reading of this manuscript and helpful comments.

1 Broudy was one of Whitehead's last students, and according to friends who knew Broudy well, Whitehead's influence on him was reflected in his thinking and way of life.
2 In his books as the 'Real World', 'Truth and Credibility', 'The Citizens Dilemma', 'Paradox and Promise' and 'The Uses of Schooling'.
3 Neo-Aristotelianism can be traced in his writings in North Adams and in his 1961 book *Building a Philosophy of Education*.
4 In his later years he devoted much time to the problems of higher education and served for several years as the staff director for the Chancellor's commission on the Reform of Undergraduate Learning and Living.
5 Established in 1982.

See also

In this book: Eisner
In *Fifty Major Thinkers on Education*: Aristotle, Dewey, Plato, Whitehead

Broudy's major writings

'History without Hysteria', *School and Society*, 58, 1943.
The Real World of the Public Schools, New York: Harcourt, Brace, 1972a.
Enlightened Cherishing: An Essay on Aesthetic Education, Urbana, IL: University of Illinois Press, 1972b.
'How Basic Is Aesthetic Education? Or Is 'Rt the Fourth R?', *Educational Leadership* 35, 2, p.139, 1977.
The Role of Imagery in Learning, Los Angeles, CA: The Getty Center for Education in the Arts, 1987.
The Uses of Schooling, London: Routledge and Kegan Paul, 1988.

Further reading

Bresler, L., 'Harry Broudy's Aesthetics and Music Education', *Research Studies in Music Education*, December, 2001.
Colwell, R., 'Goodness and Greatness: Broudy on Music Education', *Journal of Aesthetic Education*, 26, 4, pp.37–48, 1992.
DiBlasio, M., 'The Road from Nice to Necessary: Broudy's Rationale for Art Education', *Journal of Aesthetic Education*, 26, 4, pp.21–35, 1992.
Margonis, F., 'Harry Broudy's Defense of General Education', unpublished MA thesis, Champaign, University of Illinois, 1986.
Smith, R., 'On the Third Realm – Harry S. Broudy: A Life Devoted to Enlightened Cherishing', *Arts Education Policy Review*, 101, 2, pp.34–8, 1999.
Vandenberg, D., 'Harry Broudy and Education for a Democratic Society', *Journal of Aesthetic Education*, 26, 4, pp.5–19, 1992.

LIORA BRESLER

SIMONE WEIL 1909–43

> Contrary to what is commonly believed, one moves from the general to the particular, from the abstract to the concrete. (This has important consequences for teaching.) ... It is art which, best of all, gives us the idea of what is particular. ... And art has its origin in religion. It is due to religion and art that one can arrive at a representation of what is individual; it is due to feeling (friendship, love, affection) that one human being is different from others. To label, classify someone one loves, that is impious.[1]

Simone Weil was born in Paris into a wealthy Jewish family. At the age of ten she declared herself a communist; her sympathy with the poor and oppressed is a constant theme in her life and writings. She attended university at the Sorbonne, where her asceticism and political views earned her the nickname of 'the red virgin'. On graduation she taught in a secondary school in Le Puy. Her spare-time work with the unemployed, and her refusal to cram her students for exams in the conventional way, led to her dismissal. After a grim year as a factory worker she went to Spain to fight on the side of the anarchists in the Spanish Civil War; an accident with cooking oil brought her involvement in the war to an end. In 1942 the Weil family escaped from the Nazi persecution of the Jews to America. Simone Weil travelled from there to England with the intention of joining the Free French forces. In England she contracted tuberculosis, probably exacerbated by her refusal to eat more than the rations allowed to her compatriots in occupied France, and died in a sanatorium in Ashford, Kent. Her writings were all published posthumously.

Simone Weil is best understood as a kind of neo-Platonic, Christian mystic, despite her Jewish origins. Her view of humankind is that we naturally tend to surround ourselves with the comfort of fantasy. We are like the prisoners in Plato's Cave (*Republic*, Book VII), mistaking shadows for reality and reluctant to struggle free of our chains, to leave the warmth of the fire that casts those shadows and emerge into the harsh light of the sun. She calls this pervasive condition 'gravity': it is as natural to us as the more familiar gravity by which objects fall. Our intelligence and capacity for reason are unreliable guides to us here, for we may use them in the wrong *spirit*, as mere cunning self-deceivers, for example. Or like Oedipus, that emblem of humankind, we may possess only the kind of cleverness that solves riddles and puzzles but altogether lacks self-knowledge and insight.

We require a kind of re-orientation rather than increased intellectual powers, and that re-orientation lies in the de-centring or 'unselfing' that Simone Weil calls *décréation*. 'Each man imagines he is situated in the centre of the world',[2] and it may take unusual powers to give up that position, for we hold it not only intellectually but in the imaginative part of our soul. We need to see things and people in their unique particularity, not as instances of general categories. 'The soul empties itself of all its own contents in order to receive into itself the being it is looking at, just as he is, in all his truth.'[3] Countering the demands of our selfish, nagging egos leads to a heightened sense of reality, and that heightened sense in turn diminishes our egoism further.

This *décréation* is especially necessary when we come up against the suffering of others:

> Those who are unhappy have no need for anything in this world but people capable of giving them their attention. The capacity to give one's attention to a sufferer is a very rare and difficult thing; it is almost a miracle; it *is* a miracle. Nearly all those who think they have this capacity do not possess it.[4]

It is very hard to experience other's afflictions accurately and truthfully: consequently we are inclined to sentimentalize them, or perhaps to be horribly fascinated by them. Our own more grievous sufferings too are almost impossible for us to attend to properly. Pitfalls here include varieties of masochism, and the fantasy that suffering is somehow automatically redemptive. And only the saintly can resist passing on their suffering to others.

The soul is freed from its state of gravity by love and especially by the apprehension of beauty, which may be the nearest most of us can come to love.[5] Here again we see similarities to Plato's account, in which we may make the pilgrimage from the love of a beautiful boy to love of art-objects (which serve so well to give us 'the idea of what is particular'), onwards to love of the Form of Beauty and finally to love of the Good itself. A major difference is that for Simone Weil the particular things of this world are redemptive, and not simply to be transcended in the course of a pilgrimage to higher things. 'The contemplation of particular things is what elevates a man, and distinguishes him from animals.'[6] The pilgrim's love of the world takes him back into the Platonic cave, just as Simone Weil herself left her philosophical studies to join the poorest factory workers in France.

The crucial idea here is that of *attention*. To attend properly is to look on the world in the light of the Good, struggling free of the miasma of private anxiety and fantasy that usually occludes our perception and judgement. It is to see in a steady and purified kind of way rather than 'through a glass darkly'.

> Attention consists of suspending our thought, leaving it detached, empty, and ready to be penetrated by the object; it means holding in our minds, within reach of this thought, but on a lower level and not in contact with it, the diverse knowledge we have acquired ... [7]

Attention is not to be thought of as a matter of act of will. We must indeed continually work at the business of moral discernment, yet moral discernment may come, almost *ex nihilo*, when the quality of our attention is sufficiently just and true. Such a state is what Simone Weil calls *grace*. It is the state in which, to use the title of one of her works, we must 'wait on God'.

These are, we may think, essentially religious ideas, reminiscent of the mysticism of Julian of Norwich, or of the Zen Buddhism whose guiding idea according to Simone Weil is 'to perceive purely, without any admixture of reverie'.[8] Yet she insists that these ideas should be grounded in our most ordinary educational practices. She writes that 'the development of the faculty of attention forms the real object and almost the sole interest' of school study.[9] An exercise in writing Latin prose, or a geometry problem, can be a training in the right attending that can one day be of inestimable value to our fellow human beings in their hour of need. School study can thus have powerful spiritual effects, Simone Weil insists, 'quite apart from any particular religious belief'.[10] The connection with love is found here too:

> Intelligence can only be led by desire. For there to be desire, there must be pleasure and joy in the work. The intelligence only grows and bears fruit in joy. ... It is the part played by joy in our studies that makes of them a preparation for spiritual life.[11]

Perhaps the exercise of craft skill may work in the same way. When we exercise skills of this sort we open ourselves to our materials, attuned to the quality of the wood we are planing or the wallpaper we are hanging. We use our craft knowledge but are only peripherally aware of it, if at all. There can be a kind of unselfconscious harmony in gardening, cooking, even in driving a car. Done in the right way we may find these activities, as we say, spiritually refreshing. It is not only in academic study but also in vocational training that attention can be nourished.

The philosopher Iris Murdoch has drawn on and developed elements of Simone Weil's account. *The Sovereignty of Good* has a famous example of how a woman may scrutinize her perceptions and come to see that her 'pert, familiar, tiresomely juvenile' daughter-in-law can equally, and perhaps preferably, be seen as spontaneous and delightfully youthful. Here is the attempt to perceive justly rather than impetuously, to attend without envy, prejudice or neurosis. We might consider the importance of this dimension of the moral life in education, noting that for children grasping the distinction between *bullying* and *teasing*, for example, is perhaps less a matter of understanding facts or of thinking 'whether you would like it if someone did that to you': it is more a matter of seeing the facts in a different light, with a different quality of attention. So too for the teacher there is a difference between seeing a pupil or student as on the one hand lazy and uninterested and on the other lacking in confidence and consequently reluctant to commit himself or herself.

Certainly Simone Weil's ideas point quite directly to a particular emphasis in our rearing and education of the young. We would for example share Iris Murdoch's concern for the way that television and other new technologies blunt our ability to see the detail of our surroundings;[12] whatever is the World Wide Web, and our urgent clicking on its links and impatience with downloading, doing for the quality of our attention? Perhaps we should teach children 'not only how to paint but how to *look* at paintings'.[13] Good teachers teach accuracy and truth, and meditation, the capacity for quiet contemplation undistracted by our habitual background ego-racket, should be taught in schools. The following passage from Iris Murdoch vividly expresses the spirit of Simone Weil's philosophy of education and reminds us how far from it we are in our contemporary schools and universities:

> Learning is moral progress because it is an asceticism, it diminishes our egoism and enlarges our conception of truth, it provides deeper, subtler and wiser visions of the world. What should be taught in schools: to attend and get things right. Creative power requires these abilities. Intellectual and craft studies initiate new qualities of consciousness, minutiae of perception, ability to observe, they alter our desires, our instinctive movements of desire and aversion. To attend is to care, to learn to desire to learn.[14]

Notes

1   *Lectures on Philosophy*, p.59.
2   'Reflections on the Right Use of School Studies with a View to the Love of God', in *Waiting on God*, trans. E. Crauford, New York: G.P. Putnam's Sons, p.114, 1951
3   Ibid., p.115.
4   Ibid.
5   *Notebooks*, trans. A.F. Wills, New York: G.P. Putnam's Sons, p.384, 1956.
6   *Lectures on Philosophy*, p.59.
7   Reflections on the Right Use of School Studies with a View to the Love of God, in *Waiting on God*, op cit., p.108.
8   Ibid., p.406.
9   Ibid., p.109.
10 Ibid., p.116.
11 Ibid., p.109.
12 Iris Murdoch, *Metaphysics as a Guide to Morals*, London: Chatto & Windus, p.330, 1992.
13 Ibid., p.329.
14 Ibid., p.179.

See also

In *Fifty Major Thinkers on Education*: Plato

Weil's major writings

Waiting on God, trans. E. Crauford, New York: G.P. Putnam's Sons, 1951.
Gravity and Grace, trans. A. Wills, New York: G.P. Putnam's Sons, 1952.
The Need for Roots, trans. A. Wills, New York: G.P. Putnam's Sons, 1953.
The Notebooks of Simone Weil, trans. A. Wills, 2 vols, New York: G.P. Putnam's Sons, 1956.
Lectures on Philosophy, trans. H. Price, Cambridge: Cambridge University Press, 1978.

Further reading

Le Roy Finch, H., *Simone Weil and the Intellect of Grace*, New York: Continuum, 1999.
Little, J.P., *Simone Weil: Waiting on Truth*, Oxford: Berg, 1988.
McLellan, D., *Utopian Pessimist: The Life and Thought of Simone Weil*, New York: Poseidon Press, 1990.

RICHARD SMITH

JOSEPH J. SCHWAB 1910–88

> [C]urriculum is brought to bear, not on ideal or abstract representations, but on the real thing, on the concrete case, in all its completeness and with all its differences from other concrete cases, on a large body of fact concerning which the theoretic abstraction is silent.[1]

Joseph Schwab stands as one of the more important curriculum theorists of the second half of the twentieth century. A direct philosophical descendant of John Dewey, Robert Maynard Hutchins and Richard McKeon, his work engages the same tensions and paradoxes inherent in the ideal of an education in a democracy as is apparent in their writings. Schwab, like Dewey, argued that curriculum should be grounded in the reasoned consideration of culture or the informed and reflective participation in the exchange of ideas that is central to a participatory political and social community. The shaping of such an education, however, invokes a fundamental tension: the reasoned consideration of such a culture involves developing a deep appreciation of the artifacts of that culture. This is in direct opposition to an American egalitarian ideal.

Schwab was to resolve such a paradox by emphasizing the importance of context and inquiry. He states in his essay 'The Practical: a Language for Curriculum':[2]

> The materials of a concrete curriculum will not consist merely of portions of 'science,' of 'literature,' of 'process.' On the contrary,

their constituents will be particular assertions about selected matters couched in particular vocabulary, syntax and rhetoric. They will be particular novels, short stories, or lyric poems, each for better or for worse, with its own flavor. They will be particular acts upon particular matters in a given sequence. ... Above all, the supposed beneficiary is not the generic child, not even a class or kind of child out of the psychological or sociological literature pertaining to the child. The beneficiary will consist of very local kinds of children and, within the local kinds, individual children.

Instincts of this kind have through all of his career as a teacher and a scholar driven Schwab inward to *this* classroom, to a careful analysis of the characteristics of the students he had *this* semester, and always to a concern with the here-and-now of the next class, in this course, in *this* programme. Schwab's writings reflect this: they were written usually for a particular occasion or to work out a particular preoccupation and only rarely were they conceived to develop a theme that went beyond the essay at hand.

For nearly fifty years Joseph J. Schwab worked in the University of Chicago and lived in Hyde Park, the university's community. Entering the university at fifteen, he graduated in 1930 with a baccalaureate in English literature. In the fall of 1931 he began graduate work in biology, and he received his doctorate in genetics in 1939. He left Hyde Park for a year in 1937 to accept a fellowship in science education at Teachers College, Columbia University, where he explored the development of the field of psychometrics and assisted in curriculum development while completing his doctoral research. In 1938 he returned to Chicago as an instructor and examiner in biology in the university's undergraduate college. He retired from the university in 1974 as William Rainey Harper Professor of Natural Sciences in the College. Subsequently he became a fellow at the Center for the Study of Democratic Institutions in Santa Barbara, California, an independent institute founded by Robert Maynard Hutchins, the president of the University of Chicago from 1929 to 1951.

During his early years at the University of Chicago under the presidency of Robert Maynard Hutchins, Schwab was an integral part of Hutchins' attempts to redefine and reinvigorate the concept of liberal education. Schwab's later writing can only be understood as a reflection of this early formative work. The reforming era in the College, which had begun in the 1930, had run its course by the early 1950, but for Schwab the collegiality, the forms of thought, and the practices of that period stayed with him, so much so that all of his subsequent writing and much of his later professional activity can be seen as successive efforts to explore the implications of his years in the College in broader and more varied contexts.

By 1940, when he was thirty-one, Schwab had become one of the key members of the group of faculty at Chicago committed to the reforming concerns of Hutchins. As a scientist with a sophisticated interest in general education he was prized by a group around Hutchins, Adler and Clarence Faust, dean of the college from 1941; the integration of science into a scheme for general education had always been a fundamental goal of the general education movement but it had proved to be elusive. Schwab's early writings on the nature of science and the role of the scientists reflect his efforts towards this. Schwab's conception of liberal education, however, was essentially inchoate in 1940. He believed in discussion teaching, in the potential importance of the Great Books, and in the tractability of science for general education; he was passionately concerned with the relationships between science, values and education – the theme of his first published paper on education (1941). He had not developed, however, a coherent framework into which to place his ideas and concerns. It was not until he worked with Richard McKeon, a student of John Dewey, in 1942, in the course of the planning of the four-year college that was initiated in that year that he gave the intellectual structures he needed to bring his ideas into focus.

The central educational and, therefore, curricular tasks as they were seen by McKeon, and his colleagues were based on three key notions. One was the idea of culture and its elements while the second centred on the development of an understanding of what was problematic in the culture and on the nature of changes that have taken place in the manner in which cultural elements are seen and experienced. Both of these concepts found their focus in the third idea – that of the person experiencing, and seeking to resolve, problems given by the culture. It was an argument of this kind, with its foundations in the notions of *culture*, the *person*, and *community*, and its synthesis in the conception of *experience*, which justified at the theoretical level, the 1942 curriculum. In particular Richard McKeon was concerned, most fundamentally, with the problem of knowing how experienced thought about a problem can be understood. The traditional discipline which has concerned itself with the task of the extraction of meaning from complex scriptural and philosophical texts is *hermeneutics* or *interpretation*, and this discipline more than any other was a primary concern of McKeon's. The hermeneutic tradition offered McKeon both techniques and methods that could be used for the interpretation of semantic structures of expression, and potentially, educational means. To read a text requires concern for both the text itself and the interpretive categories which the interpreter brings to that text. A curriculum which uses interpretation as its core method entails, then, a necessary focus on both the semantic problems inhering in the work being read and on the consciousness of students as readers.

While others were interested in the consequences of McKeon's thinking for their disciplines, Schwab was to seize upon the implications of McKeon's outline for teaching, as well as for the theory and practice of curriculum. It fell on Schwab to search in these terms for a way of giving a complete expression to his emerging conception of what liberal education might be. It was through the influence of McKeon that Schwab became familiar with John Dewey's thought. Dewey's corpus provided a framework which was compatible with Schwab's most basic concerns and convictions. The commerce of ideas that was so integral a part of Dewey's thought was the way of seeing and accounting for the importance of the community and conversation which Schwab cherished; Dewey's descriptions of the process of inquiry captured what was happening in Schwab's world. Increasingly Dewey was to become the thinker whose influence was fundamental to Schwab's thought. Schwab found that Dewey did not offer a 'theory' of knowing or of education in any accepted sense, but rather an invitation to inquiry, an *approach* to the task of persuasion of his readers to embark upon a practice.

In 1949, Schwab was appointed to the university's Department of Education, and there Ralph Tyler, the chairman of the department, urged him to turn his attention to the formal exploration of the rationale for liberal education. Schwab's gradually increased involvement in teaching the philosophy of education in the Department of Education also pushed him in the same way, that is to seek generalizations of his experiences and concerns. In 1951, Schwab published his first paper examining ideas of curriculum writ large. The paper, 'Dialectical Means vs. Dogmatic Extremes in Relation to Liberal Education', provided a comprehensive mapping of a territory of a given subject matter by means of a set of *topics* or *commonplaces* which ordered the possibilities that orators might need to consider as they sought to develop their arguments. This topical style was to become the hallmark of Schwab's thought and writing, and when it was joined with the Aristotelian categories which he was beginning to use habitually as a source of commonplaces and with Dewey's construction of experience, it provided Schwab with a distinctive way of approaching the problems of curriculum which concerned him.

The essay, 'Eros and Education' represents a shift in focus away from the intellectual arts that concerned Hutchins and McKeon and towards the ideas of the person and liberal personhood and experience. Here, in Schwab's conception of education, we clearly see the influence of Dewey's emphasis on the place of continuity and growth in experience. Man has a rational faculty, that is, a capacity for reason, and an emotional, sensual faculty. Human behaviour has its origins in both of these sources, but a developed, virtuous character is one in which the emotional faculties are formed so that they lead the person to take pleasure in those acts which make people good. Human behaviour results from reason motivated by desire and desire formed by reason, and the developing personality is achieved by the training or habituation of the irrational faculties such that the person behaves in accord with the good.

Schwab, with Dewey, emphasizes again and again the discretionary aspects of individual and group behaviour. He describes again and again *how* problems are to be encountered and resolved, but not *what* the solutions are or, in a specific sense, should be. In this manner, all of Schwab's writing searches for a *characterization* rather than a prescription of what teaching might be like, what a liberal education might be, how a curriculum might be developed. But there is a dilemma inherent in any emphasis of this kind on discretionary intelligence, a dilemma that Schwab acknowledged in 'Science and Civil Discourse' couched in terms of the needs of élites and the needs of the masses of the population.

Beginning in 1959 Schwab began to spend less time with the University of Chicago. He turned to work at places such as the Mellon Research Center of the Jewish Theological Seminary and federally funded science curriculum initiatives such as the Biological Sciences Curriculum Study. All of this stimulated Schwab to begin the task of rethinking the work on science he had done ten years earlier and at the same time pushed his concerns in new directions, to thinking about community, tradition and informal education.

During these years of the early 1960s the curricular concerns of

American schools centred on the content of school science. The slogan that became associated with this concern was 'structure of the disciplines'. Given his long-standing interest in the nature of appropriate curriculum for liberal education in and through sciences, Schwab was seen as a spokesman for the importance of discipline-based teaching of science in the schools. His essay 'The Concept of the Structure of a Discipline' became a basic text for the structuralists. Such work and the series of 'practical' essays that followed in the 1970s should be seen in the same light as Schwab's early work at the University of Chicago in which he worked to define what was important in any discipline for creative inquiry. They represent arguments for this process and for ways of representing the materials necessary for such a process.

As always in these essays of the 1960s Schwab is asking the perennial curricular questions: Is this way of organizing the disciplines, the ways of knowing, the most appropriate one? Why? Is this way of rendering the subject matter an appropriate one? Why? In 'Education and the Structure of the Disciplines' (a reworking of the earlier structure essay) we see him exploring two themes from the broad set he had considered in his teaching in Chicago. First, he focuses on the question 'How might subject matters be rendered?' and, as he explores this, he asks us to consider what kind of claim it might be that we are asked to examine. It follows that to appreciate the significance of a claim or observation in a text or a scientific report one must have a way of understanding its character, intent and context. Having made this point, Schwab goes on to explore one way by means of which a reader can understand the twists and turns of the contexts and characters of scientific disciplines.

Also in the 1960s, during the student protests, Schwab again took up the question of the value of a liberal education. The result of his thinking was *College Curriculum and Student Protest*, an impassioned tract that takes as its occasion the protest movement but has as its most basic purpose the restatement of Schwab's beliefs about the nature of liberal education. The outcome is a statement of his concern for the intellectual arts and disciplines with the notion of *habit*, so that the primary focus of this book is the examination of the relationships between the curriculum in its manifold aspects and the education of a person of prudent and intelligent character.

Schwab's final writing in the 1970s took two turns. The first became a series of three essays on the 'practical' as a language within the terms of which curriculum development might be undertaken. The occasion was his perception of the failure of the educational research to find a way of effecting the schools. His own career in education had been motivated always by a desire to act and (in his own words) 'do good' – although experience had taught him not that impulse needed to be tempered by both prudence and hard thinking. Neither of these traits were, it seemed, honoured by educational research as he knew it. Finally he returned to his most fundamental concern, the shape and process of education in a democratic society:

> First, community can be learned. It is not merely a matter of place, of village or small town, but a body of propensities toward action and feeling, propensities which can be expressed in many social circumstances. Second, human learning is a communal enterprise.

The knowledge we learn has been garnered by a community of which we are only the most recent members and is conveyed by languages of work and gesture devised, preserved, and passed on to us by that community. ... Even experience as a form of learning *becomes* experience only as it is shared and given meaning by transactions with fellow human beings.[3]

Joseph Schwab to the last engaged the reader in the process of inquiry he advocated. He never told us what to think but rather invited us to think very hard. That defines Schwab's intent, and his rhetorical problem, as a writer and teacher. Always he sought ways in which he could achieve mutuality with his readers so that each reader could find something of his own concerns reflected in the particular essay. It is this mutuality which allows us as readers to overcome any puzzles and quibbles we might have about the particulars of an argument and to move along with it to the point at which we have to reflect on whether we accept or reject, agree or disagree and why. In other words Schwab's essays are invitations to inquiry and reflection about the choices and alternatives that we must face as we think about the meaning of general education, the nature of science and the character of educational thought.

Notes

1 Schwab, *The Practical: A Language for Curriculum*, p.12.
2 Ibid., p.13.
3 Schwab, 'Education and the State: Learning Communities', p.235.

See also

In this book: Bruner
In *Fifty Major Thinkers on Education*: Dewey

Schwab's major writings

'The Role of Biology in General Education: The Problem of Value', *Bios*, 12, pp.87–97, 1941.
'Dialectical Means vs. Dogmatic Extremes in Relation to Liberal Education', *Harvard Educational Review*, 21, pp.37–64, 1951.
'Eros and Education', *Journal of General Education*, 8, pp.54–71, 1954.
'Science and Civil Discourse: The Uses of Diversity', *Journal of General Education*, 9, pp.132–43, 1956.
'The Concept of the Structure of a Discipline', *Educational Record*, 43, pp.197–205, 1962.
College Curriculum and Student Protest, Chicago, IL: University of Chicago Press, 1969.
'The Practical: A Language for Curriculum', *School Review*, 78, pp.1–23, 1969.
'The Practical: Arts of the Eclectic', *School Review*, 79, pp.493–542, 1971.
'The Practical 3: Translation into Curriculum', *School Review*, 81, pp.501–22, 1973.
'Education and the State: Learning Communities', *The Great Ideas Today, 1976*, Chicago, IL: Encyclopedia Britannica, pp.234–71, 1978.
'Education and the Structure of the Disciplines', *Science, Curriculum and Liberal*

Education, Ian Westbury and Neil Wilkof (eds), Chicago, IL: University of Chicago Press, pp.229–72, 1978.
Science, Curriculum and Liberal Education, Ian Westbury and Neil Wilkof (eds), Chicago, IL: University of Chicago Press, 1978.

Further reading

Westbury, I. and Wilkof, N.J., 'Introduction', *Science, Curriculum and Liberal Education: Selected Essays*, J.J. Schwab, Chicago, IL: University of Chicago Press, 1978.

IAN WESTBURY AND MARGERY D. OSBORNE

CLARK KERR 1911–

> The basic reality, for the university, is the widespread recognition that new knowledge is the most important factor in economic and social growth. We are just now perceiving that the university's invisible product, knowledge, may be the most powerful single element in our culture, affecting the rise and fall of professions and even of social classes, of regions and even of nations.[1]

Widely considered one of the twentieth-century's leading experts on higher education, Clark Kerr was born in 1911 and grew up on a farm in Stony Creek, Pennsylvania. Clark's father and mother had a strong influence on his life, instilling in him an appreciation for hard work, the courage to be an independent thinker, and a life-long love for learning.[2] Kerr entered Quaker-affiliated Swarthmore College in the fall of 1928 and led a busy life as a student participant in the debate team, athletics, the student newspaper and government, and numerous service projects. During his junior and senior years, Kerr participated in an honours programme designed to encourage intellectual excellence in his chosen major field of political philosophy in the social sciences division. Kerr also explored Quakerism, eventually choosing to join the Quaker faith before finishing school. Summarizing Kerr's decision to join the Quakers, Stuart (1980) explained,

> Kerr felt a strong affinity for the values he found at Quaker Swarthmore: pluralism, pragmatism, principled action, and the balance between the autonomous individual and the group consensus. He loved his years at Swarthmore, readily acknowledging the importance of those years in his life. ... [But] Swarthmore values were not new to him. ... Kerr did not convert to Quakerism as much as he found a social structure which most nearly reflected his own beliefs and values. It was tremendously important for the rural farmboy to discover that the broader world affirmed and validated the values his mother and father had instilled within him. Understanding this point does much to explain the self-confidence and certainty which consistently remained with Kerr throughout his life.[3]

Kerr continued to graduate school immediately after finishing Swarthmore, completing a master's degree in economics at Stanford University in 1933, and then attending University of California at Berkeley (UC-B) to pursue a doctorate in economics and labour relations from 1933 to 1939. During his doctoral studies, Kerr became involved in California's labour movement, especially self-help cooperatives. Stuart observed, '[I]nvolvement in labor relations satisfied his concern for the welfare of the needy. In a very practical way, he combined intellectual endeavor with public service'.[4] During this period he also took a one-year teaching appointment in economics at Antioch College in 1936–37, and travelled to Europe to study at the Graduate Institute of International Relations, Geneva, 1935–36, and the London School of Economics in 1935–36 and again in 1938–39. While abroad, Kerr taught about the cooperative movements in America, Russia and western Europe, and he returned to the United States at the start of the Second World War. His constant travel companion was wife Catherine Spaulding, a talented and politically active woman in her own right. Married in 1934, the couple had three children: Clark Edgar, Alexander William and Caroline Mary.

After a year as Acting Assistant Professor at Stanford in labour economics in 1939–40, Kerr took a position as Assistant and later Associate Professor of Economics at the University of Washington from 1940–45. Besides teaching, Kerr became involved in labour arbitration associated with settling industrial disputes during the Second World War, including the War Manpower Commission (1942) and the Regional War Labor Boards in San Francisco (1942–43) and Seattle (1943–45). In 1945 Kerr returned to UC-B as an Associate Professor of Economics in the School of Business Administration and as the founding Director of the Institute of Industrial Relations, an organization dedicated through teaching and research to moving labour–management relations from conflict to cooperation.

Applying his knowledge as a keen negotiator to collegiate dilemmas, Kerr experienced a rapid rise from faculty to administration, beginning with the California loyalty oath controversy in 1949–50, a dispute between the Regents and faculty over an oath concerning non-employment of Communist Party members. Careful negotiations involving Kerr yielded resolution to the loyalty oath issue, bringing Kerr to the attention of the entire faculty, administration, and Regents. Due in large part to his successful dealings with the Regents, the faculty supported Kerr to assume the newly created position of Chancellor of UC-B in 1952. During his five-year tenure, Kerr oversaw tremendous growth while nurturing increased cohesion among faculty and students. Freedom of inquiry, unity of curriculum, and diversity of extracurricular activities were important to Kerr. He believed this combination would prepare a student to become 'a well-balanced individual, capable of both specialized work *and* democratic citizenship, alike at ease with diversification *and* firmly committed to the underlying permanence of [western democratic] values'.[5] In 1957 the Regents sought a successor to retiring president, Robert Sproul, and turned to Kerr for the job, recognizing the impressive changes he had made as Chancellor of UC-B in a relatively short period. Specifically, in 1957 twenty-four departments of UC-B were rated outstanding in a national poll and the campus was ranked third in the nation, after Harvard and Yale.[6]

Kerr accepted the Regents offer in 1958 and served as President of the University of California (UC) system for nine years. As president he initiated, lobbied for, and oversaw the university's greatest era of expansion. He lead the UC system towards growth and prosperity by adding new campuses, specifically Irvine, San Diego and Santa Cruz. Kerr was credited with mass-producing low-cost, high-quality education and, this accomplishment was credited to Kerr's central role in the California Master Plan, also known as the Donohoe Act, which was signed into law by then California Governor, Edmund 'Pat' Brown, Jr, in 1960. This now-famous Plan was designed to reduce rivalry, tension and power struggles emerging between the three public segments of higher education: the University of California, the State College (now known as the California State University) and the Junior Colleges (now known as California Community Colleges). The Plan had four main principles: (1) to differentiate the functions for the three public higher segments, thus creating a hierarchically segmented system which legitimized the role of junior colleges; (2) to institute differential selectivity with respect to admission standards; (3) to provide 'something for everybody', i.e., a monopoly on awarding doctorates for the University, a solid post-baccalaureate status for the state college system, and inclusion in the higher education system for the junior colleges;[7] and (4) to ensure that no student would be denied access to any segment because of inability to pay fees.[8]

During his tenure as President, Kerr encouraged a federal role in support of research, leading the UC system into prominence as a world-leader in research and speaking about the importance of research for all leading universities in the United States. He coined the term 'multiversity', a term he introduced during a series of Godkin Lectures at Harvard University in 1963. In these lectures Kerr developed a philosophy to define the modern university as the multiversity, characterized as an inharmonious institution made up of numerous communities, including the community of the undergraduate, graduate, social scientist, scientist, non-academic personnel and administrator.[9] Despite his increasingly high profile on a national level and successes in expanding the UC system on the state level, Kerr encountered serious problems on the campus level in the mid 1960s. After a series of failed negotiations with the Regents, faculty and students during the Free Speech Movement, Kerr submitted his resignation in 1967, and the Regents, with avid support from newly elected California Governor Ronald Reagan, promptly accepted it. Though a tremendously difficult period for Kerr, he rebounded to national prominence almost immediately. Five days after his dismissal, Kerr was appointed to lead the Carnegie Commission on Higher Education, a high-profile project of the Carnegie Foundation for the Advancement of Teaching.

From 1967–73, as chairman and executive director of the Carnegie Commission, Kerr led the largest-scale assessment of American higher education ever undertaken, engaging a prestigious group of thinkers in documenting, debating, evaluating and proposing improvements for higher education in America. One output of this effort was the Carnegie Classification of Institutions of Higher Education (1970) which was created 'to provide more meaningful and homogeneous categories than are found in other existing classifications'[10] and differentiate institutions according to a simple schema identifying level and control. Widespread adoption of the Carnegie Classification came quickly and it has continued to the present as a blueprint for higher education on the state level. Only now, after thirty years of existence, are substantive changes planned for the Classification to provide a more flexible and comprehensive system.[11]

From 1974–79 Kerr continued as chairman of the Carnegie Council on Policy Studies in Higher Education, extending his influence to an international level. Altogether, between 1967 and 1980, the Carnegie Commission and Council produced 175 documents that had a profound impact on the perception, operation and organization of higher education, influencing institutional leaders as well as policy-makers, classrooms and the courts. In 1980, Kerr retired from his post as Chairman of the Carnegie Commission and returned to UC-B where he has conducted various studies of labour economics and higher education; engaged in labour negotiations, including the US Postal Service; and engaged in public speaking across the globe. Since the mid 1980s, he has published at least eight books, including texts on the future of higher education and industrial societies. Recognizing his vast contributions, Kerr has been honoured with thirty-eight honorary degrees from universities in the United States and abroad. To this day, he maintains an office and staff on the UC-B campus as he completes his memoirs, 'The Gold and the Blue', to be published by the University of California Press.

At the peak of his career, Kerr's leadership of the UC system and later the Carnegie Commission provided him a platform to articulate his theories focused on leading and improving higher education in America. Stuart aptly referred to Kerr as an 'action intellectual', characterizing him as a self-assured intellectual who attained access to the powerful élites who to a great degree managed and influenced the direction of society.[12] Throughout his life Kerr embraced a liberal ideology, celebrating the American ideals of democracy, freedom and liberty. His faith in progress embraced free enterprise, the scientific method and liberal pluralism as a means of dealing with the complexities and inequalities of a growing industrial society. Ever the skilful negotiator, Kerr saw higher education as the primary vehicle for achieving equality of opportunity – not egalitarianism – through a stratified system of higher education that would provide access for all while preparing the most academically capable, resulting in higher productivity and an increased standard of living for the nation. The means for accomplishing this lofty goal were first introduced in the California Master Plan and Kerr was considered the main architect of that effort, creating 'excellence in diverse and well-defined areas in each sector of American public higher education including academic, as well as vocational, training; promotion of research; and support for the education of an élite of talent'.[13]

Leadership of higher education has been a passion for Kerr since his early work in administration at UC-B, culminating in his study of the subject in the 1980s. He has advocated that higher education leaders be planners, mediators, consensus builders, visionaries and pragmatists. He believes leaders should maintain stability within their institutions while moving them forward toward the future. He contends they should walk the fine line between critic and loyalist. To do so, he has argued, requires knowing how to distinguish one's own personal beliefs from those of the institution.

Martin Trow, UC-B professor of public policy, summarized Kerr's philosophy as follows:

> [Kerr's] views are that university presidents and chancellors have a perfect right to speak out on any issue as private citizens, but they should not speak for their institutions on contentious political issues in their official capacity. Moreover, while they have the right and obligation to press their views on a board before a decision is made, they do not have the right to attack those positions publicly after they are made. Throughout his writings, Kerr stresses the importance of the university president as a builder of consensus.[14]

Advocate for equality of opportunity and protector of freedom of inquiry, Kerr was arguably the nation's most instrumental person in creating the modern American research university. He is credited with developing a vocabulary and philosophy that is captured best in his description of the multiversity. Kerr argued that the multiversity could withstand enormous strain because its many and diverse communities, each having contradictory goals and interests, could be dissected and reassembled with little effect on the whole. Needless to say, the concept of the multiversity was criticized because it challenged classical views of the pristine teaching college and the pure research university, but Kerr was not deterred in expressing his opinions. His vision has flourished and it has accurately portrayed the future for many higher education institutions.

Through combining his love for higher education with his deep appreciation for economics, particularly labour relations, Kerr expressed strong beliefs about the potential higher education offered to advancing industrial societies and obtaining individual progress and freedom. Kerr coined the phrase 'life-long learning' decades before it was used on college and university campuses to signify the importance of education through a lifetime. He believed that education could help integrate people into society and reduce isolationism that could contribute to conflict between people, groups and social classes. Stuart observed,

> [Kerr] saw education in a dual and balancing role in industrial society: that of providing the new basic knowledge and new skills upon which industrialism depended and that of safe-guarding progress and liberty through academic freedom and the education of individuals into a democratic society. ... Kerr believed industrialism was a revolutionary force in the world because it increased productivity and created a higher standard of living.[15]

In a speech given in 2000, Kerr reflected upon his 1963 Godkin Lectures at Harvard, questioning whether the future 'city of intellect'[16] should be led by 'hedgehogs' or 'foxes' where the fox knows many things and the hedgehog knows one big thing or two, making reference to Isaiah Berlin's famous essay.[17] He observed that the twentieth century was good for colleges and universities, referring to the period as 'the golden age of higher education in all American history'.[18] He reflected on the three greatest changes that occurred during the past one hundred years: universal access where institutions moved from being a class-oriented institution for the élite to a market-oriented one for all, scientific advancement through federal investment in research and 'leading research professors became world citizens', and enormous resources conferred through national wealth and prosperity for higher education and good jobs for graduates.[19] Recognizing that challenges remain, he cautioned against 'fractionalization of the academic guild', where subject matter is broken up in finer and finer detail and a 'free-for-all' environment where external influences drive internal decisions. Among many recommendations, he encouraged leaders of the next century to pay attention to the globalization of economic markets, fluctuation in rates of return to a college education, older students seeking job advancements, new electronic technology, the rise of the biological sciences, the power of non-academic authorities in governance, and the rise of for-profit competitors. Displaying the enormous sense of optimism that defines his character, Kerr ended his speech with a final thought about the future, ultimately siding with the foxes,

> What incredible opportunities these foxes have to explore the intricacies of a century of so many discontinuities, of so many alternative scenarios; opportunities to turn challenges into triumphs; opportunities to explore and create solutions.
>
> To the hedgehogs of the 1960s of which I was one: Rest in Peace; to the foxes of the 21st century: Great expectations for success with your solutions![20]

Notes

1 Kerr, *The Uses of the University*, Cambridge, MA: Harvard University Press, pp.vii–viii, 1963.
2 Mary Clark Stuart, 'Clark Kerr: Biography of an Action Intellectual', unpublished doctoral dissertation, University of Michigan, Ann Arbor, 1980, p.13.
3 Ibid., pp.44–5.
4 Ibid., p.59.
5 Kerr, 'Public Education in California – The Next Quarter Century', Address to Phi Delta Kappa, May 1953, *Phi Delta Kappa Journal*, p.311, October 1953.
6 http://sunsite.lib.berkeley.edu/CalHistory/chancellor.kerr.html.
7 C. Condren, *Preparing for the Twenty-First-Century: A Report on Higher Education in California*, California Post-secondary Education Commission Report 88–1, Sacramento, CA: California Post-secondary Education Commission, p.30, 1988.
8 T. Hayden, *A New Vision for Higher Education in California. Beyond the Master Plan*, Sacramento, CA: Joint Publications Office, Subcommittee on Higher Education, California State Legislature, 1986.
9 Kerr, *The Uses of the University*, Cambridge, MA: Harvard University Press, 1963.
10 Alexander C. McCormick, 'Bringing the Carnegie Classification into the 21st Century', *AAHE Bulletin*, p.1, January 2000.
11 Ibid., p.3.
12 Stuart, op cit., pp.1–3.
13 Ibid., p.158.

14 Letters to the editor, 'The Role of Trustees and Presidents', *The Chronicle of Higher Education*, 15 August, 1997.
15 Stuart, op cit., pp.129, 143.
16 Kerr, *The Uses of the University*, Cambridge, MA: Harvard University Press, 4th edn, 1995, chap. 3, 1963.
17 Kerr, 'The City of Intellect in a Century for the Foxes?', paper presentation given at The Future of the City of Intellect Conference, University of California, Riverside, p.13, 17 February 2000.
18 Ibid., p.10.
19 Ibid., pp.5–10.
20 Ibid., p.36.

Kerr's major writings

Kerr, C., Harbison, F.H., Dunlop, J.T. and Myers, C.A., *Industrialism and Industrial Man: The Problems of Labor and Management in Economic Growth*, Cambridge, MA: Harvard University Press, rev. edn, 1975, 1960. Original volume translated into eight languages.
The Uses of the University, Cambridge, MA: Harvard University Press, 3rd rev. edn, 1982, 1963. Original version translated into six languages.
Marshall, Marx, and Modern Times: The Multi-dimensional Society, London: Cambridge University Press, 1969. Original version translated into three languages.
The Great Transformation in Higher Education, 1960–1980, Albany, NY: State University of New York Press, 1991.
Troubled Times for American Higher Education: The 1990s and Beyond, Albany, NY: State University of New York Press, 1994.

Further reading

Clark Kerr was a primary author of numerous volumes published by the Carnegie Commission on Higher Education. Selected Carnegie volumes that demonstrate the depth and breadth of Kerr's understanding and influence are: *A Chance to Learn* (1970), *New Students and New Places*, including the Carnegie Classification of Institutions in Higher Education (1970), *Less Time, More Options: Education beyond High School* (1971), *Governance of Higher Education* (1973) and *The Purposes and Performance of Higher Education in the United States: Approaching the Year 2000* (1973).

Levine, A., *Higher Learning in America: 1980–2000*, Baltimore, MD: Johns Hopkins University Press, 1993.
—— 'Clark Kerr: The Masterbuilder at 75', *Change*, 19, 2, March/April 1987, pp.12–30, 35.
Stuart, M.C., 'Clark Kerr: Biography of an Action Intellectual', unpublished doctoral dissertation, University of Michigan, Ann Arbor, 1980.
Wills, G., 'Antitype Clark Kerr', *Certain Trumpets: The Call of Leaders*, New York: Simon & Schuster, 1994.

DEBRA D. BRAGG AND FRANKIE S. LAANAN

BENJAMIN S. BLOOM 1913–99

> Psychologist and authority in educational measurement, Benjamin Bloom has influenced a whole generation of researchers. His research into the importance of early childhood education has challenged educators to reconsider present procedures for organising schools and allocating resources. His recent work on Mastery Learning promises to open a new set of approaches to the education of all children.[1]

Benjamin S. Bloom was born in Lansford, Pennsylvania in 1913 into a Jewish family which had emigrated from a climate of discrimination in Russia a few years earlier. The father was a poor tailor and Ben like many others with his background wanted to become a teacher, a way of climbing the social ladder. After graduation from Pennsylvania State College in 1935 he became a research assistant in the American Youth Commission. After a short stay with the Cooperation Study in General Education he became employed in the historical Eight-Year Study by Ralph Tyler who at the time had become chairman of the School of Education at the University of Chicago. He enrolled in the doctoral programme there and completed his Ph.D. in 1942. After serving as a researcher on the Board of Examiners at the University of Chicago; and as examiner at the college of the University, Bloom became Professor of education in Chicago in 1940. He stayed there until retirement in 1990. Early in his career, Bloom became involved in international projects in India and Israel and was one of the founding members of the International Association for the Evaluation of Educational Achievement (IEA) in 1961. He belonged to the Panel that established the Research and Development Centres in the US in the 1960s and served as Chairman of the American Educational Research Association (AERA) 1965–66. Among his many recognitions was his receipt of the AERA-Phi Delta Kappa Award for distinguished contributions to education in 1970.

Working under Ralph Tyler, Bloom gained deep insights into the theory and practice of educational evaluation, a term coined by the task that evaluators set themselves. Bloom set about the task of translating the goals of instruction via concrete behaviours into instruments of measurement, a task that was particularly difficult when one had to deal with goals in the affective domain, i.e. in assessing attitudes and interests. In the 1950s he served as chairman of a committee on taxonomy of educational objectives set up by the AERA. The first book, covering the cognitive domain, authored by Bloom and David Krathwohl, *Taxonomy of Education Objectives*, was published in 1956. Another eight years elapsed until volume II, covering the affective domain, came out in 1964.

In the late 1960s Bloom began to develop a theory of 'mastery learning'. According to this theory the great majority of students, say 90–95 per cent, are able to learn basic principles, concepts and skills – if they are given enough time. Bloom's point of departure for research on mastery learning was the model of school learning which has been advanced by John Carroll at Harvard University and later Educational Testing Service in Princeton. According to Carroll the most important differentiating factor behind school achievement was *time* not differences in some kind of scholastic aptitude. One reason why differences in school achievements have traditionally been seen as due to some kind of aptitude is that the tests given to students are usually time limited. This is the main explanation, Bloom maintained, why test scores are distributed according to the famous bell-shaped Gaussian curve, i.e. distributed 'normally'. But students who have the privilege of getting individual instruction, which traditionally has been the case in privileged social strata, are being allowed enough time to learn what is required. The differences which can be noted during the first year of formal schooling increase considerably as the students move up in the system. By radically individualizing instruction and the pace of learning with regard to the starting point in each case one would be able to get 90 per cent of the students to reach the goals of instruction. This was of course, to challenge the axiom of individual differences which had a central position in educational psychology.

As mentioned above, in 1970 Bloom got the AERA with Phi Delta Kappa award for outstanding contributions to educational research. The following year he was invited by AERA to give the lecture about a self-selected topic. The formulation of the topic was provocative: 'Individual Differences: A Vanishing Point?', even with the question mark. Research based on the concept of mastery learning is centred on three main factors which, according to Bloom, explain about 90 per cent of the differences in achievements brought about by conventional school instruction. The first was what has been referred to as cognitive entry behaviour, the competence the student has when faced by a new learning task. By diagnosing these original differences and adapting the learning-teaching to them, the final differences can be reduced by some 50 per cent. Second, the affective entry behaviour should be considered so as to avoid the setbacks due to initial failures which strongly affect the motivation for further learning. By stimulating an optimal initial motivation, differences in final achievements can be reduced by some 25 per cent. Third, one can adapt the instruction with regard to media and time and not least encouragement and individualization. Thereby another 25 per cent of the final differences can be taken care of.

After some years of further research on mastery learning, in 1976 Bloom tried to 'take stock' after his didactical model had been used both inside and outside the United States. This summing up was done in his book *Human Characteristics and School Learning*. In the Preface he accounts for the philosophy of mastery learning in three simple points. When he started his research career in educational measurements the prevailing thesis was:

1   There are good learners and there are poor learners.

Then came Carroll's model for school learning:

2   There are faster learners and there are slower learners.

Bloom and others began to wonder whether extra time and help would bring a far greater proportion of students up to a competence level higher than that achieved by the conventional model. This lead to the conclusion:

3   Students become much more similar with regard to learning ability, rate

of learning and motivation for further learning if provided with favourable learning conditions.

Bloom finishes the first chapter of the 1976 book by the antimeritocratic thesis that modern societies cannot any longer be satisfied by making a selection of able students. They must find means of *developing* able ones.

A 'Primer for Parents, Teachers and other Educators' on the topic of mastery learning came out in 1980 under the title *All Our Children Learning*.

The next step in Bloom's research was the attempt to find a way of revolutionizing classroom instruction by developing methods which would make a certain type of group instruction as effective as one-to-one tutoring. He used to refer to it as the '2 sigma problem'. In 1984 he published the outcomes of try-out experiments with various methods of instruction with group methods. The 2 sigma problem could be solved by several of them, i.e. it was possible to bring students in groups up to the level of plus 2 sigma which otherwise was considered to be possible only be means of one-to-one tutoring.

In the early 1980s Bloom entered upon a five-year research study of talent development which focused on 120 gifted young people who had reached world-class status in mathematics, neurology, swimming, tennis, music and art. Few of these top performers had been regarded as child prodigies. Bloom carefully identified the learning conditions, the hard work and the support provided by parents and others necessary to rise to the top. These and other studies of the 'gifted' were reported in *Developing Talent in Young People* in 1985.

Studies pertaining to educational objectives and theories and methods of evaluation were, as mentioned, inspired by the involvement in the Eight-Year Study as well as the work on the reform of undergraduate education at the University of Chicago. The common denominator for much of this work was studies of individual differences – how large they are and what causes them.

In 1964 Bloom published a monograph *Stability and Change in Human Characteristics* where he, as he did in following books, challenged the established thesis about what changes can be brought about by educational measures.

After the appointment of President Lyndon Johnson in the USA, a major Task Force headed by John Gardner, a psychologist with strong educational interests and later Secretary of State for Health, Education and Welfare was established. The overriding mandate for the Task Force was to come up with proposals about what the Federal government could do in order to improve American school education without coming into conflict with the Constitution. Bloom provided the Task Force with expert knowledge which played an important role relating to the proposals it made. Gardner's committee, among other things, suggested a programme of compensatory education which became part of the War Against Poverty by allocating resources to school districts with a high percentage of children who were growing up in poverty or being linguistically hampered by not having English as their mother tongue. Bloom in 1965 (along with Alison Davis and Robert Hess) published a monograph about these problems, *Contemporary Education for Cultural Deprivation*.

Given Bloom's experiences in the field of educational evaluation acquired during his years as university examiner at the University of Chicago, he not surprisingly became involved in international co-operation in the field. In the early 1960s he was one of the founding members of the International Association for the Evaluation of Educational Achievement (IEA). Later during that decade he was asked by UNESCO to prepare an international seminar on evaluation. This was implemented through a seminar in Gränna, Sweden, in 1971, with participation from some twenty-five developing countries. Bloom himself acted as director of the seminar and leading experts in the field, including Ralph Tyler and John Goodlad served as lecturers. In the same year the book *Handbook on Formative and Summative Evaluation* came out. It was followed a decade later by *Evaluation to Improve Learning*. To return to my opening quotation, Benjamin Bloom was indeed psychologist and authority, who influenced generations in their quest to improve educational quality.

Note

1   Award presentation by Phi Delta Kappa and the American Educational Research Association 1970. Quoted in the Phi Delta Kappa Monograph 1971 which published Bloom's lecture at the AERA Meeting in New York City, 6 February 1971, the title of the lecture: 'Individual Differences in School: A Vanishing Point?'

See also

In this book: Goodlad, Tyler

Bloom's major writings

Benjamin S. Bloom was the author or co-author of seventeen major books. The main ones are:

Taxonomy of Educational Objectives: Volume I Cognitive Domain, New York: David McKay and Co., 1956.
Stability and Change in Human Characteristics, New York: John Wiley and Sons, 1964.
Benjamin S. Bloom, with D.B. Masia and D. Krathwohl, *Taxonomy of Educational Objectives: Volume II, The Affective Domain*, New York: David McKay and Co., 1964.
with J.T. Hastings, G. Madaus *et al.*, *Handbook on Formative and Summative Evaluation of Student Learning*, New York: McGraw-Hill 1971.
All Our Children Learning: A Primer for Parents, Teachers and other Educators, New York: McGraw-Hill, 1980.
Benjamin S. Bloom, with A. Sosniak, *et al.*, *Developing Talent in Young People*, New York: Ballatine, 1985.

In the early 1990s Bloom was a member of the task force appointed by the International Academy of Education, of which he was one of the founders, which looked into the problem of the home–school relationship from the point of view of educational research. The report was published under the title *The Home Environment and School Learning*, San Francisco, CA: Jossey Bass, 1993, with Thomas Kellaghan *et al.*

Bloom reported several of his seminar ideas and outcomes of preliminary studies in various scholarly and educational journals. The following list makes no claim of being representative but presents certain key articles.

'Individual Differences in School Achievement: A Vanishing Point?', award lecture at the Annual Meeting of AERA, 1971, Bloomington, IN: *Phi Delta Kappa International* 1971.
'Innocence in Education', *School Review*, 80, 3, pp.1–20, 1972.
'The State of Research on Selected Alterable Variables in Education', Mesa Seminar, 1980, B.S. Bloom, Department of Education, University of Chicago 1980.
'The 2 Sigma Problem: The Search for Methods of Group Instruction as Effective as One-to-One Tutoring', *Educational Researcher*, 13, 6, pp.4–15, 1984.
'Helping All Children Learn Well in Elementary School – and Beyond', *Principal*, pp.12–17, March 1988.

Further reading

'In Memoriam: Benjamin Bloom (1913–1999)', *IEA Newsletter*, 34, December 1999.
'Never too Young to Learn', *Newsweek*, 22 May 1972.

TORSTEN HUSÉN

JEROME S. BRUNER 1915–

> Education is not simply a technical business of well-managed information processing, not even simply a matter of applying 'learning theories' to the classroom or using the results of subject-centered 'achievement testing'. It is a complex pursuit of fitting a culture to the needs of its members, and its members and their ways of knowing to the needs of the culture.
> (Jerome Bruner, *The Culture of Education*, p.43)

In the late 1980s, I attended an international conference on education in Paris. One evening I found myself having dinner with half a dozen persons, representing half a dozen different nations, none of whom I had known before. As we spoke, a remarkable fact emerged. All of us had been drawn to a life in education because of our reading, years before, of psychologist Jerome Bruner's remarkable volume *The Process of Education*.[1]

At some point in their professional lives, many psychologists become involved in educational issues. Such engagement is especially likely in the United States, where educational theory and practice have been heavily influenced by contemporary work in psychology. It is possible that psychologists like B.F. Skinner or E.L. Thorndike have had more influence on specific educational policies, such as testing; when it comes to enlarging our sense of how children learn and what educators could aspire to, Jerome Bruner has no peers.

Born in New York City in 1915, Jerome Bruner's professional life has been that of a prolific and versatile psychologist. Trained at Duke and Harvard Universities, his first paper, published in 1939, was on 'the effect of thymus extract on the sexual behavior of the female rat'.[2] During the Second World War, Bruner participated as a social psychologist, investigating public opinion, propaganda and social attitudes. Thereafter, as one of the leaders of the post-war 'cognitive revolution' his focus has been chiefly on human perception and cognition.

During the half century since the war, Bruner has investigated in turn a series of loosely related topic areas. In his work on the 'new look' in perception, he emphasized the role of expectation and interpretation on our perceptual experiences.[3] Maintaining this focus on the active role of the subject, he turned next to the role of strategies in the processes of human categorization.[4] Becoming increasingly concerned with the development of human cognition, Bruner and colleagues at Harvard's newly formed Center of Cognitive Studies undertook a series of studies of the modes of representation used by children.[5]

In 1970, Bruner moved from Harvard to Oxford University. There he continued his developmental studies of infant agency[6] and began a series of investigations of children's language.[7] Following his return to the United States a decade later, he has shown a heightened concern with social and cultural phenomena. Rejecting the excessive computationalism of the cognitive perspective that he helped to found, he has directed attention to human narrative and interpretive capacities[8] – most recently in the law.[9] And he has helped to launch yet a third revolution in psychology – one centred around the practice of cultural psychology.[10]

It is important to sketch Bruner's contributions as a psychologist because they frame his involvement in educational issues. Reflecting his catholic research interests and his own wide learning, Bruner has approached education as a broad thinker rather than as a technician. He has considered the full range of human capacities that are involved in teaching and learning – perception, thought, language, other symbol systems, creativity, intuition, personality and motivation. He construes education as beginning in infancy and, especially in recent writings, has emphasized the role assumed in education by the gamut of cultural institutions. He has drawn on our knowledge of early hominids and has consistently viewed education from a cross-cultural perspective. (In the 1990s, he began to work regularly with the pre-schools of Reggio Emilia and other Italian communities.) Indeed, in his most recent writings on cultural psychology, Bruner has proposed education as the proper 'test frame' for constructing a full-fledged cultural psychology.

In the late 1950s, Jerome Bruner became explicitly involved in precollegiate education in the United States. At that time, following the Russian launching of the satellite Sputnik, many Americans felt that a greater portion of national resources must be devoted to education, particularly in science, mathematics and technology. This interest occurred at the very time that the cognitive revolution, partly under the charismatic leadership of Bruner, had been launched. The influential National Academy of Sciences and the National Science Foundation called a meeting of scientists, other scholars, psychologists and educators at Wood's Hole, Massachusetts in September 1959. Bruner was the obvious chair for this meeting.

In his landmark book, *The Process of Education*,[11] Bruner eloquently described the chief themes that had emerged at the conference. Against the widespread notion that youngsters should be learning facts and procedures, the conferees argued for the importance of the structure of scientific (and other) disciplines. If a student understood the principal moves in a subject area, he or she could go on to think generatively about new issues. ('Knowing how something is put together is worth a thousand facts about it.'[12]) Against the view of the child as an assimilator of information, and as a little adult, the conferees (inspired by the work of Jean Piaget and Bärbel Inhelder), put forth a still unfamiliar view of the child: the child as an active problem-solver, who had his or her own ways of making sense of the world. Against the notion that certain subjects should be avoided until secondary school or later, the conferees argued for a spiral curriculum, in which topics were introduced in appropriate ways early in school and then revisited, with added depth and complexity, at later points in schooling. This argument inspired the most quoted (and most controversial) line in the book: 'We begin with the hypothesis that any subject can be taught effectively in some intellectually honest form to any child at any stage of development.'[13]

The response to the Bruner report was swift and electrifying. The book was praised as 'seminal', 'revolutionary' and 'a classic' by a range of scholars and policy leaders. It was translated into nineteen languages and was for many years the best-selling paperback issued by the Harvard University Press. Perhaps most important, *The Process of Education* catalyzed a range of important educational programmes and experiments, both in the United States and abroad. As Bruner speculated some years later: 'I think the book's "success" grew from a worldwide need to reasssess the functions of education in the light of the knowledge explosion and the new postindustrial technology'.[14]

While he might have chosen to return to the psychological laboratory, Bruner instead became directly involved in educational efforts, first in the United States, and later in Great Britain. He joined a number of committees and commissions, serving for a while as a member of the Education Panel of the President's Science Advisory Committee under Presidents Kennedy and Johnson. By far his deepest involvement was as chair and architect of a new curriculum for social studies to be used in the middle grades.

In 1964–66, under the auspices of a government research-and-development laboratory called Educational Services Inc., Bruner led the effort to design and implement 'Man: A Course of Study'. This ambitious effort to produce a full-fledged curriculum drew on the most current thinking in the newly emerging behavioural sciences. As conceptualized by Bruner, the curriculum sought to address three fundamental issues: 'What is uniquely human about human beings? How did they get that way? How could they be made more so?'

Reflecting Bruner's belief that even young children could tackle difficult issues, the curriculum presented themes that were 'alive' in the behavioural sciences of the era. In the light of linguistic analyses of Charles Hockett and Noam Chomsky, youngsters explored the nature of communication systems. Taking into account Sherwood Washburn's discoveries about the tool use of early man, students investigated ancient and modern tools and media. Inspired by discoveries about the social relations of primates (Irven DeVore) and humans (Claude Lévi-Strauss), students explored kin relations and social organizations of cultures. There was ample material on the art, myths and childrearing practices of diverse groups. The ideas and themes were presented through rich ethnographic and filmic case studies, drawing in particular on the Netsilik Eskimos of Pelly Bay and the !Kung bushmen of the Kalahari Desert.

Years later Bruner wistfully recalled: 'In the heady days of 1962, anything seemed possible'.[15] As a young member of the research team, I can attest to the excitement that permeated this curriculum effort.[16] Scholars, psychological researchers, curriculum planners, master teachers and eager fifth graders worked shoulder-to-shoulder each day to create and revise curricula that would engage and instruct. The resulting materials were made widely available and circulated through much of the United States and abroad in the late 1960s and early 1970s.

However, the euphoria surrounding such educational experimentation did not last. Within the United States, issues of poverty and racism erupted on the domestic front, and the increasingly frustrating and divisive war in Vietnam sapped the energies of reform. The Bruner curriculum was directly attacked by conservative political and social groups, which took objection to the intellectual aspirations (read: 'élitist') and cross-cultural (read: 'relativistic') sweep of the materials.[17] Eventually, the National Science Foundation withdrew its support for curriculum. Bruner conceded that the fault did not lie entirely with external critics. The curriculum worked best with well-prepared teachers working in schools with advantaged students. Bruner was fond of remarking: 'We never quite solved the problem of getting the materials from Widener (library at Harvard University) to Wichita (largest city in Kansas, the heartland of America).'

Bruner's involvement in education yielded a set of thoughtful essays on learning and instruction, which were gathered together in *Towards a Theory of Instruction*[18] and *The Relevance of Education*.[19] In these writings, Bruner put forth his evolving ideas about the ways in which instruction actually affects the mental models of the world that students construct, elaborate on and transform. Drawing on his collaborative developmental studies, he highlighted three ordered ways in which children transform experiences into knowledge: through action, through imagery and, eventually, through a range of symbolic systems. Much of education involves a negotiation, and sometimes conflict, among these modes of representation. Increasingly influenced by the writings of the Soviet psychologist Lev Vygotsky, Bruner stressed the ways in which much of learning involves the internalization of tools and media that have been constructed over the years by other human individuals and groups. And he continued to reveal an interest in under-explored issues, such as motivation, affect, creativity and intuition.

Looking back on his educational work of the 1960s and early 1970s, Bruner has come to recognize certain limitations. Part of the limitation represented the psychology of the era: an excessive focus on solo, intrapsychic processes of knowing. A complementary limitation came from a failure to recognize the depth and pervasiveness of societal problems, including poverty, racism and widespread alienation. As Bruner commented: 'it was taken for granted [at that time] that students lived in some sort of educational vacuum, untroubled by the ills and problems of the culture at large'.[20]

By the 1970s and 1980s, Jerome Bruner had emerged as a chief critic of the cognitive revolution. He saw it as an unwarranted reduction of human thought to a set of computational routines. With other colleagues, he called for the construction of a cultural psychology, in which the historical background and current forces of a culture were given weight. In Bruner's view, such a rejuvenated psychology should discover what is meaningful to individual and groups – and why it is meaningful.

In light of this framework Bruner revisited educational issues in his 1996 book *The Culture of Education*. He proposed that education is not properly viewed simply as a function of the school, directed at the mind of individual students: 'schools as now constituted are not so much the solution to the problem of education as they are part of the problem'.[21] One is more likely to achieve educational progress, if one sees education as the function of the culture-at-large, and if one looks for learning amidst the interactions and joint constructions of students attempting to construct knowledge. No longer should educational theorists ponder the individual child (Piaget's 'epistemic subject'), puzzling about conservation of liquid or the subtlety of kinship relations. Rather, educationalists should direct their attention to groups of children attempting together – often with the aid of computer networks and remote experts – to understand the processes of biology, the nature of law and even the ways in which they themselves learn. Successful students should tell one another what they have learned about the world and about the operations of their individual and collective minds.

As this necessarily rough sketch should suggest, Jerome Bruner has served a vital role in the educational discourse of our time: bringing to bear the latest thinking in psychology on the contemporary problems of the society; always on the lookout for the nagging problems and the most promising paths to their solution; zestfully open to new currents of thought. At the same time, students of Bruner call attention to the powerful themes that permeate a career in psychology that is entering its seventh decade: a belief in the active agency of the human being, a conviction about the construction of knowledge, a perennial concern with purpose, goals and means, a virtually unerring taste for which issues are important and how best to tackle them, and an unflinching optimism that withstands personal and societal setbacks.

It remains to say that Jerome Bruner is not merely one of the foremost educational thinkers of the era; he is also an inspired learner and teacher. His infectious curiosity inspires all who are not completely jaded. Individuals of every age and background are invited to join in. Logical analyses, technical distinctions, rich and wide knowledge of diverse subject matters, asides to an ever wider orbit of information, intuitive leaps, pregnant enigmas pour forth from his indefatigable mouth and pen. In his own words 'Intellectual activity is anywhere and everywhere, whether at the frontier of knowledge or in a third-grade classroom'.[22] To those who know him, Bruner remains the Compleat Educator in the flesh: in his own words 'Communicator, model, and identification figure'.[23]

Notes

1 Bruner, *The Process of Education*, Cambridge, MA: Harvard University Press, 1960.
2 J.S. Bruner and B. Cunningham, 'The Effect of Thymus Extract on the Sexual

Behavior of the Female Rat', *Journal of Comparative Psychology*, 7, pp.333–6, 1939.

3 J.S. Bruner and C.C. Goodman, 'Value and Need as Organizing Factors in Perception', *Journal of Abnormal and Social Psychology*, 42, 1, pp.33–44, 1947; Bruner, 'On Perceptual Readiness', *Psychological Review*, 64, pp.123–52, 1957.

4 J.S. Bruner, J. Goodnow and G. Austin, *A Study of Thinking*, New York: Wiley, 1956.

5 J.S. Bruner, R.R. Olver and P.M. Greenfield, *Studies in Cognitive Growth*, New York: Wiley, 1966.

6 Bruner, *Processes of Cognitive Growth: Infancy*, Worcester, MA: Clark University Press, 1968.

7 Bruner, *Child's Talk*, New York: Norton, 1983; A. Ninio and J. Bruner, 'The Achievement and Antecedents of Labelling', *Journal of Child Language*, 5, pp.1–15, 1978.

8 Bruner, *Actual Minds, Possible Worlds*, Cambridge MA: Harvard University Press, 1986; Bruner, *Acts of Meaning*, Cambridge, MA: Harvard University Press, 1990.

9 A.G. Amsterdam and J.S. Bruner, *Minding the Law*, Cambridge, MA: Harvard University Press, 2000.

10 J.S. Bruner, *Acts of Meaning*, op cit.; J.S. Bruner, *The Culture of Education*, Cambridge, MA: Harvard University Press, 1996.

11 Bruner, *The Process of Education*, op cit.

12 Bruner, *In Search of Mind: Essays in Autobiography*, New York: Harper & Row, p.183, 1983.

13 Bruner, *The Process of Education*, op cit., p.33.

14 Bruner, *In Search of Mind*, op cit., p.185.

15 Ibid., p.190.

16 H. Gardner, *To Open Minds: Chinese Clues to the Dilemma of Contemporary Education*, New York: Basic Books, chap. 2, 1989.

17 P. Dow, *Schoolhouse Politics: Lessons from the Sputnik Era*, Cambridge, MA: Harvard University Press, 1991.

18 Bruner, *Toward a Theory of Instruction*, Cambridge, MA: Harvard University Press, 1966.

19 Bruner, *The Relevance of Education*, New York: Norton, 1971.

20 Bruner, *The Culture of Education*, op cit., p.xiii.

21 Ibid., p.198.

22 Bruner, *The Process of Education*, op cit., p.14.

23 Ibid., p.91.

See also

In this book: Piaget, Vygotsky

Bruner's major writings

The Process of Education, Cambridge, MA: Harvard University Press, 1960.

Bruner, J.S., Oliver, R.R. and Greenfield, P.M., *Studies in Cognitive Growth*, New York: Wiley, 1966.

Toward a Theory of Instruction, Cambridge, MA: Harvard University Press, 1966.

The Relevance of Education, New York: Norton, 1971.

Beyond the Information Given, J. Anglin (ed.), New York: Norton, 1973.

In Search of Mind: Essays in Autobiography, New York: Harper & Row, 1983.

Acts of Meaning, Cambridge, MA: Harvard University Press, 1990.

The Culture of Education, Cambridge, MA: Harvard University Press, 1996.

Further reading

Bakhurt, D. and Shanker, S. (eds), *Jerome Bruner: Language, Culture, Self*, London: Sage, 2001.

Bruner, J.S., *On Knowing: Essays for the Left Hand*, Cambridge, MA: Harvard University Press, 1979.

Dow, P., *Schoolhouse Politics: Lessons from the Sputnike Era*, Cambridge, MA: Harvard University Press, 1991.

Olson, D.R. (ed.), *The Social Foundations of Language and Thought: Essays in Honor of Jerome S. Bruner*, New York: Norton, 1980.

Olson, D.R. and Torrance, N., *The Handbook of Education and Human Development*, Cambridge, MA: Blackwell, 1996.

HOWARD GARDNER

TORSTEN HUSÉN 1916–

> It is relatively easy to proof read life, but very difficult to
> predict it.
> (an oft-repeated saying of Torsten Husén)

Torsten Husén was born on 1st March 1916 in Lund, Sweden. His mother had trained as a telegraphist after having completed her secondary education. His father had five years of half-time primary education, a form of education that was typical in rural areas at that time. He was the manager of a sawmill. Husén grew up in southern Sweden and began primary school at the age of six, one year before the official age of entry to school. He had learned to type at home and therefore told his primary school teacher that he could do this so that it was not necessary for him to learn how to write by hand. He proceeded to his secondary school studies in the Gymnasium in Växjö where he opted to specialize in mathematics and the natural sciences. It was also the tradition that all pupils learned three foreign languages (indeed, it was an entry requirement to upper secondary school). In Husén's case this was German, English and French in that order. His German was so good that he was able to accompany his father on business trips to Poland and Germany where he acted as his interpreter. Although he learned English he was never able to practise it and it was only when he went to England in 1946 as a member of a Swedish delegation that he was actually able to practise speaking English. It was in the 1950s that he began to write some of his books and articles in English. In the end, his English was probably the foreign language in which he was most fluent although his German remained faultless.

In 1935, at the age of nineteen, he entered the University of Lund. He began by studying mathematics, then literature (his first publication was on the influence of French clinical psychology and psychiatry on the work of Strindberg) and history and finally psychology. He has always said that he regarded (and hoped that others would do likewise) the university as a large smorgasbord where one should be able to choose dishes to satisfy intellectual curiosity. It was in his university days that he began to 'write each day' and his way of life soon became *nulla dies sine linea*. It must have been at about the same time that he developed other traits that helped him on his way: the conviction that 'nothing was impossible' in the sense that he never let bureaucracy stand in his way, and the ability to give full concentration to the task in hand. (This writer has seen him spend a whole day in very frustrating and taxing meetings and then go and sit down at his typewriter for two hours and write an article!)

Husén's doctoral thesis, some 500 pages long, in 1944 was entitled *Adolescensen* (but the book store edition bore the title *Svensk Ungdom*[1]). It was based on test and questionnaire data collection of 1000 young persons between the ages of seventeen and twenty as they entered military service. Each aspect of adolescence was described including citations from works in German, English and even French. By the age of twenty-eight, he was conversant in three foreign languages, had learned the methods of literary criticism and historical analysis, and had studied the psychological approaches of Wundt, Meumann, and the philosophy of the Vienna Circle. Indeed he had spent time studying with Kretschmer. In psychology he had learned various methodological approaches and was versed in the psychology of perception as well as in psychophysiology. By the end of 1944 he had published three books and some sixty articles.

During his last two years at the university, Torsten Husén became involved with a team in Stockholm charged with the development of a series of psychological tests for military purposes, a task requiring him to learn psychometrics. He moved to Stockholm in 1944. One extra outcome of this work was an individual adult intelligence test. In 1948 Husén published a book[2] on the relationships between social background, intelligence as measured by the military tests and schooling. Husén was not only involved in the construction of the first tests for military use in Sweden but during his ten years as senior psychologist in the defence department he was instrumental in organizing and implementing the application of the results of the work. One could regard him as the father of Swedish military psychology.

In 1938, all children born in 1928 in the city of Malmö were tested. This was to be the beginning of a longitudinal study that still continues at the end of the twentieth century. In 1950, there was a major report[3] on the Malmö study attempting to assess the influence of schooling on the growth of intelligence from ten to twenty years of age. It also touched on the problem of the 'reserves of ability' that was to become a hot issue in Sweden in the following years. At the same time, there was other work by one of Husén's students, Kjell Haernqvist, that examined the 'pool of ability'.[4] The major tenet of these publications was that selective secondary schooling did not favour the development of manifold talents present in the society coupled with the notion of the 'reserve of talent' in society. Neither of the studies was able to identify the two different academic and practical talents so inherent in the thinking about selective education. These findings had a profound effect on the political debate on education in Sweden and also in other countries. All of this led Husén to interest himself in the interaction between research and policy-making. His thinking and publications had effects around the world.

The Malmö study continued and several of Husén's doctoral students undertook the analyses and reporting of the various time-series data. The first comprehensive report of the Malmö data was published in 1969.[5] At the end of the 1980s another of his students, Tuijnman, was able to demonstrate that the continuing education of adults had an effect on their later job choice and remuneration.[6]

In the meantime (1953) Husén had become a Professor of Education and Educational Psychology at Stockholm University. In those days it was insufficient for a professor of education simply to conduct empirical studies in education or to be specialized in developmental and differential psychology. He was also expected to be proficient in philosophy of education and the history of education. Ever faithful to his maxim of *nulla dies sine linea* he spent his evening writing three books on the history of primary education in Sweden with emphasis on the work of Fridtjuv and Anders Berg.[7] These two had promoted special educational approaches for the teaching of orthography and thus it was not a surprise when, at the same time, Husén published a book reporting the results of an empirical psychological study of orthography.[8]

At the same time, Husén was interested in the eternal nurture–nature debate. He analysed data on monozygotic and dizygotic twins (about 600 pairs) from military data collected in 1948 to 1952. He examined[9] the intra- and inter-pair patterns of differences in aptitude, school achievement, height weight, laterality and writing. The approach he used was different from many earlier ones.

From 1953 onwards and especially after 1956 when he became the first professor in Sweden of educational research, Husén and his students became engrossed in various educational research projects. These involved the major debate concerning selective versus comprehensive education,[10] an analysis of educational needs as a basis for curriculum reform,[11] and research into the eternal problem of class size and the homogeneity of classes,[12] to mention but some of the projects. As these results had to be used by policy-makers for the reform of education, Husén became interested in the relationship between research and researchers and policy-making. This interest led him to examine this relationship in several countries and resulted in two books nearly twenty years apart. The first was in 1967 together with Gunnar Boalt[13] and the second in 1984 together with Maurice Kogan.[14] The various modes in which research relates to policy-making in different contexts are exemplified.

Between 1956 and 1982, Husén supervised thirty-eight students who successfully defended their doctoral theses. It should be recalled that then the Swedish doctorate was akin to the German Habilitation and the French Doctorat d'Etat. Thus the amount of work involved in the early theses was enormous. Husén had a great knack for identifying young researchers who would profit from training in order to undertake a doctoral thesis. As head of IEA, he put in motion the famous Gränna seminar for teams of six curriculum specialists from each of twenty-three countries. This had a profound effect on curriculum development in many countries of the world. He also was instrumental in the organization of the three European Seminars on Learning and the Educational Process (SOLEP) following on from those organized by Lee Cronbach in Stanford.

In the early 1950s Husén had been invited to Germany to participate in a workshop on the role of psychological research in the resolution of educational problems. The impact of empirical research methods on researchers trained in hermeneutics should in theory have produced some fine research conceptualization. Since Husén had published several books and articles in English, his name was known to researchers outside Sweden and in 1958 Husén's research group decided to affiliate itself with the emerging International Association for the Evaluation of Educational Achievement (IEA). In 1962, Husén became the chairman of IEA, edited its first major publication[15] and guided it along its way from then until 1978. In the 1960s and 1980s this organization carried out the largest sample survey research studies in education. It was clear that counting the number of graduates from the last grade of secondary schools was a bad proxy for the educational productivity of nations' school systems and that what was required was a measure of what they had achieved in terms of knowledge, skills and values. Although the results of the studies were continuously used by ministries of education in some twenty countries, it was only in the 1990s with the publication of the TIMSS study results that IEA 'hit' the media. The standards of research set by the IEA studies in the 1960s and 1970s set the scene for the standards required in later international achievement studies conducted by ETS and OECD.

In the 1960s he was increasingly requested to advise ministries of education, the International Institute for Educational Planning (IIEP) in Paris (he was chairman of the board of this institute from 1971 for ten years), the UNESCO Institute for Education in Hamburg, OECD, UNESCO, the International Council for Educational Development (of which he was a member for many years), as well as to such conferences as that initiated by President Johnson in Williamsburg, Virginia. He taught at the Institute for Humanistic Studies in Aspen, Colorado. He enjoyed his regular visits to Stanford either as a Fellow at the Behavioural Sciences Center or at the university, that continued past his retirement.

In 1982 he became an Emeritus professor but still continued with many of his activities and even took on new tasks. He continued to publish books and even became co-editor-in-chief of both the first (10 volumes)[16] and second (12 volumes)[17] editions of the International Encyclopedia of Education. He was the senior author of the first educational publication[18] of the Academia Europaea. He was a founding member of and chairman (1986–98) of the International Academy of Education.

Husén is a most affable person and is able to pour oil on troubled waters in many of the groups with which he has worked when there has been friction. Indeed, he is able to foresee trouble when chairing meetings and possesses the superlative gift of being able to divert the discussion in such a way that the trouble either does not occur or is dissipated quickly. He has a clarity of expression that is essential in international meetings. His knowledge and skills in both the philosophy of education and empirical research in education make him a rare person who commands great respect.

It would not have been possible for him to run the many research projects without competent teams of research workers and money. His 'never regarding anything as impossible' approach was essential for the success of the projects.

Husén was very closely involved in the research accompanying the Swedish school reforms in the 1950s and 1960s. This was noticed in other countries and he became a member of the Governing Board of the Max Planck Institut für Bildungsforschung in Berlin. He was also invited several times by Anthony Crosland in Britain to discuss structures of educational systems. He could also be said to be one of the foundling fathers of comparative education in Europe and contributed to these kinds of studies through his chairmanship of IEA.

Husén is an interdisciplinary thinker. His knowledge of the history of educational ideas coupled with his wide knowledge of literature and his empirical approach in education led to a breadth of vision that was breathtaking. His ability to refer to psychological, sociological and economic studies in education when focusing on a particular aspect of education resulted in the problem being looked at from many angles. His writing concerning what schools as institutions can and cannot do, how the various contexts in which young people find themselves impact what they can learn, the structure of school systems, and the notion of lifelong education have all had an important influence in many countries. Three publications (and translated into several languages) that had a wide readership concerned these issues.[19]

In all, he has written fifty-five books and some 1500 articles.

Notes

1 *Svensk Ungdom* [Adolescence]. *Psykologiska undersökningar av ynglingar I äldern 17–20 ar*, Stockholm: Gebers, 1944.

2 *Begavning och Miljö* [Aptitude and Milieu]. *Studier i begåvningsutvecklingen och begåvningsurvalets psykologisk – pedagogiska och sociala problem.* Stockholm: Gebers, 1948.

3 T. Husén, *Testresultatens prognosvärde. En undersökning av den teoretiska skolningens inverkan på testresultaten, intelligenstestens prognosvärde och de sociala faktorenas inverkan på urvalet till högre läroanstalter,* Stockholm: Gebers, 1950.

4 K. Haernqvist, *Reserverna för högre utbildning*, Stockholm: Ecklesiastikdepartementet, SOU 1958, 11. K. Haernqvist, *Individuella differenser och skoldifferenttiering*, Stockhom: Ecklesiastikdepartementet, SOU:1960, 13.

5 T. Husén, with the assistance of I. Emanuelsson, I. Fägerlind and R. Liljefors, *Talent, Opportunity, and Career*, Stockholm: Almqvist & Wiksell, 1969.

6 A.C. Tuijnman, *Recurrent Education, Earnings, and Well-being: A Fifty-year Longitudinal Study of a Cohort of Swedish Men*, Stockholm: Almqvist & Wiksell, 1989.

7 T. Husén, Fridtjuv Berg, 'folkollärarkåren och stavningsreformerna', *Pedagogiska skrifter*, 192, 1946. T. Husén, Fridtjuv Berg, 'och enhetsskolan', *Pedagogiska skrifter*, 199, 1948. T. Husén, Anders Berg 'under folkskolans pionjärår', *Pedagogiska skrifter*, 205, 1949.

8 T. Husén, 'Rättstavningsförmågans psykologi. Några experimentella bidrag', *Pedagogiska skrifter*, 207–9, 1950.

9 T. Husén, *Tvillingstudier*, Stockholm: Almqvist & Wiksell, 1953. T. Husén, *Psychological Twin Research: A Methodological Study*, Stockholm: Almqvist & Wiksell, 1959.

10 N.-E. Svensson, *Ability Grouping and Scholastic Achievement*, Stockholm: Almqvist & Wiksell, 1962.

11 U. Dahllöf, *Kursplaneundersökningar I matematik och modersmålet*, Stockholm: Ecklesiastildepartementet, 1960.

12 S. Marklund, *Skolklassens storlek och struktur*, Stockholm: Almqvist & Wiksell, 1962.
13 T. Husén, and G. Boalt, *Educational Research and Educational Change: The Case of Sweden*, Stockholm: Almqvist & Wiksell, and New York: John Wiley, 1967.
14 T. Husén, and M. Kogan, (eds), *Educational Research and Policy: How do they Relate?*, Oxford: Pergamon Press, 1984.
15 T. Husén (ed.), *International Study of Achievement in Mathematics: A Comparison of 12 Countries*, vols 1 and 2. Stockholm: Almqvist & Wiksell, 1967.
16 T. Husén and T.N. Postlethwaite (eds), *International Encyclopedia of Education*, vols 1–10, Oxford: Pergamon.
17 T. Husén and T.N. Postlethwaite (eds), *International Encyclopedia of Education*, vols 1–12, Oxford: Pergamon, 1994.
18 T. Husén, A. Tuijnman and W. D. Halls (eds), *Schooling in Modern European Society: A Report of the Academia Europaea*, Oxford: Pergamon, 1992.
19 T. Husén, *The School in Question: A Comparative Study of the School and its Future in Western Societies*, London and New York: Oxford University Press, 1979. T. Husén, *An Incurable Academic: Memoirs of a Professor*, Oxford and New York: Pergamon Press, 1983. T. Husén, *Education and the Global Concern*, Oxford: Pergamon, 1990.

See also

In this book: Cronbach

Husén's major writings

Adolescensen (Adolesence), Stockholm: Almqvist & Wiksell, 1944.
Predictive Value of Intelligence Test Scores, Stockholm: Almqvist & Wiksell, 1950.
Psychological Twin Research, Stockholm: Stockholm University Press, 1959.
International Study of Achievement in Mathematics I-II, ed. and author, New York: John Wiley, 1967.
Talent, Opportunity and Career, Stockholm: Almqvist & Wiksell, 1969.
Talent, Equality and Meritocracy, The Hague: Nijhoff, 1974.
The School in Question, London: Oxford University Press, trans. into eleven languages, 1979.
Husén, T., with Kogan, M., *Educational Research and Policy*, Oxford: Pergamon Press, 1984.
The Learning Society Revisited, Oxford: Pergamon Press, 1986.
Education and the Global Concern, Oxford: Pergamon Press, 1990.
Husén, T., with Tuijnman, A. and Halls, W.D., *Schooling in Modern European Society: A Report of the Academia Europaea*, Oxford: Pergamon Press, 1992.
The Role of the University: A Global Perspective, ed. and author, Paris: UNESCO, 1994.

Further reading

Husén, Torsten, 'A Marriage to Higher Education', *Journal of Higher Education*, 51, pp.15–38, 1980.
Husén, Torsten, *An Incurable Academic: Memoirs of a Professor*, Oxford: Pergamon Press, 1983.
Postlethwaite, T. Neville (ed.), *International Educational Research: Papers in Honor of Torsten Husén*, Oxford: Pergamon Press, 1986.
Tjeldvoll, Arild, *Listening to Torsten Husén: A Comparative Education Researcher*, a book reporting fifteen hours of interviews, 1999.

Also see *International Who's Who*, London: Europa Publications, *Who's Who in Europa: Dictionnaire Biographique*, ed. Servi-Tech, Waterloo: Belgium, and *Who's Who in the World*, Chicago, IL: Who's Who Marquis).

T. NEVILLE POSTLETHWAITE

LEE J. CRONBACH 1916–

Lee Cronbach begins his contribution to the *History of Psychology in Autobiography*[1] by saying: 'Psychology caught me early. I was born in 1916, just before Lewis Terman's disciples fanned out to spread the gospel of mental testing.' He could have added that Terman's revision of the Binet–Simon Intelligence scale (Stanford–Binet) came out the same year under the title *The Measurement of Intelligence*.[2] He mentions, however, that by the age of five he was tested by a lady school psychologist, and with an IQ of 200 he was registered as one of the 'gifted' children ('Terman's kids') who were then followed by Terman well into the 1950s. Anyhow, his gifts were such that he was able to finish high school in Fresno, California (where he was born) at the age of fourteen and the state college in the same place at eighteen. His father was a Jewish silk dealer. The family could not afford to send him to the university which meant that he, as was the case with many others with the same background, enrolled at the Fresno State College to be trained as a teacher. He soon became interested in psychology having majored in mathematics and as he himself puts it became interested in 'engineering analysis of psychological measuring devices'. He taught mathematics for two years at Fresno High School. After a year at Berkeley, which resulted in an MA, he went on in 1938 to the University of Chicago, which had been developed as a leading institution in educational psychology by C.H. Judd and F.N. Freeman, both trained in Leipzig and with strong empirical and experimental traditions. Cronbach completed his Ph.D., at Chicago in 1942 profiting from courses by Ralph Tyler and serving for a couple of years as research assistant on the Eight-Year Study headed by Tyler. On the study staff Cronbach was regarded 'as all-purpose methodologist'. After an interlude as a college teacher and a military psychologist, Cronbach returned to the University of Chicago as an assistant professor where he gave an introductory course in educational psychology which generated the basis for his *Educational Psychology* which came out in its first but by no means last edition in 1949. He points out himself in the autobiography that he 'settled into a style that became both the main strength and the main weakness' of his scholarly production namely the specialization on 'measurement and individual differences'.

In 1948, he was appointed to the University of Illinois, Urbana, as a professor of education psychology where he had as colleagues Raymond B. Cattell in the psychology department and N.L. Gage in the education department. The recruitment of those mentioned was part of the 'leap to prominence' by the University taken at the time. The Illinois measurement programme in psychology and education had, as Cronbach puts it, 'few rivals'.

In 1964, after a year at the Centre for Advanced Study in the Behavioural Sciences at Stanford, Cronbach was appointed to a professorship in education at Stanford University. He retired in 1980. During that period of his career he authored some seven books.

The contributions that Cronbach made to the theory and methodology in educational measurement are reflected in the fact that he is strongly represented in the *International Encyclopaedia of Education*.[3] He is quoted in forty-seven entries primarily for his contributions to research methodology and theory. He is, for example, cited in articles about abilities and aptitudes, measurement of attitudes, decision theory in educational testing and aptitude-treatment interaction.

Right from the outset as a researcher in the behavioural sciences, Cronbach specialized in educational measurement and psychometric problems. Rightly so then, he was primarily seen as a methodologist. The level of competence he reached as a researcher and the range of subjects that he covered was reflected in the fact that he over a period of ten years was elected both as President of the American Psychological Association (APA) and the American Educational Research Association. In the APA, he, in the 1950s, led a committee on test standards and as an educational research along with P. Suppes conducted a study on 'Research for Tomorrow's Schools' (1969). Cronbach advanced a generalizability theory which replaced the classical theory in psychological measurement of 'true score' by a 'universal score' which defines a person's mean score over all acceptable observations. A generalization occurs from a sample to a universe.

At an early stage in his career Cronbach became interested in problems of psychological measurement and started to use decisions theory in assessing psychological and educational measurements. He conducted studies of test reliability which contributed to basic clarifications. Some of this was brought together in the book *Psychological Testing and Personnel Decisions* which he published together with G.C. Gleser in 1957. As chairman of the APA committee on test standards he contributed to the clarification of the concept of validity. His distinctions between various kinds of validity are still the prevailing ones.

Perhaps the most well known of Cronbach's contributions to educational research is the development of the Aptitude-Treatment Interaction paradigm (ATI) which was first presented in his and Gleser's book but more fully developed in a book that he published with his Stanford colleague Richard Snow in 1977, *Aptitudes and Instructional Methods: A Handbook for Research on Interactions*. Relevant research was reviewed and a new theory was launched about the relationship between individual differences and learning variables. The background was the model about selection and placement of individuals that Cronbach had developed with Gleser in the book about the use of decisions-theory. The word 'treatment' was used to refer to what was done with the students within the framework of particular programmes and instructional methods. In the ATI (aptitude-treatment interaction) approach the emphasis was on what learning methods would be most adequate given a certain aptitude.

As one of Ralph Tyler's outstanding students, and because of his practical training in the Eight-Year Study, educational evaluation was another field to which Cronbach devoted his research. At Stanford,

Cronbach developed an evaluation course in which each student planned an evaluation. Part of his work in this field was an evaluation of Stanford's undergraduate programme entitled 'Values, Technology and Society'. This work, in what in Bloom's terminology is called 'formative evaluation' has a strong impact on the practical applications in the field.

In the study Cronbach conducted with P. Suppes (1969) for the US National Academy of Education he made the distinction between decision-oriented and conclusion-oriented research and rejected the classical distinction between 'pure' and 'applied'. In the methodology of psychological measurements he was responsible for the revision of the reliability theory. Lee Cronbach has made a truly outstanding contribution to theory and methodology in educational measurement and psychology. While his contributions to educational scholarship have consisted to a large extent in advancing research methodology in the field, he has undoubtedly also contributed to wider philosophical perspectives on our understanding of education.

Notes

1 G. Lindzey (ed.), *History of Psychology in Autobiography*, 8, 64–93, pp.64, 1989.
2 L. Terman, *The Measurement of Intelligence*, London: Harrap and Co, 1989.
3 T. Husén (Editor in Chief) and T.N. Postlethwaite, *The International Encyclopedia of Education*, 1–12, Oxford: Pergamon, 1993.

See also

In this book: Bloom, Tyler

Cronbach's major writings

Essentials of Psychological Testing, New York: Harper & Row, 1949, rev. edns 1960, 1970, 1984, 1990.
'Coefficient Alpha and the Internal Structure of Tests', *Psychometrika*, 16, pp.297–334, 1951.
Educational Psychology, New York: Hartcourt and World Brace, 1954, rev. edns, 1963, 1977.
Cronbach, L.J., with Meehl, P.E., 'Construct Validity in Psychological Tests', *Psychological Bulleting*, 52, pp.281–303, 1955.
'The Two Disciplines of Scientific Psychology', *American Psychologist*, 12, pp.671–84, 1957.
Cronbach, L.J., with Gleser, G.C., *Psychological Testing and Personnel Decisions*, Urbana, IL: University of Illinois Press, 1957, new edn, 1965.
Cronbach, L.J., with Gleser, G.C. and Rajataratnam, N., 'Generalizability of Scores Influenced by Multiple Sources of Variance', *Psychometrika*, 30, pp.395–418, 1965.
'Heredity, Environment and Educational Policy', *Harvard Educational Review*, 39, pp.338–47, 1969.
Cronbach, L.J., with Patrick Suppes, *Research for Tomorrow's Schools: Disciplined Inquiry in Education*, New York: Macmillan, 1969
Cronbach, L.J., Gleser, G.C., Nanda, H. and Rajaratnam, N., *The Dependability of Behavioural Measurements: Theory of Generalizability for Scores and Profiles*, New York: Wiley, 1972.

'Beyond the Two Disciplines of Scientific Psychology', *American Psychologist*, 30, pp.116–27, 1975.
'Five Decades of Public Controversy over Mental Testing', *Amercian Psychologist*, 30, pp.1–14, 1975.
Cronbach, L.J., with Snow, R.E., *Aptitudes and Instructional Methods: A Handbook for Research on Interactions*, New York: Irvington, 1977.
Toward Reform in Program Evaluation, San Francisco, CA: Jossey-Bass 1980.
'Abilities and Ability Testing: Recent Lines of Thought', *Evaluación Psicológica*, 1, 1–2, pp.79–97, 1985.
'Internal Consistencies of Tests: Analyses Old and New', *Psychometrika*, 53, pp.63–70, 1988.

Further reading

Lindzey, G. (ed.), *History of Psychology in Autobiography*, 8, pp.64–93, 1989.
Husén, T. (Editor in Chief) and Postlethwaite, T.N., *The International Encyclopaedia of Education*, 1–12, Oxford: Pergamon, 1993.

TORSTEN HUSÉN

DONALD THOMAS CAMPBELL 1916–96

In this chapter we shall examine the validity of 16 experimental designs against 12 common threats to valid inference.[1]

Was there ever a more dry beginning to a best-seller? More than 300,000 copies of this treatise on experimental methods have been sold. Co-authored with Julian C. Stanley, it appeared originally as a chapter in Gage's *Handbook of Research on Teaching*. On this alone could rest Campbell's reputation as a methodologist, particularly in education. But he was much more.

Campbell's father had been raised in a fundamentalist church in Pennsylvania, although he was not an active churchgoer as an adult. Campbell was sent by his mother to Sunday School during his childhood but he rejected religion while nevertheless recognizing its evolutionary role. He had: 'considerable respect for the quality of lives led by those devout believers who combined subtle understanding of themselves with high ethical standards'.[2]

He finished high school at the age of eighteen, knowing that he wanted to be a scientist, but without a chosen field, and then spent a year working for $40 a month plus room and board on a turkey ranch near Victorville, California. Giving us a glimpse of family influence, he noted that family ideology favoured 'broadening experiences'.

The next year he lived at home and attended San Bernardino Valley Junior College for his freshman and sophomore years. He was taught by a zoologist who published articles on squirrel fur colour that were relevant to evolutionary theory. From him and other teachers at the junior college he declared that he gained his image of the work of scientists.

Campbell subsequently completed his first degree at the University of

California at Berkeley, graduating first in the class of 1939 (and his younger sister graduating second). He was a Naval reserve in the Second World War and then returned to obtain a Ph.D. in Social Psychology at Berkeley completing this in 1947 at the age of thirty-one.

Campbell's work in these early years was in data collection and theory development relating to attitude formation, with propaganda never far from a consideration, as these were post-war years. He then spent three years at Ohio State University, but took up a post at the University of Chicago for the next three years, 1950–53.

During Campbell's final year at Chicago, he was relieved of all teaching duties to participate in James G. Miller's 'Committee on Behavioural Sciences'. This focused on cybernetics, information theory and general systems theory. Although he greatly valued this broadening opportunity at Chicago he was critical of much of his experience there. His comments should be noted by anyone with responsibility for setting up systems of management, control and accountability:

> Most obvious to me is that I found the scholarly life much less enjoyable, overall, than I had found it at Ohio State. At Chicago, the tenure pressures were extreme. ... Publications were every-thing. ... Worse still, we were explicitly told that our publications had to be works of genius. This requirement reduced productivity for all.

Northwestern offered Campbell a five-year term as Associate Professor. He saw it as:

> an opportunity to return to a mutually affirming scholarly atmosphere, where worker scientists were honoured and where I would earn my living through teaching. (By the time I became aware that publications were necessary at Northwestern, I had overcome the logjam, still shamelessly using un-refereed journals.)

He eventually stayed at Northwestern for thirty-six years then subsequently took up an appointment at Lehigh University.

Campbell received many honorary degrees and awards from various professional groups such as the universities of Stanford, Oxford, Harvard and Yale, the American Psychological Association, the National Academy of Arts and Sciences, the Society for the Psychological Study of Social Issues, Evaluation Research Society and the American Educational Research Association.

His obituary appeared in *The New York Times*, 12 May 1996.[3] It began:

> Donald T. Campbell, a nimble-minded social scientist who left his mark on half a dozen disciplines and helped revolutionize the fundamental principles of scientific inquiry common to them all, died on Monday in a hospital near his home in Bethlehem, Pa. He was 79.

His wife, Barbara Frankel, said the cause was complications from surgery for colon cancer.

The obituary ended: 'In addition to his wife, a retired professor of anthropology at Lehigh, he is survived by two sons from a previous marriage ... a sister, ... and two grandchildren.'

Some four years after his death the Campbell Collaboration was named in his honour and launched in Philadelphia in February 2000 at a meeting attended by an international group representing many social science researchers and chaired by Robert Boruch.[4] Like the Cochrane Collaboration in medicine (Maynard and Chalmers 1997) it has the goal of being a source of information on evidence that is of as high a quality as possible.

Perhaps each discipline to which Donald Campbell contributed saw him as their own, as a philosopher of science, an organization theorist, a social science methodologist, an epistemologist, a theoretical biologist, etc. In education, certainly, students in the 1960s and 1970s fell in love with Donald Campbell for the clarity and excitement of his writings. If one could have done a degree in Campbell one would have. In addition to *Experimental and Quasi-Experimental Designs for Research*, another widely cited article was undertaken with Donald Fisk and entitled *Convergent and Discriminant Validation by the Multi-Trait – Multi-Method Matrix* (1959). This early article exemplified a commitment to validity not as a false dichotomy, a decision that something is valid or not, but to the *measurement* of the *degree of* validity. Far from a mechanistic, deterministic precision, Campbell espoused wisdom and judicious judgements, aware of what we do know, but also massively aware of what we don't know.

Although he generally collaborated with statisticians and promoted randomized controlled trials the stereotype that, sadly, is often wrongly attributed to such work cannot be applied to Campbell. He knew the messiness of field experiments and did not seek to hide this. Furthermore the following quotation from a joint publication with Robert Boruch illustrates their commitment to using all sources of evidence:

> The subjective impressions of the many participants and observers of the social experiment acquire a relevance equal to that of the computer output. If ... the qualitative impressions are markedly at variance with the computer output, the validity of the latter should be suspected fully as much as the validity of the former; in particular, an attempt should be made to understand the source of the discrepancy.[5]

Campbell was committed to broad-ranging evaluation with tremendous respect for the practitioner who would know a great deal from being close to the data, as well as an insistence on the best possible designs to tease out cause and effect.

Writing of the danger of 'researchers becoming a self-serving élite, often excluding practitioners by adopting complex statistical procedures that make our conclusions immune from criticism, even from well-placed competent observers who saw the program in action', he advised:

> To avoid such biases, we must devise ways that are readily comprehensible to the participating staffs, recipients, and other well-placed observers, for them to collect, formulate, and summarise their estimations of program effectiveness. ... We must recognise that such summaries may have a validity comparable to the statistical analysis of more formal measures. Usually, these perspectives will agree, but where they do not, we should remember that the statistical analyses involve simplifying assumptions that may be seriously in error.[6]

Campbell showed the tolerance for detail and thorough investigation that typifies science, and yet he also had the grand vision of a society which conducts experiments to find out if its social policies are likely to work. 'Reforms as Experiments' is the title of another important and influential article.[7]

Campbell saw the research scientist as belonging to a 'disputatious community' and not espousing eternal truths but tentative conclusions. He expressed concern at what we might now call academic spin-doctors.

> Government asks what to do, and scholars answer with assurance, quite out of keeping with the scientific status of their fields. In the process, the scholar-advisers too (along with the politicians), fall into the over-advocacy trap. Certainly the idea that one already knows precludes finding out how valid one's theories are.[8]

During his time at Ohio State, he was involved in 'indirect attitude measurement', which generally implies misleading the respondent as to the purpose of the questionnaire in order to get at attitudes that would not be otherwise expressed. This methodology apparently worried him since years later, in one of the books in his honour to which he contributed a chapter, he listed objections that an ethics committee would be interested to hear, including:

The deceptive-deprecatory-exploitative attitudes of psychologists towards subjects.
The failure to do the research implied in the introduction of indirect tests.
The disappointing nature of the research results.[9]

In reading Campbell's account of his research, it seems as though extraordinary amounts of time were spent collecting survey data and discussing the nature of science. The survey data was used for scholarly articles, not as feedback to practitioners. Perhaps his work reflected primarily his early training in social psychology which, although it is a serious experimental science, seems to experiment in order to validate theories rather than to develop theories that are driven by data that has been collected because it is socially useful.

Campbell lived through the politically stressful times of the Second

World War and official segregation and racism in the United States and this may explain some of his lengthy efforts to collect data on the nature of prejudice in social attitudes. He notes that:

> At Northwestern – in contrast to other contemporaneous social science communities – the leftward politicisation of our ablest students was not accompanied by an anti-scientistic, anti-quantitative, humanistic turn. Instead, they continued to make contributions to better quantitative methods for real-world hypothesis testing as well as atheoretical ameliorative programme evaluations.[10]

A theoretical integration led to a well-funded research grant on 'Varieties of Projection in Trait Attribution', National Institutes of Health. The account presented by Campbell provides a cautionary tale. Several research associates including good statisticians and computer managers were hired and the work went ahead.

> We were a high morale team, working on the best integration of theory and data collection I have ever achieved, with an extensive enough sample size to be definitive.
>   The results were crushingly negative and threw me, at least, into a temporary depression. Our research report write-up began 'This thorough, tedious, expensive and disappointing study ...'[11]

Perhaps social scientists need to think extremely carefully about the value of theories. At least Campbell tested his against data.

This lack of productivity arising from a well-funded, well-theorized, well-planned research project, is in contrast to that arising from a 'fun' activity, a weekly social event – the social-psych-sack lunch. Held in the social psychology space on the top floor of Kresge Hall, this lunch evolved into a game in which researchers came up with novel, oddball methods. It led to another publishing success and an original contribution to methodology, a book entitled *Unobtrusive Measures*, published first in 1966 with a revision in 1981.[12]

Campbell recounts periods of depression that coincided with being unable to keep up with ongoing over-commitments. He thanks numerous friends for taking over his teaching, research administration, and so on, during bouts of depression. Writing about over-commitment as an occupational hazard he simply noted:

> Most will have known me as uniformly good-natured, optimistic, expansive, with the only pathology (perhaps unnoted as such) being the delusion that I had time to engage fully each one of my shared intellectual interests. Probably that *has* been my mood during 90 per cent of the scholarly career. ... But I somehow feel it would be less honest and less useful to others if I left (the Blues) out.[13]

Campbell gave valuable warnings on the use of indicators in social science.

> Measures that have been valid for describing the state of society become invalid when they start being used for political decision-making. Moreover, such use often leads to destructive corruption of the social process that the indicator was designed to measure. ... Thus, achievement tests once valid for describing educational status have become less valid when used as the basis of rewards to students or teachers.[14]

The philosophical community has taken considerable note of Campbell's concept of evolutionary epistemology and BVSR (blind variation and selective retention) by which he summarized those mechanisms for the evolution of societies and knowledge. Organization researchers McKelvey and Baum, in a book in Campbell's honour[15] stated that Campbell's 1965 paper 'Variation and Selective Retention in Socio-cultural Evolution' stood out as *having the most pervasive influence on organization* science'.

The website for *Principia Cybernetica* cites his work:

> the modifications or variations are blind, are random, are individually nonappropriate, are not of the order of corrections. But by chance there do occur those which provide better fit, and these survive and are duplicated. While Darwinian theory of evolution has undergone considerable elaboration and modification, and while there has been disagreement as to the mechanism and magnitude of the variations involved, his basic model of natural selection is uniformly accepted today, and stands as one of the great conceptual achievements of the 19th century. In its abstract or formal aspects, it is a model which may be applied to other adaptive processes, or other apparently teleological series of events in which modifications seem guided by outcome.
>
> (Campbell 1956, p.330)[16]

In a quotation that could be the herald of monitoring systems Campbell wrote that: 'Rather than foresighted variation, hindsighted selection is the secret of rational innovation'.[17] Espousing realism Campbell rejected the concept that the world as we see it exists only in our minds, calling this viewpoint 'ontological nihilism'.[18] Bertrand Russell often termed it 'cosmic impiety'.

Much of what Campbell wrote was very idealistic, but we can apply Soros's principle of reflexivity[19] and hypothesize that in so writing he made the world more idealistic. If people believe that financial rewards dominate behaviour, this becomes a pervasive belief in society and it may not be consistent with reality. Campbell recounted that Polanyi persuaded him that the attraction of being able to tell the truth was a dominant motive in the support journalists gave to the Hungarian Uprising:

> These élite Communist journalists, well-rewarded by their establishment with power and wealth, were motivated by the pain of

continually having to write lies about the promise of a society in which they could not write the truth as they saw it.[20]

In this contribution I have tried to let Donald Campbell's words speak for him. This may not be good style but it provides unadulterated data. In conclusion, let me suggest that in the blind variation and diversity of the disputatious academic community, many will selectively retain Campbell's wisdom and his commitment to improving the world through good (social) science.

Notes

1 The opening sentence in D.T. Campbell and J.C. Stanley (1963) *Experimental and Quasi-Experimental Designs for Research*, p.171.
2 Campbell, in Brewer and Collins, *Scientific Inquiry and the Social Sciences*, p.483.
3 *New York Times*, Sunday, Late Edition – Final, 12 May 1996, Section 1, p.37.
4 Campbell Collaboration: http://campbell.gse.upenn.edu.
5 Campbell and Boruch, 'Making the Case for Randomized Assignment to Treatments by Considering the Alternatives', p.199.
6 Campbell and Boruch, 1975, in Campbell and Erlebacher, 1970.
7 Campbell, 'Reforms as Experiments'.
8 Cited by Dunn, *The Experimenting Society*, p.25.
9 Kidder and Campbell 1970, p.333, p.466.
10 Brewer and Collins, op cit., p.482.
11 Ibid., p.475.
12 Webb, Campbell, *et al.*
13 Brewer and Collins, op cit., p.478.
14 Dunn 1998, pp.55–6.
15 'Variations in Organization Science: In Honor of Donald T. Campbell', http://www.mgmt.utoronto.ca/.
16 Website of Principia Cybernetica: http://134.184.131.111/SEARCH.html.
17 Campbell 1977, p.506, found on Website of Principia Cybernetica: http://134.184.131.111/SEARCH.html.
18 *The Experimenting Society*, p.28. Russell wrote of 'cosmic impiety' and Popper was a 'realist'.
19 Chaps 3 and 4 in G. Soros, *The Crisis of Global Capitalism: The Open Society Endangered*, London: Little Brown and Company, 1998.
20 Brewer and Collins, op cit.

See also

In this book: Cronbach
In *Fifty Major Thinkers on Education*: Russell, Thorndike

Campbell's major writings

Campbell, D.T. and Fiske, D.W., 'Convergent and Discriminant Validation by the Multitrait-Multimethod Matrix', *Psychological Bulletin*, 56, 2, p.81–105, 1959.
Campbell, D.T. and Stanley, J.C., *Experimental and Quasi-experimental Designs for Research*, Chicago, IL: Rand McNally, 1966.
'Reforms as Experiments', *American Psychologist*, 24, pp.409–29, 1969.

MAXINE GREENE

'Methods for the Experimenting Society', *Evaluation Practice*, 12, 3: pp.223–60, 1971/1991.

Webb, E.J., Campbell, D.T., *et al.*, *Unobtrusive Measures: Nonreactive Research in the Social Sciences*, Chicago, IL: Rand McNally, 1972.

'The Nature of Man and what Kind of Socializaiton Process is Needed', *American Psychologist*, 30, 1103–26, pp.341–84, 1975.

Campbell, D.T. and Boruch, R.F., 'Making the Case for Randomized Assignment to Treatments by Considering the Alternatives: Six Ways in Which Quasi-Experimental Evaluation in Compensatory Education Tend to Underestimate Effects', in C.A. Bennett and A.A. Lumsdaine (eds), *Evaluation and Experiment*, New York: Academic Press, pp.195–296, 1975.

Cook, T.D. and Campbell, D.T., *Quasi-Experimentation: Design and Analysis for Field Settings*, Chicago, IL: Rand McNally, 1979.

Campbell, F.A. and Ramey, C.T., 'Effects of Early Intervention on Intellectual and Academic Achievement: A Follow-up Study of Children from Low-income Families', *Child Development*, 65, pp.684–98, 1994.

'Unresolved Issues in Measurement Validity: An Autobiographical Overview', *Psychological Assessment*, 8, pp.363–8, 1996.

Further reading

Brewer, M.B. and Collins, B.E. (eds), *Scientific Inquiry and the Social Sciences: A Volume in Honor of Donald T. Campbell*, San Francisco, CA: Jossey-Bass Publishers, 1981.

Dunn, W.N. (ed.), *The Experimenting Society: Essays in Honor of Donald T. Campbell*, New Brunswick: Transaction Publishers, 1998.

McKelvey, B. and Baum, J.A.C., 'Variations in Organisation Science: In Honor of Donald T. Campbell': http://www.mgmt.utoronto.ca/, 1999

Website of *Principia Cybernetica*: http://134.184.131.111/SEARCH.html.

Website: http://www.psych.nwu.edu/academics/social/campbell.htm.

Website: http://www.edfac.unimelb.edu.ac/AJE/editorial.

CAROL TAYLOR FITZ-GIBBON

MAXINE GREENE 1917–

> To feel oneself en route, to feel oneself in a place where there are always possibilities of clearings, of new openings, this is what we must communicate to the young if we want to awaken them to their situations and enable them to make sense of and to name their worlds.[1]

Maxine Greene has been described as 'the preeminent American philosopher of education today'[2] and 'one of the most important figures of any generation to have written and taught and lectured'[3] in the field of education. The influence Greene has exerted through a distinguished career as a social critic, educational philosopher, teacher and mentor reverberates in a remarkable variety of fields: arts and aesthetics, literacy, cultural studies, school improvement, teacher education, social justice, civil rights, women's studies. Greene presents an unwavering critical consciousness, scrutinizing the events of a life lived within particular cultural, social and historical contexts, searching for meaning and consequence.

Born in Brooklyn, New York, in 1917, Maxine Greene's early experience conformed to the cultural expectations which shaped the lives of American women early in the twentieth century. The daughter of 'a family that discouraged intellectual adventure and risk',[4] Greene found occasions to break through the still surface of daily life through the act of writing and the opportunity to attend concerts, plays and museums. She earned a Bachelor of Arts degree in American history and philosophy at Barnard College, in 1938. Soon after, she eloped with a young physician, and worked in his office until he was called to war and she went to work at 'odd jobs, none glorious, some lowly, some hard'[5] to support herself and her young daughter. After the war, Greene divorced and remarried, and began to take courses toward the Master of Arts degree she earned in 1949 from New York University. Greene's choice of educational philosophy as a field of graduate study was accidental, if fortuitous, determined largely by what class was available to take during the hours when her daughter was at school. Six years later, with a newly awarded Ph.D. from NYU, Greene entered the emerging (and predominantly male) field of educational philosophy. For many years, she was the only woman scheduled to present papers at meetings of the Philosophy of Education Society. Greene became the first female President of that organization in 1967, and the first woman to preside over the American Educational Research Association in 1984.

Greene has lectured at universities in the United States and abroad, but her primary faculty appointments have been in the New York area. Following one year as a professor of English at Montclair State College in 1956–57, Greene served from 1957–65 as a professor of education at NYU. In 1965, Greene joined the faculty at Columbia University, initially as editor of the journal, *Teachers College Record*, and subsequently as an exceptionally versatile teacher, responsible for courses in social philosophy, the philosophy and history of education, literature, writing, aesthetics and other educational issues. From 1975–94, Greene held the William F. Russell Chair in the Foundations of Education at Teachers College. Now Professor Emerita, she continues to teach and maintains active involvement with both the Lincoln Center Institute for the Arts in Education, where she has been philosopher-in-residence for more than two decades, and the recently established Center for the Arts, Social Imagination, and Education at Teachers College.

Testimonies to Maxine Greene's vital engagement as a teacher multiply, many appearing in two edited volumes recently published in her honour. William Ayers recalls,

> Like an intimate conversation with an old friend that is picked up, carried on, and then interrupted to be continued in the future, Maxine Greene's lecture was filled with spontaneity, intimacy, incompleteness, and forward motion ... because she harvested her teaching from her own lived experience, it always had an improvisational feel to it ... fresh and vital and inventive, yes, but also firmly rooted in a coherent ground of core beliefs and large purposes.[6]

Others describe the vividness of encounters with Maxine Greene, the sense of being called upon and challenged to approach philosophy as something that is done rather than merely read. Despite the density of her writings, the frequency of references to a daunting assortment of philosophers, artists and critics, Greene exerts a similar attraction, and exacts similar demands, on her readers.

Recipient of numerous awards and honorary degrees, Greene was twice named 'Teacher of the Year' by Phi Delta Kappa, and received the Teachers College Medal. Her book, *Teacher as Stranger*, was awarded the Delta Kappa Gamma Award in 1974 as the 'Educational Book of the Year'.

Greene has been politically and socially active since her student days when her concern with labour issues lead to a term as Legislative Director of the American Labor Party in Brooklyn. Her involvement with the cause of Republican Spain, with the civil rights and peace movements, and her arrival at Teachers College amid the student protests of the 1960s reinforced Greene's inclination to focus on events occurring beyond the sheltered space of the university and alerted her to the importance of understanding the multiple subjective interpretations that emerge from events experienced in common. Greene's work is distinguished by the extent to which she has recognized and addressed the complex and changing contexts in which American schooling occurs.

Greene is the author of five books, more than one hundred articles and chapters in anthologies on various topics, and numerous prefaces and introductions to texts by authors including venerable figures such as Seymour Sarason,[7] and relative newcomers such as Dianne Dubose Brunner[8] and Deborah P. Britzman.[9] Her second book, *Existential Encounters for Teachers*, published in 1967 was a compilation of passages selected from the writings of continental philosophers including Martin Heidegger, Rainier Maria Rilke, John-Paul Sartre, Albert Camus, Martin Buber, Søren Kierkegaard and others, on such topics as the individual, others, knowing, choosing and situations. Greene's comments are interspersed among these selections. Implicit in this project, as in all of Greene's work, is respect for the intellectual capacity and curiosity of teachers, coupled with a firm resistance to the kinds of Instrumentalism that would confine educational discourse to the immediately practical and verifiably effective. As she remarked recently, 'I believe a good teacher is the kind who can get fascinated by many sorts of ideas even though she won't have much chance to teach Habermas.'[10]

Greene's first book, *The Public School and the Private Vision*, appeared in 1965; she is currently at work on a revision of this text. Greene characterizes the book as a critique of 'a changing American culture as seen from the perspective of imaginative artists as well as educational reformers'.[11] Like much of the work to follow, this text drew upon imaginative literature to 'enable readers to see further and, at once, to visualize alternative possibilities',[12] well beyond those problems articulated by Dewey and others who had considered the relationships of school and society before her. The unique (and somewhat renegade) character of Greene's approach to educational theorizing, and many of the themes which would continue to emerge as insistences in her work, were clearly established in this text.

Greene appropriated the central concept of her 1973 book, *Teacher as Stranger*, from the phenomenological sociologist Alfred Schutz:

> I wanted to suggest that the stranger's vision brought a kind of acuity unlikely to be found in a person whose vision was dulled by familiarity. In effect, I was asking the teacher to take the view of the critical onlooker, someone attentive to inequities, false pieties, groundless promises.[13]

Greene's belief in the primacy of existential questions for those who would teach reflectively is evident in this project, with its emphasis on the necessity of the 'struggle against unthinking submergence in the social reality that prevails'[14] and the continual questioning of the basic assumptions that undergird teaching-as-usual.

With the 1978 publication of *Landscapes of Learning*, Greene emphasized the necessity for teachers to cultivate wide-awakeness – an attitude of engagement in the world and full attentiveness to people and events. The intensity of this presence to experience represents a logical extension of the existential situation Greene described in her previous book, *Teacher as Stranger*. She further develops an aesthetic approach to education, quite distinct from the forms of aesthetic education formulated in the late 1970s in the discourse of arts education. Greene's interest in the arts focuses almost exclusively on the meanings they convey, their human import, rather than the sensory, formal, or technical issues they address. In this text, as in those that follow, 'Greene advocates the educational use of the arts to combat that numbing objectification that characterizes contemporary society.'[15]

The Dialectic of Freedom, Greene's next book, reproduces the text of the John Dewey Lecture she was invited to present in 1988 and testifies to her longstanding devotion to many of Dewey's ideas. The text was published at the end of the Reagan administration, a time Greene recognized as hostile to her concerns and encouraging of a widespread resignation to 'a climate of self-centered, self-righteous individualism that disdained the merits of an individual's responsibility to others in community or a commitment to social action'.[16] The gravity of the situation is clear in the questions Greene poses:

> What is left for us then in this positivist, media-dominated, and self-centered time? How, with so much acquiescence and so much thoughtlessness around us, are we to open people to the power of possibility? How, given the emphasis on preparing the young for a society of high technology, are we to move them to perceive alternatives, to look at things as if they could be otherwise? And why? And to what ends?[17]

Greene suggests that the prevailing American vision of freedom as the absence of constraint or obligation must be replaced in the minds of teachers and learners by the more positive sense of freedom as possibility, as the capacity to choose and create themselves, to discover new ways of looking at things, to resist knowledge that is too easily given and received. She stresses here, and in subsequent writings increasingly responsive to postmodern critiques of the American devotion to individualism and personal identity, that community is strengthened and made possible when individuals become mindful of their own perspectives in contrast to others' and to the validity of multiple constructions of reality:

> Freedom shows itself or comes into being when individuals come together in a particular way, when they are authentically present to one another (without masks, pretences, badges of office), when they have a project they can mutually pursue.[18]

Greene's most recent book, *Releasing the Imagination: Essays on Education, the Arts, and Social Change*, published in 1995, suggests that imagination – the capacity to see things as they might be, to envision alternatives to the way things are – is fundamental to meaningful educational and social reform. 'Greene envisions classrooms and communities that value multiple perspectives, democratic pluralism, life narratives, and ongoing social change. This is best accomplished, she believes, through literary, artistic, and phenomenological experiences that release the imagination.'[19] Again, Greene's enduring interest in aesthetic education is evoked as she recommends the use of imaginative literature and other works of art as means to stimulate students to imagine, to think otherwise, to encounter the 'other' concretely in the guise of a character in a novel or play, to remain within a reality removed from their own for the time required to apprehend a work of art. Inspired by the accounts of aesthetic transactions offered by John Dewey, Mikel Dufrenne, Arthur Danto, Wolfgang Iser and others, Greene proposes the constitution of an artwork in the consciousness of a viewer as a metaphor for the learning process.

Reflecting on those themes that have animated her work over the course of her long career, Greene writes,

> I have spoken on various themes that concerned me, popular or not: the problem of meaninglessness; student rebellion; civil rights and the matter of 'invisibility'; moral choosing and 'wide-awakeness'; curriculum issues; the articulateness (or inarticulateness) of the public; educational standards; and, always, the arts, with a special concern for literature.[20]

She maintains a vigilant critical perspective, thoughtfully considering even those developments which seem congenial at first glance; for example, she notes her concern with the 'incipient determinism'[21] of many of the revisionist histories written in the 1960s as groups traditionally marginalized began to find their voices. This scepticism is consistent with Greene's determined resistance to the bureaucratic structures that erode the individual's sense of agency, the social circumstances Greene equates with the plague Camus describes, with Hannah Arendt's concept of 'rule by Nobody'. She questions the depersonalization that accompanies the scientific method and the unexamined rise of technology, acknowledging in both the potential to isolate and erode community, as she upholds the deeper significance of those personal and cultural contexts which inevitably shape experience.

Notes

1 Maxine Greene, *Releasing the Imagination*, San Francisco, CA: Jossey Bass, pp.149–50, 1995.
2 William C. Ayers and Janet L. Miller (eds), *A Light in Dark Times: Maxine Greene and the Unfinished Conversation*, New York: Teachers College Press, p.4, 1998.
3 William F. Pinar, 'Notes on the Intellectual: In Praise of Maxine Greene', in Ayers and Miller, op cit., p.108.
4 Maxine Greene, 'An Autobiographical Remembrance', in William F. Pinar (ed.), *The Passionate Mind of Maxine Greene*, London and Bristol, PA: Falmer Press, p.9, 1998.
5 Ibid., p.9.
6 William C. Ayers, 'Doing Philosophy: Maxine Greene and the Pedagogy of Possibility', in Ayers and Miller, op cit., pp.3–4, 6.
7 Seymour Sarason, *Teaching as a Performing Art*, New York: Teachers College Press, 1999.
8 Dianne Dubose Brunner, *Inquiry and Reflection: Framing Narrative Practice in Education*, Albany, NY: State University of New York Press, 1994.
9 Deborah P. Britzman, *Practice Makes Practice: A Critical Study of Learning to Teach*, Albany, NY: State University of New York Press, 1991.
10 Mark Weiss, Candy Systra and Sheila Slater, 'Dinner with Maxine', in Ayers and Miller, op cit. p.30.
11 Maxine Greene, 'The Educational Philosopher's Quest', in Derek L. Burleson (ed.), *Reflections: Personal Essays by 33 Distinguished Educators*, Bloomington, IN: Phi Delta Kappa, p.202, 1991.
12 Ibid., p.203.
13 Ibid., p.204.
14 Maxine Greene, *Teacher as Stranger*, Belmont, CA: Wadsworth, p.269, 1973.
15 Anne E. Pautz, 'Views Across the Expanse: Maxine Greene's Landscapes of Learning', in Pinar, op cit., p.33.
16 Jon Davies, 'The Dialectic of Freedom', in Pinar, op cit., p.41.
17 Maxine Greene, *The Dialectic of Freedom*, New York: Teachers College Press, p.55, 1988.
18 Ibid., p.17.
19 Patrick Slattery and David M. Dees, 'Releasing the Imagination and the 1990s', in Pinar, op cit., p.46.
20 Maxine Greene, in Burleson, op cit., p.208
21 Ibid., p.203.

See also

In *Fifty Major Thinkers on Education*: Dewey

Greene's major writings

Teacher as Stranger, Belmont, CA: Wadsworth, 1973.
Landscapes of Learning, New York: Teachers College Press, 1978.
The Dialectic of Freedom, New York: Teachers College Press, 1988.
Releasing the Imagination: Essays on Education, the Arts, and Social Change, San Francisco, CA: Jossey-Bass, 1995.

Further reading

Ayers, W.C. and Miller, J.L. (eds), *A Light in Dark Times: Maxine Greene and the Unfinished Conversation*, New York: Teachers College Press, 1998.
Pinar, W. (ed.), *The Passionate Mind of Maxine Greene*, London and Bristol, PA: Falmer Press, 1998.

CHRISTINE THOMPSON

R.S. PETERS 1919–

> Education, then, can have no ends beyond itself. Its value derives from principles and standards implicit in it. To be educated is not to have arrived at a destination; it is to travel with a different view.[1]

Richard Stanley Peters is the founding father of British philosophy of education as practised in the second half of the twentieth century. He was born in 1919 and educated at Clifton College and Oxford University, where he read classics. During the Second World War he joined the Friends Ambulance Unit and engaged in social relief work. At the end of the war he became a schoolmaster at Sidcot School while studying philosophy part-time at Birkbeck College, London. He was appointed to Birkbeck as lecturer in philosophy, then reader in philosophy and psychology, specializing in ethics, philosophy of mind, political philosophy and the history and philosophy of psychology.

After 1962 these interests bore fruit almost exclusively in the field of philosophy of education. For it was in that year that he was appointed to the post with which he became most closely identified – the Chair of Philosophy of Education at the Institute of Education, University of London. For the next dozen or so years he worked with extraordinary energy to transform the philosophy of education from a minor intellectual interest of a handful of scholars into an influential new sub-discipline of philosophy. In all the developments which followed he was aided by his new colleague and later co-author Paul Hirst. Hundreds of advanced students from Britain and from English-speaking countries across the world participated in the new Diploma and MA courses or embarked on doctorates, before taking posts in colleges or universities in which they would teach the subject in their turn to teachers or trainee-teachers. Peters and Hirst ensured that philosophy of education became a major component, along with other disciplines of education, in British initial teacher education, including the newly created Bachelor of Education courses.

The rapidly growing numbers of trained philosophers of education made it possible for Peters and Hirst to launch the Philosophy of Education Society of Great Britain in 1964. From 1964 until 1975 Peters was the Chairman of PESGB. From 1966 until 1982 he also edited its annual *Proceedings* and its successor *The Journal of Philosophy of Education*. Since 1986 Richard Peters has been President of PESGB.

During these remarkably fertile years, Peters also produced a stream of influential books and articles laying the foundations of new-look philosophy of education. Several of his edited collections and early volumes of the *Proceedings* contain essays by leading British philosophers of the time – such as David Hamlyn, Michael Oakeshott, Anthony Quinton and Gilbert Ryle – whom he encouraged to apply their thinking to educational issues. In 1973 he edited the volume on *Philosophy of Education* in the prestigious series Oxford Readings in Philosophy. This proved the high-water mark of his attempt to establish the subject as a sub-discipline of philosophy on a par with, say, philosophy of law or philosophy of religion.

After the mid 1970s, however, swiftly failing health led to a marked decline in the number of his publications. It also put an end to his indefatigable committee work in the cause both of his subject and also, more widely, the place of educational studies in teacher education. He retired from his post at the Institute of Education in 1983.

Richard Peters' philosophy of education was many-sided. Like Israel Scheffler, his counterpart at Harvard, where he had spent some time as a Visiting Professor in 1961, he sought to apply to educational issues the clarity and analytical power of mainstream philosophical thinking of his day. Since the war and until his appointment to the Chair in 1962, the prevailing interest in general philosophy had been in what came to be called 'conceptual', or sometimes 'linguistic', analysis. This meant concentrating on key concepts in the field – e.g. the notions of knowledge, moral obligation, God, causality, law, the state, mind and other mental concepts – with the intention of breaking them down into their component elements and thus revealing their interconnections with related concepts. One route into this area, followed further by some philosophers than others, was via an examination of the ways in which the concepts being analysed were expressed in ordinary language. Hence the narrower concern with 'linguistic' within the broader remit of 'conceptual' analysis.

Part of Peters' initial overall project was to apply 'analytical' techniques to specifically educational concepts. While Scheffler focused on the concepts of teaching and learning, and other British philosophers, encouraged by Peters, investigated these and other notions such as play, indoctrination, training, growth and socialization, Peters specialized in analysing the concept of education itself. This led him to claim that for education – as distinct from other things like training or indoctrination – to be taking place, three criteria have to be met. These are:

[i]   that 'education' implies the transmission of what is worth-while to those who become committed to it;
[ii] that 'education' must involve knowledge and understanding and some kind of cognitive perspective, which are not inert;
[iii] that 'education' at least rules out some procedures of transmission, on the grounds that they lack wittingness and voluntariness.

(Peters 1966, p.45)

Education, on this account – and as elaborated elsewhere in his early writings – consists in the initiation of the uninitiated into activities which are worthwhile pursuing for their own sake. Prominent among these are activities concerned with the pursuit of truth like science, history, literature and philosophy. Educated people are not blinkered specialists in one such domain but understand the broader perspectives that these disciplines cast on other fields and on human life more generally.

Under pressure from other philosophers it soon became clear that Peters' account was no neutral, objective 'analysis' of *the* concept of education, but a delineation of a particular view – most at home in certain university and élite secondary school circles of the time – of what education *should* be like.

Awareness of this caused increasing difficulties around the end of the 1960s and into the 1970s – both for Peters' theory and for the new philosophy of education itself. While Peters attempted to refine his analysis so as to overcome the problem, the wider project of establishing philosophy of education as a new sub-area of philosophy found itself in jeopardy. For a branch of philosophy to count as a relatively autonomous field within the parent discipline, it had, in the heyday of the post-war analytic school, to possess its own key concepts. Thus philosophy of law revolved around the concept of law and related concepts, and philosophy of religion around God and connected ideas like immortality. From the start Peters saw the concept of education as the keystone of the new sub-discipline, supported by other concepts mentioned above like teaching, training and learning. But if 'analysis' of the concept of education was yielding so little fruit (and the harvests from its sister-concepts teaching, indoctrination, training etc. were also proving meagre), how could philosophy of education make out its claim for special status?

But Richard Peters' main claim to be the architect of late twentieth-century British philosophy of education lay elsewhere than in carving out a new sub-discipline of philosophy. 'Applied philosophy' and 'applied ethics' came on the scene largely after Peters' productive years had ended, offering philosophical, especially ethical, perspectives on issues in, for instance, medicine, law, war and peace and the environment. Yet Peters was in effect one of the first British applied philosophers. He was deeply concerned to help teachers and teacher-educators to become clearer about the philosophical dimensions of their work. This took several forms. It meant opening teachers' eyes to the philosophical inadequacies of fashionable educational theory, not least the kind of 'progressive' theory that found its way into the Plowden Report of 1967. It meant encouraging them to question the justifiability of current practices – to do with discipline and punishment, for instance. It meant opening their eyes to wider issues – about democracy in schools, educational aims, equality, moral education, the education of the emotions, the role of the headteacher, the nature of educational disciplines.

This applied aspect of Peters' work helped to set the broad agenda for British – and not only British – philosophy of education for the rest of the twentieth century. He bequeathed to it a problem-centred approach. Unlike other ways of philosophizing about education – the tradition of historical scholarship found today in, for instance, the German speaking countries and Japan – the school that Peters helped to shape has been rooted in educational practice and dedicated to its improvement. But it would be wrong to put all the weight on contemporary relevance. This is only a part of Peters' legacy. More central were the connections he made between surface issues and deeper layers of philosophical thinking, especially in the philosophy of mind and in ethics. In the latter area Peters underpinned his arguments about curriculum subjects, moral development, equality of educational opportunity and other topics with a fully fledged moral philosophy, explicitly indebted to Kant. First-order moral judgements – that corporal punishment is wrong, for instance – have to be tested against, among other things, higher-order moral principles of benevolence, freedom, impartiality and truth-telling. Why these? Peters sought to show that all these ultimate moral principles are capable of a 'transcendental' justification, in that any rational inquirer asking why they should be followed must be committed to them by virtue of his or her attachment to rationality itself.

Peters also used a similar pattern of argument in the justification of curriculum activities. As mentioned above, he saw education as initiation into such intrinsically worthwhile activities as history, science, literature and philosophy. But what makes intellectual pursuits like these worthwhile, rather than, say, playing golf or lying in the sun? In a much discussed chapter in Peters 1966, he argued that it is the concern with the pursuit of truth embedded in the former which means that the serious inquirer who questions their credentials cannot reject them without undermining a central element in the rationality to which he or she is committed.

Whether this or any of the other 'transcendental' arguments stand up is doubtful. Much of the critical discussion of Peters' ideas has focused on them. The Kantian ethics on which he based his philosophy of education lost ground in the last quarter of the twentieth century to Aristotelian perspectives. Peters' philosophy of education is centred, to borrow part of the title of one of his most well-known edited collections, on 'the development of reason'. The rational life, devoted to a concern for truth, is his lodestar, in philosophy as in life. He is all-too-conscious of the fragility of this ideal, of, as he termed it, 'the thin crust of civilisation'. Emotions and desires beneath the psychic surface constantly threaten the rule of reason and need to be brought under its sway. Education is a process of initiation into rationality's demands.

In many quarters Peters has been seen – and saw himself – as the person who brought the techniques of post-war Oxford's 'analytic' philosophy to bear on concrete educational issues. But as the most perceptive of commentaries on his work, written for his Festschrift by his former colleague Ray Elliott, suggests, he is more 'a philosopher in the older style'.[2] Peters wrote that his eyes 'are more likely to be fixed on the brass tacks under the teacher's desk than on the Form of the Good'.[3] Yet for all his avowed rejection of broad metaphysical approaches to education, his philosophical stance, in its universalism, attachment to truth and reason, and emphasis on self-control, is, in Elliott's eyes, akin to that of the Stoics. Like the Stoics, too, Peters has a keen awareness of the human predicament – in his case, of our need to make sense of our lives against the contingency of the world.

Notes

1 Peters, *Education as Initiation*, p.47.
2 See Cooper, *Education, Values and Mind*, pp.41–68.
3 Peters, *Education as Initiation*, p.8.

See also

In this book: Hirst, Scheffler

Peters' major writings (on education)

Education as Initiation, inaugural lecture, London: University of London Institute of Education, 1967; 1st pub. London: Harrap, 1964.
Ethics and Education, London: Allen and Unwin, 1966.
The Concept of Education, ed., London: Routledge & Kegan Paul, 1967.
Perspectives on Plowden, ed., London: Routledge & Kegan Paul, 1969.
Peters, R.S., with Hirst, P.H., *The Logic of Education*, London: Routledge & Kegan Paul, 1970.
Peters, R.S., co-editor with Dearden, R.F. and Hirst, P.H., *Education and the Development of Reason*, London: Routledge & Kegan Paul, 1972.
The Philosophy of Education, ed., Oxford: Oxford University Press, 1973.
Psychology and Ethical Development, London: Allen and Unwin, 1974.
Moral Development and Moral Education, London: Allen and Unwin, 1981.

Further reading

Collits, M., 'R.S. Peters: A Man and his Work', unpublished Ph.D. thesis, University of New England, Armidale, New South Wales, Australia, 1994.
Cooper, D.E. (ed.), *Education, Values and Mind: Essays for R.S. Peters*, London, Routledge, 1986.

JOHN WHITE

JOHN I. GOODLAD 1920–

> So those two things – one, trying to raise the level of what teaching is all about; and two, trying to keep public education available for everybody. Advancing these goals has been my mission.[1]

John I. Goodlad has taught at every grade level from the first grade through to advanced graduate seminars. He began his professional career in a one-room rural school in British Columbia, Canada. Receiving his teaching license in 1939, he was a teacher before becoming a principal in 1941. In 1946 he went to the University of Chicago, where he received his Ph.D. in 1949. In addition to being a professor at Emory University, the University of Chicago, the University of California at Los Angeles and the University of Washington, he has held many leadership positions in universities and other educational and research organizations, such as the Director of the Center for Teacher Education of the University of Chicago, the Director of the University Elementary School at UCLA, the Dean of the Graduate School of Education at UCLA, the Director of the Center for Educational Renewal at the University of Washington, and the President of the independent Institute for Educational Inquiry based in Seattle. He also served as the

President of the American Educational Research Association and the American Association of Colleges for Teacher Education.

Goodlad is a prolific writer. His inquiry into, and reflection upon, education has resulted in more than thirty books, 200 journal articles, and eighty book chapters and encyclopedia entries. As an educator, Goodlad is unique in the sense that he is a researcher, an activist and a philosopher. He conducts empirical studies on schooling and education, engages in putting his innovative ideas into practice, and reflects philosophically upon the social phenomenon called 'education'. The combination of being an empirical researcher, a philosophic thinker, and an activist of educational renewal is uncommon in education.

As to empirical research, Goodlad has many interests. Shen reviewed Goodlad's enormous body of publications and sorted out the following major themes – (1) non-grading, (2) curriculum inquiry, (3) schooling, (4) teacher education, and (5) strategies for educational renewal.[2] However, Shen acknowledged that these five themes are just a convenient organizational structure for discussing Goodlad's ideas, because the themes are closely interconnected in his career.

Non-grading is Goodlad's first and sustained research theme based on his personal professional experience in education. It is from this research theme that others evolved. On a September morning in 1939, Goodlad faced his first class in Woodwards Hill School of the Surrey Municipality in British Columbia. It was a one-room, eight-grade school, consisting of thirty-four children, the youngest was not yet six and the oldest had just turned seventeen. In this one-room school, Goodlad became painfully aware of the relentless intrusion of the norms of graded schooling into his classroom: the requirement of teaching each subject to each grade (adding up to fifty-six lessons a day, an average of seven subjects with each of eight grades), and the pass/fail system that had already resulted in condemning Ernie, a thirteen-year-old boy, to spend seven years in the first grade. Several years later, as the director of education in the British Columbia Industrial School for Boys, Goodlad discovered that the incarcerated juvenile delinquents with whom he worked were nearly all several grades retarded in their school placement. Goodlad's doctoral dissertation was a study of the effects of promotion and non-promotion, a regularity of schooling that confounded not only his life as a teacher in the one-room school but also the lives of his students who were subjected to non-promotion. He found that the social and personal adjustment of the matched promoted second-graders and non-promoted first-graders were significantly different. He concluded that the evidence supports promotion over non-promotion as the more defensible educational practice. The idea of non-grading was born. By 1972, Goodlad had developed a more comprehensive theoretical framework by including moral concern, economic efficiency, psychological reasons and pedagogical and experiential grounds as factors which supported non-grading.[3]

As far as the substance of Goodlad's curriculum inquiry is concerned, his work has been developed at three levels. First, he investigates curriculum practice. His research on the first level includes inquiries into the curriculum reform movement in the 1950s and 1960s, core curriculum, and comprehensive description and analysis of the elementary and secondary curriculum. He has argued that core curriculum is at the very heart of our society's responsibility to ensure for all elementary and secondary students common encounters with the most significant domains of human experience. Second, with continuing inquiry into curriculum practice, Goodlad became concerned with a framework by which the central problems of curriculum could be systematically identified and related to each other. He held that conceptual systems which identified the major questions to be answered in developing a curriculum must be rigorously formulated, and he first employed a framework differentiating the societal, institutional, and instructional levels in 1960. Later on he refined his conceptual system for curriculum in *Curriculum Inquiry: The Study of Curriculum Practice* (1979). Goodlad's conceptual system includes three elements – substantive, political-social and technical-professional – and further develops the Tyler rationale. Finally, Goodlad has also been reflecting on curriculum as a field of study, reviewing its status and making recommendations for its improvement. Based on comprehensive reviews of curriculum as a field of study, Goodlad has argued that we should separate 'ought' questions from 'what' questions. He observed in 1979 that 'It has been my contention for some years that curriculum inquiry must move back to basics, and there is nothing more basic for study than what people practice or do, good or bad, right or wrong.'[4] Goodlad's curriculum inquiry has covered all three levels, from investigating curriculum practice and trends, to delineating curriculum as a field of practice, and to meta-analysing curriculum as a field of study. It is uncommon for a researcher to cover all three levels.

In addition to his research on non-grading and curriculum, Goodlad has also investigated many other topics pertaining to schooling, such as school aim, school goal, school function, school and classroom ambience, early schooling and the history of elementary schools. When addressing the question of what schools are for, he differentiates three aspects – goals (what schools are asked to do), functions (what schools do or are used for), and aims (what schools should do). According to Goodlad, the aim of schools is to develop rational people who do not sin against themselves and their kind. Goodlad's aim of schooling emphasizes both the individual and humankind. The rational individual is not self-centred. The individual ideally develops his or her talents to the full potential and contributes to the welfare of humankind. Schools always exist in a specific social context and are expected to advance specific goals. The expectations are expressed as, in Goodlad's terms, the goal of schooling. In 'A Study of Schooling', Goodlad and his associates condensed the school goals into four categories: (1) academic, embracing all intellectual skills and domains of knowledge; (2) vocational, geared to developing readiness for productive work and economic responsibility; (3) social and civic, related to preparing for socialization into a complex society; and (4) personal, emphasizing the development of individual responsibility, talents, and free expression. What schools actually do is another area in which Goodlad has made major contributions. There is a large amount of information about the condition of American schools in *Early Schooling in the United States* (1973), *Looking behind the Classroom Door* (1974) and, particularly, *A Place Called School* (1984).

Teacher education is another major theme in Goodlad's professional life. His work in this area has three characteristics. First, as early as in the 1960s, Goodlad proposed an insightful proposition that 'teaching is a synthesis' and paid special attention to value judgements in the synthesis of teaching.[5] Against the trend of increasing technification in teacher education, Goodlad argues for the moral dimensions of teaching and the moral mission of schooling. Second, he conducted a comprehensive study to understand both the history (as reported in *Places Where Teachers Are Taught*) and current status of teacher education (as reported in *Teachers for Our Nation's Schools*). Third, based on the understanding of the history and current status of teacher education, Goodlad proposes twenty postulates which stipulate the necessary conditions for sound teacher education.

The theme of strategies of educational renewal has a unique position in Goodlad's professional career. It is not only an independent, important part of his research, but also the bridge between the research and practice. Goodlad has devoted much of his time to probing into various aspects of schooling and teacher education, and his strategies for educational renewal link these two areas. Goodlad proposed the following interrelated concepts as strategies for educational renewal – the school as the centre of renewal, the principal as the key to renewal in a school setting, a school–university partnership and the linking of partnerships in a binding relationship to form networks. Goodlad has tested his theory of the educational renewal process. The educational arena is dominated by the RDDE (research, development, dissemination, and evaluation) model. Effective in agriculture and industry, RDDE is a linear and rational model for change embodied in the Western, industrial and highly technological culture. Goodlad argued that for renewal to occur, there must be some combination of internal responsiveness and external stimulation; for renewal to continue, there must be some continual, productive state of tension between these two essential sets of forces. He proposed the model of dialogue, decisions, actions and evaluation (DDAE) for educational renewal. The DDAE model is not instrumental to some external goal; rather, it is a state of existence. It seeks institutional renewal and an increasingly healthy and satisfying state of being.

Goodlad's empirical studies as discussed above are guided by his moral vision of what education, schooling and teaching should be. As Sirotnik put it: 'he has been consistently concerned with matters of fair play, of equity, of social justice in the treatment of all children and in ensuring their access to excellent public education'.[6] When discussing the moral dimensions of teaching, Goodlad emphasizes facilitating enculturation, providing access to knowledge, building an effective teacher–student connection, and practising good stewardship, with moral imperatives embodied in each of them. Goodlad maintains that education is an inalienable right for each individual and education should facilitate a personal journey of self-transcendence. His agenda for educational renewal is based on the incongruence between his moral principles of what education, schooling and teaching should be and his empirical findings of how education, schooling and teaching function.

Goodlad is not only an empirical researcher and a reflective thinker, he is also active in putting ideas into practice. For example, during the early days of his career, he was actively innovating teacher education programmes at Emory University and the University of Chicago, and helping develop nongraded schools. In 1966 he created the League of Cooperating Schools, which was a tripartite agreement for educational renewal among nineteen school districts in southern California, the University of California at Los Angeles, and the Research Division of the Institute for the Development of Educational Activities. The agenda of the League was both to put new ideas into practice and to study the dynamic process of educational change. The largest renewal project that Goodlad has led is the National Network for Educational Renewal, which consists of thirty-three colleges and universities, more than 100 school districts, and over 500 partner schools across the United States. Guided by the twenty postulates for sound teacher education, the moral dimensions of teaching and principles of educational renewal, the mission of the network is to simultaneously renew both K-12 (kindergarten to the 12th grade) schools and the education of educators in a democracy.

Goodlad's professional achievements have been recognized in twenty honorary degrees from colleges and universities, and many awards from professional societies. His *A Place Called School* received the first Distinguished Book-of-the-Year Award from Kappa Delta Pi and the Outstanding Book Award from the American Educational Research Association in 1985. Recently he received the Harold W. McGraw Jr Prize in Education and the James B. Conant Award for his contribution to education.

Goodlad has left his marks on American education. The following quote summarizes Goodlad's influence rather well – 'This gentle scholar, long associated with calling for the best in schooling, is welcome at every educator's meeting, and his books, monographs, and shorter writings are in every teachers' room and in every teacher training institution.'[7] Facing many pendulum swings and educational fads, Goodlad has been consistent in his message and optimism about the future of education and public schooling. His consistent message is driven by his ideal of what education, schooling and human life should be and is based on his knowledge about the current status of education and schooling. This is the reason why the editors of a book in honour of Goodlad entitled it *The Beat of a Different Drummer*. Goodlad has also influenced the international scene. His writings have been translated into Chinese, French, Hebrew, Italian, Japanese and Spanish. Just like John Dewey's visits to China between 1919 and 1921, Goodlad's visit to China in 1981, when China began to open her door, left its marks on the Chinese educational system.[8]

In the introduction to *Facing the Future: Issues in Education and Schooling*, Ralph Tyler summarized the characteristics of Goodlad's professional career:

> I am impressed not only with the scope of Goodlad's knowledge and experience, but even more with the effective way in which he operates in three related but different roles. He demonstrates competence in the role of researcher; collecting, examining, and interpreting information about the realities of education.
>
> Goodlad also presents a view of what education and schooling ought to be that is very attractive, actually inspiring. His utopia seems both sound and comprehensive, and possible of eventual attainment. In this sense, he is authentically prophetic.

Goodlad's knowledge of the realities of education and schooling and his conception of the ideal are joined by his design for progressive improvement and strategy for action. ... He has clearly demonstrated competence as a leader in the practice of education. The combination in one person of the three roles – researcher, prophet, and mover – is very rare indeed.[9]

And Tyler's observation was made without the benefit of Goodlad's career during the concluding quarter of the twentieth century.

Notes

1 Carol Tell, 'A Conversation with John Goodlad', *Educational Leadership*, 56, 8, May 1999, p.19.
2 J. Shen, 'Connecting Educational Theory, Research, and Practice: A Comprehensive Review of John I. Goodlad's Publication', *Journal of Thought*, 34, 4, Winter 1999, pp.25–96.
3 J.I. Goodlad, *Speaking of Nongrading*, two-cassette album, Code No. 07–079425-X, New York: McGraw-Hill, 1973.
4 J.I. Goodlad, *Curriculum Inquiry: The Study of Curriculum Practice*, New York: McGraw-Hill, p.46, 1979.
5 Goodlad said: 'Teaching demands that the teacher make value judgments of many kinds that lead to employing the most promising techniques for stimulating and guiding teaching.' Please refer to John I. Goodlad, 'The Professional Curriculum of Teachers', *Journal of Teacher Education*, 11, December 1960, p.454.
6 K.A. Sirotnik, 'On Inquiry and Education', in K.A. Sirotnik and R. Soder (eds), *The Beat of a Different Drummer: Essays on Educational Renewal in Honor of John I. Goodlad*, New York: Peter Lang Publishing, p.5, 1999.
7 Cited in C. Frazier, 'Goodlad and Educational Policy', in ibid., p.245.
8 Z. Su, 'John I. Goodlad and John Dewey: Implications of Their Ideas for Education and Democracy In China', in ibid., pp.151–63.
9 R.W. Tyler, 'Introduction', in J.I. Goodlad, *Facing the Future* (New York: McGraw-Hill, p.xi, 1976.

See also

In this book: Tyler

Goodlad's major writings

Goodlad, J.I. and Anderson, R.H., *The Nongraded Elementary School*, New York: Harcourt, Brace & Co., 1959.
Goodlad, J.I. and Associates, *Looking behind the Classroom Door*, Worthington, OH: Charles A. Jones Publishing Company, 1974.
The Dynamics of Educational Change: Toward Responsive Schools, New York: McGraw-Hill Book Co., 1975.
Goodlad, J.I. and Associates, *Curriculum Inquiry: The Study of Curriculum Practice*, New York: McGraw-Hill Book Co., 1979.
What Schools Are For, Bloomington, IN: Phi Delta Kappa Educational Foundation, 1979.
A Place Called School: Prospects for the Future, New York: McGraw-Hill Book Co., 1984.

Teachers for Our Nation's Schools, San Francisco, CA: Jossey-Bass, 1990.
Educational Renewal: Better Teachers, Better Schools, San Francisco, CA: Jossey-Bass, 1994.
In Praise of Education, New York: Teachers College Press, 1997.

Further reading

Shen, J., 'Connecting Educational Theory, Research, and Practice: A Comprehensive Review of John I. Goodlad's Publication', *Journal of Thought*, 34, 4, Winter, pp.25–96, 1999.
Sirotnik, K.A. and Soder, R. (eds), *The Beat of a Different Drummer: Essays on Educational Renewal in Honor of John I. Goodlad*, New York: Peter Lang Publishing, 1999.

JIANPING SHEN

PAULO FREIRE 1921–97

> The pedagogy of the oppressed [is] a pedagogy which must be forged with, not *for*, the oppressed (be they individuals or whole peoples) in the incessant struggle to regain their humanity. This pedagogy makes oppression and its causes objects of reflection by the oppressed, and from that reflection will come liberation.[1]

Paulo Freire was one of the most important and influential writers on the theory and practice of critical education in the twentieth century and remains extremely influential today. He was born in Recife in north-eastern Brazil on 19 September 1921. He first became internationally known as an adult educator because of the literacy programmes he developed and out of which came his core ideas about critical education. Ultimately, his critical approach extended well beyond the area of adult education. His focus on the role of education in the struggles of oppressed people was characterized by a rare combination. His political commitments and radical perspectives were combined with personal humbleness, a powerful ethical outlook and an impressive intellectual coherence.

Freire was involved with social movements and adult education, in particular movements linked with popular culture and 'base community movements' within the Catholic Church. Working with peasants and workers mainly in the impoverished areas of north-eastern Brazil, it was here where he first developed his influential methods for dealing with the problem of illiteracy. After these experiences and after organizing several well-known adult literacy programmes, Freire was invited by the Brazilian Ministry of Education to organize a national literacy programme. In spite of its success, his work was interrupted by a military dictatorship in 1964. Freire was arrested and exiled to Chile. During his time in exile, Freire worked in a considerable number of geographical areas. He engaged in literacy struggles and in other educational programmes in Chile, Angola, Mozambique, Cape Verde, Guinea-Bissau, Nicaragua and other places. He also worked as a consultant for UNESCO and with the Department of

Education of the World Council of Churches in Geneva. As his influence grew throughout the world, he was invited to take a position at Harvard University. Freire also became an honorary fellow at numerous universities and received a considerable number of awards from universities throughout the world.

After Brazil declared an amnesty in 1979, those people who had been exiled were able to return to Brazil. Freire too returned and accepted a position to teach at the Pontifical Catholic University of São Paulo and the University of Campinas. The years in exile had not dimmed his political and educational passion. Freire immediately became a member of the Workers' Party and quickly became a central figure in its policies over literacy and culture. After the Workers' Party won the municipal elections in São Paulo in 1989, Freire was appointed Secretary of Education. Under his administration, many progressive programmes in adult education, curricular restructuring, community participation and an ambitious set of policies for democratizing schools were implemented.

After leaving his position as Secretary of Education, he spent the last six years of his life devoting himself to writing and speaking both nationally and internationally. This was a time of considerable intellectual ferment for him. He wrote a number of provocative and even more personal books that had an extremely wide readership throughout the world. In these books and in his many interviews and articles, he sought to raise questions about his and others' work that demanded attention. It was almost as if he knew that he had little time to live. He died in 1997, but his legacy and his thought remain alive throughout the world. The reason for the continuing power of his work has much to do with the cogency of his ideas. Perhaps his most generative idea is that education is always a political act. This idea was not a mere slogan for him. Indeed, it is central to the understanding of Freire's theory of education. For him, education always involves social relations and, hence, necessarily involves political choices. Freire insists that questions like 'what?', 'why?', 'how?', 'to what end?', 'for whom?' are central to any educational activity. These are not meant to be abstractions. Every educator has to ask these questions and answers to them will be crucial guides to any critical educational project. Hence, not only is it impossible to remain neutral in education, but one has to constantly realize that all educational policies and practices have social implications. They either perpetuate exclusion and injustice or they assist us in constructing the conditions for social transformation.

For Freire, most social relations in capitalist societies such as our own – including those involved in education – are based on relations of oppression. In the Brazilian context where Freire developed his theory and practice, the reality was one of massive political, social and economic inequalities in which millions of people were excluded from economic, social and educational capital. This oppression and the relationships between oppressor and oppressed were compelling for Freire. They motivated much of his work with impoverished people both in Brazil and later on in many other countries.

Even in his earliest writings, he realized that the dominant ideas in education would not reverse the reproduction of the forms of exclusion that so deeply characterized these societies. Because of this, Freire insisted on the need for a new conception of education, one that would derive from both a radically different standpoint and worldview and that would require a radically different epistemological approach. Hence, an essential grounding of Freire's conception of education and of the methodology he developed is the fact that he chose to put the culture, knowledge and conditions of the disadvantaged, the excluded and the oppressed first.

The conception of education offered by Freire did not stop inside the classroom. While he understood the importance of the classroom activity both for reproduction and transformation, he went further to insist that new educational techniques alone will not create a radically new school or society. Education can help us to understand the world we live in and can make us better prepared to transform it, but only if we deeply connect education to the larger realities in which people live, and to struggles to alter those realities. In response to this, he proposed a new epistemological approach.

Emancipatory education for Freire is never a simple transmission of knowledge. Knowing is not accumulating facts or information, what he called 'banking'. Rather, knowing is constructing oneself as a subject in the world, one who is able both to rewrite what one reads and to act in the world to radically alter it. Thus, Freire's idea of literacy went well beyond the subject's capacity to read words. Rather, the act of reading must be about the ability to 'read' the world.

Underneath Freire's proposals for an emancipatory education was a crucial anthropological claim. He believed that men and women are producers of culture and, therefore, producers of history. Human beings are uncompleted beings and have an 'ontological vocation' to become more fully human. Teachers and students as well are unfinished human beings and both have much to learn from each other in the educational process. This does not mean that the teacher should deny her or his role as the one who conducts the process of learning. But the process must be based on critical dialogue and mutual knowledge creation.

Freire emphasized the role of teachers as critical cultural workers. Teachers should struggle with the dominant cultural values that are present both in the society and inside themselves in order to understand their cultural and political function. This dual struggle could lead teachers to work in reflexive and transformative ways. And, once again, such transformative work would necessarily go beyond the classroom. In his words:

> To the extent that I become clearer about my choices and my dreams, which are substantively political and attributively peda-gogical, and to the extent that I recognize that though an educator I am also a political agent, I can better understand why I fear and realize how far we still have to go to improve our democracy. I also understand that as we put into practice an education that critically provokes the learner's consciousness, we are necessarily working against myths that deform us. As we confront such myths, we also face the dominant power because those myths are nothing but the expression of this power, of its ideology.[2]

The ethical and political meanings behind this are clear. If it is true that dialogical education presupposes a political understanding of what I already know as a teacher, it is also true that it demands a profound respect for the students and their knowledge. 'There is a strong tendency that pushes us to state that what is different is inferior. ... This is intolerance. It is the irresistible tendency of opposing the differences.'[3]

Yet the school is one of the major institutions that embody such ideologies of inferiority. The school takes dominant knowledge and de-historicizes and naturalizes it. It makes such dominant knowledge into the only visible and socially acceptable knowledge. For Freire, this is simply wrong. He insisted that knowledge is historical. According to him, there is no knowledge that is not historically and socially produced, within political, cultural, and economic relations. This relational understanding is very important to his argument that the 'different', what is called 'popular' knowledge, is not valued and is not considered legitimate for dominant conservative models of education. Emancipatory education must not reproduce the kind of practice that is so very common in traditional schools. In opposition to this, a Freirean model of education for liberation considers the knowledge of the students to be fully legitimate, values it and historicizes it. But it does not stop there. Freire's approach uses the knowledge already possessed by students to give them the power to re-appropriate dominant knowledge for their own emancipation. For instance, in this perspective, students may learn what is socially defined as the 'norm' in language usage. But a truly critical education must go beyond this. As he says,

It is necessary that, in learning the so-called 'norm', [the students] understand that they are learning it not because their language is ugly and inferior, but because in mastering the 'norm' they acquire tools to [use in] the struggle for the necessary reinvention of the world.[4]

Given his commitment to a dialectical relation between practice and theory, Freire always based his practices on cogent theoretical ideas, which in turn were profoundly connected with his practical actions. Thus, he spent his entire life pursuing a pedagogical praxis, one without *a priori* definitions of contents, textbooks, or pedagogical techniques. Instead, his intention was to build a pedagogical process, what he called 'conscientization', that was grounded in the cultural and social realities of teachers and students. From these realities, the thematic elements, the contents, the pedagogical decisions – in other words, the curriculum and the teaching – would come. This joining together of theory and practice contributed to the power and influence of Freire's ideas.

In concrete terms, his method of 'conscientization' with adults in literacy programmes was basically constituted by a process of coding/decoding linguistic and social meanings, organized through a number of steps. First, generative themes are developed. They emerge from informal and personal contacts with communities, and are then discussed in Culture Circles using a dialogical procedure. From these discussions, a thematic universe is generated and from it the teachers extract a vocabulary universe, constituted by several words socially and culturally relevant for those communities. From this vocabulary universe, a minimum vocabulary universe is obtained, constituted by seventeen or eighteen generative words that are phonemically rich and ordered in increasing phonetic difficulty. Finally, specific steps are taken to achieve the process of reading, which consists of a process of decoding written words taken from a coded existential situation. This connection to the real existential situation is a crucial step and is one of the keys to enabling students from oppressed groups to use their newly gained knowledge to reconstruct their lives.

Because of the fact that the use of this approach with oppressed people spread throughout the world, Freire was always worried that his ideas would become simply a 'method', a recipe to be followed uncritically. Thus, Freire was aware of the dangers associated with the essentialization of theories. He knew that the origins of his critical educational theories and practices – the decision to intervene in the world, in a very unjust Brazilian reality – must never be forgotten. This is in keeping with the main thrust of his theory, the constant reminder that what seems as the mere learning of the alphabet or of mathematics is in fact a complex political relation. For him, the very fact that education is usually not seen as political is part of the problem and the transformation of this situation is in itself part of a specific political project. To reduce his theory to a simple methodology to be replicated is to negate the nature of Freire's enormous contribution to education.

Notes

1 Paulo Freire, *Pedagogy of the Oppressed*, Harmondsworth: Penguin, p.25, 1982.
2 Paulo Freire, *Teachers as Cultural Workers: Letters to Those who Dare Teach*, Boulder, CO: Westview Press, p.41, 1998.
3 Ibid., p.71.
4 Paulo Freire, *A educação na cidade*, São Paulo: Editora Cortez, p.46, 1991.

Freire's major writings

Pedagogy of the Oppressed, trans. M.B. Ramos, Harmondsworth: Penguin, 1982; New York: Seabury Press, 1970.
Cultural Action for Freedom, Cambridge, MA: The Harvard Educational Review Monograph Series, no. 1, 1970.
Education for Critical Consciousness, New York: Seabury Press, 1973.
Pedagogy in Process: The Letters to Guinea-Bissau, trans. C. St. John Hunter, New York: Seabury Press, 1978.
Pedagogy of Hope: Reliving Pedagogy of the Oppressed, trans. R.R. Barr, New York: Continuum, 1994.
Teachers as Cultural Workers: Letters to Those Who Dare Teach, Boulder, CO: Westview Press, 1998.

Further reading

Collins, D.E., *Paulo Freire: His Life, Works and Thoughts*, New York, Paulist Press, 1977.
Freire, P., Fraser, J.W., Macedo, D., McKinnon, T. and Stokes, W. (eds), *Mentoring the Mentor: A Critical Dialogue with Paulo Freire*, New York: Peter Lang, 1997.

Horton, M. and Freire, P., *We Make the Road by Walking: Conversations on Education and Social Change*, Philadelphia, PA: Temple University Press, 1990.

McLaren, P. and Leonard, P. (eds), *Paulo Freire: A Critical Encounter*, New York: Routledge, 1996.

Shor, I. and Freire, P., *A Pedagogy for Liberation: Dialogues on Transforming Education*, Westport, CT: Bergin & Garvey, 1987.

Taylor, P.V., *The Texts of Paulo Freire*, Buckingham: Open University Press, 1993.

MICHAEL W. APPLE, LUÍS ARMANDO GANDIN
AND ÁLVARO MOREIRA HYPOLITO

SEYMOUR B. SARASON 1919–

> Introducing, sustaining, and assessing an educational change are political processes, because they inevitably alter or threaten to alter existing power relationships. ... Few myths have been as resistant to change as that which assumes that the culture of the school is a non-political one, and few myths have contributed as much to the failure of the change efforts.[1]

Seymour Sarason, who was at the time of publication, still writing prolifically in his eighties, is one of the world's leading thinkers and writers on the culture of the school, particularly in terms of its relationship to educational change. Drawing on a background and training in clinical psychology, Sarason has, over his life, developed an extended oeuvre and eclectic perspective that both critiques a psychological view of educating while combining this view with more historical, cultural and political forms of understanding. The large number of books Seymour Sarason has written encompass subjects as diverse and interconnected as school culture, educational change and reform, teacher education, the role of the arts in teaching and learning, mental handicap and deficiency (as it was once known), counselling, careers, ageing and, not least, his own professional autobiography.

Seymour B. Sarason was born in 1919 in Brooklyn, New York, the son of Jewish immigrant parents. His father, a 'cutter of children's clothes'[2] was liked, though not especially respected in the family. He was 'much more Jewish in a religious sense'[3] than his mother. His more 'Americanized' mother 'met many of the stereotypes of the Jewish mother: loving, overprotective, guilt producing and ambitious'[4] who regarded the past as 'something to be overcome, not to be passed on'.[5] In his autobiography, Sarason reflects that his lifelong feelings of being an outsider and of historical rootlessness may be traced to these origins.[6] So too might his distinctive intellectual contributions to understanding the role and inter-relationship of culture, change and history in education – the progeny of a parental marriage between progress and tradition.

Sarason's Jewish immigrant roots and the fact that he was on the leading edge of the first Jewish cohort to be appointed to the faculties of major American universities influenced not only his sense of what it meant to be culturally different, but also his preoccupation with American identity, and with the distinctive, but rarely acknowledged nature of American psychology as a community that became 'the Romans of the modern era, building roads of psychology literally across the earth'.[7] If immigrant Jewishness spawned an insider/outsider ambivalence of identity in Sarason's life and work, so too did his contraction of polio during two of his high school junior years when his upper body was encased in a brace or a cast. The impact of this crippling disease, which left Sarason with a lifetime legacy of disability, had a direct bearing on his early career interest in people who also had disabilities – in their case, ones of mental retardation. More subtly, the disability that disqualified Sarason from active service in the Second World War, helped shape his concerns about how clinical psychology and government policy treated the war's physically wounded veterans. And more subtly still, when polio precluded Sarason from participating in the competitive games and rituals of adolescent masculine rivalry, it also led him, indirectly, to exclude himself in adulthood from the intellectually competitive and institutionally conformist cultures of masculine professorial life and career development in the university.[8]

It is only fitting that this ambitious outsider, rooted in tradition yet riveted by change, should make his entry to the university professorship obliquely. Sarason commenced his post-secondary education at DANA College, Newark, as an 'economically impoverished' sixteen-year-old student in 1935. DANA first made Sarason want to become part of the world of ideas and it was here that briefly, he became a Marxist and a member of the Socialist Workers' Party, whose form of Leftism he rejected because of its missionary obsession, its failure to understand American complexity, its reluctance to embrace styles and positions on injustice that could command wider public respect, and its sheer humourlessness.[9] Here, Sarason severed his ties to the cabals of Leftist conformism with all their ideological predictability, and began to beat his own politically critical path.

In 1939, Sarason secured a scholarship to graduate school in Clark University, Worcester, Massachusetts, where he was taught by, among others, British psychologist and exponent of factor analysis, Raymond Cattell.[10] At the end of his second year, he was able to obtain a then unique attachment or 'externship' to the nearby Worcester State Hospital for mental illness where he first became interested in community psychology. Graduating from Clark, he passed a civil service examination for psychologists and at the age of twenty-three, took a position at a new and innovative institute, the Southbury Training School. Here, Sarason developed his humanistic view of mental retardation, cultivated a scepticism about the misuses of IQ tests for political, social and organizational purposes, became fascinated by how the innovative impetus of new 'settings' such as Southbury faded so quickly; and first learned how art, through the dedicated work of teachers like Professor Henry Schaefer-Simmon, could unlock hidden gifts in those who had been designated as mentally incompetent.

Unusually, Seymour Sarason worked in just one university for his entire life – moving to Yale's department of psychology in 1945 where he worked for over forty-five years. His first book on *Psychological Problems in Mental Deficiency*[11] was published in 1949, followed by a text on *The Clinical Interaction* in 1956.[12] Working in the Institute of Human Relations at Yale offered possibilities for interdisciplinary learning. Close associates included the life history expert John Dollard, the innovative and celebrated cultural anthropologist Thomas Gladwin, with whom Sarason co-authored a monograph on mental subnormality, and Sarason was even interviewed as a subject for the Kinsey Report on male sexual behaviour, by Kinsey's senior colleague, Pomeroy.

Two extended episodes during Sarason's long career at Yale are especially significant. One was a long-term relationship initiated by Burton Blatt, the incoming chair of special education at nearby New Haven State College in the mid 1950s. Through this relationship, Sarason was able to solidify his emerging interest in education in the real worlds of activism and teacher education which Blatt valued – this led to their joint publication of *The Preparation of Teachers: An Unstudied Problem in Education*[13] where they criticized teacher education for being ahistorical, unsociological and unwilling to confront the 'force of societal tradition (which) pervades and determines what schools are as cultural entities'.[14]

The second extended episode was the decade which Sarason calls his 'Camelot Years'[15] when he founded and ran the Yale Psycho-Educational Clinic – a new setting of action, intervention, observation and reflection – that he wanted to create to abate his sense of restlessness and put an end to 'running a research factory'.[16] The clinic was distinctive in the way it took staff out to create or alter real community settings such as schools, to understand them and assist those within them, and to do so with due sensitivity to their unique cultural and historical characteristics. Sarason's experience of creating and running the clinic forms much of the experiential basis for his groundbreaking book on *The Creation of Settings and the Future Societies*.[17]

Throughout his work, Seymour Sarason returns with persistent, insistent and sometimes perseverating regularity to a small number of core concerns. First, is the uncritical nature of American clinical psychology and its co-option as a tool of administrative control (a position that anticipated others' later critiques of psychometric testing). Second, is the repeated tendency of 'big government', even when motivated by the best intentions, to try and change large organizations such as schools and school systems without understanding the complexity and resilience to change of their cultures. Third, is the misguidedly ahistorical and culture-free nature of American psychology which has defined psychological problems in ways that make them amenable to individual intervention and remediation rather than as problems that have a deep-rooted history, sociological complexity and inescapably American quality about them. Fourth, Sarason has dealt repeatedly with the issues involved in creating (and sustaining) new organizational settings such as schools, mental health units and, in his own case, the Psycho-Educational Clinic at Yale University. Fifth, he speaks repeatedly about the personal and intellectual impact in his early adult and career development of the Depression, the Second World War and their aftermath on a subsequent era of social and institutional change that was simultaneously characterized by the most optimistic visions of progress and redemption, and by the most spectacular calamities of political and organizational overreach in pursuit of those goals.[18] Sixth, Sarason repeatedly worries and despairs about the quality and character of teacher education and its inability to create a more educationally productive culture of schooling. Last, is Sarason's abiding concern with understanding and advocating for 'underdogs' in education – professors who challenge scholasticism, teachers who teach against the cultural grain, and students with mental disabilities who display hitherto unforeseen gifts, talents and raw perspicacity, when their experiences are taken more seriously.

The style through which Sarason raises these themes is consistently critical, courageously provocative, and even iconoclastic. He challenges endless conventional wisdoms (though rarely by criticizing their individual protagonists). Indeed, his writings are rarely encumbered by any felt necessity to refer to copious lists of references! Sarason's inspiration, rather, comes more from reflection on a wealth of practical experience and on the world around him, than on exhaustive syntheses of literature or accumulations of empirical evidence.[19] In his own words, 'I was far more interested in ideas than I was in research. I was more a critic than I was an investigator. I was more a philosopher than I was a psychologist.'

Seymour Sarason, indeed, has been as much of an activist as an analyst; working as a practitioner and a leader in the field of mental health, and as the founder of his own unique Psycho-Educational Clinic at Yale University. As activist and analyst though, Sarason confesses in his autobiography to feeling very much an 'outsider'[20] who has struggled to create a more historical, political psychology of educating. While this has led him, even in his eighties, to feel professionally alone in important respects (personal communication), there are great benefits and indeed obligations of being a public intellectual who, as Palestinian cultural theorist Edward Said[21] observes, is never completely 'at home in one's home'. Perhaps the way Sarason praises his three intellectual 'heroes' in the field of psychology – John Dewey, William James and Sigmund Freud – best expresses the distinctive quality and cast of mind that can be seen in the work and life of Sarason himself:

> What they had in common was an education, a fund of knowledge, a restless cast of mind, a generalizing cast of mind, and a kind of courage that enabled each in his lifetime to undergo dramatic transformations in thinking and outlook. The extent of their knowledge of human history was awesome, to someone like me utterly humbling and a source of envy. From their truly Olympian heights, they could see a past and envision a very different future. And they wrote – did they ever write – in the endeavour to make their ideas public and influential. They were always questioning. In the case of each, the world had difficulty pigeonholing him.[22]

Among Seymour Sarason's numerous contributions to the fields of education and psychology, four texts in particular have left, or promise to leave, a lasting intellectual legacy. The first, on *The Culture of the School and the Problem of Change*[23] was not published until Sarason was fifty years of age. This book has become one of the great classics of educational change and of the organizational culture of schooling. It presented a powerful critique of large-scale innovations such as new mathematics in the 1960s and their failure to address the deep-seated and historically arbitrary 'regularities' of schooling such as scheduling, class organization and the traditions of teacher isolation. The culture of the school, this text showed, was highly impervious to systemic change. School change efforts rarely addressed the politics of the school, school leadership, the community and policy context of schooling, or the trenchant culture of teacher individualism which made schools poor places for the teacher learning that was essential for change efforts to be successful.

Today, what is undoubtedly Sarason's most influential book stands alongside a small number of other key texts on the pedestal of school culture and educational change. These are Willard Waller's *Sociology of Teaching*[24] which, strangely, Sarason does not cite in the first edition of his book; and two others to which he does make passing reference in his 1982 revision, Dan Lortie's *Schoolteacher*[25] and Michael Fullan's *The Meaning of Educational Change*[26] which became available as Sarason's own second edition went to press.

In both editions and also in the rewritten 1996 version, *Revisiting 'The Culture of the School and the Problem of Change'*,[27] it is fair to say that Sarason's text has never quite had the worldwide impact of Waller, Lortie or Fullan. The reason for this is not to be found in the quality of the analysis, but in Sarason's determination to address the specifically American quality of the change issues he confronts, and to locate them in American policy debates. Admirable as this effort might have been, it also undermined the global accessibility and transportability of his work. This is a pity since so many of the matters raised by Sarason articulately presage major debates in the ensuing analysis of educational change by others. Thus, on the importance of the change process, Sarason argues that:

> we cannot have relevant descriptions and studies until we recognize that the description of the change process involves ... the most fundamental ... assumptions determining three general types of social relationships: those among the professionals within the school setting, those among the professionals and pupils, and those among the professionals and the different parts of the larger society.[28]

On the cultural politics of change, Sarason warns that 'few myths have been as resistant to change as that which assumes that the culture of the school is a nonpolitical one'.[29] He repeatedly pleas for time issues to be addressed in allowing teachers to adjust to the implementation of change, complaining that the time perspective of change is 'determined not by people in the schools but by federal policy makers' (p.79). To someone like myself, who has co-authored a book on *What's Worth Fighting For Out There?*[30] beyond the school, Sarason presents a much earlier and sobering analysis of the importance of the school's ecological relationships with its environment. And writing as someone who has tried to construct an original analysis of teaching and guilt,[31] I find it salutary to return to Sarason's most important work and see him talk about teachers being engaged in 'constant giving in the context of constant vigilance' which leads to 'guilt feelings because the teacher cannot give all that he or she feels children need'.[32] The powerful implication for professional learning, Sarason notes, is that 'to sustain the giving at a high level requires that the teacher experience *getting*.[33] In short, there is almost nothing in the subsequent literature of educational change that has not, in some way, already been mentioned by Sarason himself in this landmark text of the field.

Just one year after *The Culture of the School and the Problem of Change*, Sarason wrote another book of devastating originality. Drawing on his experiences of witnessing how innovation faded at the Southbury Training School and of establishing and leading the Psycho-educational Clinic at Yale, as well as on his observations of how innovative efforts in schools or mental health systems fared over time, Sarason wrote a superb analysis of *The Creation of Settings and the Future Societies*.[34]

The book might more aptly have been titled 'The Collapse of Settings'. It describes the naïve ways in which administrators and policy-makers approach the creation of such settings. It highlights the arrogance of architects in their belief that buildings and design values will shape the communities within them. It points to how new settings threaten and are frequently sabotaged by existing ones, the importance and difficulties of managing 'foreign relations' with settings elsewhere, the actual and attributed feelings of superiority held by members and leaders of the new settings, and the dangerous tendency of members of the setting to see administrative questioning and political scepticism as moral affronts.

New settings, he stresses, draw people together who want excitement, challenge and the freedom to be innovative, but who soon find themselves bogged down with budgets, space problems and bureaucratic delay. New settings often start small with shared understandings among intimate communities, but can rapidly become victims of their own success as they expand, differentiate and break into warring factions. There are myths of unlimited resources and difficulties in allocating value and these problems congeal around the leadership of the new setting as custody of that leader's organizational 'baby' becomes contested by others, as conflicts break out and as the leader feels increasingly alone.

The Creation of Settings has profound implications for why innovation rarely lasts; why, in the main, model schools, beacon schools, schools of the future and pilot projects are, over time, the unsustainable creations of administrative innocence or conceit. Three decades after its publication, *The Creation of Settings* remains a highly influential source for those who study the history of educational innovation and the fate of model school experiments today.[35]

In later years, Seymour Sarason applied his educational insights to more thoroughgoing critiques of educational policy.[36] *The Predictable Failure of Educational Reform*[37] is the most incisive and succinct of these texts. In it, Sarason makes four key and interrelated points. First, while educational change efforts often promise quality and improvement, they rarely try to alter the fundamental regularities or deep structures of schooling that persistently impede improvement efforts. Second, these regularities, like all aspects of schooling, are systemically interrelated. 'Trying to change any parts of the system requires knowledge and understanding of how the parts are interrelated.'[38] Indeed, when problems such as leadership, curriculum, strategies of teaching or school organization are 'posed and attacked separately', then 'the chances of failure are high'.[39]

Third, Sarason argues that these systemic regularities of schooling are underpinned by deeply entrenched power relationships. One of his most memorable contentions is that 'schools will remain intractable to desired reform as long as we avoid confronting ... their existing power relationships', including those of the classroom.[40] Last, and consistently with his earlier work, Sarason reminds his readers that 'it is virtually impossible to create and sustain over time conditions for productive learning for students when they do not exist for teachers'[41] in terms of professional development, feelings of empowerment, and opportunities for collegiality. Few books draw together, as effectively as this one, the value of viewing schools as historical and politicized forms of organization, if one wants to understand the persistent intractability of educational change initiatives.

In what is, at the time of writing, one of his most recent books, Seymour Sarason returns to two of the abiding themes of his career – teacher education,[42] and the artistry of teaching. In *Teaching as a Performance Art*,[43] Sarason argues that teaching amounts to more than exercising technique or addressing standards. It is a performance art, a passionate activity that moves those it touches and loses the classroom audience in the performance itself. Teaching, Sarason stresses, amounts to more than quiet facilitation or indirect coaching as computer advocates insist, but in line with my own research, also involves, direct, dramatic and arousing engagements with students, even in the case of the most progressive teachers.[44]

Sarason spells out the implications of his analysis by arguing that teacher education initiatives should select their professional talent more carefully through selection procedures that involve some kind of audition, that organizations should refrain from stifling or squandering the talent of their teachers, and that schools should offer teachers continuing opportunity for role variety and development so they do not become stale and 'typecast'.

Sarason's conception of teaching and of teachers drives his understandings about, and recommendations regarding, both teacher education and educational change. The conception of the teacher as a performing artist is very different from the politically popular one of the teacher 'as a kind of civil drill sergeant required to enforce educational standards'.[45] It is a conception where:

> the teacher wants the audience of students to find that teacher interesting, stimulating, believable, someone who helps see themselves and their world in a new and enlarged way, someone who satisfies their need for new experiences that take them out of their ordinary selves.[46]

Such teachers, he regrets, 'teach in a system that only pays lip service to the necessity of their understanding what the teacher's role requires'.

Seymour B. Sarason: historical and political psychologist, original thinker, intellectual iconoclast and self-acknowledged outsider. This outsider status is heightened even more today as politically critical perspectives and scholarship are increasingly marginalized in a standardized, normalizing educational universe where conservatism and retrenchment repeatedly masquerade as worthwhile reform. The value of Sarason's legacy will be that of bearing witness to the arrogant folly of most reform efforts, providing succour to those who must endure or subvert them, and reactivating memories of more humanistic, empowered and democratic forms of educational being that represent the best of what we can achieve as educators.

Notes

1 Seymour B. Sarason, *The Culture of the School and the Problem of Change*, 2nd edn, Boston, MA: Allyn & Bacon, p.71, 1982.
2 Seymour B. Sarason, *The Making of an American Psychologist: An Autobiography*, San Francisco, CA: Jossey-Bass, p.17, 1988.
3 Ibid., p.29.
4 Ibid., p.28.
5 Ibid., p.28.
6 Ibid.
7 Ibid., p.9.
8 Ibid.
9 Ibid., pp.90–8.
10 Ibid., p.116.
11 Seymour B. Sarason, *Psychological Problems in Mental Deficiency*, New York: Harper & Row, 1949.
12 Seymour B. Sarason, *The Clinical Interaction*, New York: Harper & Row, 1956.
13 Seymour B. Sarason, K. Davidson, and B. Blatt, *The Preparation of Teachers: An Unstudied Problem in Education*, Cambridge, MA: Brookline Books, 1987, originally published in 1962.
14 Sarason, *The Making of an American Psychologist: An Autobiography*, op cit., p.340.
15 Ibid., p.353.
16 Ibid., p.356.
17 Seymour B. Sarason, *The Creation of Settings and the Future Societies*, San Francisco, CA: Jossey-Bass, 1972.
18 Sarason, *The Making of an American Psychologist*, op cit.
19 Ibid., p.233.
20 Ibid., p.29.
21 E.W. Said, *Representations of the Intellectual*, New York: Random House, p.57, 1994.
22 Sarason, *The Making of an American Psychologist*, op cit., pp.329–30.
23 Sarason, *The Culture of the School and the Problem of Change*, op cit.
24 Willard Waller, *The Sociology of Teaching*, New York: Wiley, 1932.
25 Dan Lortie, *Schoolteacher*, Chicago, IL: University of Chicago Press, 1975.
26 Michael Fullan, *The Meaning of Educational Change*, New York: Teachers College Press, 1980.
27 Seymour B. Sarason, *Revisiting 'The Culture of the School and the Problem of Change'*, New York: Teachers College Press, 1996.
28 Sarason, *The Culture of the School and the Problem of Change*, op cit., p.59.
29 Ibid., p.71.
30 Andy Hargreaves and Michael Fullan, *What's Worth Fighting For Out There?*, New York: Teachers College Press, 1998.
31 Andy Hargreaves, *Changing Teachers, Changing Times*, London: Cassell; New York: Teachers College Press, 1994.
32 Sarason, *The Culture of the School and the Problem of Change*, op cit., p.200.
33 Ibid.
34 Sarason, *The Creation of Settings and the Future Societies*, op cit.
35 Dean Fink, *Good School/Real School*, New York: Teachers College Press, 2000.

36 Seymour B. Sarason, *Schooling in America: Scapegoat and Salvation*, New York: Free Press, 1983; Seymour B. Sarason, *Letters to a Serious Education President*, Newbury Park, CA: Corwin Press, 1993; Seymour B. Sarason, *Barometers of Social Change*, San Francisco, CA: Jossey-Bass, 1996.
37 Seymour B. Sarason, *The Predictable Failure of Educational Reform*, San Francisco, CA: Jossey-Bass, 1990.
38 Ibid., p.15.
39 Ibid., p.27.
40 Ibid., p.5.
41 Ibid., p.145.
42 Sarason, *et al.*, *The Preparation of Teachers*, op cit.; Seymour B. Sarason, *The Case for Change: Rethinking the Preparation of Educators*, San Francisco, CA: Jossey-Bass, 1993.
43 Seymour B. Sarason, *Teaching as a Performance Art*, New York: Teachers College Press, 1999.
44 Andy Hargreaves, Lorna Earl, Shawn Moore and Susan Manning, *Learning to Change: Teaching Beyond Subjects and Standards*, San Francisco, CA: Jossey-Bass, 2001.
45 Sarason, *Teaching as a Performance Art*, op cit., p.6.
46 Ibid., p.36.

See also

In *Fifty Major Thinkers on Education*: Dewey

Sarason's major writings

Psychological Problems in Mental Deficiency, New York: Harper & Row, 1949.
The Clinical Interaction, New York: Harper & Row, 1956.
Sarason, S.B., with Davidson, R. and Blatt, B., *The Preparation of Teachers: An Unstudied Problem in Teacher Education*, Cambridge, MA: Brookline Books, 1987; originally pub. 1962.
Sarason, S.B., with Levine, M., Goldenberg, I., Cherlin, D. and Bennett, E., *Psychology in Community Settings*, New York: Wiley, 1966.
The Creation of Settings and the Future Societies, San Francisco, CA: Jossey-Bass, 1972.
The Culture of the School and the Problem of Change, 2nd edn, 1982; Boston, MA: Allyn & Bacon, 1971.
Schooling in America: Scapegoat and Salvation, New York: Free Press, 1983.
The Making of an American Psychologist: An Autobiography, San Francisco, CA: Jossey-Bass, 1988.
The Predictable Failure of Educational Reform, San Francisco, CA: Jossey-Bass, 1990.
The Case for Change: Rethinking the Preparation of Educators, San Francisco, CA: Jossey-Bass, 1993.
Barometers of Social Change, San Francisco, CA: Jossey-Bass, 1996.
Teaching as a Performance Art, New York: Teachers College Press, 1999.

Further reading

Fullan, M., *The Meaning of Educational Change*, New York: Teachers College Press, 1980.
Hargreaves, A., *Two Cultures of Schooling: The Case of Middle School*, Lewes: Falmer Press, 1986.

Hargreaves, A., *Changing Teachers, Changing Times: Teachers' Work and Culture in the Postmodern Age*, London: Cassell and New York: Teachers' College Press, 1994.

Hargreaves, A., Lieberman, A., Fullan, M. and Hopkins, D. (eds), *The International Handbook of Educational Change*, The Netherlands: Kluwer Press, 1998.

Hargreaves, D., *The Challenge for the Comprehensive School*, London: Routledge & Kegan Paul, 1982.

Huberman, M., *The Lives of Teachers*, London: Cassell and New York: Teachers College Press, 1993.

Lieberman, A. (ed.), *Building a Collaborative School Culture*, New York: Teachers College Press, 1988.

Lortie, D., *Schoolteacher*, Chicago, IL: University of Chicago Press, 1975.

Nias, J., Southworth, G. and Yeomans, A., *Staff Relationships in the Primary School*, London: Cassell, 1989.

Waller, W., *The Sociology of Teaching*, New York: Wiley, 1932.

Woods, P. *Sociology and the School*, London: Routledge & Kegan Paul, 1985.

ANDREW HARGREAVES

ISRAEL SCHEFFLER 1923–

> Critical thought is of the first importance in the conception and organization of educational activities.[1]

Israel Scheffler is Victor S. Thomas Professor of Education and Philosophy, Emeritus, at Harvard University. He joined the Harvard faculty in 1952, and retired from it in 1992. He received his BA and MA degrees from Brooklyn College, and his Ph.D. in Philosophy from the University of Pennsylvania under the direction of the eminent philosopher Nelson Goodman, with whom Scheffler became a life-long friend, collaborator and philosophical protagonist.

Scheffler has been a key figure in philosophy of education in the United States, and indeed, along with R.S. Peters in Great Britain, is the pre-eminent philosopher of education in the English-speaking world in the second half of the twentieth century. His contributions to the subject are of two sorts. First, Scheffler greatly influenced the methodology of philosophy of education, by bringing to it the methods, techniques and outlooks common in general philosophy. Second, he developed substantive, highly influential views of key educational concepts and issues, including the concepts of teaching and of education itself, and of central topics, including the fundamental matter of the ultimate aims and ideals of education. Those substantive views reflect Scheffler's commitment to conceiving of education in fundamentally *moral* terms, in which the obligation to treat students with respect, as persons, is paramount.

The analytic approach developed by Scheffler greatly influenced successive generations of philosophers of education. His earliest paper in the philosophy of education, 'Toward an Analytic Philosophy of Education', offers a conception of philosophy of education as 'the rigorous, logical analysis of key concepts related to the practice of education'. Here 'logical analysis' is understood as careful attention to and sophistication concerning 'language, and the interpenetration of language and inquiry', which attempts 'to follow the modern example of the sciences in empirical spirit, in rigor, in attention to detail, in respect for alternatives, and in objectivity of method'; which emphasizes argumentative rigour; and which makes full 'use of techniques of symbolic logic brought to full development only in the last fifty years' where relevant and appropriate.[2] A 'sense of community of investigation, unified by method rather than doctrine', and 'a common search for clarity on fundamental issues' characterize the analytic approach to philosophy, an approach which Scheffler argued should be central to philosophy of education. Scheffler illustrated this sort of logical analysis with two celebrated examples from general philosophy: Russell's theory of definite descriptions, taken from philosophy of language to clarify issues in the theories of meaning and reference; and Hempel's paradox of the ravens, taken from philosophy of science, in order to help clarify the character of confirmation. Scheffler's idea was to apply this analytic approach to education, both by applying the results of analysis to further autonomous research, and by applying the method of analysis to educational concepts and issues. Both require that philosophy of education be in intimate contact with the method and substance of general philosophy.

Scheffler's first book in philosophy of education, guided by the analytic approach, was his edited anthology, *Philosophy and Education: Modern Readings*, which attracted considerable interest and called attention to a new direction in the field. His first sustained effort at clarifying educational terms and concepts in this way appeared in his book, *The Language of Education*. In this book Scheffler offered analyses of three different kinds of educational locutions: educational slogans, such as 'teach children, not subjects'; educational metaphors, such as 'education as growth'; and educational definitions, the definitions of key educational terms, such as 'curriculum'. In all of Scheffler's discussion, he aimed to produce analyses sufficient to permit the serious logical appraisal of these types of educational locutions. For example, his analysis of educational slogans made it clear that while, for example, 'teach children, not subjects' is literally false (since, in being taught, children must be taught something), it nevertheless has significant practical import; and he showed that definitions likewise can be both descriptive and programmatic, and need to be evaluated on both scores. Distinguishing between the literal slogan and its practical import enables us to appraise the slogan more adequately. Similar points apply to the use and study of metaphors, definitions, and other educational locutions. In all this, Scheffler applied insights from the philosophy of language to the analysis of educational concepts.

Notice that *appraisal* is key here. We want to judge these sayings, and evaluate them. It is a mistake to think that analysis attends only to the meanings of words, and is irrelevant to questions of value or to normative concerns. On the contrary, for Scheffler the point of careful analysis is exactly that it enriches our understanding of education, and helps us to achieve more defensible educational conceptions, theories and practices. This is clearly brought out in Scheffler's analysis of teaching, a concept which is thoroughly normative and value-laden. For Scheffler, 'teaching' is more narrow than the broad notion of 'fostering of beliefs', since beliefs can be fostered in non-teaching ways, for example by indoctrination or brainwashing. Teaching, according to Scheffler, carries with it restrictions of *manner*, requiring acknowledgement of the student's sense of reasons. Thus the concept of teaching has a fundamental *moral* component, which is wrongly lost, in Scheffler's view, by conceiving of it as a rote series of behaviours or movements designed to have particular outcomes. Teaching focuses on *reasons* and *rationality*: the teacher tries to get the student to believe *for good reasons*, and the teacher must do so in ways which respect the student's independent judgement. The student's own sense of reasonableness must be appealed to in genuine teaching, and the teacher's broad task is to enhance and enrich the student's sense of what constitutes a good reason. In this way, rationality is the key aim of education, as indicated in the opening citation above and in the following oft-quoted passage: 'Rationality ... is a matter of *reasons*, and to take it as a fundamental educational ideal is to make as pervasive as possible the free and critical quest for reasons, in all realms of study.'[3]

This conception of education invites, on the part of the teacher *and* on the part of the student, the reasoned criticism of everything educational: not only the content of the curriculum, but also the nature and organization of the school, and of the broader culture within which education takes place. In this respect, Scheffler's ideal of education is challenging and idealistic: no culture has systematically solicited and welcomed its own criticism in a quest for genuine improvement. This suggests a sense in which the educational ideal of rationality which Scheffler espouses is indeed an ideal – something which can perhaps never be completely achieved, but which nevertheless provides a guiding focus for educational affairs.

The work discussed to this point, on the notions of teaching and of education, and of the fostering of students' rationality as a fundamental educational aim and ideal, is at the heart of Scheffler's philosophy of education. A collection of his essays first published in 1973, *Reason and Teaching*, captures the variety of educational contexts in which these themes may be played out. Of particular note is Scheffler's work on the themes of teacher education and the role of the teacher, developed in his classic essays 'Philosophical Models of Teaching' and 'University Scholarship and the Education of Teachers'; and the important statement of his view of rationality as a central educational ideal offered in his 'Moral Education and the Democratic Ideal', all of which are reprinted in that collection.

Speaking of the goodness of reasons is another way of speaking about justification: to ask 'Do I have a good reason for believing this?' is in effect to ask, 'Am I justified in believing this?' Justification is a key concern of epistemology, that branch of philosophy concerned to understand the nature, scope and limits of knowledge. In his book *Conditions of Knowledge: An Introduction to Epistemology and Education*, Scheffler offers a systematic treatment of epistemology and its central problems and concepts – knowledge, truth, belief, evidence, reason, justification and the like – as these relate to education. This book still serves as an excellent introduction to the subject of epistemology, and is unique in its systematic interrelating of epistemological and educational concepts and concerns.

Scheffler's concern for *objectivity*, of both judgement and method, is manifested in two important books in the philosophy of science. *The Anatomy of Inquiry* is a work devoted to issues at the heart of the philosophy of science: the nature of explanation, of cognitive significance and of confirmation. Here Scheffler demonstrates the ability of careful analysis to shed light on outstanding questions pressed by philosophy of science. *Science and Subjectivity* is a sustained discussion of the objectivity of science and its method, and offers both a detailed critical reaction to philosophical efforts to discredit science's claim to objectivity and an original reconceptualization of that key notion. In both these books, Scheffler deals directly with issues in philosophy of science; philosophy of education is not mentioned in either of them. But in both contexts, Scheffler is centrally concerned with the rationality of belief and judgement and the objectivity of method. In this general way, Scheffler's wide-ranging philosophical interests – science, knowledge, language and education – are united by overlapping issues and emphases. This also makes clear why, in Scheffler's view, philosophy of education must be pursued in close contact with its parent discipline.

Scheffler's book *The Language of Education* endeavoured to bring the insights of philosophy of language to bear on the language of education. In *Beyond the Letter: A Philosophical Inquiry into Ambiguity, Vagueness, and Metaphor in Language*, Scheffler makes a major contribution to philosophy of language proper, as his earlier books contributed to philosophy of science and epistemology proper. His book *Four Pragmatists*, although it occasionally deals with education, is likewise primarily a contribution to our understanding of the philosophical movement of Pragmatism, which offers a sympathetic critique of selected aspects of the work of Peirce, James, Dewey and Mead. In his book *Of Human Potential*, Scheffler returns to philosophy of education and offers a systematic analysis of the notion of human potential and its proper role in our conception of education.

In the books mentioned thus far, and in three additional collections of essays – *Inquiries: Philosophical Studies of Language, Science, and Learning*; *In Praise of the Cognitive Emotions* (in which he rejects a sharp distinction between the cognitive and the affective); and *Symbolic Worlds* (dealing with art, science, language, ritual and play) – Scheffler has contributed enormously to philosophy in general, and philosophy of education in particular. One of Scheffler's most recent books, *Teachers of My Youth: An American Jewish Experience*, offers an autobiographical account of his early years and educational experiences, and complements in a highly personal way his more impersonal, philosophical discussions of education. Another, *Work, Education and Leadership*, co-authored with V.A. Howard, once again takes up central issues in the philosophy of education.[4] He has made important contributions to epistemology, philosophy of science, philosophy of language and to the study of Pragmatism, in addition to his towering stature and fundamental contributions to the philosophy of education. If I may add a brief personal aside, it has been my pleasure and good fortune to have been a student of Scheffler's. His philosophical excellence is overshadowed only by his excellence as a teacher and as a human being, who regularly exhibits the care, concern and respect for his students that in his philosophical writings he urges us all to exhibit to our own.

All important philosophers of education have bridged the gap between philosophy of education and general philosophy, and made clear the relevance to philosophy of education of larger philosophical issues and methods. It is an unfortunate institutional fact that, in the United States,

Great Britain and elsewhere, since the time of Dewey philosophers of education have for the most part had institutional homes in departments and schools of education rather than in departments of philosophy. This has on the whole had a detrimental effect upon philosophy of education, for philosophy of education requires intimate contact with its parent discipline. Scheffler's work in epistemology, philosophy of language and philosophy of science has greatly enhanced his work in philosophy of education. That work manifests a level of philosophical sophistication typically not found in the work of philosophers of education who are less centrally connected to, or motivated by, mainstream philosophical issues. Moreover, because Scheffler's work in philosophy of language, philosophy of science and epistemology is highly regarded in the broader philosophical community, his work in philosophy of education enjoys and has brought to philosophy of education a respectability it might not otherwise enjoy. As one interested in fundamental philosophical issues, who contributes to general philosophy, who places philosophy of education issues in the context of broader philosophical concerns, and whose treatment of issues in the philosophy of education benefits from a sophisticated appreciation of, and talent for, the parent discipline, Scheffler provides a model to which philosophers of education would do well to aspire. Philosophy of education is well served by cultivating a strong connection to general philosophy, while at the same time maintaining its basic focus on the practice of education and the philosophical issues arising out of that practice. In this respect philosophers of education are well advised to emulate Scheffler's integration of philosophy of education, general philosophy and educational practice. The health of philosophy of education as a discipline can be measured largely by the ability of its practitioners to approach the level of sophistication of Scheffler's integration on this score.

By way of summary, let me mention again four major contributions to philosophy of education Scheffler has made. First is his introduction of methods of logical analysis – attention to language, clarity, objectivity of method and careful and rigorous argumentation. Second is his utilization of these methods to pursue issues of value in an effort to develop our most defensible conceptions of education, teaching and so on, so as to have the best possible understanding of education, and of educational aims and ideals, which in turn most adequately serve educational practice. Third is his development of specific accounts of key educational concepts: (1) *education*, namely, the conception of education aimed at the fostering of rationality; and (2) *teaching*, namely, as an activity restricted by manner such that the teachers must submit their teaching and the substance of what is taught to the independent judgement of the student, respect the student's sense of reasons and reasonableness, and treat students with respect, and as a concept with a deeply moral component, which cannot be understood or analysed behaviouristically. Fourth is his demonstration of the benefits to be gained by bringing philosophy of education into close contact with general philosophy, and the mistake of removing philosophy of education from contact with its parent discipline.

There are, of course, possible challenges to be made to Scheffler's work. As with any broad philosophical position, there is room for critical reaction, and philosophers have criticized various aspects of Scheffler's views. In particular, some have questioned whether logical analysis should indeed be emphasized as a fundamental method in the philosophy of education; whether philosophy of education need be as intimately connected with general philosophy as Scheffler suggests; whether teaching is rightly analysed in moral rather than behavioural or other terms; and whether the fostering of rationality really is as basic to education as Scheffler argues. These and other dimensions of Scheffler's work, and these and other criticisms of that work, are considered (among many other places) in a special issue of the journal *Synthese*, and in the anthology *Reason and Education: Essays in Honor of Israel Scheffler*. The wide-ranging set of papers in that collection critically examine Scheffler's work on education, teaching and rationality, and apply that work across a broad range of educational and philosophical contexts: philosophy of science and science education, moral philosophy and moral education, philosophy of religion and religious education, philosophy of language and the language of education, the emotions, human potential, educational policy and many more. With all this Scheffler should be pleased, since his insistence on rigorous analysis and criticism surely applies to his own work as well as to everything else. The bulk of his work will in all likelihood stand well the test of time and critique. Even if it does not, however, there is no denying the fundamental importance of his work for philosophy of education. Scheffler has set a standard for serious work in philosophy of education that, in its way, is his most important contribution of all. [5]

Notes

1 Israel Scheffler, *Reason and Teaching*, p.1.
2 This emphasis on symbolic logic differentiates Scheffler's brand of analytic philosophy from Peters', which is in the tradition of 'ordinary language' analysis. While Scheffler's analyses always took full notice of ordinary meanings and usages, he did not hesitate to utilize logical techniques to supersede ordinary language when philosophical understanding and theory could benefit from such utilization.
3 Israel Scheffler, 'Concepts of Education: Reflections on the Current Scene', reprinted in Scheffler, *Reason and Teaching*, p.62, emphasis in original.
4 A complete bibliography of Scheffler's publications, through 1992, appears in *Synthese*, 94, 1, pp.139–44, 1993.
5 This article is drawn from my talk, 'Israel Scheffler', recorded on cassette tape: William Hare (ed.), *Twentieth Century Philosophy of Education: Four Lectures on John Dewey, Bertrand Russell, Israel Scheffler, and R.S. Peters*, Dalhousie University Learning Resource Services, 1990.

See also

In this book: Hirst, Peters
In *Fifty Major Thinkers on Education*: Dewey, Russell

Scheffler's major writings

'Toward an Analytic Philosophy of Education', *Harvard Educational Review*, 24, pp.223–30, 1954.

Philosophy and Education: Modern Readings, editor, Boston, MA: Allyn and Bacon, 2nd edn, 1966, 1958.
The Language of Education, Springfield: Charles C. Thomas, 1960.
The Anatomy of Inquiry, New York: Alfred A. Knopf, 1963.
Conditions of Knowledge: An Introduction to Epistemology and Education, Chicago, IL: Scott, Foresman, 1965.
Science and Subjectivity, 2nd ed., Indianapolis, IN: Hackett Publishing Company, 2nd edn, 1982; 1st pub., Indianapolis, IN: Bobbs-Merrill, 1967.
Reason and Teaching, Indianapolis: Hackett Publishing Company, 1989; 1st pub., London: Routledge & Kegan Paul, 1973.
Four Pragmatists, London: Routledge & Kegan Paul, 1974.
Beyond the Letter: A Philosophical Inquiry into Ambiguity, Vagueness, and Metaphor in Language, London: Routledge & Kegan Paul, 1979.
Of Human Potential, London: Routledge & Kegan Paul, 1985.
Inquiries: Philosophical Studies of Language, Science, and Learning, Indianapolis, IN: Hackett Publishing Company, 1986.
In Praise of the Cognitive Emotions, New York: Routledge, 1991.
Teachers of My Youth: An American Jewish Experience, Dordecht: Kluwer, 1995.
Symbolic Worlds, Cambridge: Cambridge University Press, 1997.
Scheffler, I., and Howard, V.A., *Work, Education and Leadership*, New York: Peter Lang, 1995.

Further reading

Siegel, H., *Educating Reason: Rationality, Critical Thinking, and Education*, London: Routledge, 1988.
—— *Rationality Redeemed?: Further Dialogues on an Educational Ideal*, New York: Routledge, 1997.
—— (ed.), *Reason and Education: Essays in Honor of Israel Scheffler*, Dordrecht: Kluwer.
Synthese, 94, 1, 1993. A special issue of the journal devoted to discussion of Scheffler's philosophical work, guest-edited by Catherine Elgin.

HARVEY SIEGEL

JEAN-FRANÇOIS LYOTARD 1924–98

> Postmodern knowledge is not simply a tool of the authorities; it refines our sensitivity to differences and reinforces our ability to tolerate the incommensurable. Its principle is not the expert's homology, but the inventor's paralogy.[1]

Jean- François Lyotard was one of the principal French philosophers and intellectuals of the twentieth century. He is considered by many scholars as one of the leading figures in the 'postmodern debate' in philosophy. When Lyotard's *The Postmodern Condition: A Report on Knowledge* (1984) was first published in France in 1979, it became an instant classic. The book is, as Lyotard wrote in his introduction, 'a report on knowledge in the most highly developed societies'.[2] *The Postmodern Condition* is an original contribution of the changing development and status of knowledge, science and education in advanced societies. Lyotard synthesizes for the first time

148

philosophical ideas from diverse and separate studies on postmodern culture and defines the 'postmodern' position as 'incredulity toward metanarratives'.[3] That is, Lyotard rejects the 'Grand Narratives' of Western culture such as the dialectis of the Spirit, the hermeneutics of meaning, the emancipation of the rational or working subject, or the creation of wealth which claim they offer solutions that remain neutral and uncontaminated by the interests of domination. Instead, Lyotard examines the collapse of such 'Grand Narratives' and suggests that they must give way to less ambitious *petits récits*, little narratives that resist closure and totality. As he elaborates in *The Differend* (1988) 'a universal rule of judgment between heterogeneous genres is lacking in general',[4] and '[t]here is no genre whose hegemony over others would be just'.[5] Only by means of repeated testimony as *petits récits* can we celebrate variation, multiplicity and difference in our lives. This marks a quest that reaches out for the new, for new questions that will generate new inquiries; a quest that is an agonistics of celebrating the ill-defined, the unknowable, the irreducible, the unpresentable, that resists global categorization. This view determines Lyotard's ultimate vision of science, knowledge and education as a search not for consensus, but precisely for 'instabilities', as a practice of paralogism, in which the end is not to reach agreement but to celebrate our differences and to bear witness to them (an ethical obligation).

Jean-François Lyotard was born in Versailles in 1924. He studied phenomenology with Merleau-Ponty, and his first philosophical publication, *La Phénoménologie* (1954) translated into English in 1991 dealt primarily with the work of his mentor. He taught philosophy in secondary schools for ten years (1949–59), including a short period in an Algerian lyceé at Constantine (a city in the north-east) from 1950 to 1952 just before the outbreak of the Algerian war. The years 1954–64 represent Lyotard's active political involvement. In 1954 he joined the radical Marxist group Socialisme ou barbarie from which he left in 1963 to join Pouvoir ouvrier, a revolutionary workers' organization; he remained a member of the latter for two years. For the next twenty years, Lyotard taught in several higher education institutions (Sorbonne, Nanterre, CNRS and Vincennes). During this time, while a lecturer at the University of Nanterre, Lyotard initiated Le Mouvement du 22 Mars, a movement opposing the Fouchet's reforms of 1967 and one committed to the freedom of expression and democratic participation by students and staff in university affairs. Lyotard was politically active during the events of May 1968 and he defended the students' desire for genuine democratic participation. In 1971, Lyotard received his Docteur ès lettres; his doctoral thesis was entitled 'Discours, figure' and it marked a conscious shift away from Marxism. Later, Lyotard secured a post as professor of philosophy at the University of Paris VIII (Saint-Denis) which he held until his retirement in 1989. Lyotard served as a council member of the Collège International de Philosophie in Paris. He had been a Visiting Professor at the universities of Wisconsin, Minnesota, Yale, Johns Hopkins, Montreal, São Paolo and Turin, among others. Lyotard was Professor Emeritus at the University of Paris, and was for several years Professor of French at the University of California, Irvine. He moved from that position to Emory University in Atlanta, where he was Professor of

French and Philosophy. He passed away in Paris during the night of 20–1 April 1998.

Lyotard's work constitutes a seminal contribution to what has become known as the modernity/postmodernity debate, a debate that has involved many of the most prominent contemporary philosophers and social theorists.[6] This debate developed an important philosophical interpretation of the origin and change of knowledge, contemporary science, technology and education in postindustrial societies. Lyotard, explains Michael Peters, signalled a break 'not only with the so-called "modern era" but also with various traditionally "modern" ways of viewing the world'.[7] Lyotard points out that his use of the word 'postmodern' does not merely imply a linear temporal sequence, that is, 'modernity' followed by 'postmodernity'. On the contrary, the postmodern is already implied by the modern, because 'a work can become modern only if it first postmodern. Postmodernism thus understood is not modernism at its end but in the nascent state, and this state is constant'.[8] There are parallels and shared assumptions in other contemporary ideas such as poststructuralism and deconstruction as developed by Foucault, then later Barthes, Kristeva, Derrida and Deleuze. The creative interdisciplinary approach which Lyotard brings to his project has affected not only the philosophical domain, but also an entire spectrum of the human sciences, including education.[9]

Lyotard's work directly addresses the concerns of education, especially in the areas of educational philosophy and theory, and of educational policy. His ideas analyse the future status and role of education and knowledge and in many ways they have been proven prophetic in predicting how the status of knowledge is altered as societies enter the postindustrial age. Lyotard argues that the state of the Western culture and knowledge is permanently altered 'following the transformations which, since the end of the nineteenth century, have altered the game rules of science, literature and the arts'.[10] Lyotard places these transformations within the context of the crisis of the 'Grand Narratives', especially the Enlightenment metanarratives concerning meaning, truth and emancipation which have been used to legitimate both the rules of knowledge in the sciences and the foundations of modern institutions of education. These transformations have altered not only the game rules, but also the practices for the transmission and production of knowledge. Most fundamentally, they have altered the game rules for the discourse of legitimation of knowledge. The postmodern condition, Lyotard argues, represents a legitimation crisis of the modern ways of the production of knowledge. Knowledge has already become the principal force of production, changing the composition of the workforce in developed countries. The commercialization of knowledge and its new ways of circulation, he suggests, raise new ethical, political and legal problems between the nation-state and the information-rich multinationals, as well as widening the gap between the so-called developed and third-world countries.[11]

The issue for Lyotard is one of understanding and providing a critique of 'the transformation of language into a productive commodity' which reduces phrases to encoded messages with an exchange value messages that can be stored, retrieved, packaged, manipulated and transmitted. He describes this in terms of the performativity principle, a sense of efficiency measured according to an input/output ratio. This implies a tendency to subject all discourses to only one criterion, that of efficiency. The performativity principle, maintains Lyotard, treats all language games as consummerable. He suggests that such an approach obscures the plurality of language games as well as cultural and societal differences. The concept behind performativity is the optimization of the system's performance efficiency. 'The application of this criterion', in Lyotard's view, 'to all of our games necessarily entails a certain level of terror, whether soft or hard: be operational (that is, consummerable) or disappear.'[12]

Lyotard opposes the legitimacy of education through performativity, because he believes that the supporters of performativity urge that education should impart only the knowledge and skills necessary to preserve and enhance the operational efficiency of society. The logic of the performativity principle, of optimizing the system's overall performance and its criterion, is technological, it cannot provide us with a rule of judging what is true or what is beautiful. What is taught, then, is determined by the technological requirements of the system, and educators are evaluated by how efficiently they convey what they teach. When education is legitimated through performativity, Lyotard points out, knowledge is not thought to have any intrinsic worth. Instead, knowledge is valued only as a commodity which can be sold, it no longer possesses 'use value' but only 'exchange value'.[13]

Lyotard argues that legitimation through performativity is problematic and has questionable consequences for society. Postmodern education and science, according to Lyotard, are legitimated neither by a criterion of efficiency nor by search for universal consensus. Rather, in Lyotard's view, legitimation comes from plurality, dissensus, innovation, imagination and creativity: or what he terms 'the quest for paralogy'.[14] Lyotard maintains that 'consensus is only a particular state of discussion, not its end. Its end, on the contrary is paralogy'.[15] Looking for a different way of legitimation, Lyotard indicates that '[t]he only legitimation that can make this kind of request [i.e., the paralogical activity] admissible is that it will generate ideas, in other words, new statements'.[16] The goal of postmodern education and science is the discovery of these new ideas and concepts.

Lyotard's contribution to a richer understanding of postmodern education and the changing status of knowledge should not be allowed to overshadow the significance of his other works. Lyotard wrote twenty books and many scholarly articles, spanning a range of philosophical fields, themes, styles and topics. Lyotard's thought developed over the years drawing on a number of thinkers as diverse as Merleau-Ponty, Freud, Nietzsche, Kant, Wittgenstein and Deleuze. His early work in the 1950s was influenced by phenomenological thinkers (Merleau-Ponty, Heidegger and Levinas). For Lyotard there was a 'gap' between our experience and the language we use to speak about this experience. In 'Discours, figure', Lyotard criticizes theoretical constructs that banish history in favour of timeless, universal categories of thought that remain independent of the particularities of our life-world experience. Lyotard's association during the 1960s with the radical Marxist group Socialisme ou barbarie reinforced his distrust of any theory that ignored the critique of historical materialism and the freedom of political praxis.[17]

After 1966 Lyotard discontinued his active political affiliation with any radical Marxist group and his autobiographical account 'A Memorial for Marxism: For Pierre Souyri'[18] represents intellectually, on the one hand, a disagreement with Marxism and, on the other, a turn to philosophy.[19] Michael Peters (1995) argues that Lyotard's turn away from Marxism and his turn to philosophy needs to be seen in the historical context of the French intellectual life in the 1950s and the 1960s, and, especially, the struggle against humanism and 'universal' human development (communist or capitalist) expressed in the assumed neutrality of 'progress'. In *Economie libidinale* (1993, orig. 1974) Lyotard criticizes the underlying notion of the dialectic and argues that there is no truth arrived at through the supposed ethical and social truths of Marxism, because those truths are no better that the falsehoods it wants to overcome. Lyotard uses the notion of Freud's economy of libidinal energy and transfers it to the context of Marxist political economy to show the impossibility of choosing one political position over another, since we can never decide the correct one. The experience of a (political or philosophical) position, according to Lyotard, does not necessarily imply its exhaustion or its development into another position where it is both conserved and suppressed. In *The Differend* (1988) Lyotard expands the ideas he introduces in the *Postmodern Condition* and argues that a 'differend' (a radical difference) cannot be equitably resolved by some appeal to universal consensus without doing violence to the interests of the weaker party. Lyotard clearly rejects Habermas' vision of an evolutionary social leap into a new type of rational society defined as the communication community that reaches consensus based on the best arguments. This, Lyotard argues, is the unacceptable remnant of a 'totalizing' philosophical tradition in which conformists are valorized and anti-conformists are 'terrorists' of the ideals of consensus. Habermas' position, according to Lyotard, leaves critically unquestioned the very context of argumentation, which is always marked by the effects of power, status, networking and influence.

The major theme in Lyotard's work is the legitimation of knowledge in the postmodern age, a theme that is directly relevant to central concerns in education. Lyotard's views provide a sound critique of the neo-liberal commercialization of education in terms of the systemic, self-regulatory nature of global capitalism, the commitment by world agencies such as the World Bank and the International Monetary Fund to monetarism and supply-side economics is a strong indication of the neo-liberal strategies for capital accumulation.[20] The emphasis on private and individual, instead of public investment, commodifies education and views it as a means to increase labour flexibility and efficiency, thus improving the competitiveness of the economy. Education, in this model, is viewed as a leading sector of the economy and is defined by the principle of performativity. Lyotard stands against the legitimation of education in terms of performance of a system as a whole. Performativity functions as a reigning metanarrative according to which educational policies must be shaped. Lyotard theorizes the legitimation of knowledge and education based on difference understood as paralogy, where 'the little narrative remains the quintessential form of imaginative invention'.[21]

In the emerging postmodern society, the central concerns about the legitimation of knowledge and education are perhaps more compelling today than they were ever before: the principle of performativity is more prevalent now in education than previously, thus Lyotard's ideas can be a powerful tool of critiquing the priorities and foundations of modern educational institutions.

Notes

1 J.-F. Lyotard, *The Postmodern Condition: A Report on Knowledge*, trans. G. Bennington and B. Massumi, Minneapolis, MN: University of Minnesota Press, p.xxv, 1984, 1st pub. in France 1979. Henceforth referred to as *PMC*.
2 *PMC*, p.xxv.
3 *PMC*, p.xxiv.
4 J.-F. Lyotard, *The Differend: Phrases in Dispute*, trans. G. Van den Abbeele, Minneapolis, MN: University of Minnesota Press, p.xi, 1988, 1st pub. in France 1982.
5 Ibid., p.158.
6 M. Peters, *Poststructuralism, Politics and Education*, New York: Bergin & Garvey, 1996.
7 M. Peters, 'Education and the Postmodern Condition: Revisiting Jean-François Lyotard', *Journal of Philosophy of Education*, 29, p.387, 1995.
8 *PMC*, p.79.
9 R. Kearney and M. Rainwater, *The Continental Philosophy Reader*, London, Routledge, 1996.
10 *PMC*, p.3.
11 See Peters, *Education and the Postmodern Condition*, op cit.
12 *PMC*, p.xxiv.
13 *PMC*, pp.4–5.
14 *PMC*, p.66.
15 *PMC*, pp.65–6.
16 *PMC*, p.65.
17 R. Kearney and M. Rainwater, *The Continental Philosophy Reader*, London: Routledge, 1996.
18 J.-F. Lyotard, 'A Memorial for Marxism: For Pierre Souyri', in *Peregrinations: Law, Form, Event*, New York: Columbia University Press, 1988.
19 M. Peters, 'Emancipation and Philosophies of History: Jean-François Lyotard and Cultural Difference', unpublished manuscript, University of Auckland, 1998.
20 M. Peters, 'Education and the Postmodern Condition: Revisiting Jean-François Lyotard', *Journal of Philosophy of Education*, 29, pp.393–4, 1995.
21 *PMC*, p.60.

See also

In this book: Habermas, Wittgenstein
In *Fifty Major Thinkers on Education*: Kant, Nietzsche

Lyotard's major writings

Libidinal Economy, Bloomington, IN: Indiana University, 1993, Fr. 1974.
Lyotard, J.-F., with Thebaud, J.-L., *Just Gaming*, Minneapolis, MN: University of Minnesota Press, 1985, Fr. 1979.
The Postmodern Condition, Minneapolis, MN: University of Minnesota Press, 1984, Fr. 1979.
The Differend, Minneapolis, MN: University of Minnesota Press, 1988, Fr. 1982.

The Postmodern Explained, Minneapolis, MN: University of Minnesota Press, 1992, Fr. 1986.
Heidegger and the Jews, Minneapolis, MN: University of Minnesota Press, 1990, Fr. 1988.
The Inhuman: Reflections on Time, Stanford, CA: Stanford University Press, 1991, Fr. 1988.
Peregrinations: Law, Form, Event, New York: Columbia, 1988.
The Lyotard Reader, Cambridge, MA: Blackwell, 1989.
Lessons on the Analytic of the Sublime, Stanford, CA: Stanford University Press, 1994, Fr. 1991.
Toward the Postmodern, Atlantic Heights, NJ: Humanities Press, 1993.
Political Writings, Minneapolis, MN: University of Minnesota Press, 1993.

Further reading

Benjamin, A. (ed.), *Judging Lyotard*, London and New York: Routledge, 1992.
Bennington, G., *Lyotard: Writing the Event*, New York: Columbia, 1988.
Peters, M. (ed.), *Education and the Postmodern Condition*, New York: Bergin & Garvey, 1995.
Readings, B., *Introducing Lyotard: Art and Politics*, London and New York: Routledge, 1991.

MICHALINOS ZEMBYLAS

LAWRENCE A. CREMIN 1925–90

We do not, it seems to me, study the history of education merely for its possible value in avoiding mistakes, in recognizing the inefficiencies of the monitorial system, for example, or the parochialism of ecclesiastical education, or the fragility of academic freedom, though history can have such value. We study history to become aware of our presuppositions and commitments in education by examining the origin of those presuppositions and commitments. I genuinely believe that if our national leaders had had a richer and more accurate history of American education at their disposal during the last twenty-five years, they would have possessed a much greater range of options as to where to intervene for the better and how. ... We study history, not because in its absence there will not be any history, but rather because in its absence we shall have a corrupt history; we shall have the myths, the distortions, and the ideologies that flourish in the absence of critical scholarship. It is this, I think, that Socrates had in mind when he taught that the unexamined life is unfit to be lived by man. And it is this that propels those of us who study the past, even though we can never know it fully.[1]

Cremin was a historian, teacher and leader whose work had a profound effect on educational history in particular and educational research in general. He was born in New York City in the United States in 1925. After attending Towsend Harris High School, a public high school for gifted youth, he matriculated at the City College of New York (CCNY) in 1942.

He entered the US Army Air Corps before his senior year and returned to finish undergraduate college after the Second World War. He was elected to Phi Beta Kappa and graduated from CCNY with a BS in social science. His father and mother who founded the New York School of Music wanted him to become a concert pianist, but Cremin was ultimately drawn to the humanities and social sciences, particularly the field of history. The availability of the GI Bill allowed him to enter graduate school at Teachers College, Columbia University in September 1946. At Teachers College he took a wide range of graduate courses, including courses on the social and philosophical foundations of American education from such eminent scholars as John L. Childs, George Counts, R. Freeman Butts and R. Bruce Raup. He received his MA in 1947 and his Ph.D. in 1949.[2]

Cremin is best known for his long-standing efforts to improve the quality of scholarship and teaching in history of education and to broaden the parameters of inquiry for educational historians. Moreover, he devoted much of his career to establishing history of education as a disciplined-based field inextricably linked to the main currents of historical scholarship. As he entered the field in the early 1950s, writings in the history of education lacked rigorous methodological and theoretical foundation and tended to be pedantic, parochial and uncritical. It recorded the origins and development of public education in a vacuum with virtually no regard for the larger social and economic context that shaped the structure and content of formal schooling. Further, Cremin found that historians of education were prone to romanticize public education as the 'great equalizer' of democratic societies. While chronicling the development of public schooling as part of an unfolding pageantry of modern democracy, historians of education easily omitted the undemocratic experiences of Native Americans, slaves, immigrants, ordinary workers, women and ethnic minority groups. This way of writing about the origins and development of American education came to be known as the Cubberly tradition, named after its greatest exemplar, Ellwood P. Cubberly, long-time Dean of the School of Education at Stanford University. The 'Cubberly School' of educational history fostered a pattern of historical scholarship that characterized the genesis, rise and triumph of the common school as the engine of modern democracy. Written mainly by education professors without rigorous training in the methods and techniques of historical research, it was appropriately categorized as 'in-house' history and marked by its romantic and myopic view of the complex and troubled past of public schooling. As it was written to promote particular forms of public education, much of it was inherently motivated by specific ideological commitments, even as its proponents saw their advocacy as dedication to sound professional standards. The heirs of the Cubberly tradition played a significant role in shaping Cremin's views of the role of history in educational policy and practice. However, he rebelled against their fundamental conception of historical scholarship as he worked to usher in a new and different standard of disciplined-based educational history.

Cremin's importance to the transformation of the role of history in the field of education can be understood primarily through an appreciation of the leading role he played on two important fronts. First, he played a critical role in improving the quality of scholarship and teaching in the field of history of education. Second, influenced by the conceptual framework of historian Bernard Bailyn, he broadened the parameters of social and intellectual history for historians of education. During the late 1950s a self-conscious effort was made by the Fund for the Advancement of Education, a subsidiary of the Ford Foundation, to improve the quality of scholarship and teaching in the field of history of education. In 1961, with the publication of *The Transformation of the School: Progressivism in American Education, 1876–1957*, Cremin became an exemplar of the Ford Foundation's campaign to involve more discipline-based scholars in the study of educational history. The book linked the history of progressive education to mainstream intellectual and social history of the progressive era and it assumed a major place within the larger field of American history. Winner of the Bancroft Prize in American History in 1964, *Transformation* was viewed as a model of the new historiography in educational history. Following its publication Cremin was offered a joint appointment in Columbia University's Department of History and invited to become a member of the Ford Foundation's Committee on the Role of Education in American History. He had become the embodiment of the Committee's emphasis on first-rate scholarship in the field of educational history and a model for the new emphasis on disciplined-based historical studies in education. His work ultimately carried international appeal as historians in varying geo-political contexts grappled with the relationship between progressive politics and educational change.[3]

In 1960, Bernard Bailyn, in *Education in the Forming of American Society*, proposed a significantly broader definition of educational history away from an exclusive focus on formal schooling toward a study of all institutions and agencies, formal and informal, that shaped cultural beliefs and social behaviour over time. Cremin's acceptance of Bailyn's conception of educational history was well illustrated in the former's publication of *The Wonderful World of Ellwood Patterson Cubberly* in 1965. Concurring in the criticisms of the historical studies of education offered by Bailyn, he called for a history of education beyond the school to a host of other institutions that educate, including families, churches, libraries, museums, publishers, benevolent societies, youth groups, agricultural fairs, radio networks, military organizations and research institutes. This view not only marked a sharp break with the study of educational history as practised within the Cubberly tradition, it differed significantly from the focus of Cremin's earlier works. In *The American Common School: An Historic Conception* (1951) and *Public Schools in Our Democracy* (co-authored with Merle Borrowman in 1956), as well as in *Transformation* (1961), Cremin's scholarship focused almost exclusively on the history of public schools. Soon after the publication of *The Wonderful World of Ellwood Patterson Cubberly*, he was invited by the Carnegie Corporation of New York to write a comprehensive history of American education to celebrate the centennial of the US Office of Education. This new study of educational history was conceptualized mainly around his broadened definition of education as formal and informal enculturalization.

Beginning his masterful three-volume study in 1964, each volume was built around the new definition of education he adopted from Bernard Bailyn. For these volumes he defined the study of educational history as the deliberate, systematic and sustained effort to transmit, evoke, or acquire knowledge, values, attitudes, skills and sensibilities, as well as any learning that results from that effort, direct or indirect, intended or unintended. Clearly, with this focus there was little distinction between Cremin's concept of education and traditional anthropological definitions of culture itself. Indeed, for Cremin the line between educational history and cultural history virtually evaporated. His comprehensive history of American education yielded three great books: *American Education: The Colonial Experience* (1970), *American Education: The National Experience* (1980) and *American Education: The Metropolitan Experience* (1988). For the second volume, *American Education: The National Experience*, he won the Pulitzer Prize for history in 1981. Having won the Bancroft Prize and the Pulitzer Prize he stood as America's most prominent historian of education and one of the most recognized scholars in the field internationally. Without question, Cremin's three volumes personified the earlier concerns of the Ford Foundation, that educational history could become integrated into the main discipline of intellectual and social history.

The field of educational history flamed into vigorous life in America during the second half of the 1960s. Cremin, as much as any scholar, had helped to infuse new life into a field that had become moribund by the mid twentieth century. Although he was in vital respects the 'Dean' of the new history of American education, many of the young scholars of the late 1960s were influenced by the critical perspectives of the Civil Rights Movement, the 'new' radical social history, the women's movement, and the free speech and anti-war movements on college campuses. They lived and became educated as historians in a radically different social context than the immediate post-Second World War era of Cremin's generation. Thus, as Cremin did for his generation, the younger scholars in the field began to write a new and different history that was more consistent with the questions inherent in the experiences of their generation. The emergent fields of social history, working-class history, ethnic history and women's history connected the particular field of educational history to the general field of social and intellectual history in ways different than defined by Bailyn and Cremin. Instead of moving away from the study of schools toward a study of other formal and informal agencies, the new scholars focused a more critical lens on Cubberly's 'Wonderful World' of common schools. They transformed the old in-house history of the genesis, rise and triumph of the great democratic common school system into an analysis of the undemocratic role of class, race, gender and bureaucracy in shaping the basic structure and content of public education. Instead of juxtaposing the history of school systems with the history of libraries, churches, museums and benevolent societies, the new historians of education sought to integrate the origins and development of school systems into the overall contradictions of social and economic development. Themes of class domination and social inequality emerged along side traditional themes of democracy and individual opportunity. This new history not only challenged Cubberly's belief that the genius of American civilization lay in its development of public education, it redefined the historical meaning of public education and reset the parameters of historical inquiry as defined by Cremin. In short, it conceptualized public schooling as a subordinate institution that generally reinforced dominate patterns of social inequality and defined the primary role of educational history as an investigation of the role of formal schooling in the larger social order. Although some studies focused on education in non-school social settings, on balance, they moved away from the course chartered in Cremin's three-volume masterpiece. Today there is more balance between the two conceptions, but the main emphasis in educational history remains on formal schooling rather than on families, churches, libraries, museums, publishers, benevolent societies, youth groups, agricultural fairs, radio networks, military organizations and research institutes.

Despite the heated controversy that arose over what became known as 'revisionist' educational history during the late 1960s and early 1970s, the improvement of the quality of scholarship and teaching in the field from the late 1960s to the late 1980s grew significantly. Moreover, educational history was taken seriously enough internationally to find a more comfortable place in the larger field of intellectual and social history. Indeed, the history of education underwent a transformation from the sterile and narrow in-house histories of the mid twentieth century to a rich and vibrant field during the latter third of the twentieth century. Without question, Cremin played a decisive role in setting the broad debate and through his writings and teachings he, as much as anyone, transformed educational history into a more disciplined-base inquiry. He helped found the History of Education Society and the National Academy of Education, two organizations that have advanced the scholarship in educational history in particular and educational research in general. After assuming the presidency of the Spencer Foundation, Cremin helped to advance the quality of educational research in general through increasing grants for basic disciplinary research in the field of education. Moreover, by focusing more attention on studies that might illuminate problems of educational equity, and directing additional funds to fellowship programmes that could help to renew the educational research community, he translated his long-standing commitment to improving the quality of scholarship in education into strong institutionalized programmes. Many national and international students of educational research, inside and outside schools of education, have benefited from the fellowship and research programmes he developed within the Spencer Foundation. Further, during his tenure as Frederick Barnard Professor of Education at Teachers College, he produced some of the outstanding scholars in educational history. Through several of his former students such as Patricia Albjerg Graham (historian and former president of Spencer Foundation), Ellen Condliffe Lagemann (historian and current president of Spencer Foundation) and Mary Ann Dzuback (historian and president elect of the History of Education Society), Cremin leaves a powerful legacy that continues to shape significantly the course of scholarship in the field of education. Finally, as a prolific writer, he produced a large body of first-rate scholarship that remains a must read for all students of educational history.

Notes

1 Cremin, 'American Education: Some Notes Toward a New History', Monograph

LAWRENCE A. CREMIN

for American Educational Research Association–Phi Delta Kappa Award Lecture – Bloomington, IN: Phi Delta Kappa International, pp.17–18, 1969.
2 Ellen Condliffe Lagemann and Patricia Albjerg Graham, 'Lawrence Cremin: A Biographical Memoir', *Teachers College Record*, 96, 1, Fall, pp.102–11, 1994; Diane Ravitch, 'Lawrence A. Cremin', *The American Scholar*, 61, 1, Winter, pp.83–9, 1992.
3 Peter Cunningham, *Curriculum Change in the Primary School Since 1945: Dissemination of the Progressive Ideal*, London and New York: Falmer Press, 1988; Ron Brooks, *King Alfred School and the Progressive Movement, 1898–1998*, Cardiff: University of Wales Press, 1998; Shirley Dennis, *The Politics of Progressive Education: the Odenwaldschule in Nazi Germany*, Cambridge, MA: Harvard University Press, 1992; John Shotton, *No Master High or Low: Libertarian Education and Schooling in Britain 1890–1990*, Bristol: Libertarian Education, 1993; Joachim Liebshner, *Foundations of Progressive Education: The History of the National Froebel Society*, Cambridge: Lutterworth Press, 1991.

Cremin's major writings

'Toward a More Common School', *Teachers College Record*, LI, pp.308–19, 1949–50.
The American Common School: An Historic Conception, New York: Bureau of Publications, Teachers College, Columbia University, 1951.
'The Curriculum Maker and His Critics: A Persistent American Problem', *Teachers College Record*, LIV, pp.234–45, 1952–53.
Cremin, L.A., with Freeman Butts, R., *A History of Education in American Culture*, New York: Henry Holt and Company, 1953.
Cremin, L.A., Richardson, C.C., Brule, H. and Synder, H.E., *The Education of Teachers in England, France, and the USA*, Paris: UNESCO, pp.225–48, 1953.
'The Revolution in American Secondary Education, 1893–1918', *Teachers College Record*, LVI, pp.295–308, 1954–55.
Cremin, L.A., with Merle L. Borrowman, *Public Schools in Our Democracy*, New York: Macmillan, 1956.
'The Problem of Curriculum Making: An Historical Perspective', in *What Shall High Schools Teach?*, Washington, DC: Association for Supervision and Curriculum Development, pp.6–26, 1956.
The Republic and the School: Horace Mann on the Education of Free Men, New York: Bureau of Publications, Teachers College, Columbia University, 1957.
'The American Common School in Theory and Practice', *The Year Book of Education 1957*, New York: World Book, pp.243–59, 1957.
'The Progressive Movement in American Education: A Perspective', *Harvard Educational Review*, XXVII, pp.251–70, 1957.
'L'Avvenire della Scuola Pubblica Americana', *Problemi della Pedagogia*, Luglio-Ottobre, I, pp.37–54, 1957.
'The Writings of William F. Russell', *Teachers College Record*, LIX, pp.172–8, 1957–58.
'The Recent Development of the History of Education as a Field of Study in the United States', *History of Education Journal*, 11, VII, pp.1–35, 1955–56.
The American School, Madison, WI: Americana Press, 1958.
'John Dewey and the Progressive-Education Movement, 1915–1952', *The School Review*, LXVII, pp.160–73, 1959.
'What Happened to Progressive Education?', *Teachers College Record*, LXI, pp.23–9, 1959–60.
The Transformation of the School: Progressivism in American Education, 1876–1957, New York: Alfred A. Knopf, 1961.
'L'Ecole Pour Tous', *Education Americaine*, Paris: Nouveaux Horizons, pp.i–40, 1963.

159

The Genius of American Education, Pittsburgh, PA: University of Pittsburgh Press, 1965.
The Wonderful World of Ellwood Patterson Cubberley, New York: Bureau of Publications, Teachers College, Columbia University, 1965.
Cremin, L.A., with the Committee on the Role of Education in American History, *Education and American History*, New York: The Fund for the Advancement of Education, 1965.
'John Dewey's My Pedagogic Creed', in Daniel J. Boorstin (ed.), *An American Primer*, 2 vols, Chicago, IL: University of Chicago Press, IL, pp.608–20, 1966.
'American Education: Some Notes Toward a New History', Monograph for American Educational Research Association – Phi Delta Kappa Award Lecture, Bloomington, IN: Phi Delta Kappa International, 1969.
American Education: The Colonial Experience, 1607–1783, New York: Harper & Row, 1970.
'Curriculum-Making in the United States', *Teachers College Record*, LXXIII, pp.207–20, 1971–1972.
'The Family as Educator: Some Comments on the Recent Historiography', *Teachers College Record*, LXXVL, pp.250–65, 1974–75.
'Public Education and the Education of the Public', *Teachers College Record*, LXXVII, pp.1–12, 1975–76.
Public Education, New York: Basic Books, 1976.
Traditions of American Education, New York: Basic Books, 1977.
American Education: The National Experience, 1783–1876, New York: Harper & Row, 1980.
'The Problematics of Education in the 1980s: Some Reflections on the Oxford Workshop', *Oxford Review of Education*, 9, 1, pp.9–20, 1983.
'Grading the Nation's Schools', *The World Book Year Book*, Chicago, IL: World Book-Child Craft International, pp.66–83, 1983.
'The Popularization of American Education Since World War II', *Proceedings American Philosophical Society*, 129, 2, pp.113–20, 1985.
American Education: The Metropolitan Experience, 1876–1980, New York: Harper & Row, 1988.
Popular Education and Its Discontents, New York: Harper & Row, 1990.

Further reading

Bailyn, Bernard, *Education in the Forming of American Society*, New York: Random House, 1960.
Bowles, Samuel and Gintis, Herbert, *Schooling in Capitalist America: Educational Reform and the Contradictions of Economic Life*, New York: Basic Books, 1976.
Bullock, Henry Allen, *A History of Negro Education in the South: From 1619 to the Present* New York: Praeger, 1970.
Burgess, Charles O. and Borrowman, Merle L., *What Doctrines to Embrace: Studies in the History of American Education*, Glenview, IL: Scott, Foresman, 1969.
Church, Robert L., *Education in the United States: An Interpretive History*, New York: The Free Press, 1976.
Clifford, Geraldine Joncich, *Edward L. Thorndike: The Sane Positivist*, Middletown, CT: Wesleyan University Press, 1984.
Cohen, Sol, *Progressives and Urban School Reform: The Public Education Association, of New York City, 1895–1954*, New York: Bureau of Publications, Teachers College, Columbia University, 1964.
Cubberly, Ellwood P., *Public Education in the United States*, 2nd edn rev., Boston, MA: Houghton Mifflin, 1934.
Dzuback, Mary Ann, *Robert M. Hutchins: Portrait of an Educator*, Chicago, IL: University of Chicago Press, 1991.

Fisher, Berenice M., *Industrial Education: American Ideals and Institutions*, Madison, WI: The University of Wisconsin Press, 1967.

Graham, Patricia Albjerg, *Progressive Education from Arcady to Academe: A History of the Progressive Education Association, 1919–1955*, New York: Teachers College Press, 1967.

Kaestle, Carl F., *The Evolution of an Urban School System: New York City, 1750–1850*, Cambridge, MA: Harvard University Press, 1973.

Karier, Clarence J., Violas, Paul and Spring, Joel, *Roots of Crisis: American Education in the Twentieth Century*, Chicago, IL: Rand McNally, 1973.

Katz, Michael B., *Irony of Early School Reform: Educational Innovation in Mid-Nineteenth Century Massachusetts*, Boston, MA: Beacon Press, 1968.

Krug, Edward A., *The Shaping of the American High School, 1920–1941*, 2 vols, Madison, WI: University of Wisconsin Press, 1972.

Lagemann, Ellen Condliffe, *The Politics of Knowledge: The Carnegie Corporation, Philanthropy, and Public Policy*, Middletown, CT: Wesleyan University Press, 1989.

Lazerson, Marvin, *Origins of the Urban School: Public Education in Massachusetts, 1870–1915*, Cambridge, MA: Harvard University Press, 1971.

Mattingly, Paul H., *The Classless Profession: American Schoolmen in the Nineteenth Century*, New York: New York University Press, 1975.

Perkinson, Henry, *The Imperfect Panacea: American Faith in Education, 1856–1965*, New York: Random House, 1968.

Ravitch, Diane, *The Great School Wars: New York City, 1805–1973*, New York: Basic Books, 1974.

Schultz, Stanley K., *The Culture Factory: Boston Public Schools, 1789–1860*, New York: Oxford University Press, 1973.

Spring, Joel, *Education and the Rise of the Corporate State*, Boston, MA: Beacon Press, 1972.

Tyack, David B., *The One Best System: A History of American Urban Education*, Cambridge, MA: Harvard University Press, 1974.

JAMES D. ANDERSON

BASIL BERNSTEIN 1925–2000

> We are moving from secondary schools where the teaching roles were insulated from each other, where the teacher had an assigned area of authority and autonomy, to secondary schools where the teaching role is less autonomous and where it is a shared or co-operative role. There has been a shift from a teaching role which is, so to speak, 'given' (in the sense that one steps into assigned duties), to a role which has to be *achieved* in relation with other teachers. It is a role which is no longer made but *has to be made*. The teacher is no longer isolated from other teachers, as where the principle of integration is the relation of his subject to a public examination. The teacher is now in a complementary relation with other teachers at the level of his day-to-day teaching.[1]

This quotation is from an article called 'Open Schools, Open Society', first published in the popular journal, *New Society*, in 1967.[2] The title of the article, and indeed the journal, spoke of a desire for a less class-based open society where competence rather than class background might be more important in negotiating educational futures. The article came out at a high point in promulgating such desired futures and must be understood in the historical context in which it was located. Much of Bernstein's *oeuvre* has to be understood in this way, not because there is an absence of timeless authenticity in his writing, but because of the wide spectrum of misunderstandings and misapplication of his theories.

The British context in which Bernstein began writing grew out of the post-war 'age of austerity' which followed the Second World War. In 1945, a Labour Government was elected with a programme of mildly Socialist reconstruction to rebuild British society from the desolation of six years of world war. All social groups having fought side-by-side, the 'we are in it together' spirit of war carried over for a time into an egalitarian impulse within social relations which was expressed in political aspirations.

The aspirational mission of the Labour Government to build a 'New Jerusalem' in Britain took place in a cultural terrain vividly divided by regional and class differences. Growing up as a working-class school student in the 1950s – as I did – was to be reminded at every stage of one's origin and likely destination. This may be particularly difficult for North American readers to conceptualize, so the following quotation seeks to capture the 'structures of feeling' that were part of working-class experience of schooling at the time:

> Yet, from the beginning I experienced odd contradictions, for while I was supposed to learn, most of the questions to which I inarticulately and tentatively sought answers were not on the school's agenda. They were, it is true, mainly childish questions, but they turned on my understanding of the world at the time. They were things that we talked about at home: Why did my father work so hard? Why did I not see him in the mornings, or until late in the evening? Why did my mother go to work 'to support me'? Why were all the fields I played in being developed by more and larger council estates? Why did we have to walk (or later, ride) more than three miles to school? Why was the school in a 'posh' village and not in my village? Why were the children from my village treated differently from the children from the immediate school locality?
>
> These then were aspects of my world; but why did we never talk about them, let alone learn about them at school?
>
> My concerns about schooling increased when I went to secondary school. I passed the 11+ and was sent off to a grammar school (again, miles away from my village). All my friends now went to *our* village's school: a secondary modern. The long ride to the grammar school through the council estates wearing a blue Venetian blazer and a hat with a yellow tassel cemented an incurable fascination with schooling. (The fascination lasted longer than the blazer and hat, which I took to packing in my bike saddle bag and putting on in the school's bike shed.)
>
> At the grammar school the curriculum made my sense of disconnectedness and dichotomy at the primary school seem childish. Here, not only was the content alien and dull but the very form of transmission and structure (the discursive formation no less) was utterly bewildering. I experienced schooling as if I were

learning a second language. A major factor in this cultural displacement was the school's curriculum.[3]

Bearing witness through scholarly examination and exhumation to the experiences of class and region in British schooling became a primary project for a generation of sociologists. Bernstein was, by far, the most persuasive, generative and articulate of this generation. In a famous phrase, Bernstein argued that 'education cannot compensate for society'.[4] The problem, he argued, was not educational and cultural coding systems *per se* but access to those systems. Above all, what Bernstein achieved 'was to show up the mechanism by which access to elaborated code was a function of social class'.[5]

Bernstein's route into this kind of intellectual inquiry has been fairly well documented. Born in 1925, some of his earliest experiences of working-class culture came as a resident worker at the Bernhard Baron Settlement in the East End of London. The Settlement movement grew out of a kind of missionary concern to bring cultural and spiritual enlightenment to disadvantaged regions. In this case, the missionary zeal was to bring Reform Judaism to a predominately Orthodox Jewish community. Bernstein was involved in family casework and later wrote: 'This experience in more ways than one had a deep influence upon my life. It focused and made explicit an interest I always seemed to have had in the structure and process of cultural transmission.'[6]

Bernstein read sociology at the London School of Economics. At the time, 'LSE' was training a cohort of sociologists, a good number of whom investigated the impact of social inequality in applied fields, such as education, health and welfare. Bernstein, choosing education, then went on to train as a teacher. His first teaching assignment was from 1954 to 1960 at the City Day College. He has recorded his fascination at the challenge of teaching students released for the day from industrial life to undertake education and training. The gap between theoretical discourse and practical engagement must have been especially fascinating in his class on car mechanics: Bernstein has been a lifelong non-driver, so theory must have led practice here (the non-driver status is remarkably common among social theorists – even those residing in the USA – for example: Studs Terkel, Derek Sayer, Gordon Wells, Philip Corrigan, Dick Hebdige).

The workers that Bernstein taught at City Day College had been failed by the formal school system. The interest in language use and the relationship to social class were investigated in a two-year stay in the Department of Phonetics at University College London in the early 1960s. The work of Bernstein's colleague there, Frieda Goldman-Eisler, was important, but perhaps most significant of all was the influence of the socio-linguist M.A.K. Halliday.

These influences and the institutional location in a phonetics department may have consolidated the emerging focus on language and social class.

By now, Bernstein's research programme was clearly defined in a range of published papers and received institutional expression in the founding of the Sociological Research Unit at the London University Institute of Education in 1963. Appointed as a Senior Lecturer in the Sociology of Education,

Bernstein has remained here throughout the rest of his academic career conducting research and supervising doctoral and post-doctoral studies.

The difficulty of summarizing Bernstein's contribution is captured by one of the most eloquent commentators on his work, Paul Atkinson: 'Bernstein suffered the fate of many original thinkers – he was best known for things he had never said or written.'[7] This fate has to be read against Atkinson's general conclusion:

> He is one of the best known and most influential of British sociologists. His work is known throughout the world by sociologists, linguists and educationalists. His writings have been widely reported, reproduced, anthologized and debated. His ideas have been the subject of interest and dispute for many years, and generations of students have been acquainted with at least some version of them. Bernstein's name appears time and time again in textbooks on education and language.[8]

The early work on language and social class became famous, but often in the form of a shorthand misrepresentation. His work on coding systems was indeed his 'lifework', but early on he developed a distinction between 'elaborated codes' (often employed by the middle class) and 'restricted codes'. Similarly, he developed a distinction between 'formal language' and 'public language'. Typically, a middle-class child could speak in both languages, while working-class children were restricted in codes of public language.

This coding theory was open to vulgarization of a number of sorts. Notably, that working-class children were operating with 'linguistic deficits' and (a further step in the naming and blaming process) that these deficits explained their failure in schools. Hence, the locus of blame was neatly shifted from schooling to cultural location, but the variety of misreadings and misinterpretations was manifold. M.A.K. Halliday has tried to unscramble what happened:

> In relation to the general theory of codes, the slogan 'deficit or difference' is entirely beside the point. ... If attaining social equality depends on being educated, and in order to be educated you have to operate with elaborated code, then anyone who has no access to elaborated code, for whatever reason, is being denied social justice: either their access to it must be opened up, or the processes of education must be changed.[9]

But this was not how coding theory was read and received.

> He was by this time being subjected to vicious attacks by (mainly American, but with some fellow-travellers from elsewhere) socio-linguists and educators, for (as they alleged) putting forward a 'deficit' theory of linguistic variation (see for example Labov, 1970). His concept of restricted code was denounced as imputing inferior

intelligence to the working classes, and an entire mythology was built up around the issue of deficit versus difference in which Berstein's assigned role was as whipping-boy for the deficit cause. So consigning the codes to the realm of performance was a way of saying that they had nothing to do with the underlying potential of the system.[10]

This displacement of Bernstein's work should not be allowed to stand: it was a displacement for socio-political purposes to move our gaze from social analysis and diagnosis towards trivial controversy. In fact, Bernstein's concerns were those of the classic sociologists. Above all, he 'has been concerned with cultural transmission' and social reproduction (as has his French counterpart, Pierre Bourdieu). Bernstein's coding theory sits at the heart of his life work:

It was nothing less than a sustained attempt to comprehend the systemic relationships between social class, culture and socialization. Codes were used to express general principles of structuring and reproduction that linked together an array of analytic levels: the division of labor, the distribution of roles and identities, the construction of messages and meaning, the exercise of social control.[11]

Bernstein himself,[12] in the excellent Festschrift organized by Alan Sadovnik,[13] has pronounced on his view of his lifework:

The main drive of my own work developed towards explicating the distinctly sociological regulations on communication. ... My drive was explicitly motivated by the desire to conceptualise code so that its definition would integrate levels of analysis and their cultural regulation. Embedded in the earlier work is a distinction between orientation to meaning and the form of its realisation. *Orientation to meaning* was the fundamental feature with respect to the crucial dimension, context dependence/independence. Form of realisation referred to the regulation of the interactional practice on the *actualising* of the orientation to meaning in speech and conduct. Thus positional and personal forms of familial or school forms of control could be different realisations of the *same* orientation to meaning: elaborated.
    Positional and personal forms of control allowed for differences in *code modality*. Codes regulate more that explicitness and specificity. Users are positioned and oppositioned in contexts which vary in the way power is articulated and subjectivities are constructed and revealed. Positional and personal, however, did not permit the vital distinction between power and control. The higher-order concepts classification and framing were developed in 1971; power relations constructed the principle of the classification and control relations constructed the principle of framing. In this way, orientation to meanings is regulated by classification and

165

framing values. Code modalities transform distributions of power and principles of control into contextually regulated communications.

The research moved towards the construction of specialised semiotic codes, essentially pedagogic codes (provided the latter are broadly defined), in the wider contexts of forms of symbolic control.[14]

This quote provides a reasonable chronological summary of Bernstein's concerns. The early period was primarily concerned with language. In 1971,[15] the work on classification and framing was published and a later paper (1977) on visible and invisible pedagogues.[16] This later paper presages his work on pedagogic discourse (1986,[17] 1990[18]).

The work on classification and framing and pedagogic discourses grows from the concern to extend coding theory into an understanding of the 'message systems' of curriculum and pedagogy. Curriculum defines what counts as valid knowledge, and pedagogy what counts as valid transmission of knowledge. To these, Bernstein added 'evaluation' which defines what counts as valid realization of knowledge by those who have been taught.

In Durkheimian terms, Bernstein sees a move, an evolution from mechanical to organic solidarity. Classification refers to the boundaries between curriculum categories. Strong classification denotes a curriculum that is differentiated and separated into traditional subject knowledge: weak classification denotes an integrated curriculum with weak boundary maintenance. These two types are characterized as collection and integrated codes.

Framing refers to the transmission of what counts as valid school knowledge through pedagogic practices. There, the degree of control that teachers and students possess over the selection and overall organization of school knowledge is analysed. Strong framing limits these options; weak framing implies a wider range of options.

Later work analyses how the 'pedagogic device' is a coding of power where valid school knowledge is differentially distributed among social groups. Here, the concern is to analyse 'the social class assumptions and consequences of forms of pedagogic practices'.[19] The continuities at the heart of Bernstein's work on cultural transmission and social reproduction are evident, in spite of the extending range of his concerns. How, over the years, has this monumental life work been received and recognized? Again, changing historical contexts play a major part in the story. Atkinson et al. state:

It is, indeed, remarkable that a sociologist who has prefigured and reflected fundamental themes and issues in contemporary social thought should not be regarded more widely as a central figure in the academy. The reasons are not hard to find, however. For despite the evident importance of his chosen themes, and the affinities with other scholars who enjoy greater international esteem, Bernstein has always ploughed his own intellectual furrow. He has avoided aligning himself with fashionable positions just for the sake of invoking totemically potent authorities. His research and publications remain unmistakably his own.[20]

His friend, Brian Davies,[21] judges:

> That he is a major, and now lonely figure, is not in dispute. That his complex and still evolving work on the school has not yet been widely appreciated and understood is certain. That these things are a convoluted mixture of his own style, strengths and weaknesses, the times, and the only company that there has been to keep is a proposition worth addressing.[22]

Both these commentaries concentrate on personal characteristics above all, but Davies does mention 'the times' *en passant*.

Perhaps sociological judgements have a tendency to be ahistorical, but here the historical context is a crucial part of the judgements that are called forth. Bernstein has worked all his life on one of the great taboos of our society – the persistent patterns of disadvantage that underpin the social order. In the 1960s and 1970s, for a short time, these taboos were more lightly patrolled than before or since – classification and framing, so to speak, weakened a little. Since then, the tightenings have been persistent and perceptible. The changing regime of English schooling is deeply symptomatic. These changes may be more important explanatory frameworks in terms of Bernstein's life work than questions of personal style. Davies makes the point with regard to recent schooling discourses:

> Within this obsessive equality debate, now largely driven by North American School effectiveness agendas, there is little wonder that those who like technologisable answers have become school improvers. This roughly amounts to a situation where having abandoned 'what makes students able?' – or never having seriously posed it – we find ourselves going on to ask: 'what makes them abler?'[23]

Or, put alternatively, having seen the school to be an effective dispenser of privilege and disadvantage, we ask only how can we make the school more effective.

But having tried to locate personal style in historical context, let me at least respect it and give Bernstein, who died in the year 2000, the final word on the current contexts:

> What stands out is the increasing power of the state over its agencies of symbolic control and the form this power takes – the introduction and celebration of the market as a crucial decentralised relay of state control. Whether this is necessarily always a relay of class ideology remains to be seen. Today the left seems more responsive to social movements, feminism, sexual orientation,

and regionalism as it attempts to create a language freed from the pollution of collectivism and redemptive individualism. It certainly is difficult to talk about class and culture, let alone class culture.[24]

Revisiting the quote at the beginning of this piece, let us think of it as a statement of 'devices and desires', not an anachronism but a testimony to what could once be thought, but for the moment is once again unthinkable, because:

On the one hand, the pedagogic discourse of schools is now more strongly classified, subject boundaries, specialised competencies, basic skills, and teacher rather than student pedagogic relations are emphasised, specific vocational education has little or no place in the national curriculum. What we now have resembles a traditional grammar school model. On the other hand, schools are placed in a competitive market situation, academic success is made public by publishing test and examination results, the administration has been decentralised, and a market orientation is changing the managerial culture. The new decentralised schools, together with the management culture, are the product of the neoliberal wing of the new right *but* the pedagogic discourse and selectivity is the product of more traditional conservatism. Thus tensions within contemporary conservatism at the level of the state are reproduced in tensions in the culture of the school. The state's national testing programme reflects the tensions within contemporary conservatism and between contemporary conservatism and the educational establishment. This culminated in the refusal of teachers to carry out national testing of 14-year-old students, and, finally, in a revision of the whole testing programme for schools.[25]

Notes

1 Bernstein, *Class, Codes and Control: Towards a Theory of Educational Transmissions*, vol. 3, London: Routledge & Kegan Paul, p.71, 2nd edn, 1975.
2 Bernstein, 'Open Schools, Open Society', *New Society*, pp.351–3, 14 September, 1967.
3 Goodson, I.F., 'A Genesis and Genealogy of British Curriculum Studies', in A.R. Sadovnik (ed.), *Knowledge and Pedagogy: The Sociology of Basil Bernstein*, Norwood, NJ: Ablex Publishing Corp, pp.360–1, 1995.
4 Bernstein, *Class, Codes and Control: Applied Studies Towards a Sociology of Language*, vol. 2, chap. 10, London: Routledge & Kegan Paul, 1973.
5 Halliday, M.A.K., 'Language and the Theory of Codes', in A.R. Sadovnik (ed.), *Knowledge and Pedagogy: The Sociology of Basil Bernstein*, Norwood, NJ: Ablex Publishing Corp, p.134, 1995.
6 Bernstein, 'Introduction', in B. Bernstein (ed.), *Class, Codes and Control: Theoretical Studies Towards a Sociology of Language*, vol. 1, London: Routledge & Kegan Paul, p.2, 2nd edn, 1974.
7 Atkinson, P., Davies, B. and Delamont, S., *Discourse and Reproduction: Essays in Honor of Basil Bernstein*, Cresskill, NJ: Hampton Press Inc, p.xi, 1995.
8 Atkinson, P., *Language, Structure and Reproduction: An Introduction to the Sociology of Basil Bernstein*, London: Methuen, p.1, 1985.

9   Halliday, 'Language and the Theory of Codes', op cit., p.134.
10 Ibid., p.133.
11 Atkinson *et al.*, *Discourse and Reproduction*, op cit., pp.x–xi.
12 Bernstein, 'A Response', in A.R. Sadovnik (ed.), *Knowledge and Pedagogy: The Sociology of Basil Bernstein*, Norwood, NJ: Ablex Publishing Corp, pp.385–424, 1995.
13 Sadovnik, A.R., *Knowledge and Pedagogy: The Sociology of Basil Bernstein*, Norwood, NJ: Ablex Publishing Corp, 1995.
14 Bernstein, 'A Response', op cit., p.399.
15 Bernstein, *Class, Codes and Control: Theoretical Studies Towards a Sociology of Language*, vol. 1, London: Routledge & Kegan Paul, 1971.
16 Bernstein, 'Class and Pedagogies: Visible and Invisible', in B. Bernstein (ed.), *Class Codes and Control: Towards a Theory of Educational Transmissions*, vol. 3, London: Routledge & Kegan Paul, pp.116–56, 2nd rev. edn, 1977.
17 Bernstein, 'On Pedagogic Discourse', in J. Richardson (ed.), *Handbook of Theory and Research in the Sociology of Education*, New York: Greenwood Press, pp.205–40, 1986.
18 Bernstein, *Class, Codes and Control: The Structuring of Pedagogic Discourse*, vol. 4, London: Routledge & Kegan Paul, 1990.
19 Ibid., p.63.
20 Atkinson *et al.*, *Discourse and Reproduction*, op cit., p.ix.
21 Davies, B., 'Bernstein, Durkheim and the British Sociology of Education', in A.R. Sadovnik (ed.), *Knowledge and Pedagogy: The Sociology of Basil Bernstein*, Norwood, NJ: Ablex Publishing Corp., pp.39–57, 1995.
22 Ibid., p.40.
23 Ibid., p.46.
24 Bernstein, 'A Response', op cit., p.389.
25 Ibid., p.390.

Bernstein's major writing

'Open Schools, Open Society', *New Society*, 14 September, pp.351–3, 1967.
Class, Codes and Control: Theoretical Studies Towards a Sociology of Language, vol. 1, London: Routledge & Kegan Paul, 2nd edn, 1974, 1971.
Class, Codes and Control: Applied Studies Towards a Sociology of Language, vol. 2, London: Routledge & Kegan Paul, 1973.
Class, Codes and Control: Towards a Theory of Educational Transmission, vol. 3, London: Routledge & Kegan Paul, 1975.
Class, Codes and Control: The Structuring of Pedagogic Discourse, vol. 4, London: Routledge & Kegan Paul, 1990.
Pedagogy, Symbolic Control, and Identity: Theory, Research, and Critique, London and Washington: Taylor & Francis, 1996.

Further reading

Atkinson, P., *Language, Structure and Reproduction: An Introduction to the Sociology of Basil Berstein*, London: Methuen, 1985.
Atkinson, P., Davies, B. and Delamont, S., *Discourse and Reproduction: Essays in Honor of Basil Bernstein*, Cresskill, NJ: Hampton Press Inc, 1995.
Sadovnik, A.R. (ed.), *Knowledge and Pedagogy: The Sociology of Basil Bernstein*, Norwood, NJ: Ablex Publishing Corp, 1995.

IVOR F. GOODSON

MICHEL FOUCAULT 1926–84

> The central issue of philosophy and critical thought since the
> eighteenth century has always been, still is, and will, I hope,
> remain the question, *What* is this Reason that we use? What are
> its historical effects? What are its limits, and what are its dangers?
> How can we exist as rational beings, fortunately committed to
> practising a rationality that is unfortunately criss-crossed by
> intrinsic dangers ...[1]

Michael Foucault was born in Poitiers in 1926 and he died of AIDS in 1984
at the age of fifty-seven years. In his short life span Foucault became an
emblem for a generation of intellectuals – someone who embodied in his
work the most pressing intellectual issues of his time. Jürgen Habermas was
to remark: 'Within the circle of the philosophers of my generation who
diagnosed our times, Foucault has most lastingly influenced the *Zeitgeist*.'[2]
Yet to characterize his work and his ideas is very difficult, because not only
did he change the direction and emphasis of his thought over his lifetime but
also he did not fit into any of the normal academic categories. Georges
Dumèzil, the historian of religion – a mentor and strong intellectual
influence upon Foucault – said that there were a thousand Foucaults: 'he
wore masks, and he was always changing them'.[3] Indeed, Foucault himself
indicated the difficulty of locating his politics in traditional terms:

> I think I have in fact been situated in most squares on the political
> checkerboard, one after the another and sometimes simulta-
> neously: as anarchist, leftist, ostentatious or disguised marxist,
> nihilist, explicit or secret anti-marxist, technocrat in the service of
> Gaullism, new liberal etc. An American professor complained
> that a crypto-marxist like me was invited to the USA, and I was
> denounced by the press in Eastern Europe for being an accomplice
> of the dissidents. None of these descriptions is important by itself;
> taken together, on the other hand, they mean something. And I
> must admit that I rather like what they mean.[4]

Foucault had attended both Kojève's and Hyppolite's lectures on Hegel.
In his inaugural lecture at the Collège de France he named as his closest
supports and models, Dumèzil, Canguilhem (the philosopher of biology
who succeeded Gaston Bachelard at the Sorbonne) and Hyppolite. He was a
student of both Louis Althusser and Maurice Merleau-Ponty. He grew
up in the tradition of a history of philosophy that dominated the French
university, a history that gave pride of place to Hegel and helped to
legitimate the, then, contemporary emphases on phenomenology and
existentialism, especially as it developed in the thought of Jean-Paul Sartre.
He was classified by the popular press as a member of the structuralist Gang
of Four, along with Claude Lévi-Strauss, Jacques Lacan and Roland
Barthes. Foucault indicated his intellectual debts in an early essay entitled
'Nietzsche, Freud, Marx'[5] yet his relationship to Marx and Marxism was
more complex and problematic, than his engagement with Nietzsche, whose
Genealogy of Morals (1887) provided a model for historical study. Foucault

is quoted as saying 'I am simply Nietzschean'.[6] He came to Nietzsche through the writings of Georges Bataille and Maurice Blanchot, both of whom exercise tremendous influence upon his work. Yet it was Nietzsche and Martin Heidegger, whose thought, together, helped Foucault to frame up his life's work as the history by which human beings become subjects and to change the emphasis of his early work from political subjugation of 'docile bodies' to individuals as self-determining beings continually in the process of constituting themselves as ethical subjects.

As a child, Foucault attended local state schools and received his *baccalauréat* at a Catholic school. Later he took his *licence de philosophie* at the *École Normale Supérieure* and was awarded his *agrégation* at the age of twenty-five. In 1950 he took his *licence de psychology* and worked in a psychiatric hospital. Two years later he obtained a diploma in psycho-pathology, publishing a book on mental illness and personality in 1954 – republished in 1966 as *Mental Illness and Psychology* (1976).

Both in this early work and an introduction ('Dream, Imagination and Existence') to the work of the Heideggerian psychotherapist, Ludwig Binswanger, Foucault worked through approaches in phenomenology and existential psychiatry. He went on to work in French departments in Swedish, Polish and German universities, completing his doctorate under Georges Canguilhem in 1959 at the University of Hamburg on a study of madness that became the basis for *Folie et déraison: Histoire de la folie à l'âge classique* (translated as *Madness and Civilization: A History of Insanity in the Age of Reason*, 1992), first published in 1961. In the classical age madness was a legal issue but not yet a medical one. The eighteenth century saw the birth of the asylum as a specific site for madness and the substitution of medical for juridical power. This 'medicalization' of madness based upon the practice of dividing the normal and the pathological, foreshadowed themes that Foucault was to vigorously pursue later in a reformulated fashion in *Naissance de la clinique: Une Archéologie du regard médical*, published in 1963 (translated as *The Birth of the Clinic: An Archaeology of Medical Perception*, 1973) and *Raymond Roussel* (1963).

In the following decade he became the renown iconoclastic philosopher-historian, moving from his first chair as Professor of Philosophy at University of Clemont-Ferrand, to the University of Vincennes, and eventually to the prestigious Collège de France as Professor of the History of Systems of Thought, a self-designation that reflected his own innovative but 'structuralist' leanings that he clearly differentiated from the history of ideas. Indeed, the 'archaeological' distinguished Foucault's method as focusing on the conditions under which a subject is constituted as a possible object of knowledge. In 1966 Foucault's *Les Mots and les choses* (translated as *The Order of Things: An Archaeology of the Human Sciences*, 1970) was published. As he argued in that text: 'Structuralism is not a new method; it is the awakened and troubled consciousness of modern thought.'[7] Yet in the Foreword to the English edition, Foucault also remarked:

> The problem of the subject. In distinguishing between the epistemological level of knowledge (or scientific consciousness) and the archaeological level of knowledge, I am aware I am advancing in a direction that is fraught with difficulty. ... I do not

wish to deny the validity of intellectual biographies, or the possibility of a history of theories, concepts, or themes. It is simply that I wonder whether such descriptions are themselves enough, whether they do justice to the immense density of discourse, whether there do not exist, outside their customary boundaries, systems of regularities that have a decisive role in the history of the sciences.[8]

The Order of Things proposes an archaeology of the human sciences based upon discovering the laws, regularities and rules of the formation of systems of thought which emerged in the nineteenth century. Foucault distinguishes three *epistemes* or system of thought, each with its own distinctive structure: the Renaissance, the classical age and the modern age. Strongly influenced by Nietzsche's *Genealogy of Morals* (1887) and his 'critique of humanism', Foucault embraces a variation of the 'death of God' when he suggests: 'In our day, and once again Nietzsche indicated the turning-point from a long way off, it is not so much the absence or death of God that is affirmed as the end of man ...'[9] and continues 'As the archaeology of our thought easily shows, man is an invention of recent date. And one perhaps nearing its end.'[10]

In their study of Foucault's work, Dreyfus and Rabinow (1982) propose four stages: a Heideggerian stage (typified by his study of madness and reason), an archaeological or quasi-structuralist stage (characterized by *The Archaeology of Knowledge* and *The Order of Things*), a genealogical stage and, finally an ethical stage. The shift from the archaeological to the genealogical stage in Foucault's writings is well represented in *Discipline and Punish*, a work that has direct relevance to educational theory. Like *The History of Sexuality*, *Discipline and Punish* exhibits a Nietzschean genealogical turn focused upon studies of the *will to knowledge* understood as reflecting both discursive and non-discursive (i.e., institutional) practices and, in particular, the complex relations among power, knowledge and the body. *Discipline and Punish*, is concerned with the body as an object of certain disciplinary technologies of power and Foucault examines the genealogy of forms of punishment and the development of the modern penal institution, discussing in turn torture (beginning with the gruesome account of Damien the regicide), punishment (with clear echoes of Nietzsche's famous list of meanings in the *Genealogy*[11]), discipline, and the prison.

The section on 'discipline', organized into three sections, respectively 'docile bodies', 'the means of correct training' and 'panopticism', includes an account of the ways during the seventeenth and eighteenth centuries the disciplines became general formulas of domination. Foucault claims that this new political anatomy was evidenced in a multiplicity of often minor processes at different locations that eventually coalesced into a general method: 'They [i.e., disciplinary techniques] were at work in secondary education at a very early date, later in primary schools; they slowly invested the space of the hospital; and, in a few decades, they restructured the military organization.'[12] Foucault talks of disciplinary techniques in terms of 'the art of distributions', the monastic model of enclosure became the most perfect educational regime and 'partitioning' (every individual had his or her own place). 'The rule of *functional sites*' refers to the ways that architects designed space to correspond to the need to supervise and to prevent 'dangerous communication'. Foucault argues 'the organization of a serial space was one of the great technical mutations of elementary education'[13] that made it possible to supersede the traditional apprenticeship system where the pupil spends a few minutes with the master while the rest of the group remains idle.

Foucault also details 'the control of activities', including the timetable, what he calls 'the temporal elaboration of the act' (e.g., marching), and the correlation of the body and the gesture (e.g. 'good handwriting ... presupposes a gymnastics'), as well as other aspects. He writes:

> To sum up, it might be said that discipline creates out of the bodies it controls four types of individuality, or rather an individuality that is endowed with four characteristics; it is cellular (by play of spatial distribution), it is organic (by the coding of activities), it is genetic (by the accumulation of time), it is combinatory (by the composition of forces). And, in doing so, it operates four great techniques; it draws up tables; it prescribes movements; it imposes exercises; lastly, in order to obtain the combination of forces, it arranges 'tactics'.[14]

He discusses the means of correct training in terms of 'hierarchical observation', as he suggests 'the school building was to be a mechanism for training ...', a 'pedagogical machine',[15] normalizing judgement, and the examination. The examination 'transformed the economy of visibility into the exercise of power', introduced 'individuality into the field of documentation', and 'surrounded by all its documentary techniques, ... [made] each individual a "case"'.[16] Most famously, Foucault discusses 'panopticism' – a system of surveillance, based on Jeremy Bentham's architectural figure, that operates by permitting the relentless and continual observation of inmates at the periphery by officials at the centre, without them ever being seen.

Discipline and Punish is concerned with the operation of technologies of power and their relations to the emergence of knowledge in the form of new discourses, based around modes of objectification through which human beings became subjects. It is a theme that Foucault develops further in his work on the history of sexuality. Foucault asks:

> Why has sexuality been so widely discussed and what has been said about it? What were the effects of power generated by what was said? What are the links between these discourses, these effects of power, and the pleasures that were invested by them? What knowledge was formed as a result of this linkage?[17]

It is in the course of his inquiries into sexuality and the proliferation of associated discourses that Foucault coins the term 'bio-power' considered as a kind of anatomo-politics of the human body and control of the population at large.

In his so-called final 'ethical' phase, Foucault is said to move 'back to the subject', to the ethics of self-formation considered as an ascetic practice. Focuault argues that 'work' done on the self is not to be understood in terms of traditional left wing *models of liberation* but rather as (Kantian) *practices of freedom*, for there is no essential, hidden, or true self, for Foucault, 'concealed, alienated, or imprisoned in and by mechanisms of repression'[18] that is in need of liberation but only a *hermeneutics of the self*, a set of practices of self-interpretation. Foucault emphasizes that freedom is the ontological condition for ethics and, in his works on the history of sexuality, he returns to the Stoics to entertain the notion of 'care for the self' which has priority over and develops earlier than 'care for others'.

The significance of Foucault's thought in relation to education is that he provides theoretical and methodological means to study the field of education, part of the emergent human sciences, focusing on the power/knowledge relations and conditions under which subjects are constituted objects of knowledge. Educationalists are only at the beginning of exploring the relevance and promise of Foucault's thought to their own field.

Notes

1   Michel Foucault, 'Space, Knowledge and Power: Interview', *Skyline*, March, p.19, 1982.
2   Jürgen Habermas, 'Taking Aim at the Heart of the Present', in David Cousens Hoy (ed.), *Foucault: A Critical Reader*, Oxford: Blackwell, p.107, 1986.
3   Cited in Didier Eribon, *Michel Foucault*, trans. Betsy Wing, Cambridge, MA: Harvard University Press, p.xi, 1991.
4   Michel Foucault, 'Polemics, Politics and Problematisation', in *The Foucault Reader*, New York: Pantheon Books, pp.383–4, 1984.
5   Michel Foucault, 'Nietzsche, Freud, Marx', in *Nietzsche*, 'Proceedings of the Seventh International Philosophical Colloquium of the Cahiers de Royaumont', 4–8 July, 1964, Edition de Minuit, Paris, pp.183–200, 1967.
6   Cited in Françoise Dosse, *History of Structuralism, Vol. 1, The Rising Sign, 1945–1966*, Minneapolis, MN and London: University of Minnesota Press, p.374, 1997.
7   Michael Foucault, *The Order of Things*, New York: Vintage, p.208, 1970.
8   Ibid., pp.xiii–xiv.
9   Ibid., p.385.
10 Ibid., p.387.
11 Friedrich Nietzsche, *The Birth of Tragedy* and *The Genealogy of Morals*, trans. Francis Golffing, New York: Anchor Books, p.213, 1956.
12 Michel Foucault, *Discipline and Punish*, trans. Alan Sheridan, Harmondsworth: Penguin, p.138, 1991.
13 Ibid., p.147.
14 Ibid., p.167.
15 Ibid., p.172.
16 Ibid., p.187ff.
17 Michel Foucault, *The History of Sexuality*, vol. 1, London: Allen Lane, Penguin, p.11, 1978.
18 Michel Foucault, 'The Ethics of the Concern for the Self as a Practice of Freedom', in Paul Rabinow, *Michel Foucault: Ethics, Subjectivity and Truth*, London: Penguin, p.283, 1997.

See also

In this book: Heidegger
In *Fifty Major Thinkers on Education*: Nietzsche

Foucault's major writings

The Archaeology of Knowledge, trans. A.M. Sheridan, London: Tavistock, 1977.
The Birth of The Clinic: An Archaeology of Medical Perception, trans. A.M. Sheridan, London: Tavistock, 1973.
Discipline and Punish: The Birth of the Prison, New York: Vintage, 1977.
'On Governmentality', *Ideology and Consciousness*, 6, pp.5–21, 1979.
The History of Sexuality, vol. I, New York: Vintage, 1980.
The Use of Pleasure: The History of Sexuality, vol. II, New York: Vintage, 1985.
The Care of the Self: The History of Sexuality, vol. III, New York: Vintage, 1990.
'Governmentality', in G. Burchell, C. Gordon and P. Miller (eds), *The Foucault Effect: Studies in Governmentality – With Two Lectures by and an Interview with Michel Foucault*, Brighton: Harvester Wheatsheaf, pp.87–104, 1991.
Madness and Civilization: A History of Insanity in the Age of Reason, trans. Richard Howard, London: Routledge, 1992, 1961.
'Michel Foucault: Ethics, Subjectivity and Truth', *The Essential Works of Michel Foucault 1954–1984*, vol. 1, Paul Rabinow (ed.), London: Allen Lane, Penguin, 1997.
Power/Knowledge: Selected Interviews and Other Writings 1972–1977, Colin Gordon (ed.), London: Harvester, 1980.
Politics, Philosophy, and Culture: Interviews and Other Writings, 1977–1984, M. Morris and P. Patton (eds), Routledge: New York, 1988.

Further reading

Dreyfus, H. and Rabinow, P., *Michel Foucault: Beyond Structuralism and Hermeneutics*, Brighton: Harvester Press, pp.208–26, 1982.
Macey, D., *The Lives of Michel Foucault: A Biography*, New York: Pantheon Books, 1993.
Marshall, J., *Michel Foucault: Personal Autonomy and Education*, Dordrecht: Kluwer, 1996.
Smart, B. (ed.), *Michel Foucault: Critical Assessments*, vols 1–3, London: Routledge, 1994.

MICHAEL PETERS

MARGARET DONALDSON 1926–

> some of the skills which we value most highly in our education system are thoroughly alien to the spontaneous modes of functioning of the human mind.[1]

Margaret Donaldson is a developmental psychologist whose theories about the nature and development of the human mind have far-reaching implications for education. She was born in the Scottish town of Paisley, near Glasgow, on 16 June 1926, the eldest of three children. When she was six her family moved from Paisley to a village in Perthshire, where she attended the local primary school and later went to secondary school in Callander. At the age of seventeen she embarked upon a degree in French and German at the University of Edinburgh, thus starting a life-long and distinguished association with the University and city of Edinburgh. After obtaining a first-class degree in 1947, she undertook an M.Ed. in psychology and education, graduating with distinction in 1953. At this point she decided not to become a teacher of French and German, but to pursue her growing interest in children's thinking and learning; she took an assistant lectureship in the Department of Education and completed a Ph.D. on children's thinking in 1956. In 1958 she obtained a lectureship in the Department of Psychology at Edinburgh, and remained there for the rest of her academic career, being appointed to a Readership in 1969 and a Professorship in 1980. She is currently Emeritus Professor of Developmental Psychology at the University of Edinburgh.

At the time when Donaldson was embarking on her career in developmental psychology, British psychology was very much dominated by behaviourist theories. Donaldson, however, became more interested in different theoretical approaches which were emerging from other parts of the world. In 1957, for example, she spent a term in Geneva working with the Swiss psychologist Jean Piaget and his team: she came back impressed by his methods and the scale of his theorizing, but not convinced he was necessarily right. Donaldson was also influenced by the newly emerging work of Soviet psychologists such as Lev Vygotsky and Alexander Luria, and by that of the American psychologist Jerome Bruner. Indeed, she spent several summers during the 1960s working with Bruner and his colleagues at Harvard.

One of Donaldson's early concerns was with the kind of items used in intelligence tests. She became interested in why children find particular questions difficult, and spent time trying to elicit the reasons behind children's responses to such questions.[2] She found that children often failed to provide correct answers because they did not stick strictly to the information provided in the question. Instead they would import ideas of their own – which often made human sense – but which were irrelevant to the task at hand. As we shall see, this is a theme, which was to recur strongly in Donaldson's later work.

During the 1960s Donaldson became particularly interested in the thinking and language of pre-school children. She set up a nursery within the Psychology Department at Edinburgh which was attended by local children aged between three and five years. These children were studied intensively by Donaldson, her colleagues and her students. The insights created by these studies formed the basis of *Children's Minds*, Donaldson's best-known and most highly acclaimed book, which was published in 1978.

The central idea of *Children's Minds* is the distinction between thinking which is 'embedded' within contexts that make human sense and thinking which is not embedded in this way. According to Donaldson, thinking which takes place within the context of familiar or readily understandable human purposes is relatively easy for us. In such contexts, humans are usually able to reason or think logically about problems, particularly if the conclusion that is reached is not in conflict with their existing knowledge or beliefs. Indeed, examples of such reasoning can be seen among children as young as three or four years of age. However, when we are required to move 'beyond the bounds of human sense', so that our thinking is no longer sustained by the supportive context of meaningful events, then even adults encounter considerable difficulties. This kind of thinking Donaldson referred to as 'disembedded', a term which she hoped would convey the notion that 'this is thought which has been prised out of the old primitive matrix within which originally all our thinking is contained'.[3]

This distinction between 'embedded' and 'disembedded' thinking is well illustrated by comparing two tasks used to study young children's egocentrism. The term 'egocentrism' comes from the work of Piaget[4] and concerns the ability to take account of another person's point of view. It was Piaget's belief that children below the age of six or seven years are typically egocentric in this sense, and he devised a number of tasks which appear to demonstrate this.

In one well-known task, children are seated at a table on which there is a model of three mountains, each a different colour. A doll is placed at a different position on the table, and the child is asked to select a picture which shows the doll's view of the mountains. Piaget found that children up to the age of seven or eight years have considerable difficulty with this task, and will often select a picture showing their own view of the mountains instead of the doll's. Piaget concluded that young children's egocentrism prevents them from realizing that their own viewpoint is only one among several.

In *Children's Minds*, Donaldson contrasts the mountain task with another task devised to test children's egocentrism. In this task there are three dolls, two of which are policemen and one is a little boy. The child is then asked to hide the boy within a configuration of model walls so that he cannot be seen by either policeman. To do this successfully, children have to ignore their own view of the scene and take account of the different viewpoints of the other participants. However, despite their supposed egocentrism, children as young as three or four years are able to succeed in this task with little difficulty.[5]

According to Donaldson, these two tasks provide a good illustration of the difference between embedded and disembedded thinking. In the policeman task, the purposes and motives of the participants are clear and readily understandable to a young child: the task is embedded in a context that makes human sense. In contrast, the mountain task – like many of Piaget's tasks – is not embedded in such a context: there are no clear intentions or purposes which would make the task instantly intelligible. It is not surprising, then, that young children find it difficult.

This distinction between embedded and disembedded thinking is perhaps the single most important idea in *Children's Minds*. It is also a distinction which is of crucial importance in understanding why so many children have difficulty in school. For, as Donaldson argues, 'the better you are at tackling problems without having to be sustained by human sense, the more likely you are to succeed in our education system'.[6] As a result, we end up with a small number of educational 'successes', and a large number of educational 'failures'.

How can we avoid this state of affairs? In *Children's Minds*, Donaldson describes a number of ways in which schools might help children overcome the difficulties involved in acquiring disembedded modes of thinking. In particular, she places great emphasis on the process of reading, believing this to be of crucial importance in the early years of school. However, she stresses that this is not simply to ensure that children have the practical skill of reading texts, important though this obviously is. Rather, 'the hope, then, is that reading can be taught in such a way as greatly to enhance the child's reflective awareness, not only of language as a symbolic system, but of the processes of his own mind'.[7] Donaldson therefore emphasizes the importance of making children aware of the relationship between spoken and written language, of giving them time to reflect rather than having to respond quickly, and of allowing them to make errors and learn from them. She also advocates that children should be told about the nature of the system they are encountering at a relatively early stage – for example, that there is not a simple one-to-one correspondence between written letters and spoken sounds.

Children's Minds was extremely well received by a wide range of readers. Like all of Donaldson's writing, the arguments were presented with extreme lucidity, and they struck a resonant chord with a large number of her readers. As a result, many teachers in primary schools re-assessed the assumptions they were making about the capabilities of young children, as well as the appropriateness of such Piagetian notions as 'readiness to learn'. Developmental psychologists, for their part, began to re-examine the techniques they used to assess children's abilities, and to explore the implications of Donaldson's ideas in other areas, such as the learning of mathematics.[8]

After *Children's Minds*, Donaldson's work developed in two main directions. She continued to give substantial attention to the teaching of literacy, and in 1989 produced a powerfully argued critique of methods which were currently in vogue – such as the enthusiasm for 'real books' and the notion that learning literacy is essentially a similar process to learning to use spoken language.[9] She also wrote a number of fiction books for children, which drew on the understanding of children which she had gained through her research.[10]

Donaldson's major concern, however, was with remedying what she felt to be some of the shortcomings of *Children's Minds*. In particular, she felt that the processes involved in moving from embedded to disembedded thinking had not been adequately described, and that she had given insufficient attention to the role of emotion. She therefore embarked upon a lengthy period of intellectual inquiry which resulted in 1992 in the publication of *Human Minds*.[11]

In *Human Minds*, Donaldson proposes a model of mental development based around four main modes of mental functioning. Each mode is defined in terms of the mind's locus of concern at any particular time, or what its mental activity is about. In the first mode, which Donaldson terms the *point mode*, the locus of concern is with the immediate present (or 'here and now'): this mode of functioning starts to appear around the age of two to three months. In the second, or *line mode*, the locus of concern goes beyond the here and now to include specific events recalled from the past or anticipated in the future: this mode starts to emerge at around eight to nine months. In the third or *construct mode*, which becomes available from the age of three or four years, the locus of concern moves from the specific to the general: the concern is now with 'how things are in the world' or 'the general nature of things'. The final mode is the *transcendent mode*, in which the locus of concern has moved beyond space and time – for example, when operating in the abstract realms of mathematics or logic. This final mode, according to Donaldson, is not necessarily attained by everyone.

Donaldson's four modes of mental functioning might seem at first sight similar to Piaget's main stages of development, but in fact they are profoundly different. One very important difference is that each Piagetian stage grows out of and supersedes the previous one. By contrast, each of the modes of functioning that Donaldson defines is still available after a new one has been acquired: the modes follow one another developmentally, but do not replace each other. Thus we continue to use the early modes throughout life and end up with a repertoire of modes, not with a single 'adult' way of functioning that is quite beyond a child's reach. In this respect, then, adults are much closer to children than many people might believe.

A further important feature of Donaldson's model of development is that it gives emotion – which Donaldson defines as ' value feelings' – the same prominence as thought. In so doing, Donaldson was very aware that she was departing from the custom of modern Western culture, in which emotion is often considered to be inferior to logic or reason. In fact, as Donaldson argues, emotion and thought are often closely related. Thus in the point and line modes of functioning, emotion and thought are usually bound up with each other, as indeed they are for much of the construct mode. However, there are times in the construct mode where thought is strongly dominant, and Donaldson refers to this as the *intellectual construct mode*: for example, when performing mathematical calculations about hypothetical situations. In addition, there are also times in this mode when emotion is dominant to thinking, and Donaldson refers to this as the *value-sensing construct mode*: some emotional responses to art or music might fall into this category. In similar fashion, Donaldson makes an important distinction between the *intellectual transcendent mode* and the *value-sensing transcendent mode*. The former might include abstract reasoning in mathematics or logic: the latter, in contrast, is primarily found in accounts of spiritual or religious experiences.

As this last sentence suggests, Donaldson's argument in *Human Minds* took her well outside the realm of developmental psychology and led her to explore the history of science, the nature of Buddhism and the varieties of religious or spiritual experience. Indeed, it is this journeying through unexpected but none-the-less relevant fields which makes *Human Minds* such a distinctive and fascinating book. However, in the final chapter, Donaldson returns to consider the educational implications of her model of development. Two main ideas emerge.

First, Donaldson argues that the acquisition of the point and line modes, as well as much learning within the core construct mode, occur spontaneously and naturally: children learn much through their informal and unplanned encounters with the world around them, and particularly with more knowledgeable adults. However, learning in the higher modes – the intellectual and value-sensing modes – does not take place this way. If we want all children to acquire the potential to use these modes – and Donaldson argues strongly that we do – then we need to teach them formally and explicitly. And we should also recognize the difficulty in doing so.

Second, Donaldson argues that approaches to education which are termed 'child-centred' – those which are based around the child's interests or wishes – will not be adequate to the task. While she strongly advocates the importance of seeing things from the child's point of view, she also maintains that the child's point of view is limited: children do not know the possibilities that lie ahead of them. At the same time, she rejects the other extreme, which she terms a 'culture-centred' approach. Such an approach – which attempts to impose uniformity and standards at the expense of creativity – is also limited, as it ignores the child's point of view. She thus argues for a 'decentred' approach to education, explicitly using Piaget's term to advocate an approach which takes account both of the child's point of view and that of the culture to which they belong.

If we consider Donaldson's writings as a whole, there is no doubt that she has made a huge and far-reaching contribution to our thinking about education. She has reminded us of the importance (and limitations) of seeing the child's point of view; she has challenged orthodoxies, both in developmental theory and in teaching practice; she has put forward her own highly original theory of how the human mind develops, and she has argued for approaches to education which treat the development of both intellect and emotion with the highest regard. Above all, she has demonstrated in the clearest possible way that our educational aspirations will only be fully realized if they are based on an accurate and deeply rooted understanding of the nature of children's – and human – minds.

Notes

1 Donaldson, *Children's Minds*, London: Fontana, p.15, 1978.
2 Donaldson, *A Study of Children's Thinking*, London: Tavistock, 1963.
3 Donaldson, *Children's Minds*, op cit., p76.
4 See for example, J. Piaget and B. Inhelder, *The Child's Conception of Space*, London: Routledge, 1956.
5 M. Hughes and M. Donaldson, 'The Use of Hiding Games for Studying the Co-ordination of Viewpoints', *Educational Review*, 31, pp.133–40, 1979.
6 Donaldson, *Children's Minds*, op cit., pp.77–8.
7 Ibid., p.99.
8 See for example, M. Hughes, *Children and Number*, Oxford: Blackwell, 1986.
9 Donaldson, *Sense and Sensibility: Some Thoughts on the Teaching of Literacy*, Occasional paper 3, Reading and Language Information Centre, University of Reading, 1989.
10 See for example, Donaldson, *Journey into War*, London: Andre Deutsch, 1979.
11 Donaldson, *Human Minds: An Exploration*, London: Allen Lane, Penguin, 1992.

See also

In this book: Bruner, Piaget, Vygotsky

Donaldson's major writings

A Study of Children's Thinking, London: Tavistock, 1963.
Children's Minds, London: Fontana, 1978.
Donaldson, M., with Grieve, R. and Pratt, C., *Early Childhood Development and Education: Readings in Psychology*, Oxford: Blackwell, 1983.
Human Minds: An Exploration, London: Allen Lane, Penguin, 1992.
Humanly Possible: Education and the Scope of the Mind, in D. Olson and N. Torrance (eds), *The Handbook of Education and Human Development*, Oxford: Blackwell, pp.324–44, 1996.

Further reading

Bryant, P., 'Constraints of Context: A Review of Human Minds', *Times Higher Education Supplement*, 25 September, 1992.
Grieve, R. and Hughes, M., *Understanding Children: Essays in Honour of Margaret Donaldson*, Oxford: Blackwell, 1990.

MARTIN HUGHES

IVAN ILLICH 1926–

> Yes, my work is an attempt to accept with great sadness the fact of Western culture. Dawson has a passage where he says that the Church is Europe and Europe is the Church, and I say yes! *Corruptio optimi quae est pessima*. Through the attempt to insure, to guarantee, to Regulate Revelation, the best becomes the worst. And yet at any moment we might still recognize, even when we are Palestinians, that there is a Jew lying in the ditch whom I can take in my arms and embrace.
>
> I live also with a profound sense of ambiguity. I can't do without tradition, but I have to recognize that its institutionalization is the root of an evil deeper than any evil I could have known with my unaided eyes and mind. This is what I would call the West. By studying and accepting the West as the perversion of Revelation, I become increasingly tentative, but also more curious and totally engaged in searching for its origin, which is the voice of him who speaks. It's as simple as that ... childish if you want, childlike, I hope.
>
> (from *Ivan Illich: In Conversation*, pp.242–3)[1]

Ivan Illich, iconoclastic historian and social critic, has worked as parish priest, university administrator and professor, centre director, lecturer and author. He is best known in educational circles for the work that he did in the late 1960s and 1970s, particularly his second book, *Deschooling Society*.[2] When Illich speaks of 'the West as the perversion of Revelation', one could easily conclude that his theological beliefs have driven his social criticisms. It would be unlikely, however, for students of educational thought to arrive at this same conclusion if they limited their reading of Illich to *Deschooling Society*. Driven by his belief that any form of secular power or social activism lay beyond the specific mission of the Church, Illich declared, in an earlier essay, a need for 'radically humanist ideals' and 'consciously secular ideology' to help plan and achieve 'inventive solutions to social problems'.[3] Accordingly, until very recently, Illich, writing as a radical humanist, remained consciously secular in the language he used to discuss social problems. Nevertheless, students of Illich would be well advised to read him through both secular and theological lenses.

Born the eldest of three sons in September of 1926 in Vienna, Austria, Illich's radical devotion to the Church incubated during the turbulent years of his youth. Foreshadowing his existence as a pilgrim and a deliberately intenerate scholar, he spent part of each of the first four years of his life living in Dalmatia, Vienna, and France or wherever his parents happened to be. His grandfather's house in Vienna, however, came to be his primary place of residence during the 1930s. Throughout these early years, Illich's intellectual development benefited not only from the time he spent with a number of different governesses who taught him many of the languages in which he became fluent, and reading from his grandmother's substantial library, but also from his interactions with the many notable intellectuals included among his parents' circle of friends (e.g., Rudolf Steiner, Rainer Maria Rilke and Jacques Maritain, not to mention the family physician of Sigmund Freud). Nonetheless, the young Illich was regarded as too 'retarded' to attend school and, thus, retained.

In 1938, Hitler's armies occupied Austria. As the son of a wealthy Dalmatian engineer and a Sephardic Jewish mother, Illich was subject to the Nazi regime's fluctuating definition of Aryan and Jew. In 1941, he, along with his mother and younger twin brothers, fled Austria, staying mainly in Italy. Though he reports difficulty in explaining the decision, it was during this period in his life that Illich entered the priesthood.

By age twenty-four, he had been ordained and completed master's degrees in theology and philosophy at Rome's Gregorian University. Shortly thereafter, he earned a doctorate in the philosophy of history from the University of Salzburg. It was at Salzburg, under the tutelage of Professors Albert Auer and Michael Muechlin, that Illich developed a fascination for the study of historical method and the interpretation of old texts. Auer, whose writings on the theology of suffering in the twelfth century hold particular relevance for Illich, worked closest with Illich in helping him complete his doctoral thesis on Arnold Toynbee's philosophical and historical methods. Illich would also pursue further advanced studies in chemistry (crystallography) at the University of Florence.

Though his recognized brilliance, aristocratic sophistication, and piety marked him as an ideal candidate for the Vatican's high ranking diplomatic core, Illich's critical view of the institutional dimensions of the Church that he would later express in his writings prompted him to turn down an invitation to attend the Church's Collegio di Nobili Ecclesiastici. Instead, in 1951, he chose to leave Rome altogether to conduct postdoctoral studies on Albert the Great's work in alchemy at Princeton University.

On the evening of his arrival in New York, however, a conversation developed over dinner at a friend's house that led Illich to drop those plans. The topic of that conversation was the 'Puerto Rican problem' in New York. Shortly thereafter, he went to the office of Cardinal Spellman to request assignment to a Puerto Rican parish. The Cardinal obliged the young cleric's wishes, assigning him to the Incarnation Parish in Washington Heights, a historically Irish community that was experiencing a dramatic influx of Puerto Rican immigrants.

To the New York Archdiocese, the 'Puerto Rican problem' was an issue of 'integrating' these immigrants into American-style Catholicism – an idea that Illich regarded as chauvinistic and completely at odds with Christian love. To Illich, 'any feeling of cultural superiority is as powerful a manifestation of original sin as the confusion of tongues at Babel. The process of obtaining grace', he stressed, 'might involve a total stripping of cultural values, "a beatitude of cultural poverty".'[4]

Immediately upon reporting to Incarnation Parish, he began developing and practising an entirely different approach. First, Illich developed fluency in Spanish within three months of his arrival. An initial three-week period of training in a Berlitz programme enabled Illich to cultivate his fluency through his face-to-face interactions with the Puerto Rican immigrants themselves. Second, unlike his American counterparts, Illich immersed himself in the cultural patterns of the Puerto Ricans to better understand how he could bring himself into friendship with them. Not only did he spend tremendous amounts of time participating with the Puerto Ricans in their cultural activities in New York, he also took his vacations in Puerto Rico, where he walked, rode horseback and hitchhiked the entire length and width of the island learning about and ministering to the people's religious needs as they defined them. This cultural immersion, of course, greatly facilitated his fluency in Spanish. It enabled him, as he beautifully explains in 'The Eloquence of Silence',[5] to learn not just the sounds of the language, but also its silences. Such an approach to linguistic training would later be a hallmark of the Spanish language institutes that he went on to establish in Puerto Rico and Mexico. Finally, Illich also researched and educated himself about the distinctive character of the Puerto Rican immigration – how it differed from previous patterns of immigration to the United States, and how the historical conditions in Puerto Rico accounted for the distinctive qualities of Puerto Ricans as Catholics. He presents many of his findings on these matters in the essay, 'Not Foreigners, Yet Foreign'.[6]

As evidence of the success of his approach to ministering to the needs of the Puerto Rican immigrants in New York, we should note that it was Illich who helped pioneer what came to be known as San Juan's Day. Shortly before the first celebration of this national feast day, one police official predicted to Illich that he should expect 5,000 people to attend the Fiesta. In fact, over 35,000 people attended that first San Juan's Day celebration on the football field at Fordham University. Moreover, Illich had become the idol of his displaced flock.

Illich's success in working with the Puerto Ricans led to his being made the youngest monsignor (age twenty-nine) in the history of the American church and coordinator of the Office of Spanish–American Affairs. In 1955, he was appointed to serve as the Vice-Rector of the Catholic University of Puerto Rico at Ponce. His charge was to create a centre (Institute of Intercultural Communications (IIC)) that would immerse American priests in Puerto Rican and Latin American culture. In addition to subjecting the missionaries-in-training to very intensive training in the Spanish language, Illich also tried to insure that the patterns of daily living within the Institute would reflect, to the fullest extent possible, the patterns of Puerto Rican culture. In this way, Illich hoped, the priests would come to recognize and resist the arrogance and the violence of cultural imposition that had been historically perpetrated by the Church and its 'ecclesiastical conquistadores'.[7] After five years on the island, due to his violation of the Bishop of Ponce's ban on association with the pro-contraception gubernatorial candidate, Muñoz Marin, Illich was ordered to leave Puerto Rico.

After a brief return to New York, Illich flew to South America, where he proceeded to walk and hitchhike the three thousand miles from Santiago, Chile to Caracas, Venezuela searching for a location to establish a new centre. He hoped to create this new centre in 'a valley with excellent climate, with a town not more than an hour away from a great library and a good university, where housing and food would be cheap enough to accommodate many students'.[8] He would later find these ideal conditions in Cuernavaca, Mexico, which offered the additional attraction of being located in the most progressive parish in Latin America, headed by the controversial figure of Bishop Mendez Arceo.

With the endorsement of Bishop Arceo, Cardinal Spellman, and Fordham University, Illich established his new centre for 'de-Yankeefication' in 1961. Originally named the Center of Intercultural Formation (CIF), it would later become known as the Center of Intercultural Documentation (CIDOC). Illich created this centre as an effort to subvert President Kennedy's Alliance for Progress (which he viewed as a propagation of American-styled bourgeois appetites at the expense of cultures and livelihoods in the south) and the Papal decree ordering the American Church to send 10 per cent of its priests and religious (approximately 35,000 people) to Latin America. In essence, Illich intended CIDOC to serve many of the same purposes that IIC had served in Puerto Rico. Because the Papal order was so obviously tied to the Alliance For Progress, however, Illich brought an even greater sense of urgency to this project than he had in Puerto Rico. 'I was opposed', he explains,

> to the execution to this order: I was convinced that it would do serious damage to those sent, to their clients, and to their sponsors back home. I had learned in Puerto Rico that there are only a few people who are not stunted, or wholly destroyed, by lifelong work 'for the poor' in a foreign country. The transfer of United States living standards and expectations could only impede the revolutionary changes needed, and the use of the gospel in the service of capitalism or any other ideology was wrong.[9]

At all times, Illich believes, the Church while upholding its prophetic mission must denounce without sanctioning. Only in this way can the Church avoid legitimizing the political affairs of the world. While withdrawing itself from direct social and political endorsement, the Church must celebrate the mystery of faith out of which radical personal and social change arises. This theological stance – a commitment which prejudices that Church as She (the mystery of God's presence, the kingdom among us) over the Church as It (the institutional incarnation) – earned Illich enemies on the left and right, both within and outside of the Church. Though as a person he embraced controversial political positions, as a clergyman Illich remained deeply consigned to his theological conservatism and the surprising activity of the Holy Spirit.

In his prophetic call for a less-bureaucratic, lay-led, and more humble Church, Illich added fuel to his enemies' fire. Repeated petitions to the New York Archdiocese by ultra-conservative leaders urged his recall from Mexico. Equally enraged requests to the Vatican resulted in Illich's summons to appear before the Congregation for the Doctrine of the Faith (an offshoot of the Sacred Congregation of the Universal Inquisition) in June 1968.

In humble submission, he flew immediately to Rome. Exercising absolute canonical correctness, Illich appeared, read the long questionnaire mired in dubious accusation, withheld his defence, and returned to Cuernavaca. By his silence, Illich opted to spare the Church the embarrassment of its perverse activity. Three months later, his request for leave in order to live as a layman was granted.

In January of 1969, a Papal ban forbade all Catholic priests, monks and nuns from attending courses or seminars at CIDOC. Immediately, Illich sent details of his inquisition to the *New York Times* Religion editor. By March of that year, Illich, one of the Church's most brilliant and obedient servants, permanently resigned.

Despite the ban against CIDOC and its subsequent repeal in June of 1969, the work at the Center continued without interruption. Having worked on public schooling while in Puerto Rico, where he met Everett Reimer (the person whom he credits for having stimulated his interest in public education) Illich turned his attention to the new 'church' – schooling. From 1969–70, CIDOC hosted a series of seminars titled 'Alternatives in Education'. Reimer, Paul Goodman, Joel Spring, John Holt, Jonathan Kozol and Paulo Freire were among the many notable participants in those seminars. Several publications resulted from these gatherings, most notably, *Deschooling Society.*

Readers of Illich should know that he did not name his book *Deschooling Society.* Cass Canfield, Sr, the president of Harper's gave the book its startling name for marketing purposes. Illich did not argue for the elimination of schools, but rather for their *disestablishment.* By this he meant that public funding should not be used to support schools. To the contrary, he believed that schools should be required to pay taxes so that schooling would come to be recognized as a luxury object, thus providing the legal basis for discontinuing discrimination against people for their lack of schooling. This, in effect, would create a separation of school and state similar to the separation of church and state recognized under the US Constitution. It would also, Illich believed, lead to an improvement in the quality of education. Because education would cease to be compulsory, the pursuit of learning could be pursued with more authentic purpose and without ulterior motive by those who sought it, and it could be provided as an act of leisure and a gift of love and mercy by those in possession of the knowledge being sought.

Furthermore, readers of Illich should also understand that his thoughts and his approach toward the study of schooling and education began to shift even before the actual release of *Deschooling Society*. Methodologically, the phenomenological mode of analysis that he employed in *Deschooling* stemmed from his long-held interest in a very special branch of *ecclesiology*. For Illich, ecclesiology is 'the predecessor to sociology', in that it entails the 'scientific study of that particular community which the church conceives as its ideal, and has since the fourth century'.[10] And within ecclesiology is *liturgy*, that branch of ecclesiology focusing on rituals and the manner in which they 'create that community which then calls itself the church and is studied by ecclesiology'.[11] Hence, one of the most important chapters in *Deschooling Society* is titled 'The Ritualization of Progress'. In that essay Illich describes how:

> the school system today performs the threefold function common to powerful churches throughout history. It is simultaneously the repository of society's myth, the institutionalization of that myth's contradictions, and the locus of the ritual which reproduces and veils the disparities between myth and reality.[12]

Similar to the way that the Church as It made religion compulsory for the salvation of needy souls, schooling had become the 'New World Religion' or ritual necessary for participation in society, a means by which the educationally needy secured secular salvation.

Even prior to the release of *Deschooling Society*, however, Illich developed misgivings about his call for the disestablishment of schools. He recalls that Wolfgang Sachs and a small group of other students whom Illich met with in Germany, criticized the articles collected in *Deschooling*, claiming:

> that by making so much of the unwanted side effects of compulsory schooling, I had become blind to the fact that the educational function was already emigrating from the schools and that, increasingly, other forms of compulsory learning would be instituted in modern society.[13]

These other forms of learning (e.g., television, compulsory in-service training, workshops, etc. would not be compulsory in a legalistic sense, but they would use other means of making people believe that they are learning something.

Consequently, Illich shifted the focus of his work from the phenomen-ological process of schooling to the cultural orientation that produced it. How did people become so addicted to the idea of education? For Illich, the answer to this question rests in understanding how the assumption of scarcity, the core presupposition of the economic world-view, has led people to view as an education 'need'. Under the law of scarcity, all of our needs are great, but our means to satisfy those needs are scarce. This includes our means to satisfy our 'need' to learn. In his shift toward becoming a historian of scarcity, Illich recognized that:

By the early seventeenth century a new consensus began to arise: the idea that man was born incompetent for society and remained so unless he was provided with 'education'. Education came to mean the inverse of vital competence. It came to mean a process rather than the plain knowledge of the facts and the ability to use tools which shape a man's concrete life. Education came to mean an intangible commodity that had to be produced for the benefit of all, and imparted to them in the manner in which the visible Church formerly imparted invisible grace. Justification in the sight of society became the first necessity for a man born in original stupidity, analogous to original sin.[14]

As a historian who revels in viewing the contemporary world from the twelfth century, Illich notes how today's certainties were non-existent yesterday. In calling the history of the last 500 years 'a war against subsistence', Illich shows the careful reader how in designing our existence, people must redesign themselves to fit their new systems and creations. A cosmos formerly in the hands of God is now in the hands of man.

As a philosopher, Illich is commonly categorized as a religious, anti-technology theorist, as distinct from secular anti-technology philosophers (e.g., Junger, Marcuse, Habermas, etc.). He betrays, however, every attempt to categorize and classify. Neither anti-school, anti-institution, nor anti-technology, Illich is simply acutely conscious of those creations that limit the possibility of extending the hand of friendship to the Other just across the threshold. In all of Illich's writings the extension and cultivation of *philia*, the love born of friendship, is his principal concern.

Notes

1 David Cayley, *Ivan Illich in conversation*, Concord, Ontario: House of Anansi Publications, pp.242–3, 1992.
2 Ivan Illich, *Deschooling Society*, New York: Harper & Row, 1970.
3 Ivan Illich, *Celebration of Awareness: A Call for Institutional Revolution*, New York: Doubleday, pp.102 and 103, 1970.
4 Francine du Plessix Gray, *Divine Disobedience: Profiles in Catholic Radicalism*, New York: Vintage Books, p.245, 1971.
5 Illich, *Celebration of Awareness*, op cit., pp.41–51.
6 Ibid., pp.29–40.
7 Gray, *Divine Disobedience*, op cit., p.244.
8 Ibid., p.251.
9 Illich, *Celebration of Awareness*, op cit., pp.53–4.
10 Cayley, *Ivan Illich in Conversation*, op cit., p.65.
11 Ibid., p.66.
12 Illich, *Deschooling Society*, op cit., p.54.
13 Cayley, *Ivan Illich in Conversation*, op cit., p.70.
14 Ivan Illich, *Toward a History of Needs*, Berkeley, CA: Heyday Books, pp.75–6, 1977.

See also

In this book: Freire, Habermas
In *Fifty Major Thinkers on Education*: Steiner

Illich's major writings

A Celebration of Awareness: A Call for Institutional Revolution, New York: Doubleday, 1970.
Deschooling Society, New York: Harper & Row, 1970.
Tools for Conviviality, New York: Harper & Row, 1973.
Medical Nemesis: The Expropriation of Health, New York: Pantheon, 1973.
Energy and Equity, New York: Harper & Row, 1974.
Toward a History of Needs, Berkeley, CA: Heyday Books, 1977.
Shadow Work, London: Marion Boyers, 1981.
Gender, New York: Pantheon Books, 1982.
Illich, I., with Barry Sanders, *ABC: The Alphabetization of the Popular Mind*, Berkeley, CA: North Point Press, 1988.
In the Mirror of the Past: Lectures and addresses, 1978–1990, London: Marion Boyers, 1992.
In the Vineyard of the Text, Chicago, IL: University of Chicago Press, 1993.

Further reading

Aries, Phillipe, *Centuries of Childhood: A Social History of Family Life*, New York: Knopt, 1962.
Cayley, David, *Ivan Illich: In Conversation*, Concord, Ontario: House of Anansi Publications, 1992.
Elias, John, *Conscientization and Deschooling: Freire's and Illich's Proposals for Reshaping Society*, Philadelphia, PA: Westminster Press, 1976.
Ellol, J., *The Technological Society*, New York: Knopf, 1964.
Gray, Francine du Plessix, *Divine Disobedience: Profiles in Catholic Radicalism*, New York: Vintage Books, 1971.
Kohr, Leopold, *The Breakdown of Nations*, London and New York: Routledge & Kegan Paul, 1986.
Ladner, Gerhard, *The Idea of Reform*, Santa Fe, NM: Gannon, 1970.
Pieper, Joseph , *The Silence of St. Thomas*, New York: Pantheon, 1957.
Polanyi, Karl, *The Great Transformation*, New York: Octagon Books, 1975.
Prakash, H. S. and Esteva, G., *Escaping Education: Living as Learning within Grassroots Cultures*, New York: Lang, 1998.
Sachs, Wolfgang (ed.), *The Development Dictionary*, London: Zed Books, 1992.

DAVID A. GABBARD AND DANA L. STUCHUL

LAWRENCE KOHLBERG 1927–87

> In our research, we have found definite and universal levels of development in moral thought.[1]

Lawrence Kohlberg was an educator, psychologist and philosopher, and regarded by many as an intellectual giant who followed in the footsteps of Socrates, Jean Piaget and John Dewey. Kohlberg's work was centred on the development of moral judgement in children and adults using a cognitive developmental approach involving Piagetian stage theory. A second stream of research and publication focused on moral behaviour, and here notions of just communities and democratic action dominated his work. His influence on educational practice is found in educational curricula for moral development and in models for school administration and governance. Beyond the educational sphere, Kohlberg's work has had a profound impact on other areas of adult development, such as community-based education, religious education, prison education and education in the professions. Spanning traditional disciplinary boundaries and moving between description of empirical reality and normative philosophical principles of justice and fairness, Kohlberg was at once an objective researcher and passionate advocate of democratic and liberal values and institutions. 'The central characteristic of my theory or research programme has been its interdisciplinary nature, using empirical psychological and anthropological data to make philosophical claims, and using philosophic assumptions to define and interpret psychological, anthropological, and educational data' (Kohlberg 1985, p.505).[2]

Kohlberg himself described the genesis of his interest in morality as rooted in the experience of the Nazi tyranny during his time in boarding school and college. His interest in morality and moral education 'arose in part as a response to the Holocaust [and] the slow but continuing effort of world society to make some moral sense of [it]'.[3] His first published article in 1948 was the account of a ship crew's heroic attempt at smuggling European Jews to Palestine. As an undergraduate at the University of Chicago, he read Kantian ethics and the political philosophies of Locke, Jefferson and John Stewart Mill, related to universal human rights. During the time of his graduate studies in psychology he began to formulate his theory of moral development based on Piaget and Dewey. He completed his doctoral studies at the University of Chicago in 1958 with a dissertation on the development of modes of moral thinking and choice among adolescents. After six years in the psychology department of the University of Chicago he transferred to the Graduate School of Education at Harvard in 1968 where he completed the majority of his research and writing until his death in 1987. During his years at Harvard, Kohlberg trained groups of students and researchers who would continue, expand and critique his work, and he conducted pilot programmes of moral education in schools, prisons and other institutions. The two foci of his work are the theoretical and empirical research on moral development and the establishment of just communities – models of schools and prisons built upon democratic principles of justice and fairness that represent the most developed stages of moral thinking.

Kohlberg's concern with moral development is central to education and goes back in time at least as far as Plato's Socrates whose dialogue with Meno centres around the question of whether virtue is something that can be taught, whether it comes by practice, or whether it arises from natural aptitude or instinct. The question is central to civilized society and the lives of individuals because without virtues or morality societies will quickly degenerate into a Hobbesian 'war of every man against every man', as was witnessed during the totalitarian regimes throughout history. Values motivate behaviour and morality, thus, they are fundamental to the everyday decisions; moral judgement and thinking are second nature, whether done consciously or not. During the centuries since Plato, philosophers have proposed different answers to Meno's question and so have educators. In a seminal article in the *Harvard Education Review* in 1972, Kohlberg summarized three broad streams in the development of Western educational thought: romanticism, cultural transmission and progressivism.[4] The romantic view of education follows the philosophies of Jean Rousseau, George H. Mead and G. Stanley Hall, and is exemplified by A.S. Neill's Summerhill movement. In this view, what comes from within the child is the most important aspect of development, and education should allow the child's inner good to come to the fore – and the inner bad under control – in a permissive pedagogical environment. The cultural transmission ideology, in contrast, maintains that the primary task of education is to transfer the information, rules and values from one generation to the next so as to maintain stability and preserve the achievements of previous generations. Educational technologies and, in particular, behaviouristic theories, make up this stream of thinking about education. Progressivism, finally, forms the third stream of educational thought and the one ardently embraced by Kohlberg. Whereas romanticism uncritically assumes that whatever inborn tendencies a child possesses ought to be supported and whereas cultural transmission ideologies replicate the societal *status quo*, progressivism is seen as a dialectic interplay between the child and the environment. Progressivism, based on William James and John Dewey, holds that education should nourish the natural interaction between a child and a society or environment.

> In the progressive view, this aim requires an educational environment that actively stimulates development through the presentation of resolvable but genuine problems or conflicts. Educative experiences make the child think – think in ways which organize both cognition and emotion ... [T]he acquisition of knowledge [results in] an active change in patterns of thinking brought upon by experiential problem-solving situations. ... [T]he progressive sees the acquisition of morality as an active change in patterns of response to problematic social situations.[5]

In Kohlberg's view, there is a unity between cognitive and moral development, between the affective and intellectual domains. 'The development of logical and critical thought, central to cognitive education, finds its larger meaning in the broad set of moral values.'[6]

Kohlberg's theory is based on Piaget's approach with the following major tenets. (1) cognition in general and moral reasoning in particular are structured in the mind in the form of schemata, mental structures that are used to perceive and make sense of everyday experience. Each schema is based on assumptions about the nature of the world and reality, and it is the schema which determines how individuals perceive reality. Schemata exist from the earliest childhood onwards and never stop changing or becoming more refined. Development means change in mental structure. New experiences are either assimilated, that is integrated into existing schemata or accommodated, that is, these experiences force the creation of new schemata for understanding. Cognitive development occurs through assimilation and accommodation, through integration of experience into existing mental structures and the creation of new and more elaborate ones. (2) Cognitive and moral development occurs as children and adults move through a series of stages, each successively more sophisticated, each representing a structured whole for making sense of experience. Individuals move through the stages in an invariant sequence, they do not skip stages, rarely regress to earlier ones, and incorporate patterns of thinking of previous stages into the newly acquired one. Development and maturation occurs as a result of cognitive disequilibrium, the experience of situations that cannot be adequately understood at the present stage. (3) Higher stages are better in the sense that they allow individuals to make sense of experiences in more comprehensive ways. Not all individuals attain the higher stages of development although stage development correlates with age, at least during the early stages of cognitive development. Stage development can be retarded but not accelerated.

With regards to moral development, Kohlberg described six stages and three levels: preconventional level I consists of stage 1 (punishment and obedience orientation) and stage 2 (instrumental relativist orientation). Conventional level II consists of stage 3 (interpersonal concordance orientation) and stage 4 (society maintaining orientation); and the postconventional or principled level III consists of stage 5 (social contract orientation) and stage 6 (universal ethical principles). In defining the postconventional stages 5 and 6, Kohlberg drew extensively on social contract theory and in particular in the work of philosopher John Rawls.[7] At each stage of development, individuals will reason about what is right and why it is right in a very different way. When asked why stealing from a friend is wrong, for example, an individual at stage 1 reasoning well might answer that it is wrong because if caught one will get punished, while an individual at stage 3 might point to the fact that stealing will harm the trust relationship with the friend. At stage 5, the individual might point to the implicit contract among members of society to uphold the right to property and to act in mutually beneficial ways.

Kohlberg's empirical research focused on the development of methods to measure and to assess the validity of the theory of moral development. He developed the moral judgement interview (MJI), a protocol and scoring manual involving semi-structured interviews on hypothetical moral dilemmas, where participants are asked to decide and morally justify some course of action. Using the extensive scoring guidelines, it is possible to determine the stage of moral reasoning of the interviewee. Using the results of a twenty-year longitudinal study where subjects were interviewed every three years, Kohlberg showed stage progression step-by-step as predicted by his theory. Other longitudinal studies validated these findings. Like Piaget before him, Kohlberg carried out research to assess the cross-cultural validity of the theory. The results of studies conducted in over forty western and non-western countries, by and large showed increases in moral judgement with age and education and confirmed the majority of the stages of moral reasoning, pointing to the universality of the theory. With respect to moral education, extensive research found that such programmes promote gains in moral reasoning.[8]

Much of Kohlberg's work during the 1970s and 1980s centred on the practical implications of the theory of moral development. This involved curriculum development and reform in schools and universities, and

LAWRENCE KOHLBERG

experiments in educational democracy in prisons, schools and community-based organizations under the Just Community Approach.[9]

Kohlberg's writings have attracted a large number of prominent responses from philosophers such as Jürgen Habermas and Israel Scheffler, fellow social scientists, collaborators and former students, commenting on his work, extending the research and theory, and posing alternative and competing explanations and theoretical frameworks. Of particular interest to adult educators is the application of the cognitive developmental thinking to professional development and to development in domains other than justice reasoning, across the life-span, and at the workplace.[10] As Schrader succinctly put it: 'Certainly Kohlberg had his critics ... but even for his critics, Kohlberg's ideas warrant consideration and provide a starting point for new ideas. Kohlberg welcomed dialogue and controversy. He believed that without cognitive conflict and dialogue, we cease to develop.'[11]

Notes

1 Kohlberg, 'The Child as a Moral Philosopher', *Psychology Today*, 2, 4, September, p.8, 1968.
2 Kohlberg, 'A Current Statement on Some Theoretial Issues', in S. Modgil and C. Modgil (eds), *Lauwrence Kohlberg: Consensus and Controversy*, Philadelphia, PA: Falmer, pp.485–546, 1985.
3 Kohlberg, *The Philosophy of Moral Development*, San Francisco, CA: Harper & Row, p.407, 1981.
4 Kohlberg and R. Mayer, 'Development as the Aim of Education', *Harvard Education Review*, 42, p.449, 1972.
5 Ibid., pp.454–5.
6 Ibid.
7 J. Rawls, *A Theory of Justice*, Cambridge, MA: Belknapp Press of Harvard University, 1971.
8 J. Rest, *Moral Development: Advances in Research and Theory*, New York: Praeger, 1986.
9 Kohlberg, *The Just Community Approach to Moral Education in Theory and Practice*, in M. Berkowitz and F. Oser (eds), *Moral Education: Theory and Application*, Hillsdale, NJ: Lawrence Erlbaum, 1985.
10 For example, M. Commons, D. Sinnott, F. Richards and C. Armon, *Adult Development*, vol. 1 and 2, New York: Praeger, 1989; and J. Demick and P. Miller, *Development in the Workplace*, Hillsdale, NJ: Lawrence Erlbaum, 1993.
11 D. Schrader, 'Editor's Notes', in D. Schrader (ed.), *The Legacy of Lawrence Kohlberg*, New Directions of Child Development, 47, San Francisco, CA: Jossey Bass, 1990.

See also

In this book: Habermas, Neill, Piaget
In *Fifty Major Thinkers on Education*: Dewey, Kant, Mill, Rousseau, Socrates

Kohlberg's major writings

Kohlberg was a prolific writer who published widely in the fields of psychology, philosophy, and education. His major books include the three volume series, *The Philosophy of Moral Development* (San Francisco, CA: Harper & Row, 1981), *The Psychology of Moral Development* (San Francisco, CA: Harper & Row, 1984), and

Lawrence Kohlberg's Approach to Moral Education (New York: Columbia University Press, 1989, with C. Power and A. Higgins). With A. Colby, Kohlberg authored a two-volume scoring manual, *The Measurement of Moral Judgement* (Cambridge, MA: Center for Moral Education, Harvard University, 1987). His empirical work is summarized in a research monograph, *A Longitudinal Study of Moral Judgement* (Chicago, IL: University of Chicago Press for the Society for Research in Child Development, 1983, with A. Colby, J. Gibbs, and M. Liebermann). A comprehensive review of the theory of moral development and synopses and replies to critics is contained in L. Kohlberg, C. Levine and A. Hewer, *Moral Stages: A Current Formulation and Response to Critics* (New York: Karger, 1983).

Further reading

Berkowitz, M. and Oser, F. (eds), *Moral Education: Theory and Application*, Hillsdale, NJ: Erlbaum, 1985.

Kanjirathinkal, M.J., *A Sociological Critique of Theories of Cognitive Development: The Limitations of Piaget and Kohlberg*, Dyfed, Wales: Edwin Mellen, Lampeter, 1990.

Modgil, S. and Modgil, C. (eds), *Lawrence Kohlberg: Consensus and Controversy*, Philadelphia, PA: Falmer, 1986.

Reed, D.R.C., *Following Kohlberg: Liberalism and the Practice of Democratic Community*, Notre Dame IN: University Notre Dame, 1997.

Reimer, J., Prichard Paolitto, D. and Hersh, R.H., *Promoting Moral Growth*, New York: Longman, 1983.

Rest, J.R. and Narvaez, D.F. (eds), *Moral Development in the Professions: Psychology and Applied Ethics*, Hillsdale, NJ: Erlbaum, 1994.

Rest, J.R., Narvaez, D., Bebeau, M.J. and Thomas, J., *Postconventional Moral Thinking: A Neo-Kohlbergian Approach*, Hillsdale, NJ: Erlbaum, 1999.

Schrader, D. (ed.), *The Legacy of Lawrence Kohlberg*, New Directions for Child Development, 47, San Francisco, CA: Jossey Bass, 1990.

K. PETER KUCHINKE

PAUL H. HIRST 1927–

> analytical philosophy of education ... has ... been marked by much re-assessment and re-working of the most fundamental issues within the discipline ... (E)arlier work can now be seen to have presupposed without adequate critical examination many philosophical beliefs and forms of argument associated with the Enlightenment and particularly Kant. It is my personal view that philosophy of education is now steadily elucidating a new and more adequate characterization of education ... [as] ... not primarily education into theoretical academic disciplines but initiation into social practices in which we can ... find a fulfilling life.[1]

Paul Heywood Hirst has played a major role in the establishment of philosophy of education in the English-speaking world as a distinctive area of academic philosophy and as a contributory discipline within educational studies. He has also been highly influential in a number of institutional and policy-related developments in education and has commanded wide respect as a lucid and inspiring teacher, a lively and tenacious debater and an effective and far-sighted educational leader.

Hirst was brought up in an austere, unworldly and morally earnest home dominated by fundamentalist evangelical Christianity (his father was a member of a strict branch of the Plymouth brethren). Apart from its influence on much of his intellectual work (seen, for example, in the search for concepts and beliefs which are in some sense basic or ultimate with respect to a question at issue and an emphasis on truth) this background laid the foundations for Hirst's distinctive teaching style, his responsibilities as a preacher giving birth to a range of histrionic skills. Hirst received a very narrow and intensive academic grammar school education, focusing in its later stages almost exclusively on Mathematics and Physics, and he won entry at the age of seventeen to Trinity College, Cambridge, to read for the Mathematical Tripos. At Cambridge, Hirst began to remedy the narrowness of his earlier upbringing and education, finding in philosophy his real intellectual interest and a resource for putting his religious formation into critical perspective. He was deeply impressed by the work of A.J. Ayer (particularly its emphasis on the connection between meaning and truth) but rejected Ayer's negative verdict on the claims of metaphysics and religion, realizing that there must be different kinds of meaning and truth criteria: at this early stage, one of the central theses of Hirst's 'forms of knowledge' thesis had emerged.

After Cambridge, Hirst embarked on a career as a schoolteacher of Mathematics. His success as a teacher (several of his pupils have become distinguished mathematicians) led to Hirst's appointment in 1955 to the Department of Educational Studies at the University of Oxford, where he was responsible for the training of Mathematics teachers. Throughout his period as a schoolteacher and at Oxford, Hirst's interest in philosophy continued unabated. Oxford in the 1950s was gripped by the 'analytic revolution' in philosophy, and Hirst was swept up in the exciting philosophical atmosphere of the time, reading widely and participating in seminars for the recently established BPhil degree, where the leading philosophers of the day presented their work in progress. Hirst began to see the relevance of these philosophical developments to educational questions and he held classes for trainee teachers on the application of contemporary philosophy to education. However, Oxford offered little scope for the expansion of this work, which had now become Hirst's dominant interest, and so in 1959 he accepted an invitation from Louis Arnaud Reid to take up a lectureship in Philosophy of Education at the Institute of Education, University of London. Hirst found Reid's work stimulating (particularly in the area of art) but felt that it needed reformulation in the light of developments in analytical philosophy. Reid, however, had little sympathy with Hirst's analytic approach, and it was only when Richard Peters was appointed to the Chair of Philosophy of Education in the London Institute in 1962 that Hirst's work began to flourish.

Hirst found in Peters a congenial spirit, and their close collaboration over the next decade (during which, in 1965, Hirst was elected to the Chair of Education in King's College, London) was central to a remarkable period in the blossoming of philosophy of education in Great Britain and throughout the English-speaking world. This development became closely identified with its two leaders and 'Hirst and Peters' became household names to generations of teachers trained at this time and to educators worldwide. Hirst was deeply involved in the teaching and institutional aspects of this development, and was instrumental in the establishment of the Philosophy of Education Society of Great Britain, in which he has continued to play a leading role. In intellectual terms, Peters provided Hirst with philosophical breadth and support in the development of his own ideas (Hirst has always acknowledged a considerable intellectual debt to Peters[2]) and their interests and developing philosophical positions were complementary and compatible. Hirst's primarily epistemological concerns at the time combined with Peters' work on rational moral judgements and the nature and justification of democratic social principles to create a distinctive, powerful overall general position in philosophy of education[3] (known in certain quarters as 'the London Line') which laid the foundations for the development of the subject and which set its framework and agenda for many years.

In 1971, Hirst moved to the University of Cambridge as Professor of Education and Head of the Department of Education, with the task of establishing the study of education within the University on a proper academic and professional basis. In moving to Cambridge and to heavy responsibilities of academic leadership and administration, Hirst accepted that his contribution to philosophy of education had to take second place for the time being to more pressing concerns. Following his retirement from Cambridge in 1988, Hirst re-established a close relationship with the London Institute as Visiting Professorial Fellow and embarked on a major re-consideration and re-statement of his thought.

Hirst's thought is characteristically highly abstract (focusing on matters of fundamental conceptualization or principle), tightly wrought, dense and nuanced. Its lucidity, and the urgency and directness with which it is presented, compels and requires sustained critical attention, not least to the educational implications of the discussion, which are rich but in need of careful interpretation. Hirst's work exemplifies many features of the developing tradition of analytic philosophy of education, a concern for conceptual clarification being pursued not for its own sake but in the interests of providing justificatory support for arguments about fundamental educational questions. The early work included an articulation of the nature of educational theory which resisted its crude assimilation to a scientific model,[4] a conceptual mapping of the concept of teaching[5] and an argument to the effect that, since religion has an uncertain epistemological status, it cannot serve as a basis for common moral education[6] (Hirst's own religious views moved over time into the region of agnosticism). However, Hirst's early work is dominated by his 'forms of knowledge' thesis, first developed in his highly influential 1965 paper 'Liberal Education and the Nature of Knowledge'[7] which is arguably the most discussed and debated paper in analytic philosophy of education, not least because of the suggestive, but incomplete and programmatic, character of the arguments advanced. In this paper Hirst argued that all knowledge and understanding can be located within a number of 'forms' identifiable in terms of distinctive concepts and tests for truth (truth criteria) and that these forms (which, it was suggested, could include morality, art – conceived propositionally – and religion) have a major (though complex) bearing upon a proper understanding of the appropriate shape and structure of the school curriculum. This thesis was often misinterpreted, particularly in its educational implications (neither the direct teaching of the forms to students was intended, nor the identification of the forms with school subjects) and clarifications, re-statements and critiques of the thesis were prominent for many years.

Hirst's 'forms of knowledge' thesis can only be properly understood in the context of the broader philosophical position in which it was located. At the heart of this view (which Hirst now refers to dismissively as 'rationalist') the cognitive capacities of the person (seen in the formation of conceptual schemes enabling the achievement of justifiable or rational beliefs) are seen as structuring, and limiting the intelligible operation of, all other capacities, such as the affective and the conative, thereby making possible rational emotions and rational action: the 'rational life' to which all should aspire. The 'rational life' presented in this view was an attractive and flexible ideal. It included the notion of freedom of choice and rational autonomy (since reason was seen as leaving many matters for rational determination by the individual) but in a context in which reason had delivered some fundamental social principles, such as those of liberal democracy. This vision yielded a clear, coherent and powerful framework for the formulation of educational aims. The development and pursuit of knowledge and understanding (the various forms of which were mapped in the 'forms of knowledge' thesis) were seen as central to education not only because they were intrinsically worthwhile but because they were seen as vital to the rational development of all other human capacities in their personal and social aspects. A stipulative account of 'liberal education' as the non-instrumental initiation into the various forms of knowledge with the aim of developing the cognitive dimension of the rational mind was seen as providing the core of a wider (though subsidiary) education which was concerned with knowledge, skills and qualities of character more directly focused upon the rational life in its practical aspects. 'Education' itself was sharply distinguished from activities such as 'catechesis' (or formation in religious faith) on the grounds that properly educational influence should be governed and limited by what can be shown to be epistemologically well grounded.[8]

During the 1970s and 1980s Hirst became progressively dissatisfied with this general position under the influence of neo-Aristotelianism and philosophers such as Alasdair MacIntyre, Richard Rorty, Charles Taylor and Bernard Williams. His later work has embarked on a major re-statement of his view, emphasizing the centrality to education not of reason as in the forms of knowledge but of initiation into social practices (patterns of activity engaged in for the satisfaction of human needs and interests comprising a range of elements including knowledge, attitudes, feelings, virtues, skills, dispositions and relationships). It is important to note, however, that while the central role of reason as in the forms of knowledge in Hirst's early position was argued hard (one of Hirst's lectures in Cambridge was entitled 'All that Matters in Life is Reason') the significance of the social and of social practices was not ignored. Hirst's more recent work, where arguments against the centrality of (theoretical) reason are urged with equal force, is therefore best seen not as a wholesale repudiation of his early arguments but as drawing attention to different primary concerns and emphases (a re-conceived, though crucial, role for forms of reason and individual autonomy remain and the existence of forms of knowledge is not denied).

In his later work,[9] Hirst, in common with John White and others, has moved away from an emphasis upon epistemology as providing the basis of our proper understanding of education. In his later view, Hirst presents the good life as rooted not in cognitive judgements and the theoretical knowledge based in the forms of knowledge, but in desire satisfaction, practical reasoning and involvement in the sound social practices in relation to which our lives become structured and satisfactions obtained. In this later view, reason is seen as exercised in relation to and as part of other wants and satisfactions, as directed by our interests and as primarily practical (a matter of 'know-how' rather than 'know-that', and of the tacit rather than the articulated and explicit). On this view, reason should not be conceived as separable from, or having determining status over, other capacities of the person. Education is seen as concerned with the development of the good life and as primarily requiring not the acquisition of knowledge but broad and reflective initiation into social practices (some more necessary and unavoidable than others) and the development of practical reason in relation to them. Since academic theoretical disciplines are not primarily and directly relevant to this development, study of them (as distinct from initiation into the practice of critical reflection upon practices) is seen as appropriate only for those who find such study personally satisfying.[10] The identification of a distinctive notion of liberal education is no longer considered to be important. Moral education is seen as essentially concerned not with the development of moral reason (underpinned by rationally determined moral principles universal and local) but with engagement in specific existing and rationally evolving social practices aimed at individual and social human fulfilment.[11] The precise character and defensibility of Hirst's later general overall view (in particular, its relationship to and compatibility with central elements in the liberal tradition) has yet to come into focus and its exploration (in relation, for example, to specific examples of social practices in illumination of what constitutes a successful practice) will command the continuing attention of contemporary philosophers of education.

Hirst's emphasis on practical reason and on the limitation of theoretical understanding has been apparent for some time in his developing views on the nature of the relationship between theory and practice in education and the demands of professional preparation for teaching. At the heart of these views is an insistence on the inadequacy of abstract conceptualization as a sufficient basis for rational practice and the need to generate appropriate conceptualizations (and 'practical principles') within practice itself, theoretical knowledge (such as that found in the 'disciplines' of education) having an indirect role in the reflective assessment and realignment of practice.[12] One major implication of this view is the centrality to the initial training of teachers of progressive initiation in practical contexts into professional practice with its requirements of reflection at different levels.[13]

In addition to his intellectual work, Hirst has also made a major contribution in institutional and policy terms to education. At Cambridge, Hirst brought about an unprecedented respect for Education as a subject, through course development (including a revitalization and re-orientation to practice of the moribund Post-Graduate Certificate of Education, the acceptance of Education into the Cambridge Tripos system, and the expansion of study at Masters and doctoral level), through the general transformation of the University Department of Education and the complex negotiation of a status for Homerton College within the university, and through his extensive and influential role in wider university affairs as a member of the General Board of the Faculties and other important committees. Hirst has also played an important role at national level in relation to developments in teacher training, serving as Chairman of the University Council for the Education of Teachers and co-directing a major research project exploring the role of the school in initial teacher training, where the practical implications of his thinking on the nature and development of professional practice were explored in some detail.[14] Hirst has also served on a number of bodies concerned with higher education and was an influential member of the Committee of Inquiry into the Education of Children from Ethnic Minority Groups chaired by Lord Swann.

Notes

1 P.H. Hirst, 'Philosophy of Education: The Evolution of a Discipline', in G. Haydon, (ed.), *50 Years of Philosophy of Education: Progress and Prospects*, London: Bedford Way Papers, Institute of Education, University of London, pp.16–19, 1998.
2 P.H. Hirst, 'Richard Peters's Contribution to the Philosophy of Education', in D.E. Cooper (ed.), *Education, Values and Mind: Essays for R.S. Peters*, London: Routledge & Kegan Paul, 1983.
3 P.H. Hirst and R.S. Peters, *The Logic of Education*, London: Routledge & Kegan Paul, 1970.
4 P.H. Hirst, 'Educational Theory', in J.W. Tibble (ed.), *The Study of Education*, London: Routledge & Kegan Paul, 1965.
5 P.H. Hirst, *Knowledge and the Curriculum: A Collection of Philosophical Papers*, London: Routledge & Kegan Paul, chap. 7, 1974.
6 Hirst, *Knowledge and the Curriculum*, op cit., chap. 12; P.H. Hirst, *Moral Education in a Secular Society*, London: Hodder and Stoughton, 1974.
7 P.H. Hirst, *Knowledge and the Curriculum*, op cit., chap. 3, see also chaps 4, 6.
8 P.H. Hirst, 'Education, Catechesis and the Church School', *British Journal of Religious Education*, Spring, 1981; P.H. Hirst, 'Education and Diversity of Belief', in M.C. Felderhof (ed.), *Religious Education in a Pluralistic Society*, London: Hodder and Stoughton, 1985.
9 See, in particular, P.H. Hirst, 'Education, Knowledge and Practices', in R. Barrow and P. White (eds), *Beyond Liberal Education: Essays in Honour of Paul H Hirst*, London: Routledge, 1993; and P.H. Hirst, 'The Nature of Educational Aims', in R. Marples (ed.), *The Aims of Education*, London: Routledge, 1999.
10 See, for example, P.H. Hirst, 'The Foundations of the National Curriculum. Why Subjects?', in P. O'Hear and J. White (eds), *Assessing the National Curriculum*, London: Paul Chapman, 1993.
11 P.H. Hirst, 'The Demands of Moral Education: Reasons, Virtues, Practices', in J.M. Halstead and T.H. McLaughlin (eds), *Education in Morality*, London: Routledge, 1999.
12 P.H. Hirst, 'Educational Theory', in P.H. Hirst (ed.), *Educational Theory and its Foundation Disciplines*, London: Routledge & Kegan Paul, 1983.
13 P.H. Hirst, 'The Theory and Practice Relationship in Teacher Training', in M.

Wilkin, V.J. Furlong and M. Booth (eds), *Partnership in Initial Teacher Training: The Way Forward*, London: Cassell, 1990; P.H. Hirst, 'The Demands of a Professional Practice and Preparation for Teaching', in J. Furlong and R. Smith (eds), *The Role of Higher Education in Initial Teacher Training*, London: Kogan Page, 1996.
14 V.J. Furlong, P.H. Hirst, K. Pocklington and S. Miles, *Initial Teacher Training and the Role of the School*, Buckingham: Open University Press, 1988.

See also

In this book: Peters, White

Hirst's major writings

Hirst, P.H., with Peters, R.S., *The Logic of Education*, London: Routledge, 1970.
Knowledge and the Curriculum: A Collection of Philosophical Papers, London: Routledge, 1974.
Moral Education in a Secular Society, London: Hodder and Stoughton and National Children's Home, 1974.
'Educational Theory', in P.H. Hirst (ed.), *Educational Theory and its Foundation Disciplines*, London: Routledge & Kegan Paul, 1983.
'Education, Knowledge and Practices', in Robin Barrow and Patricia White (eds), *Beyond Liberal Education: Essays in Honour of Paul H. Hirst*, London: Routledge, 1993.

Further reading

Barrow, Robin and White, Patricia (eds), *Beyond Liberal Education: Essays in Honour of Paul H Hirst*, London: Routledge, 1993.
Hirst, Paul H. and White, Patricia, 'The Analytic Tradition and Philosophy of Education: An Historical Perspective', in P.H. Hirst and P. White (eds), *Philosophy of Education: Major Themes in the Analytic Tradition, Volume 1*, London: Routledge, 1998.
Hirst, Paul H. and White, Patricia (eds), *Philosophy of Education: Major Themes in the Analytic Tradition*, 4 vols, London: Routledge, 1998.

TERENCE H. MCLAUGHLIN

PHILIP WESLEY JACKSON 1928–

> Yet having said that, I remain convinced that being a teacher has had a profound effect on my life. It has made me what I am today or at least has had a hand in doing so. That conviction explains why I went on to say that the notion that teaching has had no effect on those who teach doesn't make any sense to me. To that extent, at least, I remain in full agreement with Waller's contention about teaching's most pronounced effect being upon teachers themselves.[1]

Philip W. Jackson is the David Lee Shillinglaw Distinguished Service Professor Emeritus in the Department of Education and Psychology at the

University of Chicago. Jackson attained his Ph.D. in developmental psychology from Teachers College, Columbia University in 1955. He was appointed Assistant Professor of education at the University of Chicago in 1955 and remained there until his retirement in 1998.

Jackson's tenure at the University of Chicago was marked by a number of different roles. He not only served as professor, he also served as Chairman of the Department of Education, as Dean of the Graduate School of Education, and as Director of the University's Benton Center for Curriculum and Instruction. In addition to these administrative positions, he was Principal of the University's nursery school from 1966 to 1970.

Jackson's career in the field of education has moved gradually over the years from one focused within the confines of educational psychology to one addressing curricular, indeed philosophical issues in education. His doctoral work at Teachers College, Columbia University, was under the direction of Professor Irving Lorge, a specialist in measurement and statistics. Jackson brought to his appointment at Chicago the quantitative competencies and empirical inclinations that one might expect of a new Ph.D. under Lorge's mentorship. But Irving Lorge was not his only mentor, although he was among his most important initial ones. In the Department of Education at the University of Chicago, Jackson encountered another professor who also was a psychologist, but of a very different orientation. Jacob Getzels, a graduate of Harvard University's Department of Social Relations, had a wide social view of learning and a broad conception of cognition. Getzels played a key role in guiding the young Assistant Professor.

Getzels and Jackson's initial claim to fame emerged with the 1962 publication of their book, *Creativity and Intelligence*. *Creativity and Intelligence* represented their effort to disentangle creative thinking from a conception of intelligence that depended upon the performance of tasks that made no demands upon the test taker to display ingenious or novel forms of thinking. The conceptual aim of their research was basically to demonstrate that you couldn't be sure from one's IQ score whether or not that individual was likely to rate as high or as low on measures of creativity. In a series of ingenious tasks Getzels and Jackson assessed adolescents who were high on measures of intelligence and low on measures of creativity as contrasted with those who were high on creativity but who received low scores on measures of intelligence. They attempted to determine the background conditions, the form of home life, the sorts of dispositions that were associated with these two groups of children. At a time at which there was substantial interest in the development of creative thinking skills in America, their book was widely discussed and provided a substantial push to work in this area.

Interest in creativity as measured through testing practices, even ingenious testing practices, did not occupy a central role in Jackson's scholarship. In the mid 1960s, Jackson became interested in something that seems of obvious importance today, but at that time was a neglected arena. He wanted to understand what goes on in classrooms. This curiosity resulted in research in the Laboratory School of the University of Chicago and culminated in an extremely important book titled, *Life in Classrooms*. Regarding this project Jackson writes,

Its aim is neither to damn schools nor to praise them, nor even, necessarily, to change them. Rather the goal is simply to arouse the reader's and possibly to awaken concern over aspects of school life that seem to be receiving less attention than they deserve.[2]

And indeed it did!

In the 1960s when the initial research for this project was undertaken, there was still a dominant interest among researchers in isolating and measuring discreet dimensions of thinking and teaching. Teacher assessment measures purporting to represent a series of pedagogical virtues were to be applied to teacher performance as a rating scale. The educational research community was still under, as it is to some degree today, a scientific array of aspirations. The prospects of learning anything scientifically valuable by studying life in classrooms was not high on the agendas of empiricists committed to quantification. Jackson was among the first to study classroom practice and to provide a kind of interpretive and descriptive picture of the events that occurred in such settings.

Now the observation of classrooms like the observation of any array of social arrangements depends substantially for its quality on the level of perceptivity that the observer brings to the occasion. Jackson, if he has any virtue, and he has many, shines in this domain. He is among the most perceptive of American students of educational practice and his perceptivity combined with a literary and poetic style of writing made it possible for him both to see and to describe in trenchant terms practices that become obvious only in a recollection stimulated by the kind of evocative prose that Jackson uses. Consider the following passage from *Untaught Lessons*[3] in which he describes one of his high-school teachers.

What I remember most vividly about my early morning classes in Mrs. Henzi's room was the way she handled our homework assignments. Three or four students at a time would be sent to the blackboard at the front of the room to work out one of the problems that had been assigned the day before. These were usually textbook exercises consisting of equations to be simplified and solved for x. Mrs. Henzi, standing at the side of the room opposite the windows, her glasses flashing with reflected light, would read the problem aloud for the students at the board to copy and solve while the rest of the class looked on. As each student finished his calculation he would turn and face the front of the room, moving slightly to one side as he did so in order to make his board work visible. Mrs. Henzi would inspect each solution carefully (as would everyone else who was seated), noting not only the answer but each of the steps taken to reach it. (All of the calculations had to be displayed in detail on the board.) If everything was correct she would send the student back to his seat with a word of praise and a curt nod. If the student had made an error she would have him take a close look at his work to see if he could find his mistake. 'There is something wrong there, Robert,' she would say, 'Take another look.' If after a few seconds of scrutiny Robert wasn't able to detect his error, Mrs. Henzi would ask for volunteers (of which there were usually plenty) to point out where their hapless classmate had gone wrong.[4]

The impact of this passage is given even increased weight when combined with quantitative data, a practice Jackson employed in *Life in Classrooms*. *Life in Classrooms* is both an achievement in qualitative research and models an intelligent way in which quantitative information can be used to support and augment what has been rendered in prose.

What is important about Jackson's *Life in Classrooms* is that along with Louis Smith's and William Geoffrey's *The Complexities of an Urban Classroom*,[5] it began a movement that has not as yet terminated. The movement I speak of is the extraordinary interest among educational researchers in America in understanding the dynamic complexities of schools, classrooms, teaching practices and learning. There is, in the American educational research community, a kind of qualitative revolution designed to present incisive and insightful narratives of the practical affairs of school life in ways that cannot be revealed in numbers. Jackson, along with a few others, embarked on an approach to educational scholarship which has not abated.

Jackson's work in education has, over the years, moved gradually from the quantitative empiricism he learned at Teachers College to another kind of empiricism that is closer to the novelist, especially the essayist, than to the work of those concerned with data that can be reduced to numbers and statistically analysed. His interest in the essay as a form of expression fits well his interest in the literary use of language. His work in this form emerges in books such as, *The Practice of Teaching*,[6] published in 1986, *Untaught Lessons*,[7] published in 1992 and, *John Dewey and the Lessons of Art*,[8] published in 1998. Increasingly Jackson moved to the methodological left and in so doing provides the American educational research community with accounts of teaching and schooling that are among the most sensitive and insightful that are available.

Philip Jackson has served the field of education not only as a scholar, but as an educational leader and administrator. He is an elected member and former Vice-President of the National Academy of Education, he was President of the American Educational Research Association in 1990–91, President of the John Dewey Society in 1996–98. He served on the advisory board of the Encyclopaedia Britannica Education Corporation from 1966–68 and was appointed Fellow at the Center for Advanced Study in the Behavioral Sciences at Stanford, California in 1962–63.

Jackson's career in American education is characterized by his incisive and trenchant observations of American education; he does not suffer fools gladly and is not enraptured with misguided bandwagons, even when all seem to be happily jumping aboard. But criticism by academics of schools is easy when one has no responsibility for the day-to-day operations of a classroom or school. Jackson *was* Principal of the Laboratory School at the University of Chicago. He *did* shoulder the responsibility of running a school – if schools are indeed institutions one can run. I suspect Jackson would claim they cannot, and perhaps more important, should not be run. What he has contributed to American education is a perspective developed from a keen sensibility and an incisive mind taking apart and then reconstructing deeper analyses of the aims and means of education. Critic, researcher, essayist, poet, Philip Jackson has helped the rest of us think harder and more deeply about education. Such talent is far too uncommon.

Notes

1 Philip Jackson, *Untaught Lessons,* New York: Teachers College Press, p.73, 1992.
2 Philip Jackson, *Life in Classrooms,* New York: Holt, Rinehart and Winston, p.vii, 1968
3 Philip Jackson, *Untaught Lessons,* op cit., pp.1–2.
4 Ibid., pp.1–2.
5 Louis Smith and William Geoffrey, *The Complexities of an Urban Classroom,* New York: Holt Rinehart and Winston, 1968.
6 Philip Jackson, *The Practice of Teaching,* New York: Teachers College Press, 1986.
7 Philip Jackson, *Untaught Lessons,* op cit.
8 Philip Jackson, *John Dewey and the Lessons of Art,* New Haven, CT: Yale University Press, 1998.

See also

In *Fifty Major Thinkers on Education*: Dewey

Jackson's major writings

Jackson, P., with J.W. Getzels, *Creativity and Intelligence,* London: Wiley, 1962.
Life in Classrooms, New York: Holt, Rinehart and Winston, 1968.
The Teacher and the Machine, Pittsburgh, PA: University of Pittsburgh, 1968.
The Practice of Teaching, New York: Teachers College Press, 1986.
Untaught Lessons, New York: Teachers College Press, 1992.
John Dewey and the Lessons of Art, New Haven, CT: Yale University Press, 1998.

ELLIOT W. EISNER

JANE ROLAND MARTIN 1929–

> If there is one thing I have learned from my own research it is this: To make education rich and rewarding for every girl and boy and also as beneficial as possible for society as a whole, it is absolutely necessary to keep looking with clear and steady eyes on the girls and women in the educational landscape and on the cultural assets that have traditionally been placed in their keep.[1]

Martin is an internationally renowned philosopher whose inquiry in and about education has shaken its conceptual foundations, showing them to b deeply and consequentially gendered. For she has theorized a hidden curriculum of gender embedded in the ideal of the educated person and in basic concepts of teaching, schooling and education itself, often assumed to be gender-blind. As remedies, she has proposed a new gender-sensitive educational ideal, re-conceptualized schooling, urged activism for academic transformation and recommended public acknowledgement of multiple educational agency, with a view to preservation of a broadly conceived cultural wealth.

Daughter of a newspaperman and a home economics teacher, she grew up in New York City. She attended the Little Red School House and the Elisabeth Irwin High School, which have contributed to the great US experiment in progressive education,[2] as later Martin's own writings have done also,[3] partly because of these schools' impact upon her.[4] In 1951 she graduated from Radcliffe College with a major in political theory that gave her a memorable experience of gender bias which she only began to understand many years afterwards.[5] Later graduate coursework in education suggested that philosophical study might help her address questions posed by practical challenges she faced as an elementary school teacher.[6] But after completing the Ph.D. in philosophy and education at Radcliffe in 1961, she found that applying her philosophical proficiencies to 'the real life problems of education' would be a major challenge.[7]

Highly technical linguistic debates came to dominate analytic philosophical practice in education. Martin herself contributed prominently to those debates on the structure of explanation[8] even though, during that time, women's published contributions to educational theory have been documented as scarce.[9] Without affirmative action, too, women's tenure-line employment was infrequent, especially (as in Martin's case) when women scholars had scholar-husbands. After holding various adjunct faculty positions in education and philosophy for over a decade, she eventually moved through the academic ranks in an undergraduate philosophy department at the University of Massachusetts, Boston, where she is now professor emerita.

As the civil rights, peace and women's movements captured the attention of US campuses and as the free school movement flourished in the 1970s, Martin's inquiry began to focus on the logic of curriculum. What should be the relationship between the disciplines and curriculum? What justifies a 'god-given subject' or 'immutable basic'? What is the anatomy of a proper school subject? What part should student choice play in curriculum, and should it be left to chance? What is 'hidden curriculum'? Such analysis led Martin to critique some dogmatic assumptions under-girding the ideal of a liberal education and its most conservative advocates' objections to interdisciplinary fields such as social studies, Black studies and women's studies. Thus she began to address 'the real life problems of education' philosophically. In so doing, she showed that philosophical inquiry on curriculum need not be epistemological, as often then assumed, for significant ethical, social and political curriculum questions frequently arise as well.[10]

Martin's analyses of curriculum deployed standard philosophical methods and made no mention of women or gender. However, they did lay important conceptual groundwork for the basic research on women and education that she began in 1980 and for which she is now best known. Challenging philosophers and educators to take women's educational experiences and contributions seriously and to question their own long-standing assumptions about gender, she challenged them also to rethink the meaning of education itself, as well as their analytic approach. Thus she sparked acrimonious controversy, especially among analytic philosophers of education. Yet *Philosophy of Education: An Encyclopedia*, which cites Martin in a half dozen different entries,[11] has claimed that the feminist challenge she initiated has 'changed the face of philosophy of education'.[12]

Indeed, her boldly activist presidency of the Philosophy of Education Society marked a major turning point in the field's history in 1981. Martin first presented her new research on women with her frequently cited and republished presidential address, 'The Ideal of the Educated Person', which critiqued analytic philosopher R.S. Peters' allegedly gender-neutral account of this ideal, and with two other influential articles in *Harvard Educational Review*.[13] In *Reclaiming a Conversation* (1985), subsequently translated into Japanese by T. Sakamoto and M. Sakagami, she responded to some of these articles' challenges. Her first research on women had identified an epistemological inequality in contemporary analytic philosophy of education that excluded, distorted, and devalued women as subjects and objects of educational thought. She had documented contemporary analytic philosophers' neglect even of classics (by both men and women) from the history of thought about women's educational activities. Furthermore, Martin had shown that such neglect was consequential, insofar as it led contemporary philosophers of education not only to exclude women, but also to rule questions about child-rearing out of bounds to the field. *Reclaiming a Conversation* addressed these problems by critically reconstructing thought about women's education from neglected texts by Plato, Jean-Jacques Rousseau, Mary Wollstonecraft, Catharine Beecher and Charlotte Perkins Gilman and by acknowledging that mothering can be educating. While critiquing such thinkers' gender-blind and gender-bound educational ideals, Martin argued for a *gender-sensitive* educational ideal. This ideal required educators constantly to be aware of gender's workings in the two sexes' lives – where gender could make an educational difference and where it should make none. Sensitive to rather than prescriptive of gender, the ideal presumed no essential traits in either sex, but constituted an aim that both sexes should be educated in, about, and for both 'productive' (political, cultural, economic) and 'reproductive' (nurturing) processes of society.[14]

Martin also here proposed that historians of educational thought should question their assumptions about acceptable sources of data, methods of study, and authorship itself – thus inviting scholars to search for evidence of women's educational thought in non-standard sources: e.g., magazines, personal diaries, letters, pamphlets, newsletters, pieces of fiction, and oral sources. She suggested that historians of educational thought might then have to 'take on the role of anthropologist' in addition to the standard one of philosopher.[15] Moreover authors of educational thought might be not only individuals, but also groups who founded schools or social movements.

Martin's articles (1969–93), many re-published in *Changing the Educational Landscape* (1994) and widely anthologized elsewhere, show the further necessity of rethinking the co-educational curriculum, which she undertook in *The Schoolhome* (1992). Re-interpreting Maria Montessori's 'casa dei bambini' and critiquing William James' 'Moral Equivalent of War' while citing myriad sources from both popular and high culture, this book radically re-conceptualized school as a 'moral equivalent of home' for both 'learning to live' and learning about dominated and dominating cultures. Faulting the epistemological fallacy that reduces curriculum to mere 'spectator' knowledge, it also deployed Aristotle's golden mean to re-theorize gender-sensitivity. Moreover, it called for consciousness-raising about a miseducative phenomenon she named *domephobia*, a morbid fear and repressive hatred of things domestic that infects both culture and education in the United States to the detriment of women's and children's wellbeing.

However, Martin has lately argued that reforming schools as she recommends in *The Schoolhome*, though necessary, cannot be sufficient to address this culture's most basic educational needs. Her newest research, still in progress, is challenging two popular essentialist equations – between education and schooling and between culture and high culture. Martin is also critiquing both the 'gendered-division of educational functions' between home and school and the 'cultural loss' that ensues from these essentialist premises which educators take for granted. Drawing a strong distinction between the 'cultural wealth' and the cultural liabilities that make up the general 'cultural stock' which education may transmit, she is arguing now for a broadly defined 'multiple educational agency'. Educational agency belongs not only to schools and homes, but also to churches, neighbourhoods, workplaces, museums, libraries, concert halls, electronic and print media. On her view, if the public were to acknowledge broad educational agency, such multiple agents could and should be held accountable whenever they miseducate youth, 'for the damage they are doing in preserving and transmitting our culture's liabilities rather than its wealth'.[16]

Consistent with her new notion of multiple educational agency, Martin's theorizing has not exclusively focused upon children's education. Her most recently published book, *Coming of Age in Academe* (2000), has analysed how the second-class status of education itself as a profession and field of study reflects an 'education-gender system' in higher education. Comparing academic women to immigrants assimilated into the United States over the past two centuries, she has critiqued various academic practices that perpetuate the academy's estrangement from women's lived experience and especially from ghettoized 'women's' occupations, including teaching. Not only women suffer from this system. Martin has termed it a 'brain drain' that diverts 'the attention of society's "best and brightest" from the problems of the real world'.[17] Urging academic women to refuse assimilation, she advocated dismantling the education-gender system through 'actions great and small',[18] 'both strategic and outrageous'. Also she pleaded with liberal-arts faculty 'to think across the disciplines and across college lines in order to make common cause with scholars on education, nursing, and social-work faculties'.[19]

Thus taking the lead as a feminist pioneer in educational theory, Martin has brilliantly succeeded against strong odds at bringing her scholarship into close connection with her everyday life,[20] not only as a mother of two sons and as a professor of undergraduate philosophy.[21] Her theorizing about academic gender bias also reflects her experiences generously mentoring women graduate students around the world who, lacking any available feminist mentors in philosophy of education at their own universities,[22] have independently sought her tutelage.[23] But, ironically unlike many lesser-known white men of her generation in philosophy of education, Martin never held a tenure-line appointment at any comprehensive research university where she might have taught and advised such students.

Nonetheless, Martin's challenge to 'bring women into educational thought' today receives prominent curricular attention in teacher education.[24] Young scholars have voluntarily taken up this same challenge. For they have brought into the field Dewey's, Hegel's and Theodor von Hippel's thought on women's education as well as educational thought by many culturally diverse women: e.g., Catherine Macaulay, Ana Roque de Duprey, Anna Julia Cooper, Mabel McKay, bell hooks, Louisa May Alcott, Ntozake Shange, Toni Morrison, Margaret Fuller, Charlotte Brontë, the French novelist Colette, the Canadian novelist L.M. Montgomery and the collective voice of the American Association of University Women.[25] Now many more women are philosophers of education than ever before. Martin's challenge to the gender-blind analytic paradigm of educational thought has also made possible new philosophical discussions and debates on issues of vital concern to intelligent educational practitioners: e.g., about teaching and co-education, physical education and sex education, political correctness and cultural pluralism, role models, androgyny, sexism and gender-freedom in public education.[26] Such debates have also drawn upon a far wider range of cultural resources than ever tolerated before – novels, films, pictures, even music and the worldwide web. Martin was obviously right in 1981 to promise that the field would be reinvigorated and enriched by bringing women into educational thought.[27]

Small wonder, then, that the American Educational Research Association has honoured Martin several times and that many other organizations have honoured her as well.[28] Small wonder that Martin has received honorary doctoral degrees in both the United States and Sweden and that her work enjoys respect also in Canada and Australia. Or that she has lectured in England, Israel, Finland, The Netherlands, Norway, Sweden and Japan. Perhaps Gloria Steinem has best summed up the broad appeal – the generative power and promise – of Martin's theorizing about education: 'Jane Roland Martin brings us together to think about the energy being wasted on an old game, and the possibilities if those energies were set free'.[29]

Notes

1 Jane Roland Martin, 'Women, Schools, and Cultural Wealth', in Connie Titone and Karen E. Maloney (eds), *Women's Philosophies of Education: Thinking Through Our Mothers*, Upper Saddle River, NJ: Merrill, p.175, 1999.
2 To document this remarkable school's history, Jane Roland Martin was awarded a Spencer Foundation Grant with Helena Ragoné for a project entitled 'Remembering Progressive Education: Interviews with the Class of '43'.
3 Nel Noddings, *Philosophy of Education*, Boulder, CO: Westview, chap. 10, 1995.
4 Jane Roland Martin, *The Schoolhome: Rethinking Schools for Changing Families*, Cambridge, MA: Harvard, p.211, 1992.
5 Martin, *The Schoolhome*, op cit., p.53.
6 Jane Roland Martin, 'One Woman's Odyssey', in *Changing the Educational Landscape: Philosophy, Women, and Curriculum*, New York: Routledge, p.2, 1994.

7 Ibid.
8 Jane Roland Martin, *Explaining, Understanding, and Teaching*, New York: McGraw-Hill, 1970. Also see her 'On the Reduction of "Knowing That" to "Knowing How" ', in B.O. Smith and R.H. Ennis (eds), *Language and Concepts in Education*, Chicago, IL: Rand McNally, 1961, reprinted in *The Philosophical Foundations of Education*, ed. Steven M. Cahn, New York: Harper & Row, pp.399–410, 1970; and her 'On "Knowing How" and "Knowing That" ', *The Philosophical Review*, pp.379–87, 1958.
9 Susan Laird, 'Teaching and Educational Theory: Can (And Should) This Marriage Be Saved?', *Educational Studies*, 29, 2, Summer, p.137, 1998.
10 Jane R. Martin (ed.), *Readings in the Philosophy of Education: A Study of Curriculum*, Boston, MA: Allyn & Bacon, p. 9, 1970.
11 *Philosophy of Education: An Encyclopedia*, J.J. Chambliss (ed.), New York: Garland, p.706, 1996; analytic philosophy, civic education, domestic education, feminism, girls and women, philosophy and literature.
12 Barbara Houston, 'Feminism', in *Philosophy of Education: An Encyclopedia*, p.219.
13 All articles are reprinted in Martin, *Changing the Educational Landscape*, chaps 1, 2, 3.
14 Susan Laird, 'Martin, Jane Roland', in Lorraine Code (ed.), *Encyclopedia of Feminist Theories*, New York: Garland, 2000.
15 Jane Roland Martin, *Reclaiming a Conversation: The Ideal of the Educated Woman*, New Haven, CT: Yale, p.181, 1985.
16 Martin, 'Women, Schools, and Cultural Wealth', op cit., pp.159–75.
17 Jane Roland Martin, *Coming of Age in Academe: Rekindling Women's Hopes and Reforming the Academy*, New York: Routledge, p.133, 2000.
18 Ibid., chap. III.
19 Ibid., p.173.
20 Martin, *Changing the Educational Landscape*, op cit., p.1.
21 Martin, *Reclaiming a Conversation*, op cit., p.xi; Martin, *Coming of Age in Academe*, op cit., p.95.
22 In the United States, for example, Karen E. Maloney, 'The Theory of Education of Charlotte Perkins Gilman: A Critical Analysis', Ed.D. diss., Harvard University Graduate School of Education, 1985, and Susan Schober Laird, 'Maternal Teaching and Maternal Teachings: Philosophic and Literary Case Studies of Educating', Ph.D. diss., Cornell University, 1988. However, the students whom she has mentored include other students from the United States, Canada, Australia and Sweden.
23 Martin, 'A Professorship and Office of One's Own', in *Changing the Educational Landscape*, op cit., chap. 6. See also Susan Laird,' "Working It Out", with Jane Roland Martin', *Peabody Journal of Education*, 71, 1, pp.103–13, 1996.
24 Steven E. Tozer, Paul C. Violas and Guy Senese, *School and Society: Historical and Contemporary Perspectives*, Boston, MA: McGraw-Hill, p.351, 1995. This is one of the most widely used basic texts in historical, philosophical, and social foundations of education. Martin's *The Schoolhome* is also a frequent text in such courses.
25 Most notably, Titone and Maloney, *Women's Philosophies of Education*, op cit.; Susan Laird, 'Women and Gender in John Dewey's Philosophy of Education', *Educational Theory*, 38, 1, winter, pp.111–29, 1988; Susan Laird, 'Curriculum and the Maternal', *Journal for a Just and Caring Education*, 1, 1 January, pp.45–75, 1995; Susan Laird, 'The Ideal of the Educated Teacher: *Reclaiming a Conversation* with Louisa May Alcott', *Curriculum Inquiry*, 21, pp.271–97, 1991; Susan Laird, 'The Concept of Teaching: *Betsey Brown* vs. Philosophy of Education?', in James Giarelli (ed.), *Philosophy of Education 1988*, Normal, IL: Philosophy of Education Society, pp.32–45, 1989. Also Zandra Lesley Shore, 'Girls Reading Culture: Autobiography as Inquiry into Teaching the Body, the

Romance, and the Economy of Love', Ed.D. diss., Ontario Institute for Studies in Education at the University of Toronto, 1999; Virginia Ann Worley, 'The Educational Place of *Metissage* in Colette's *La Maison de Claudine*: A Two-Fold Pedagogy of Place Itself and of the Place-Teaching Partnership', Ph.D. diss., University of Oklahoma, 1999; Jeffrey Ayala Milligan, 'Negotiating the Relationship between Religion and Public Education: Conceptualizing a Prophetic Pragmatic Teacher from Toni Morrison's *Beloved*', Ph.D. diss, University of Oklahoma, 1998. In 'One Woman's Odyssey', op cit., p.15, p.31, n.39, n.40, n.41, n.42, n.43, n.44, Martin cites other scholars who have taken up her challenge: Inga Elgqvist-Saltzman and her students at the University of Umea; Mineke van Essen, Mieke Lunenberg, and their colleagues in The Netherlands; David MacGregor in Canada; Robert Roemer and others at a Guilford College symposium; and Mary Ann Connors at the University of Massachusetts.

26 See, for example, Ann Diller, Barbara Houston, Kathryn Pauly Morgan and Maryann Ayim, *The Gender Question in Education: Theory, Pedagogy, and Politics*, Boulder, CO: Westview, 1996.

27 Susan Laird, 'Teaching and Educational Theory: Can (And Should) This Marriage Be Saved?', *Educational Studies*, 29, 2, summer, pp.131–51, 1998.

28 For example, the John Dewey Society, Society of Professors of Education, American Educational Studies Association, Society of Women in Philosophy, and several universities, including Harvard.

29 Gloria Steinem, Foreword to *Coming of Age in Academe*, op cit., p.xvii.

See also

In this book: Peters
In *Fifty Major Thinkers on Education*: Alcott, Montessori, Plato, Rousseau, Wollstonecraft

Martin's major writings

Explaining, Understanding, and Teaching, New York: McGraw-Hill, 1970.
Reclaiming a Conversation: The Ideal of the Educated Woman, Japanese language edition, 1987; New Haven, CT: Yale University Press, 1985.
The Schoolhome: Rethinking School for Changing Families, Cambridge, MA: Harvard University Press, 1992.
Changing the Educational Landscape: Philosophy, Women and Curriculum, New York: Routledge, 1994.
Coming of Age in Academe: Rekindling Women's Hopes and Reforming the Academy, New York: Routledge, 2000.

Further reading

Diller, A., Houston, B., Morgan, K.P. and Ayim, M., *The Gender Question in Education: Theory, Pedagogy, and Politics*, Foreword by Jane Roland Martin, Boulder, CO: Westview, 1996.
Titone, C. and Maloney, K.E. (eds), *Women's Philosophies of Education: Thinking Through Our Mothers*, Upper Saddle River, NJ: Merrill, 1999.

SUSAN LAIRD

NEL NODDINGS 1929–

> Interest in preserving the lives of our children and fostering their
> individual growth provides a compelling interest in moral life and
> moral education.[1]

Like other noted philosophers, Nel Noddings has contributed to a range of
educational scholarship. In particular, the topics of her work revolve around
the analysis of caring and its place in ethics,[2] the development of school
structures that encourage caring relations,[3] efforts to reconceptualize evil
from the standpoint of women,[4] and the use of maternal interests to inform
moral education.[5] The wide influence of Noddings' work hinges on her
broad conceptions of moral reasoning, values and belief. Moreover, her
contributions have come at a critical juncture in contemporary debates over
education. Recent trends have bolstered a lively interest in moral life and
moral development. However, opportunities to affirm the ethical foundations of teaching and learning are also threatened by politically motivated
calls for schools to reassert the narrow and often nostalgic views of a
particular group. Against this threatened partisanship, Noddings provides
an understanding of ethical belief that is both more rigorous and more
inclusive than we would otherwise have today.

Noddings began her professional career as a mathematics teacher after
graduating from Montclair State College in New Jersey. Her first teaching
position was with a sixth-grade class, but she went on to teach high school
mathematics for twelve years. School had played a central role in Noddings'
life as a student herself, and her early experiences with caring teachers
contributed to a career-long interest in student–teacher relations. Her
academic passions, first mathematics and later philosophy, also originated in
her admiration for the teachers who taught them, and only afterwards in the
demands of the subject matter itself.[6]

Nodddings completed her masters degree in mathematics at Rutgers
University. She also served as a school and district administrator before
continuing her graduate work at Stanford University. After completing her
doctoral degree in educational philosophy and theory, Noddings was hired
in 1975 to direct the University of Chicago's Laboratory School. As a newly
minted philosopher of education, Noddings must have found this position
irresistible given the school's past association with John Dewey, the pre-
eminent American pragmatist whose progressive views have and continue to
influence Noddings' own work. In 1977, Noddings joined the education
faculty at Stanford University where she served in all ranks, including as
director of Stanford's teacher education programme and as acting Dean.
Noddings received several teaching awards at Stanford, and in 1992 she was
appointed to an endowed chair. After retiring from Stanford University,
Noddings taught philosophy of education at Teachers College Columbia
University until 2000.

Much of Noddings' early research is in mathematics education, a field to
which she has contributed throughout her career. Increasingly, however,
philosophy and the study of ethics became the centre of her academic work.
Her first book, *Caring: A Feminine Approach to Ethics and Moral Education*[7]
contributed to this focus. Noddings begins this book by raising a perennial

question: What is the basis for moral action? While many other ethicists have posed the same question, Noddings' approach differs from philosophical traditions of the past. In particular, she argues that neither of the two major ethical systems – utilitarian and deontological ethics – provide an adequate foundation for understanding the moral dilemmas and ethical concerns of women. Noddings does not reject decisions based on anticipated consequences (a utilitarian approach) or principled reasoning (a deontological approach). Rather, she proposes an alternative perspective grounded in natural caring, as in the care of a mother for a child. Natural caring, Noddings asserts, is a moral attitude, a longing for goodness that arises out of the experience or memory of being cared for. From this basis, Noddings develops the notion of ethical caring, a state of being in relation, characterized by receptivity, relatedness and engrossment.

The strength of Noddings' approach is its emphasis on reciprocity, a point on which she argues that ethical matters cannot be analysed simply from the perspective of an individual agent acting out of duty or in accordance with some abstract principle. Instead, the relation always includes a 'cared for', together with his or her interests, motives and affective responses. In this respect, the approach constantly looks to relations at hand. When principles such as equity and fairness are used to make decisions, their use is derived from a primary concern for persons, dialogue with those persons and the quality of relations that are formed as a result.

Noddings draws on a range of feminist theories to support her analysis, and for this reason she faces challenges similar to the challenges encountered by other feminist scholars. In the case of ethics, moral action is typically described in 'the language of the father', Noddings writes, 'in terms such as justification, fairness, justice'.[8] Scholars who emphasize maternal interests, however, enter the discussion with what Carol Gilligan called 'a different voice'.[9] The challenge of bringing a new voice to an old domain is in presenting a 'rigorous' analysis without giving up the very spirit that contributes to the analysis in the first place. The question becomes how to be 'tough-minded', so to speak, about concepts that are not strictly empirical or logical in the formal use of these terms.

Noddings meets this challenge in several ways. First, her work consistently acknowledges opposing views. She also explicitly addresses the difficulties that arise in her own analysis of caring – not just the political difficulties noted above but also the analytic difficulties entailed in the theory itself. She discusses, for example, the ways in which reciprocity – a cornerstone of care theory – becomes extremely complex in the types of unequal relationships (e.g., student–teacher) that concern educators most. Issues of time, intensity and situational variations also must be worked out, as do the questions of what it means to care for non-human entities such as plants, animals, ideas and organizations. As her work illustrates, Noddings' conviction is to think through these complexities as intelligently as possible rather than discard the theory because of them.

Second, Noddings defines her approach as feminine in the classical sense of placing its emphasis on relatedness and receptivity. In part, the aim of doing so is to separate the approach from empirical questions of gender *per se*. Women, she argues, are clearly capable of the skills that are emphasized in conventional ethics – formal reasoning and the arrangement of principles hierarchically to arrive at logical conclusions. At the same time, men have no reason to reject caring as a basis for their moral actions. Like women, they too have a vested interest in preserving life, enhancing the quality of relations and fostering individual growth. Sharing these interests, both men and women suffer from an unnecessarily narrow view of ethics.

Third, although Noddings argues that her approach is phenomenological in its method, and thus concerned with epistemology, the purpose of ethical phenomenology is not to 'prove' a moral truth. Instead, Noddings proposes that care theorists strive for conceptual knowledge and enlightened understanding, as opposed to formulaic certainty. 'The hand that steadied us as we learned to ride our first bicycle', she writes, 'did not provide propositional knowledge, but it guided and supported us all the same, and we finished up "knowing how".'[10]

Noddings' philosophical analysis of caring was followed in 1989 with *Women and Evil*,[11] a book that added to her reputation as a leading feminist scholar. This work reveals a long-standing yet ambivalent fascination with Judeo-Christian theology, a set of traditions that have defined evil largely in terms of disobedience and sin. Noddings argues that this approach creates the problem of reconciling human miseries with a benevolent and all-powerful God. Moreover, efforts to resolve this problem often mystify evil, and may even contribute to the forms of dominance from which evil may arise. Noddings rejects this approach but not the need for a morality that will help individuals understand and control their own tendencies toward evil. Again drawing on the experience of women, she proposes an approach that locates evil in the phenomenological conditions of pain, separation and helplessness. When evil is encountered from this perspective, evil need not be explained away, but simply faced with as much courage as our situations allow. Caring is an important source for this type of courage, serving also as a basis for dialogue and cooperation. In particular, Noddings recommends that caring teachers openly address the spiritual longing and eternal questions of all students, especially students who are socialized or aspire to dominance.

Noddings' philosophical analyses of caring and evil have made a significant contribution to ethics, phenomenology and feminist scholarship. Another side to her work, however, and one which is equally important, is represented in her recurrent emphasis on the use of philosophy to inform educational practice. This aspect of her scholarship can be labelled transformationist in the sense that Noddings explicitly takes up the aims of transforming the structures of teaching and schooling in ways that will encourage caring relations and the growth of individuals. Concerns that focus on instructional arrangements, curriculum and the profession of teaching coalesce in Noddings' book *The Challenge to Care in Schools.*[12] From one perspective, this book can be viewed as a critique of liberal education and specifically the traditions that define liberal education as the 'best' education for all students. Expanding on her earlier criticisms of Mortimer Adler's Paideia Proposal,[13] Noddings contends that the standard disciplines of liberal education embrace an overly narrow conception of human rationality, one which is based almost entirely on trained intelligence. Her arguments are not simply against requiring all students to take the same courses in mathematics, science, language and so forth, but against any curriculum that ignores the wide range of interests and talents that students develop. Given genuine differences among students, prescribing the same curriculum for everyone only requires teachers to rely on coercion, thus undermining the relationships that are so central to learning and individual growth.

Educational philosophers will recognize the influence of Dewey on these arguments, as well as on the method that Noddings uses for developing an alternative approach. Her method is to engage readers in a complex thought experiment. As parents, Noddings asks, how would we want our children to be educated if they were a large group with differing abilities and talents? Although Dewey's notion of 'the best and wisest parent'[14] has been used (or misused) by the same proponents of liberal education with whom Noddings finds fault, her interpretations shun the notion of an educational élite. Furthermore, this thought experiment is not entirely hypothetical for Noddings, the mother of five daughters and five sons. As she repeatedly acknowledges, raising a large and diverse family is a key source for her convictions that education must be broadly conceived and responsive to the students it is intended to benefit.

Noddings' proposal is to organize school curriculum around centres of care, a departure from the standard disciplines that Dewey was unwilling to make. Nevertheless, Noddings and Dewey would agree on another point. While both philosophers favour that education be tailored to student interests, they equally oppose differentiating curriculum on the basis of perceived social or occupational needs. Such forms of tracking ignore that education is more than simply preparation for life, but also an experience lived directly. Contemporary debates have raised a different issue by demonstrating that many uses of tracking also lead to serious inequities. On this point, however, Noddings cautions that we should not confuse equity with sameness. 'Human talents are wonderfully broad', she writes, 'and, if we are really concerned with equity, those talents should be treated with equal respect.'[15]

In calling for an education responsive to students, Noddings places renewed emphasis on the continuities between learning and experience. This too is a recurrent theme in her scholarship. It is also the focus of *Educating for Intelligent Belief or Unbelief*,[16] a book in which Noddings examines the connections between subject areas and the spiritual questions that adolescents often raise about themselves, life, death, nature and religion. In mathematics, for instance, Noddings notes that many great mathematicians have struggled with similar existential questions, including whether God exists, how the universe began, where life came from, and what happens after death. Because such questions seem to transcend time, place and otherwise diverse human experiences, Noddings wonders why they are almost entirely absent in the curriculum, or when present, restricted solely to courses in religion and history.

To counteract this tendency, Noddings provides a wealth of examples that illustrate how educating for intelligent belief or unbelief can be used as the backbone of a school curriculum, not just with respect to spiritual questions but as an approach to open inquiry brought to bear on a broad range of student concerns. In a sense, her proposal represents the contributions of philosophy to education across the curriculum. But for

Noddings, the aims of such inquiry are neither critical thinking *per se*, nor the type of Socratic argumentation that seeks to defeat an antagonist. Rather, she argues for forms of inquiry that will provide all participants the opportunity to take part in an eternal dialogue. 'In such a dialogue', Noddings writes, 'believer and unbeliever draw closer to one another.'[17]

In summary, while Noddings is best known for her work on ethical caring, her contributions to education span a range of contemporary theories and topics. Foremost among these contributions has to do with what teachers already know when through teaching they come to recognize their students and colleagues striving toward an ethical ideal. The sense of caring that fosters this recognition is not merely a fleeting sense of satisfaction or the 'feel-good' gratification of philanthropic deeds. Instead, Noddings teaches that caring is a moral attitude informed by the complex skills of interpersonal reasoning, that it is neither without its own forms of rigor nor somehow less professional than the calculated skills of formal logic. Most importantly, Noddings' work demonstrates that caring need not be what Wittgenstein advised we 'must pass over in silence'. On the contrary, to do so would be to miss one of the most pervasive and intriguing forms of human rationality.

Notes

1　Nel Noddings, 'Shaping an Acceptable Child', in A. Garrod (ed.), *Learning for Life: Moral Education Theory and Practice*, Westport, CT: Praeger, p.67, 1992.
2　Nel Noddings, *Caring: A Feminine Approach to Ethics and Moral Education*, Berkeley, CA: University of California Press, 1984.
3　Nel Noddings, *The Challenge to Care in Schools*, New York: Teachers College Press, 1992.
4　Nel Noddings, *Women and Evil*, Berkeley, CA: University of California Press, 1989.
5　Noddings, 'Shaping an Acceptable Child', op cit.
6　Nel Noddings, 'Accident, Awareness, and Actualization', in A. Neumann and P. Peterson (eds), *Learning from Our Lives: Women, Research, and Autobiography in Education*, New York: Teachers College Press, pp.166–82, 1997.
7　Noddings, *Caring*, op cit.
8　Ibid., p.1.
9　Carol Gilligan, *In a Different Voice*, Cambridge, MA: Harvard University Press, 1982.
10　Noddings, *Caring*, op cit., p.3.
11　Noddings, *Women and Evil*, op cit.
12　Noddings, *The Challenge to Care*, op cit.
13　Nel Noddings, 'The False Promise of the *Paideia*', *Journal of Thought*, 19, pp.81–91.
14　John Dewey, *The School and Society*, Chicago, IL: University of Chicago Press, p.3, 1902.
15　Noddings, 'Accident, Awareness, and Actualization', op cit., p.177.
16　Nel Noddings, *Educating for Intelligent Belief or Unbelief*, New York: Teachers College Press, 1993.
17　Ibid., p.144.

See also

In *Fifty Major Thinkers on Education*: Dewey

Noddings' major writings

Caring: A Feminine Approach to Ethics and Moral Education, Berkeley, CA: University of California Press, 1984.
Noddings, N., with Paul J. Shore, *Awaking the Inner Eye: Intuition in Education*, New York: Teachers College Press, 1984.
Women and Evil, Berkeley, CA: University of California Press, 1989.
The Challenge to Care in Schools, New York: Teachers College Press, 1992.
Educating for Intelligent Belief or Unbelief, New York: Teachers College Press, 1993.
Philosophy of Education, Boulder, CO: Westview Press, 1995.
Educating Moral People, New York: Teachers College Press, 2001.
Starting at Home: Caring and Social Policy, Berkeley, CA: University of California Press, 2002.

Further reading

Noddings, Nel and Witherell, Carol (eds), *Stories Lives Tell*, New York: Teachers College Press, 1991.
Stone, Lynda (ed.), *The Education Feminism Reader*, New York and London: Routledge, 1994.
Noddings, Nel, Gordon, Suzanne and Benner, Patricia (eds), *Caregiving*, Philadelphia, PA: University of Pennsylvania Press, 1996.
Noddings, Nel, Katz, Michael and Strike, Kenneth (eds), *Justice and Care in Education*, New York: Teachers College Press, 1999.

DAVID J. FLINDERS

JÜRGEN HABERMAS 1929–

> The commitment to consider all individuals as potential participants in discourse presupposes a universalistic commitment to the potential equality, autonomy, and rationality of individuals.[1]

Jürgen Habermas is the leading second generation figure of the Frankfurt School, a group of philosophers, social theorists and cultural critics who established the Institute for Social Research in Frankfurt in 1929. Habermas taught philosophy at the Universities of Heidelberg and Frankfurt, before moving to the Max Planck Institute in 1972, and subsequently, from the mid 1980s, returning to his post as professor of philosophy and sociology at the University of Frankfurt.

Though a social theorist and philosopher rather than an educationist, Habermas has exerted a profound influence on education. His early work takes forward the project of the Frankfurt School of critical theory (e.g. Horkheimer, Adorno, Marcuse) in its critique of instrumental reason and positivism as being 'scientistic' (the belief that all worthwhile knowledge is only scientific knowledge (Habermas 1972, p.4) and 'technicist' (e.g. treating people and situations as means to an end), and in its expressed political intention of emancipating disempowered individuals and groups within an egalitarian society. Habermas' early work is an attempt to base a social theory on epistemology, and is explicitly prescriptive and normative, entailing a view of what behaviour in a social democracy *should* entail. Its intention is not simply to provide an account of society and behaviour but to realise a society that is based on equality and democracy for all its members. The purpose of his theory is not merely to understand situations, power and phenomena but to change them, to eradicate inequality.

Habermas, like his former mentor and teacher Adorno, finds differential, illegitimate power and inequality to be structurally inherent in capitalism. Capitalism maintains its hegemony (where ideology and unequal power relations operate with the tacit consent of all participants, even the disempowered, contributing to their acceptance of their disempowered positions) by averting crises of motivation, legitimacy, identity, politics and economics.[2] Habermas' early work is located in the tradition of ideology critique of the Frankfurt School and is premised on fundamental principles of social justice, the promotion of social equality, the creation and nurture of 'generalizable interests', and the commitment to the achievement of democratic society. Habermas defines his notion of ideology as the 'suppression of generalizable interests'[3] in the day-to-day lives of participants, where systems or groups possessing power operate in rationally indefensible ways because their power relies on the disempowering of other groups, i.e. their principles of behaviour are not universalizable. Ideology critique, in some part, is a critique of the illegitimate operation of power and hegemony in capitalist society.

Habermas' critical theory suggests an educational agenda, and also has its own methodologies, in particular ideology critique and action research. Ideology – the values, beliefs and practices emanating from particular dominant groups – is the means by which powerful groups promote and legitimate their particular – sectoral – interests at the expense of disempowered groups. Ideology critique is designed to expose the operation of ideology in many spheres of society and education and the working out of vested interests under the mantle of the general good, which may be occurring consciously or subliminally, revealing to participants how they may be acting to perpetuate a system which keeps them either empowered or disempowered, i.e. which suppresses a generalizable interest. Situations are not natural but are the outcomes or processes wherein interests and powers are protected and suppressed, and one task of ideology critique is to expose this.

Habermas[4] suggests that ideology critique can be addressed in four stages:

Stage one: a description and interpretation of the existing situation – a hermeneutic exercise that identifies and attempts to make sense of the current situation (echoing, from Weber, the *verstehen* approaches of the interpretive paradigm).

Stage two: a penetration of the reasons that brought the existing situation to the form that it takes – the causes and purposes of a situation and an evaluation of their legitimacy, involving an analysis of interests and ideologies at work in a situation, their power and legitimacy (both in micro- and macro-sociological terms). In Habermas' early work he likens this to psychoanalysis as a means for bringing into consciousness of 'patients' those repressed, distorted and oppressive conditions, experiences and factors that have prevented them from a full, complete and accurate understanding of their conditions, situations and behaviour, and that, on such exposure and examination, will become liberatory and emancipatory. Critique here serves to reveal to individuals and groups how their views and practices might be ideological distortions that, in their effects, are perpetuating a social order or situation that works against their democratic freedoms, interests and empowerment.[5]

Stage three: the setting of an agenda for altering the situation – in order for moves to be made towards an egalitarian society.

Stage four: an evaluation of the achievement of the new, egalitarian situation in practice.

Ideology is not mere theory but impacts directly on practice. The educational methodology suggested by critical theory is action research.[6] Action research accords power to those who are operating in educational contexts, for they are both the engines of research and of practice. In that sense the claim is made that action research is strongly empowering and emancipatory. It gives practitioners a 'voice',[7] participation in decision making, and control over their environment and professional lives. Whether the strength of the claims for empowerment through action research are as strong as their proponents would hold is another matter, for action research for change and control might be relatively powerless in the face of mandated changes in education.

Habermas' theory of knowledge-constitutive interests seeks to uncover the *interests* at work in particular situations and to interrogate the legitimacy of those interests,[8] identifying the extent to which they serve equality and democracy. The intention of his theory is *transformative*: to transform society and individuals to social democracy. In this respect the purpose of critical educational research is intensely practical – to bring about a more just, egalitarian society in which individual and collective freedoms are practised, and to eradicate the exercise and effects of illegitimate power. For critical theorists and critical educationists, teachers and researchers can no longer claim neutrality and ideological or political innocence.

Habermas suggests that knowledge serves different interests and that social analysis can be conducted in terms of the knowledge-constitutive interests operating in society. Interests, he argues, are socially constructed, and are 'knowledge-constitutive', because they shape and determine what counts as the objects and types of knowledge. Interests have an ideological function,[9] for example a 'technical interest' can have the effect of keeping the empowered in their empowered position and the disempowered in their powerlessness, i.e. reinforcing and perpetuating the societal *status quo*. An 'emancipatory interest' threatens the *status quo*. In this view knowledge is not neutral. What counts as worthwhile educational knowledge is determined by the social and positional power of the advocates of that knowledge, i.e. communities of scholars. Knowledge and definitions of knowledge reflect the interests of the community of scholars who operate in particular paradigms (e.g. Kuhn 1962).

Habermas[10] constructs the definition of worthwhile knowledge and modes of understanding around three cognitive interests: (1) prediction and control; (2) understanding and interpretation; (3) emancipation and freedom. He names these the *technical, practical* and *emancipatory* interests respectively. The *technical* interest characterizes the scientific, positivist method, with its emphasis on laws, rules, prediction and control of behaviour, with passive research objects, and instrumental knowledge. The *practical* interest is exemplified in the hermeneutic, interpretive methodologies outlined in qualitative approaches to understanding and researching education (e.g. symbolic interactionism). Here research methodologies seek to clarify, understand and interpret the communications of 'speaking and acting subjects'.[11] Hermeneutics focuses on interaction and language; it seeks to understand situations through the eyes of the participants, echoing Weber's principle of *verstehen*. It is premised on the view that reality is socially constructed. Indeed Habermas[12] suggests that sociology must understand social facts in their cultural locations and as being socially determined. Hermeneutics involves revealing the *meanings* of interacting subjects, recovering and reconstructing the *intentions* of actors in a situation. Such an enterprise involves the analysis of *meaning in a social context*. Meanings rather than phenomena take on significance here.

The *emancipatory* interest subsumes the previous two interests; it requires them but goes beyond them.[13] It is concerned with *praxis*: action that is informed by reflection with the aim to emancipate. The twin intentions of this interest are to expose the operation of power and to bring about social justice, arguing that domination and repression prevent the full existential realization of individual and social freedoms.[14] The task of this knowledge-constitutive interest, indeed of critical theory itself, is to restore to consciousness those suppressed, repressed and submerged determinants of unfree behaviour with a view to their dissolution.[15]

Habermas' work impacts on education very considerably, covering, for example, curriculum design, aims, content, pedagogy, evaluation and research. At the level of *curriculum design*, Habermas' three knowledge-constitutive interests can inform three styles of curriculum design:[16]

1 a rationalist/behaviourist 'curriculum as product' view of the curriculum revealing the 'technical' knowledge-constitutive interest;[17] it is the prototypical bureaucratized and instrumental curriculum;
2 a humanistic, interpretive, pragmatic 'curriculum as practice' view of the curriculum which is identified with Stenhouse's 'process' approach to the curriculum[18] (describing and understanding the educational encounter rather than prescribing its outcome, e.g. in Eisner's 'expressive objectives'[19]), and with his Humanities Curriculum Project, embodying the hermeneutic knowledge-constitutive interest;
3 an existential, empowering and ideology-critical view of the 'curriculum as praxis'[20] which embodies the emancipatory interest. Habermas' emancipatory interest is served by rendering the curriculum problematical – for example through action research, through taking 'type three objectives'[19] – those objectives which deal with problems and problem-solving approaches – and through establishing emancipatory and critical issues in the curriculum (e.g. cultural literacy programmes as developed by Freire[21]) and social studies programmes. Above all, curricular questions such as: 'whose curricula?', 'in whose interests is this occurring?', and 'how legitimate are these interests?' are given dominance.

Knowledge is not neutral; the curriculum is ideologically contestable terrain. Here the study of the sociology of educational knowledge indicates how the powerful might retain their power through curricula, and how knowledge and power are legitimated in curricula, for example: through the definition of high status 'official' knowledge by powerful groups; and through differential access to, and uptake of, high status knowledge. The sociology of educational knowledge argues for the curriculum to be both subject to ideology critique and to promote ideology critique in students.

Emancipatory curricula serve student empowerment both in content and process, developing participatory democracies, engagement, student voice and the realization of individual and collective existential freedoms. Critique and practice combine to articulate a curriculum which interrogates cultures, lived experiences of power, domination and oppression, i.e. which subjects curriculum aims, contents and purposes to ideology critique and which sets an agenda to promote empowerment.

In terms of *curriculum content* Habermas' work suggests several substantive focuses for ideology critique, e.g.: media studies; social studies and the humanities; cultural studies; political education; citizenship education; equal opportunities; power and authority; education and the community; education and the economy; personal and social education; communication; and aesthetic education.

Habermas' work has been particularly inspirational in the field of *critical pedagogy*, influencing writers such as Giroux[22] and Apple.[23] A critical pedagogy is that which renders problematical, and which develops an ideology critique of, the selection and decision making on educational aims, curriculum design, content, teaching styles, learning styles, evaluation and development, with the intention of moving from the 'suppression of generalizable interests' and inequality to liberty, equality, social justice and fraternity, in short to individual and collective emancipation.

In terms of classroom teaching methods, eight principles of pedagogy from a Habermasian perspective can be outlined which flow from his views of knowledge-constitutive interests:[24] (1) the need for co-operative and collaborative work; (2) the need for discussion based work;[25] (3) the need for autonomous, experiential and flexible learning; (4) the need for negotiated learning; (5) the need for community-related learning in order that students can understand and interrogate a range of environments; (6) the need for problem-solving activities; (7) the need to increase students' rights to employ talk; (8) the need for teachers to act as 'transformative intellectuals',[26] promoting ideology critique.

Critical pedagogy argues that educators must work with, and on, the lived experience that students bring to the pedagogical encounter rather than imposing a curriculum that reproduces social inequality. In this enterprise teachers are to transform the experience of domination in students and empower them to become 'emancipated' in a full democracy. Students' everyday experiences of oppression, of being 'silenced', of having their cultures and 'voices' excluded from education and decision-making are to be interrogated for the ideological messages that are contained in such acts. Raising awareness of such inequalities is an important step to overcoming them. Teachers and students together move forward in the progress towards individual autonomy within a democratic and just society. In place of centrally prescribed and culturally biased curricula that students simply receive, critical pedagogy regards the curriculum as a form of cultural politics in which *participants in* (rather than *recipients of*) curricula question and critique the cultural and dominatory messages contained in curricula, and replace them with a 'language of possibility'[22] and empowering, often community-related curricula (e.g. linking schools with projects in the community that support participatory democracy). In this way curricula serve the 'socially critical' rather than the culturally and ideologically reproductive school.

Habermasian tenets suggest five principles to underpin *educational research, action research* and *evaluation*, arguing that they should be: (1) co-operative and collaborative in a consensual search for understanding; (2) adopting a problem-solving approach; (3) non-bureaucratic, with conception and execution being kept together, i.e. control being in the hands of all stakeholders; (4) emancipatory, empowering all the stakeholders to participate in an egalitarian society, realizing their own existential futures; (5) avoiding exclusive reliance on positivist methodologies. These five principles are all served in action research and feminist research.[27]

In a departure from his earlier attempt to derive a social theory from epistemology, which he acknowledges was inadequate,[28] Habermas' social theory takes a 'communicative turn' whose origins can be traced to his early work.[29] Habermas' concern to offer a vision of how to break out of the 'instrumental rationality' of Weber's 'iron cage' of bureaucracy' (as Habermas terms it, the 'colonization of the lifeworld' by 'steering media' of power, law and bureaucratization),[30] sees a way forward in 'communicative rationality' which abides by the principles of the 'ideal speech situation' whose elements comprise: (1) freedom to enter a discourse, check questionable claims, evaluate explanations, modify given conceptual structures, assess justifications, alter norms, interrogate political will, and employ speech acts; (2) orientation to mutual understanding between participants in discourses, and respect of their rights as equal and autonomous partners; (3) a concern to achieve in discussion a consensus which is based on the force of the argument alone, rather than the positional power of the participants, in particular that of dominating participants; (4) adherence to the speech-act validity claims of truth, legitimacy, sincerity and comprehensibility. Democracy and equality, for Habermas, are rooted less in the operation of power and domination and more in a search for rational behaviour and a consensus that is based on the rational search for truth, and which is achieved discursively.

In educational terms, Habermas' communicative rationality argues for the reduction of technicist, controlling bureaucratization and the increase in communication and discursive, rational ideology critique of educational, curricular and pedagogic practices, by, for example: (1) developing students' empowerment and freedoms; (2) avoiding narrowly instrumental curricula; (3) ensuring that education promotes equality and democracy; (4) developing student autonomy, voice and cultural power; (5) collaborative learning; (6) developing aesthetic education and non-instrumental forms of rationality; (7) developing flexibility and problem-solving abilities in students; (8) critically interrogating cultural and environmental contexts in which personal and community cultural biographies are embedded; (9) developing negotiated learning; (10) addressing issues of equal opportunities; (11) developing citizenship in participatory democracies; (12) undertaking political education and the study of politically sensitive issues; (13) adopting a wide view of the 'basics' in curricula, where education is its own end rather than, instrumentally, serving other ends; (14) developing interactive communication in, and through, education. The political sensitivity of this vast enterprise is recognized by many writers who are influenced by Habermas,[31] for it engages the questioning of legitimacy of curricular and pedagogical decision-making, and constitutes a challenge to existing definitions of important, high-status knowledge (Morrison 1995).

Habermas is a staunch defender of modernism[32] in the face of postmodern critics,[33] arguing that the project of modernity not only has not yet been exhausted, but that it offers a brighter prospect for the emancipation of society than does postmodernism. That aside, there are some criticisms of his work which will not be dismissed easily, for example: his over-emphasis on rationality;[33] the acceptability of the consensus theory of truth on which his work is based;[34] his understatement of the power of controlling groups to continue to exercise power;[9] the putative link between ideology critique and emancipation;[9] the pathological basis of his early work;[9] his equation of individual emancipation with societal emancipation;[9] the promotion of his own political agenda which may be as ideological as those he is criticizing;[35] the relativism of his work;[9] the ambiguity of his knowledge-constitutive interests and of the theoretical status of his knowledge-constitutive interests;[9] his neglect of managing social change;[34] the inadequacy of his problematization of subjectivity;[36] its confusion of ideology critique with social theory;[9] the utopian and generalized tenor of his work;[9] the ultimately contemplative nature of his theory;[9] the view that his theory is a philosophy of science without a science;[37] his neglect of feminist issues;[33] his over-emphasis on communication as a means of achieving societal improvement.

Despite these trenchant criticisms, Habermas' work provides a powerful theoretical underpinning to the implications of recognizing that curricula and pedagogy are problematical and political. Educational theory and educational research which are informed by Habermas' views, then, have their substantive agenda, for example examining and interrogating: the relationships between school and society – how schools perpetuate or reduce inequality; the social construction of knowledge and curricula, who defines worthwhile knowledge, what ideological interests this serves, and how this reproduces inequality in society; how power is produced and reproduced through education; whose interests are served by education and how legitimate these are (e.g. the rich, white, middle-class males rather than poor, non-white, females). Perhaps above all, Habermas' enduring concern for democracy and equality, his reworking of Marxism, and his recommendations to overcome rampant technicism as a 'steering mechanism' in 'colonizing' society, mark him out as one of the twentieth-century's leading philosophers whose work has inspired educationists.

Notes

1 Habermas 1982, p.252.
2 Habermas 1976.
3 Habermas 1976, p.113; 1984, p.10.
4 Habermas 1972, p.230.
5 See also Carr and Kemmis 1986, pp.138–9.
6 Callawaert 1999.
7 Carr and Kemmis 1986; Grundy 1987.
8 Habermas 1974, p.12.
9 Morrison 1995.
10 Habermas 1972.
11 Habermas 1974, p.8.
12 Habermas 1988, p.12.
13 Habermas 1972, p.211.
14 Habermas 1979, p.14.
15 Habermas 1984, pp.194–5.
16 For example, Carr and Kemmis 1986; Grundy 1987; Young 1989.
17 For example, Tyler 1949; Taba 1962.
18 Stenhouse 1975.
19 Eisner 1985.
20 See the work of Freire 1972; Stenhouse 1975; and Apple 1979, 1993.
21 Freire 1972.
22 Giroux 1983.
23 Apple 1979.
24 Morrison 1996.
25 Young 1989.
26 Aronowitz and Giroux 1986. Transformative intellectuals are educationists who render curricula and schooling problematical in the minds of their students, interrogating the ideologies, values and interests at work in education, with a view to raising the political consciousness of students and students' insights into their own life situations.
27 For example, Kemmis 1982; Carr and Kemmis 1986; Grundy 1987; Kemmis 1999; Cohen *et al.* 2000.
28 Habermas 1985.
29 Habermas 1970, 1979. The justification of this theory is set out in Habermas (1984, 1987a) and is premised, in large part on a theory of 'reconstructive science', a powerful critique of which is by Alford (1985).
30 Habermas 1984, 1987a.
31 For example, Apple 1979; Anyon 1981; Giroux 1983, 1992; Gore 1993.
32 Habermas 1987b.
33 For example, Giroux 1992.
34 Lakomski 1999.
35 For example, Roderick 1986, p.71.
36 Fendler 1999.
37 Miedama and Wardekker 1999, p.75.

See also

In this book: Apple, Bernstein, Eisner, Foucault, Freire, Giroux, Greene

Habermas's major writings

'Toward a Theory of Communicative Competence', *Inquiry*, 13, pp.360–75, 1970.
Towards a Rational Society, trans. J. Shapiro, London: Heinemann, 1971.

Knowledge and Human Interests, trans. J. Shapiro, London: Heinemann, 1972.
Theory and Practice, trans. J. Viertel, London: Heinemann, 1974.
Legitimation Crisis, trans. T. McCarthy, London: Heinemann, 1976.
Communication and the Evolution of Society, London: Heinemann, 1979.
'A Reply to My Critics', in J. Thompson and D. Held (eds), *Habermas: Critical Debates*, London: Macmillan, pp.219–83, 1982.
The Theory of Communicative Action. Volume One: Reason and the Rationalization of Society, trans. T. McCarthy, Boston, MA: Beacon Press, 1984.
'Questions and Counterquestions', in R. J. Bernstein, *Habermas and Modernity*, Oxford: Polity Press with Basil Blackwell, 1985.
The Theory of Communicative Action. Volume Two: Lifeworld and System, trans. T. McCarthy, Boston, MA: Beacon Press, 1987a.
The Philosophical Discourse of Modernity, Cambridge, MA: Massachusetts Institute of Technology, 1987b.
On the Logic of the Social Sciences, trans. S. Nicholsen and J. Stark, Oxford: Polity Press in association with Basil Blackwell, 1988.
Moral Consciousness and Communicative Action, trans. C. Lenhardt and S. Nicholsen, Cambridge: Polity Press in association with Basil Blackwell, 1990.

Further reading

Alford, C., 'Is Jürgen Habermas's Reconstructive Science Really Science?', *Theory and Society*, 14, 3, pp.321–40, 1985.
Anyon, J., 'Schools as Agencies of Social Legitimation', *International Journal of Political Education*, 4, pp.195–218, 1981.
Apple, M., *Ideology and Curriculum*, London: Routledge & Kegan Paul, 1979.
—— 'The Politics of Official Knowledge: Does a National Curriculum Make Sense?', *Teachers College Record*, 95, 2, pp.222–41, 1993.
Aronowitz, S. and Giroux, H., *Education Under Siege*, London: Routledge & Kegan Paul, 1986.
Bernstein R., *Habermas and Modernity*, Oxford: Polity Press with Basil Blackwell, 1985.
Callawaert, S., 'Philosophy of Education, Frankfurt Critical Theory and the Sociology of Pierre Bourdieu', in T. Popkewitz and L. Fendler (eds), *Critical Theories in Education: Changing Terrains of Knowledge and Politics*, London: Routledge, pp.117–44, 1999.
Carr, W. and Kemmis, S., *Becoming Critical*, Lewes, Falmer, 1986.
Cohen, L., Manion, L. and Morrison, K.R.B., *Research Methods in Education*, 5th edn, London: Routledge, 2000.
Eisner, E., *The Art of Educational Evaluation*, Lewes: Falmer, 1985.
Fay, B., *Critical Social Science*, New York: Cornell University Press, 1987.
Fendler, L., 'Making Trouble: Prediction, Agency, Critical Intellectuals', in T. Popkewitz and L. Fendler (eds), *Critical Theories in Education: Changing Terrains of Knowledge and Politics*, London: Routledge, pp.169–88, 1999.
Freire, P., *Pedagogy of the Oppressed*, Harmondsworth, Penguin, 1972.
Geuss, R., *The Idea of a Critical Theory*, London: Cambridge University Press, 1981.
Giroux, H., *Theory and Resistance in Education*, London: Heinemann, 1983.
—— *Border Crossings: Cultural Workers and the Politics of Education*, London: Routledge, 1992.
Giroux, H. and McLaren, P., 'Teacher Education and the Politics of Engagement: The Case for Democratic Schooling', *Harvard Educational Review*, 56, pp.213–38, 1986.
Gore, J., *The Struggle for Pedagogies*, London: Routledge, 1993.
Grundy, S., *Curriculum: Product or Praxis?*, Lewes: Falmer, 1987.
Kemmis, S., 'Seven Principles for Programme Evaluation in Curriculum Development and Innovation', *Journal of Curriculum Studies*, 14, 3, pp.221–40, 1982.

Kemmis, S., 'Action Research', in. J.P. Keeves and G. Lakomski (eds), *Issues in Educational Research*, Oxford: Elsevier Science Ltd., pp.150–60, 1999.

Kemmis, S. and McTaggart, R., *The Action Research Planner*, Victoria, Australia: Deakin University Press, 1981.

Kolakowski L., *Main Currents of Marxism Volume Three: The Breakdown*, trans. P.S. Falla, Oxford: Clarendon Press, 1978.

Kuhn, T., *The Structure of Scientific Revolutions*, Chicago, IL: University of Chicago Press, 1962.

Lakomski, G., 'Critical Theory', in. J.P. Keeves and G. Lakomski (eds), *Issues in Educational Research*, Oxford: Elsevier Science Ltd., pp.174–83, 1999.

McCarthy, T., *The Critical Theory of Jürgen Habermas*, London: Hutchinson, 1978.

Miedama, S. and Wardekker, W.L., 'Emergent Identity versus Consistent Identity: Possibilities for a Postmodern Repoliticization of Critical Pedagogy', in T. Popkewitz and L. Fendler (eds), *Critical Theories in Education: Changing Terrains of Knowledge and Politics*, London: Routledge, pp.67–83, 1999.

Morrison, K.R.B., 'Habermas and the School Curriculum', unpublished Ph.D. thesis, School of Education, University of Durham, 1995.

Morrison, K.R.B., 'Habermas and Critical Pedagogy', *Critical Pedagogy Networker*, 9, 2, pp.1–7, 1996.

Pusey, M., *Jürgen Habermas*, London: Tavistock, 1987.

Rasmussen, D. M., *Reading Habermas*, Oxford: Basil Blackwell, 1990.

Roderick R., *Habermas and the Foundations of Critical Theory*, Basingstoke: Macmillan, 1986.

Stenhouse, L., *An Introduction to Curriculum Research and Development*, London: Heinemann, 1975.

Taba, H., *Curriculum Development: Theory and Practice*, New York: Harcourt Brace, 1962.

Tyler, R., *Basic Principles of Curriculum and Instruction*, Chicago, IL: University of Chicago Press, 1949.

Young, R., *A Critical Theory of Education: Habermas and Our Children's Future*, London: Harvester Wheatsheaf, 1989.

KEITH MORRISON

CARL BEREITER 1930–

The past century has seen wave after wave of educational reforms that gathered energy for a while and then lost it. If we ignore the counter-reforms and look at those that struck people as new and exciting, we find that almost always the perceived novelty lay in a more enlightened and humane way of carrying on the process of education. It was not perceived as extending the limits of the possible. Yet what we find and indeed have come to demand in most other aspects of modern life is a continual expansion of the possible. ... But not only has this failed to occur in education, it has not even occurred to people to look for it. People cannot imagine what an extension of the limits of the possible in education would mean. I believe the work that casts students as legitimate creators of knowledge is the first in a very long time to be seriously trying to extend the limits. If it succeeds – and the indications so far are positive – this may finally herald a reform that can survive.[1]

224

Bereiter is an educational psychologist whose empirical research and theorizing have ranged over much of the territory of that field and extended beyond it into areas of policy, philosophy and technology. The connecting thread has been the desire, in his words, to 'extend the limits of the possible' in education. This objective did not take shape, however, until several years after completing his doctorate at the University of Wisconsin in 1959. Trained in quantitative methods under two of the leading psychometricians of the time, Chester Harris and Julian Stanley, Bereiter embarked on a similar career. One product of those early years, a paper titled 'Some Persisting Dilemmas in the Measurement of Change' (1963),[2] is still cited as framing conceptual problems that have not yet been resolved to everyone's satisfaction. By the time that paper appeared, however, Bereiter had abandoned the research tradition in which it was conceived, having concluded that nothing new in education could arise from research that confined itself to the analysis of existing variations, whether in people, conditions, or methods. Only more adventurous experimentation could do that. Motivated by that conviction, he moved to the Training Research Laboratory at the University of Illinois, where experiments were underway in the newly emerging field of teaching by machine.

The work at Illinois that brought him to the attention not only of educators but the mass media as well had nothing to do with technology, however. It was preschool education for disadvantaged children, a burgeoning field in which the 'limits of the possible' were not yet solidified in practice. This work gave to education the term 'direct instruction'. Although direct instruction – essentially, identifying what needs to be learned and teaching it in the most efficient manner available – was and is the method of choice in most kinds of education and training, its application to young children was novel and considered outrageous by many. Bereiter and Engelmann's *Teaching Disadvantaged Children in the Preschool* (1966)[3] became a Citation Classic, although a sizeable proportion of the citations were condemnatory. According to Bereiter the book achieved iconic status, meaning that it was considered permissible to condemn it without reading it. What the Bereiter–Engelmann preschool demonstrated, however, was that through intensive direct instruction, children for whom academic expectations were very low could be reading and doing arithmetic at mid-second grade level by the time they left kindergarten and scoring in the high normal range on intelligence tests. The impact of the preschool work is hard to assess. Direct instruction in moderate amounts is now common in kindergartens. Although the general character of the kindergarten – a garden of children – remains unchanged, there is evident a greatly altered sense of what it is possible for young children to achieve intellectually.

Bereiter's work in preschool education was explicitly atheoretical. As he argued in a 1968 article,[4] neither of the theoretical orientations then available to childhood educators – Skinnerian behaviourism and Piagetian developmentalism – made contact with fundamental questions of what to teach and how. He attached greater hope to a theoretical approach that was only beginning to appear on the educational horizon, what came to be known as cognitivism. An opportune Guggenheim Fellowship allowed him to devote a year to studying the works of this new science and, in juxtaposition, the writings of Dewey. Further advancement of the 'limits of the possible' was going to require a scientific basis – an understanding of intellectual processes sufficient to support the invention of more powerful ways to influence them.

Along with Marlene Scardamalia, he began a programme of research at the Ontario Institute for Studies in Education in Toronto that led from the psychology of writing to investigations of intentional learning to the design of computer environments and social networks that have demonstrated real qualitative leaps rather than incremental gains in children's intellectual accomplishments. Over an eight-year period, beginning in 1976, Bereiter and Scardamalia carried out scores of experiments, investigating almost the full range of cognitive issues surrounding the composing process. The question that especially intrigued them was one that no one else was investigating: How is it that children can write as well as they do, given the small amount of thinking that they evidently put into it? The answer they pieced together from varied evidence took the form of what they called the 'knowledge-telling model.' It is a model for the highly efficient generation of text that meets topic and genre constraints but that leaves the writer's knowledge virtually unaffected. This model was almost universal in children's writing and contrasted sharply with what was widely observed among expert writers which they characterized as the 'knowledge-transforming model.' Although these models were created to answer scientific questions, they raised educational issues as well. The knowledge-telling model is ideally suited to school writing assignments, where the first requirement is getting it done on time. Indeed, the standard prescription in school rhetoric handbooks for producing a research paper maps precisely on to this model: select a topic, reduce it to manageable size, collect material, organize it, produce a draft, edit it, and produce a final copy. The trouble with knowledge telling is that it is good for hardly any kind of writing other than school assignments that presuppose it.

What they observed with writing they also found in analyses of students' reading processes and it seemed to represent a pattern common across the school curriculum. School tasks and students' strategies for dealing with them co-evolve until a stable state is achieved in which the task and the students' strategies for minimizing time and cognitive effort are in harmony. Assessment practices evolve similarly, resulting in a virtually unchangeable combination of task, test and strategy. At the same time that they were discovering this phenomenon in writing and reading, other researchers were discovering the amazing extent and durability of students' scientific misconceptions. The question Bereiter and Scardamalia asked was, how could these misconceptions have gone unnoticed for so long? Like school reading and writing, school science appeared to have evolved so as to conform to what came easily to students.

Many education critics were lamenting the 'dumbing down' of the curriculum and proposing, as obvious solutions, the upgrading of content and the toughening of standards. As a result of their research, Bereiter and Scardamalia saw a deeper problem. Viewing classroom instruction as a coherent socio-cognitive process with some parts being performed by the teacher and other parts by the students, they saw both traditional and child-centred versions of 'good' teaching as ones in which the teacher performs most of the high-level cognitive functions and the students perform the lower-level ones. The methods differed mainly in how much control students were allowed over the lower-level parts of the educational process. Fundamental change would require finding ways of turning over to students more of the higher-level parts – the parts having to do with such things as goals, problems of understanding, the relating of new knowledge to old, the evaluation of individual and collective progress and the reorienting of effort on the basis of it. The summary term they used for this was 'higher levels of agency' (1991).[5]

Higher levels of agency for students could not simply be declared and expected to take hold within the established structures of school life, centred around tasks and activities (whether self-chosen or assigned by the teacher). Schooling had to be restructured around the students' own efforts to understand the world and make a place for themselves in it – an ideal often promulgated and seldom even approached in practice. Such a restructuring they believed, might at last be possible if it was grounded in an enlarged understanding of knowledge construction and if it exploited the newly emerging potentialities of network computing to restructure the flow of information in classrooms. The result was CSILE – Computer Supported Intentional Learning Environments. This project, started in 1986, immediately caught attention in the cognition and learning community because of its demonstrations of school children pursuing explanations to a depth never contemplated in curriculum guidelines. The project continues advancing the 'limits of the possible', drawing visitors from around the world to project classrooms and spawning experimental sites in a dozen countries.

Whereas the work at Illinois gave the world the term 'direct instruction', the Toronto work introduced the term 'knowledge building'. As these terms came into general use, their meanings predictably became degraded, the latter term sometimes being used merely as inflated language referring to any sort of meaningful learning. But the concept of knowledge building, as used by Bereiter, is imbedded in a larger conceptual framework that needs to be understood in order to grasp knowledge building as a distinctive activity. In a series of articles, beginning with the 1985 'Toward a Solution of the Learning Paradox'[6] and culminating in a book still in press, *Education and Mind in the Knowledge Age*, Bereiter has wrestled with the twin problems of how to account psychologically for the acquisition of increasingly complex knowledge (Piaget's problem) and how to bring into schooling the kind of deliberate knowledge production that is characteristic of science (a problem closely linked to Popper's notion of objective knowledge or, in Bereiter's preferred term, 'conceptual artifacts'). Solving the psychological problem in an educationally useful way requires, according to Bereiter, abandoning the mind-as-container metaphor common to folk psychology and conceiving of a mind that 'can support knowledgeable action without actually containing the rules, propositions, images, recorded events, and so on, that are conventionally reckoned to constitute knowledge' (Bereiter, 2000, p. 232). That is the conception of mind posited in some forms of connectionism, and Bereiter argues it is important for education in order to deal with the vast range of learning outcomes that cannot be well represented as rules, propositions and the like. Paramount among these is depth of understanding.

Knowledge building, however, is not the same as becoming knowledge-able. It is the creation of conceptual artifacts which become publicly available tools for the creation of further conceptual artifacts – the programme, in other words, of progressive disciplines. In the process of creating, testing and improving such artifacts, students gain in knowledge-ability, but at the same time they are producing things that will be of use – conceptual tools for making sense of the world. Although there have been many efforts in the past half-century to engage students in genuine inquiry, they have missed the essential dynamic of knowledge building, Bereiter claims. In Popperian terms, they have focused on world 1, the physical world, and world 2, the mental world of the student, but have ignored world 3, the world of theories and other constructions that are the object of knowledge building in the laboratories and seminar rooms of the adult world. The extensions of the 'limits of the possible' demonstrated in the CSILE project are essentially demonstrations of children at work in world 3.

Notes

1　C. Bereiter, 'Artifacts, Canons, and the Progress of Pedagogy: A Response to Contributors', in B. Smith (ed.), *Liberal Education in a Knowledge Society*, Chicago, IL: Open Court, in press.
2　C. Bereiter, 'Some Persisting Dilemmas in the Measurement of Change', in C.W. Harris (ed.), *Problems in Measuring Change*, Madison, WI: University of Wisconsin Press, pp.3–20, 1963.
3　C. Bereiter and S. Engelmann, *Teaching Disadvantaged Children in the Preschool*, Englewood Cliffs, NJ: Prentice Hall, 1966.
4　C. Bereiter, 'Psychology and Early Education', in D.W. Brison and J. Hill (eds), *Psychology and Early Childhood Education*, Monograph Series No. 4, Toronto: Ontario Institute for Studies in Education, pp.61–78, 1968.
5　M. Scardamalia and C. Bereiter, 'Higher Levels of Agency for Children in Knowledge Building: A Challenge for the Design of New Knowledge Media', *The Journal of the Learning Sciences*, 1, 1, pp.37–68, 1991.
6　C. Bereiter, 'Toward a Solution of the Learning Paradox', *Review of Educational Research*, 55, pp.201–26, 1985.

See also

In this book: Piaget
In *Fifty Major Thinkers on Education*: Dewey

Bereiter's major writings

Bereiter, C. and Scardamalia, M., *The Psychology of Written Composition*, Hillsdale, NJ: Lawrence Erlbaum Associates, 1987.
Bereiter, C. and Scardamalia, M., *Surpassing Ourselves: An Inquiry into the Nature and Implications of Expertise*, Chicago, IL: Open Court, 1993.
'Implications of Postmodernism for Science, or, Science as Progressive Discourse', *Educational Psychologist*, 29, 1, pp.3–12, 1994.
Bereiter, C. and Scardamalia, M., 'Rethinking Learning', in D.R. Olson and N. Torrance (eds), *Handbook of Education and Human Development: New Models of Learning, Teaching and Schooling*, Cambridge, MA: Basil Blackwell, pp.485–513, 1996.

Bereiter, C. and Scardamalia, M., 'Beyond Bloom's *Taxonomy*: Rethinking Knowledge for the Knowledge Age', in A. Hargreaves, A. Lieberman, M. Fullan and D. Hopkins (eds.), *International Handbook of Educational Change*, Dordrecht: Kluwer, pp.675–92, 1998.

'Keeping the Brain in Mind', *Australian Journal of Education*, 44, 3, pp.226–38, 2000.

Education and Mind in the Knowledge Age, Mahwah, NJ: Lawrence Erlbaum Associates, in press.

'Education in a Knowledge Society', in B. Smith (ed.), *Liberal Education in a Knowledge Society*, Chicago, IL: Open Court, in press.

Further reading

Brown, A.L., 'Design Experiments: Theoretical and Methodological Challenges in Creating Complex Interventions in Classroom Settings', *The Journal of the Learning Sciences*, 2, 2, pp.141–78, 1992.

Case, R. and Okamoto, Y., 'The Role of Central Conceptual Structures in the Development of Children's Thought', *Monographs of the Society for Research in Child Development*, 61, 2, serial no. 246, 1996.

Koschmann, T. (ed.), *CSCL: Theory and Practice of an Emerging Paradigm*, Mahwah, NJ: LEA, pp.249–68, 1996.

McGilley, K. (ed.), *Classroom Lessons: Integrating Cognitive Theory and Classroom Practice*, Cambridge, MA: MIT Press, 1994.

Popper, K.R., *Objective Knowledge: An Evolutionary Approach*, Oxford: Clarendon Press, 1972.

DAVID R. OLSON

PIERRE BOURDIEU 1930–

> Sociology has to include a sociology of the perception of the social world, that is, a sociology of the construction of the world-views which themselves contribute to the construction of this world.[1]

During his academic career, Bourdieu has produced theoretical and empirical work in philosophy, anthropology, sociology, education, culture and politics. In the 1960s, Bourdieu began to distance his work from the French structuralist school in which he was educated. He has since then been engaged in developing conceptual and methodological tools for research in the social sciences. Although he considers his work to be sociological, his concepts and methods are increasingly used by scholars in the various social and educational sciences across the world. Bourdieu's work has been viewed as an innovative transposition of a relational conception of the natural sciences to the social sciences that is philosophically in a tradition of realism.[2]

Bourdieu is probably best known by educators for his articulation of how the educated social groups (professional groups or classes) use cultural capital as a social strategy to hold or gain status and respect in society. *The Inheritors* (with Passeron), *Distinction*, *Homo Academicvs* and *The State Nobility* are among his best-known books, and in *Outline of a Theory of*

Practice, *The Logic of Practice* and *An Invitation to Reflexive Sociology* (with Wacquant), as well as in various essays (see, e.g., *In Other Words*), he lays out his relational approach to study society. In these works, one can explore how Bourdieu creatively weaves together multiple concepts of French and continental sociology, linguistics and philosophy into an innovative and productive intellectual project for sociology (e.g., from Bachelard, Durkheim, Marx, Mauss and Weber).

Bourdieu's 'theory' is a practical theory based in extensive research he and his associates have conducted in France over the last forty years. Bourdieu calls his own approach *reflexive sociology*. In that phrase, he captures the elements of a way to reflect not only on society but to account for the objective as well as subjective status of individuals within a social and discursive framework. The 'theory' consists of a comprehensive conceptual framework. Capital (cultural, social, economic and symbolic), legitimating principles, social field, habitus and social strategies are among the most used concepts. Epistemic reflexivity and epistemic individuals are also important concepts in Bourdieu's reflexive sociology.

To adequately enter into the theoretical position of Bourdieu we need to consider two points regarding his theoretical project. First, his theory is epistemological; that is, it orients one to a way of thinking and ordering the world under scrutiny but is not a positivistic theory of operational concepts. Second, Bourdieu's research has provided important substantive ways in which to consider the relation of education to issues of social reproduction and the mechanism through which social inclusion and exclusion are produced within a relational field as both sociological and historical 'facts'.

Bourdieu's reflexive sociology offers an approach to understand intellectual practice, whether it is in sociology, the natural sciences, or education. Central to this theory is the approach that he calls *epistemic reflexivity* and the concept *epistemic individuals*. The aim of epistemic reflexivity for the researcher is to unearth 'the epistemological unconscious of his discipline'.[3] This brand of reflexivity differs from other criticisms in at least three crucial ways: 'First, its primary target is not the individual analyst but the *social and intellectual unconscious* embedded in analytic tools and operations; second, it must be a *collective enterprise* rather than the burden of the lone academic; and, third, it seeks not to assault but to *buttress the epistemological security*' of the discipline.[4]

Epistemic individuals differ from biological individuals in that they are constructed from the epistemological characteristics they carry. That is, the epistemological unconscious of a discipline is studied through the historically and socially constructed legitimating principles operating in a *social field* which is the metaphor to explain power struggles. For instance, in the French university field that Bourdieu studied in *Homo Academicvs*, the available positions for individuals to adopt are structured according to two competing principles. He and his associates collected relevant indicators for opportunities to access, educational determinants such as schools attended, capital of academic powers, capital of scientific power, scientific prestige such as translations and citations, intellectual renown, capital of political and economic power, and political dispositions of university professors. He discovered that the French university field was organized according to two antagonistic principles of hierarchization:

the social hierarchy, corresponding to the capital inherited and the economic and political capital actually held, is in opposition to the specific, properly cultural hierarchy, corresponding to the capital of scientific authority or intellectual renown. This opposition is inherent in the very structures of the university field which is the locus of confrontation between two competing *principles of legitimation*.[5]

The attitude and methods of epistemic reflexivity provide a strategy to reflect on the epistemological and social position of the researcher, rather than enter into a subjectivist practice that is merely biographical and expressing a relationship with our beliefs and on the ways in which we have adopted certain positions (whether born with them, or achieved them).

Key concepts in the notion of epistemic reflexivity are habitus and social strategies. Bourdieu explains *habitus* as the structured and structuring mental structure through which individuals acquire their views and behaviour as a second nature. Yet habitus is not a static thing but a structuring that is continually embodied in a process of transformation, the effect of the social trajectories leading to changes in the situations of individuals, changes in relation to what counts as capital in a given social field.[6] The structures are internalized as the 'truth' to understand the world from and beliefs to fight for. Further, Bourdieu describes habitus as a collective enterprise through which the social world is produced and reproduced as a dynamic enterprise in which the being of the individual participates relative to the available capital.

Bourdieu uses the idea of *social strategies* to explain the way in which individuals engage themselves in the struggles over symbolic capital. Social strategies are, simultaneously, conscious, 'rational' choices we take to make our beliefs come true and the unconscious use of these beliefs. For instance, players in the French university field (and in any field) find certain available discursive themes and cultural practices that they can adopt as their own. They adopt them because they believe they are correct, not because they are thinking of themselves in a competition to hold or gain power in the form of capital. The way in which social strategies are, simultaneously, conscious and unconscious is, perhaps, best described in Bourdieu's own words: 'It is because agents never know completely what they are doing that what they do has more sense than they know'.[7]

The notion of social strategies also accounts very well for the fact that there always are scientists who refuse to accept what is given in their scientific field. But such innovative scientists are also players in the field as long as they participate in a struggle against what counts as capital in the field. This means that the 'object' of study (any social field) begins and ends where the effects of the legitimating principles cease, where an idea or a practice or an academic title, stops counting as symbolic capital.

Bourdieu's concepts bypass the problem of whether a structure or an agent is more important in understanding the relations between these two, that is, which one determines the other. This is so because the object of study is the interrelations between individuals and the social structure, as well as because a social field is a space of relations not consisting of predefined groups or populations. The social field, as a metaphor, is constructed by objectifying the relationship between the legitimating principles and the individuals competing in that field for what counts as symbolic capital in that field.

If we look historically at Bourdieu's conceptions, we can see that the theoretical canopy of his present work has slowly developed over many years as the theoretical 'entities' continually were brushed against and interacted with empirical research in the process of developing interpretations. Thus the concept of social field was developed later than the concept of capital. One of the last concepts is *field of power*, a metaphor for seeing the whole society. By using this concept, Bourdieu provides a way to consider the production of social hierarchies. The field of power is the arena where holders of the various kinds of capital (cultural, economic, social) compete over which of them will have the greatest chance of being symbolic or legitimate. The most common competition in most societies is between those who hold economic and cultural capital; they compete over the 'exchange rates' between those kinds of capital.[8]

Bourdieu's work on education can be compared to other contemporary researchers as these works intersect. One such comparison is to the work of Basil Bernstein who also approaches issues of the relation of social groups, knowledge and social differentiation. Important distinction in reading the two works is that Bernstein's work is heavily influenced by the analytical philosophical tradition of British intellectuals in pursuing the idea of relation whereas Bourdieu relies more on the continental philosophical traditions. A second comparison is with the work of Foucault, both interested in showing that knowledge is a 'social fact' that should undergo social and historical inquiry. Bourdieu's *The Political Ontology of Martin Heidegger* and more recent writings on the colonization of reason bring the two closer together in Bourdieu's use of genealogical inquiry. The difference lies in the fact that Bourdieu's reflections are always placed within a sociological field that focuses on the relation of knowledge and the social position of actors.[9]

Bourdieu's conceptions offer a comprehensive way of seeing the world. For the beginners of reflexive sociology there is no easy, light method to 'master' his ideas; the concepts often appear as complicated and dense, even 'blurred' and fuzzy. The reason for that is very simple: the world will always be much more complex than any conceptual way of trying to understand it.[10] And even though his work is not readily 'consumable', the playfulness (and humour) of the work gives a tone to students of his work as they begin to play with the ideas by using them. A good way to begin to study Bourdieu's work is to read some of his articles collected in *In Other Words* and his work on art, for example *Distinction*. These works should help a student to develop the possibility to actually look at how individuals employ cultural practices as social strategies to gain symbolic capital, and if not to gain any such power, at least to distinguish themselves from others by their interests. The student who begins to do some empirical observations from such a perspective will doubtless see that playing with the concepts, using them to try to understand the cultural behaviour of people (even of themselves), is not inconsistent with intellectual rigor; it is indeed the way the concepts were developed into a comprehensive, conceptual approach called reflexive sociology.

Notes

1 Bourdieu, *In Other Words*, p.130.
2 Frédéric Vandenberghe, ' "The Real is Relational" ': An Epistemological Analysis of Pierre Bourdieu's Generative Structuralism', *Sociological Theory*, 17, 1, pp.32–6, 1999.
3 Loïc J.D. Wacquant, 'Toward a Social Praxeology: The Structure and Logic of Bourdieu's Sociology', in P. Bourdieu, with L.J.D. Wacquant, *An Invitation to Reflexive Sociology*, p.41.
4 Ibid, p.36. Original emphases.
5 Bourdieu, *Homo Academicus*, p.48. Original emphasis.
6 Bourdieu, *In Other Words*, p.116.
7 Bourdieu, *The Logic of Practice*, p.69.
8 Loïc J.D. Wacquant, 'Foreword', in Bourdieu, *The State Nobility*, p.xi.
9 See, e.g., Pierre Bourdieu and Loïc J.D. Wacquant, 'On The Cunning of Imperialist Reason', *Theory, Culture, and Society*, 16, 1, pp.4–58, 1999; Pierre Bourdieu, 'The Social Conditions of the International Circulation of Ideas', in Richard Shusterman (ed.), *Bourdieu: A Critical Reader*, Oxford: Blackwell, pp.220–8, 1999.
10 Loïc J.D. Wacquant, 'Toward a Social Praxeology: The Structure and Logic of Bourdieu's Sociology', in P. Bourdieu, with L.J.D. Wacquant, *An Invitation to Reflexive Sociology*, p.23 (n.41).

See also

In this book: Heidegger, Foucault
In *Fifty Major Thinkers on Education*: Durkheim

Bourdieu's major writings

A list of Bourdieu's major writings would fill several pages and a list of all his writings a small book. We list here the books that we have referred to above, along with a few others that are accessible in English, such as collections of essays. The original publication date in French is listed after the English language edition.

Bourdieu, P., with Passeron, Jean-Claude, *The Inheritors: French Students and Their Relations to Culture*, Chicago, IL: University of Chicago Press, 1979, 1964.
Bourdieu, P., with Passeron, Jean-Claude, *Reproduction in Education, Society and Culture*, London: Sage, 1977, 1970.
Outline of a Theory of Practice, Cambridge: Cambridge University Press, 1977, 1972.
Distinction: A Social Critique of the Judgement of Taste, London: Routledge & Kegan Paul; Cambridge, MA: Harvard University Press, 1984, 1979.
The Logic of Practice, Cambridge: Polity Press; Stanford, CA: Stanford University Press, 1990, 1980
Homo Academicus, Cambridge: Polity Press; Stanford, CA: Stanford University Press, 1988, 1984.
In Other Words: Essays Towards a Reflexive Sociology, Cambridge: Polity Press; Stanford, CA: Stanford University Press, 1990, 1982–87.
The Political Ontology of Martin Heidegger, Cambridge: Polity Press; Stanford, CA: Stanford University Press, 1991, 1988.
The State Nobility: Elite Schools in the Field of Power, Cambridge: Polity Press, 1996, 1989.
Language and Symbolic Power, John B. Thompson (ed.), Cambridge: Polity Press; Cambridge, MA: Harvard University Press, 1991.

Bourdieu, P. , with Loïc J.D. Wacquant, *An Invitation to Reflexive Sociology*, Chicago, IL: University of Chicago Press, 1992.
Acts of Resistance: Against the Tyranny of the Market, New York: The New Press, 1998.

Further reading

Broady, Donald, *Sociologi och Epistemology. Om Pierre Bourdieus författarskap och den historiska epistemologin* (in Swedish), Stockholm: HLS Förlag, 1991.

INGÓLFUR ÁSGEIR JÓHANNESSON AND THOMAS S. POPKEWITZ

NEIL POSTMAN 1931–

Speech is the primal and indispensable medium. It made us human, keeps us human, and in fact defines what human means ... [t]here is no escape from meaning when language is the instrument guiding one's thought ... [m]eaning demands to be understood.[1]

Prime time. We are on the air. 'The Struggle of Ideas.' The fascinating new TV programme. 'So, who do we have on our guest list today? Not surprisingly, we have a fantastic list of friends who will enable us to enjoy a superb evening. Our first guest is no less then Professor Neil Postman, one of the greatest educational and communicational philosophers, who not only preaches better teaching, but also received the Christian Lindback Award for Excellence in Teaching. He is the author of more than twenty books and 200 articles, and he lives with us here in New York. A recipient of some of NYU's highest honours, including an appointment as University Professor in 1993 and the Paulette Goddard Professor of Media Ecology, but before we move to the first question, let us go to our commercial break.'
'And to our first question: Can you please explain to us, in simple human terms, why are you against television?' Taking a deep breath Professor Postman replies: 'It is not a war against television that I am interested in. My main concern is the connection between forms of human communication and the quality of culture. I am trying to understand the shift from the magic of writing to the magic of electronics.' 'Great!' exclaims the interviewer, 'television is indeed the magic of electronics.' Patiently, Postman continues: 'And television, like every other media, is engaged in the transformation of the way we think, the way we learn, the way we express ourselves.' 'I like it,' is the interviewer's swift response, 'you wrote that we might amuse ourselves to death. Do we?' (referring to Postman's book *Amusing Ourselves to Death*, 1985) 'We are not going to die yet, but we might end up with empty brains,' is Postman's short answer, reflecting the quick pace of television sound byte. 'So, the news of the day is that there are good news, and bad news ...'

We will stop here in this imaginary interview, which probably did or might have taken place somewhere, and which reflects Postman's view, that television is 'nothing less than a philosophy of rhetoric'.[2] That 'the best things on television *are* its junk',[3] and that 'the news of the day is a figment of our technological imagination'.[4]

Postman claims that the modern electronic communication system, which makes time and distance obsolete, the Age of Show Business, is a poor replacement for the printed Age of Exposition, a mode of thought, a method of learning and a means of expression. And this new Age of Show Business loses almost all of the characteristics that are associated with the nature of discourse. It makes us lose the sophisticated ability to think conceptually, deductively and sequentially; it makes us lose the high valuation of reason and order; the abhorrence of contradiction; the wide capacity for detachment and objectivity; and the tolerance for delayed response. And we should read *Amusing Ourselves to Death* as a warning that education is shifting from teaching as a process of dialogue to teaching as an amusing activity.

This is the deep content and insight of Marshall McLuhan's theme that the 'medium is the message' and which some would argue that Postman brought to its extreme.[5]

Postman has gone a long way toward reaching this most influential stage of being one of the most prominent philosophers and the main educational challenger of 'electronic education'. Postman's academic career began in 1959 in an English Education class called American English Grammar. In 1961, still as an Associate Professor of English Education at New York University, before becoming Chair of the Department of Culture and Communication at NYU, Postman, already recognizing the unprecedented influence of television on learning, perceived television as a most persistent and magnetic source of information and a primary source of literacy experience. But the seeds for his ideas in *Amusing Ourselves to Death* were already there. Although in his book *Television and the Teaching of English*,[6] Postman offers motivation, aid and encouragement to teachers of English who want to utilize the television, he clearly conditioned the utility of television on our responses to television being informed, discriminating and creative.

Starting his career as an elementary school teacher, Postman still perceives himself as a romantic believer in education who keeps an optimistic spirit alive, despite the debilitating affect on teaching by the current culture. Indeed, his latest book, *The End of Education*, for which he has been invited to Italy to receive the Salvatore Valitutti International Prize for the Italian translation,[7] is written with the hope of altering schooling by reintroducing to it its inherent purposes, its 'ends', but with the warning that without a serious dialogue about purposes schooling will reach its 'finish', since 'without meaning, learning has no purpose. Without a purpose, schools are houses of detention, not attention',[8] 'and the sooner we are done with it, the better'.[9]

But, to be sure, it is not schools as such that Postman is knocking, as much as society and current culture, with its oversized technology, that he focuses on, since schools are only mirrors of social beliefs, giving back what the citizen puts in front of them. Accordingly, schools are confronted with two contradicting beliefs: one belief is aimed at educating toward critical thinking, toward the development of an independent mind, and enough skill to fight and change wrongs. This is what Postman calls *Teaching as a Subversive Activity*.[10] The other belief looks at schools as a means of teaching the students to accept the world as it is, or even to subordinate themselves to culture's rules, constraints and even prejudices. This is his *Teaching as a Conserving Activity*.[11] This in fact reflects Postman's and his close writing companion for five books Charles Weingartner's dialectic approach, that for every 'true' idea they can come up with an alternative, with an opposite 'true' idea. Education is not schooling, and for Neil Postman schooling may be a subversive or a conserving activity, but it is certainly a circumscribed one. As Postman, with a bit of irony, describes the schooling time scheme: 'It has a late beginning and an early end and in between it pauses for summer vacations and holidays, and generously excuses us when we are ill.'[12] Neil Postman didn't agree with *The New York Times Magazine* when in early 1971 it identified him as a 'leading educational radical'.[13] But a year earlier Postman and Charles Weingartner did published for students aged fifteen to twenty-five a handbook for turning schools around: *The Soft Revolution*.[14]

In the early 1980s Postman forced the educational world to be aware of *The Disappearance of Childhood*[15] and of the question: *Childhood: Can It Be Preserved?*[16] Postman's response was clear. If we continue to be trapped in our own technology, our television, childhood is doomed as a social structure. Postman traces the history of childhood and, after describing the historical development of the conception and social manifestation of modern childhood from the Renaissance, and spurred by the invention of print, he points out the ways television erases the dividing line between childhood and adulthood. He argues that social pressure and especially electronic media are leading to the end of childhood as a social structure. Furthermore, American culture appears to be the enemy of childhood, leading to 'The Disappearing Child' (1983), when children look, dress, talk and behave like adults. And, again with a glimpse of irony, Postman adds that, at the same time, adults have become more like children.

Are there any social institutions strong enough and committed enough to resist the decline of childhood? Postman's optimistic reply is yes, the family and the school. Schools as we know them today, a product of the development of print, will not easily join in the assault on its parentage. In one form or another, no matter how diluted the effort, the institution of the school will stand as the last defence against the disappearance of childhood. But, fifteen years later, as we have noted above, the optimistic view of Postman was transformed to a challenging warning with the double meaning of *The End of Education*,[17] calling for redefining the values of schools as an almost last defence of schools as an educational entity. But still, Postman ends his epilogue by saying that:

> My faith is that school will endure since no one has invented a better way to introduce the young to the world of learning; that public school will endure since no one has invented a better way to create a public; and that childhood will survive because without it we must lose our sense of what it means to be an adult.[18]

The believing teacher is still there.

The perception of the technological oppression of culture brings Postman to ask if the decline of childhood signifies a general decline of American culture. Hence, the answer to the question, can a culture preserve human values and create new ones by allowing modern technology the fullest possible authority to control its destiny, is not a simple one, and the question is still open. But the challenge is that 'America has not yet begun to *think*';[19] it is still under the shocking effect of twentieth-century technology.

A decade later, *Technopoly, The Surrender of Culture to Technology*[20] can be seen as a delayed answer to this question. To be sure, Postman clearly recognizes that technology *is* a friend, but that there is a dark side to this friend. In *Technopoly*, Postman analyses when, how and why technology has become a particularly dangerous enemy. Technopoly, in Postman's view, is not only a state of culture, but also a state of mind. 'It consists in the definition of technology, which means that the culture seeks its authorization in technology, and takes its orders from technology.'[21] Technicalization, which reflects a technologic and bureaucratic amalgamation of terms and problems, is perceived as a serious form of information and language control. Postman stipulates:

> If we define ideology as a set of assumptions of which we are barely conscious but which nonetheless directs our efforts to give shape and coherence to the world, then our most powerful ideological instrument is the technology of language itself.[22]

It is, therefore, the great symbol drain. Technopoly casts aside all traditional narratives and symbols that suggest stability and orderliness, and tells, instead, of a life of skills, technical expertise and the ecstasy of consumption. Not that technological development does not have great advantages, but '[a]ll technological change is a Faustian bargain', says Postman.[23] He challenges educators not to look for cures for education's ills in new technology, because those problems are of a social, moral and spiritual, rather than technical nature. Moreover, focusing resources and energy heavily on using educational technology to teach is evading the issue of what needs to be taught.[24]

To really understand Postman's challenging attack on the impact of technology on culture in general and on education in particular, one has to grasp the linguistic conceptual basis of Postman critical analysis. Postman, the editor of *Et Cetera*, a journal of general semantics, is also the 1986 recipient of the George Orwell Award for Clarity in Language given by the National Council of Teachers of English. In *Language and Systems*,[25] and *Linguistics*[26] he and his colleagues looked at linguistics 'as a way of behaving while one attempts to discover information and to acquire knowledge about language'.[27] Furthermore, if we look at methods of scientific investigation as an expression of the necessary mode of working of the human mind, which is a continual process of inquiry that conceptualizes the linguistic enterprise, then the importance of linguistic symbols cannot be overlooked. If indeed linguistics is the exposure to and the use of symbols that shapes our mind and frames our way of thinking, the difference between reading a book and watching television becomes quite clear, and Postman's central argument is much better understood. Interestingly, school in the Hebrew language is 'beit seffer', when 'beit' means house, 'seffer' means book, thus school means the 'book house' or 'house of the book'.

Television requires perception, not conception,[28] while 'reading involves thinking, reasoning, imagining and judging'.[29] Reading material is like a blue print for a building and each reader constructs from the blueprint a structure that is, in its detail, uniquely his or her own.

> To learn to read is to learn to abide by the rules of complex logical and rhetorical tradition that requires one to take the measure of sentences in a cautious way, and, of course, to modify meaning continuously as new elements unfold in a sequence. The literate person must learn to be reflective and analytical, patient and assertive, always poised, after due consideration, to say no to the text.[30]

Way back in 1973, in *The School Book*,[31] Postman wrote that schools, as a media of communication, as a source of information, are bankrupt. Furthermore, the conventional school cannot long survive economically in competition with the electronic media; thus his prediction for the end of the millennium, which is now behind us, was that schools will become like 'learning Laundromats'. They will consist of a series of teaching–learning stations that would permit access to anything anyone wanted to learn, which would or could include not only current subjects (in 1971) in common school curricula, but a good deal more that are not. Schools would be scattered about local neighbourhoods and would be open twenty-four hours a day. Anyone could redo lessons as many times as necessary, without failing any tests or being subject to ridicule from teachers or other students for being dumb.[32] In joining Postman on the adventurous road of prediction, I would argue that when computers become everyone's commodity, cheap, friendly and accessible, they will indeed replace schools. But only for the masses, or for the poor. The select, the rich, the élite will afford education and learning in small schools, since real learning is and was, is and will be a result of a direct and live dialogue between people.

Postman's writings bring the debate to a wide and broad audience and not only to those who dwell in faculty clubs, making them a thoughtful issue for everyone who cares.

People might question if Postman provided solutions for education, although, from Postman's viewpoint, there aren't foolproof solutions around, but there is no question that Postman provokes continuous debate, challenging our thoughts, and forcing the educational world to think, to think differently. What else can one ask for?

Notes

1 Neil Postman, *Amusing Ourselves to Death, Public Discourse in the Age of Show Business*, New York: Penguin, p.9 and 50, 1985.
2 Ibid., p.17.
3 Ibid., p.16.

4 Ibid., p.8.
5 Robin Barrow, *Radical Education, A Critique of Freeschooling and Deschooling*, London: Martin Robertson, 1978.
6 Neil Postman and the Committee on the Study of Television of the National Council of Teachers in English, *Television and the Teaching of English*, New York: Appleton-Century-Crofts, 1961.
7 Neil Postman, *The End of Education: Redefining the Value of School*, New York: Alfred A. Knopf, 1997.
8 Ibid., p.7.
9 Ibid., p.xi.
10 Neil Postman and Charles Weingartner, *Teaching As a Subversive Activity*, New York: Delacorte Press, 1969.
11 Neil Postman, *Teaching as a Conserving Activity*, New York: Delta, 1979.
12 Postman, *The End of Education*, op. cit., p.ix.
13 Postman and Weingartner, *Teaching as a Conserving Activity*, p.4.
14 Neil Postman and Charles Weingartner, *The Soft Revolution, A Student Handbook for Turning Schools Around*, New York: Delacorte Press, 1970.
15 Neil Postman, *The Disappearance of Childhood*, New York: Delacorte Press, 1982.
16 Neil Postman, 'Childhood: Can It Be Preserved?', *Childhood Education*, 61, 4, pp.286–93, 1985.
17 Postman, *The End of Education*, op. cit.
18 Ibid., p.197.
19 Ibid., p.146.
20 Neil Postman, *Technopoly, The Surrender of Culture to Technology*, New York: Alfred A. Knopf, 1992.
21 Ibid., p.71.
22 Ibid., p.123.
23 Ibid., p.192.
24 Neil Postman, 'Making a Living, Making a Life: Technology Reconsidered', *College Board Review*, 76–77, pp.8–13, 1995.
25 Neil Postman and Howard C. Damon, *Language and Systems*, New York: Holt, Rinehart and Winston, 1965.
26 Neil Postman and Charles Weingartner, *Linguistics, a Revolution in Teaching*, New York: Delacorte Press, 1966.
27 Ibid., p.14.
28 Postman, *The Disappearance of Childhood*, op. cit., p.78.
29 Postman and Weingartner, *Linguistics, a Revolution in Teaching*, op. cit., p.182.
30 Postman, *The Disappearance of Childhood*, op. cit., pp.76–7.
31 Neil Postman and Charles Weingartner, *The School Book, For People Who Want to Know What All the Hollering is All About*, New York: Delacorte Press, 1973.
32 Ibid., p.116.

Postman's major writings

'The Politics of Reading', *Harvard Educational Review*, 40, 2, pp.244–52, 1970.
'Curriculum Change and Technology', Report to the President and the Congress of the United States by the Commission on Instructional Technology, Academy for Educational Development, Inc., Washington, DC, 1970.
'Media Ecology: A Growing Perspective', *Media Ecology Review*, 3, 3, pp.10–11, 1973.
'The Ecology of Learning', *English Journal*, 63, 4, pp.58–64, 1974.
Postman, Neil and Weingartner, Charles, 'Two Tests To Take – To Find Out If Yours Is a "Great" School', *American School Board Journal*, 161, 1, pp.23–6, 1974.
'Whatever I Call It, It Is', *A Review of General Semantics*, 31, 1, pp.37–44, 1974.

'What An Educator Means When He Says ...', *Journal of the International Association of Pupil Personnel Workers*, 20, 3, pp.153–6, 1976.
'Landmarks in the Literature: Where Have All the Critics Gone?', *New York University Education Quarterly*, 9, 1, pp.28–31, 1977.
'The First Curriculum: Comparing School and Television', *Phi Delta Kappan*, 61, 3, pp.163–8, 1979.
'The Information Environment', *A Review of General Semantics*, 36, 3, pp.234–45, 1979.
'Teaching as a Conserving Activity', *Instructor*, 89, 4, pp.38–42, 1979.
'Order in the Classroom!', *Atlantic*, 244, 3, pp.35–8, 1979.
'Landmarks in the Literature: The Limits of Language', *New York University Education Quarterly*, 11, 1, pp.29–32, 1979.
'Language Education in a Knowledge Context', *A Review of General Semantics*, 37, 1, pp.25–37, 1980.
' "The Ascent of Humanity": A Coherent Curriculum', *Educational Leadership*, 37, 4, pp.300–3, 1980.
Postman, Neil and Fiske, Edward B., 'Fine Tuning the Balance between Education and a Media Culture', *Teacher*, 98, 1, pp.28–30, 1980.
'Disappearing Childhood', *Childhood Education*, 58, 2, pp.66–8, 1981.
'The Day Our Children Disappear: Predictions of a Media Ecologist', *Phi Delta Kappan*, 62, 5, pp.382–6, 1981.
'Childhood's End', *American Educator: The Professional Journal of the American Federation of Teachers*, 5, 3, pp.20–5, 1981.
'Disappearing Childhood', *Childhood Education*, 58, 2, pp.66–8, 1982.
'The Disappearance of Childhood', *Children's Theatre Review*, 32, 1, pp.19–23, 1983.
'The Disappearing Child', *Educational Leadership*, 40, 6, pp.10–17, 1983.
'Engaging Students in the Great Conversation', *Phi Delta Kappan*, 64, 5, pp.310–16, 1983.
'The Disappearance of Childhood', *Childhood Education*, 61, 4, pp.286–93, 1985.
'The Educationist as Painkiller', *English Education*, 20, 1, pp.7–17, 1988.
'The Re-Enchantment of Learning', *Youth Theatre Journal*, 5, 2, pp.3–6, 1990.

Further reading

Barrow, Robin, *Radical Education: A Critique of Freeschooling and Deschooling*, London: M. Robertson, 1978.
Kincheloe, L. Joe, 'Wait a Minute Mr. Postman: TV Content Does Matter', *International Journal of Instructional Media*, 10, 4, pp.279–84, 1982/1983
Levinson, A. Bradley, 'The End of Education, Book Review', *Harvard Educational Review*, 66, 4, pp.873–8, 1966.
Olson, Renee, 'Postman Always Thinks Twice, Augmented Title: When it Comes to Technology, Interview with Neil Postman', *School Library Journal*, 42, pp.18–22, 1996.
Robinson, Sandra Longfellow, 'Childhood: Can it be Preserved? An Interview with Neil Postman', *Childhood Education*, 61, 5, pp.337–42, 1985.
Trotter, Andrew, 'Are Today's Kids Having Too Much Fun in Your Classrooms?', *Executive Educator*, 3, 6, pp.20–4, 1991.

DAN INBAR

THEODORE R. SIZER 1932–

> The school should focus on helping young people to develop the habit of using their minds well. . . . The school's academic goal should be simple: that each student masters a limited number of essential skills and areas of knowledge. The aphorism 'less is more' should dominate.[1]

The curriculum motto 'less is more', one of Theodore Sizer's renowned, more demanding dicta, represents a central precept of his education reform efforts and his emphasis on the importance of learning quality over teaching quantity. Encouraging students to perform carefully limited, but critically vital tasks to a very high standard – 'more with less' – epitomizes Sizer's challenge to schools to rethink priorities for educational goals and practices: to concentrate on intellectual and imaginative competencies which allow students to access more, not less knowledge; to be active, as opposed to passive learners; to exhibit motivation and curiosity, rather than apathy; to appreciate depth rather than shallowness, and to develop into respectfully sceptical and mindful, as opposed to mindless human beings.

Theodore Sizer, or Ted, as he is affectionately known, is an acclaimed educational reformer with a key role in putting forward a new vision for schools and schooling and in vigorously putting it into action. Sizer was born 23 June 1932 and grew up on a farm just north of New Haven, CT. He is currently Professor Emeritus at Brown University, where he served as chair of the Education Department from 1984 to 1989. He is the celebrated founder of the Coalition of Essential Schools (CES), the founding director of the Annenberg Institute for Education Reform (1993) and its director until 1996, and has been awarded honorary degrees from many universities, including Brown, Williams, Dartmouth and Connecticut College, a Guggenheim Fellowship, the James Bryant Conaut Award, and the Distinguished Service Award of the council of state school officers, among others.

After graduating in English literature from Yale in 1953, Sizer joined the army. Serving as an artillery officer, he was impressed by the army's determination to train all its recruits, even the school dropouts, and with its belief that this was an achievable goal. Following demobilization, Sizer taught English and mathematics (1955–56) at Roxbury Latin School, before entering Harvard where he was awarded his MAT in social studies (1957). This was followed by a teaching post in Australia, where he taught history and geography at Melbourne Grammar School for Boys (1958). His teaching experiences in this strictly traditional school had a profound influence on Sizer's conception of the role and impact of culture, school community and family expectations in the formation of a school.

Returning to the US, Sizer completed his Ph.D. in Education and American History at Harvard (1961). After a short spell as an assistant professor at Harvard, and director of its MAT programme (1961–64), he was appointed Dean of Harvard's Graduate School of Education (1964–72). His concern with issues of equity in education became apparent during this period, with his celebrated proposal of giving vouchers only to low-income families. In 1968, while part of the White House Task Force on Cities, his idea of chartering every public school and allowing students to take all of their public education money with them to any public school left an indelible mark on the nascent school choice policy. A radical idea at the time, the policy came ultimately to be accepted as part of the conservative agenda. Charter schools, Sizer believes, offer both competition and equal access – connoting choice. But choice, he persists, 'not as a cover for segregation, but as a powerful incentive for families, students and teachers'.[2]

By late 1971, Sizer had left Harvard to teach history and headmaster the Phillip Academy in Andover, Massachusetts (1972–81). His decision to leave Harvard, an exceptional choice for a young and successful professor, testifies to his deeply felt concern and commitment to the needs of turn-of-the-century adolescents and their schooling. As he noted, 'My world is the world of high schools – senior high schools and middle schools'.[3] The nine years spent at the Academy were highly influential for Sizer, who became even more convinced that any student, regardless of his or her cultural or social background, could perform well in the right environment and with the right kind of support.

His determination to challenge the existing school system developed largely out of this experience and was followed by a research study entitled 'A Study of High Schools' which Sizer undertook with several colleagues.[4] This study led to the publication of his highly acknowledged book, *Horace's Compromise: The Dilemma of the American High School* (1984), a renowned critique of secondary schools, and the first book in the Horace trilogy.[5]

Pressure to ascertain the nature of meaningful schools and to apply his ideas to everyday practice in a number of schools led Sizer to found the Coalition of Essential Schools (CES) in 1984. The terms 'coalition' and 'essential' capture the nature of this organization and Sizer's most precious values and goals: the establishment of a partnership of schools with a shared commitment to focusing on essentials, i.e., the intellectual core of schooling. The coalition, under Sizer's chairmanship, burgeoned from twelve high schools to a membership of over 1200 schools in both the public and private sector, and spread across thirty-eight states and two foreign countries. At least one-third of the student population hailed from minority groups.[6] To further develop his reform efforts, Sizer and the Coalition joined forces with the Education Commission of States (ECS) in a project known as 'Re:Learning'[7] and collaborated with the ATLAS Communities Project.[8]

Sizer crystallized his most fundamental values, ideas and beliefs on schooling and the approach to schooling, into nine principles. These ideas, which were published in 1983, and in 1985 became known as the Coalition's Common Principles,[9] underwent little modification over the years, and only recently was a tenth principle added to the list. In short, Sizer's vision is a call to schools to sustain intellectual focus on academic essentials which every student in the school must master; to acknowledge and meet the diverse needs of all students by focusing their learning, instruction and assessment on significant, universal and personally challenging issues; to design a curriculum that cultivates thoughtful habits of mind rather than fruitless questing after coverage of information; to view instruction and learning as both context- and student-dependent; to judge students' mastery of knowledge and skills by organizing 'exhibitions' of their work; to regard teachers as generalists (rather than as subject-matter specialists), to lower teacher–student loads and design schedules and routines that can help teachers and students improve their relations; to keep expenditure within 10 per cent of previous costs; to work in an atmosphere of high expectations, trust and respect for the school, faculty, students and parents; model democratic behaviour and honour diversity.

Unlike most educational reformers, Sizer prescribes no specific 'model' to 'implement'. Nor does he offer any standardized solutions, or specific guidance. What he does is to offer a set of thought-provoking ideas that challenge popular school routines. His approach to school change is founded on the strong belief in the unique qualities of every school, the school's specific needs, and its willingness and responsibility toward forging its own identity. Sizer sees school 'renovation' as a local phenomenon which must be addressed on a school-by-school basis, with each school committed to rethinking its priorities, thereby breathing life into the vision articulated in the principles and putting the latter into practice in a form reflecting the schools' most important values. One does not design a school, Sizer argues, 'a school grows, usually slowly and almost always painfully, as tough issues are met'.[10]

Respect for the individual and the value of diversity, are generic themes in Sizer's philosophy. These themes are reflected at all levels of the system when relating to individuals (the student, teacher, parent or educator), or groups (the classroom, school, family or community). 'People differ. Thank goodness they do. Much of the progress of humankind has come because of the restlessness of persons who have stepped beyond the predictable mold',[11] he notes. 'There are patterns to adolescent development', he argues, 'but the individual variations within these patterns are as important as the patterns themselves'. 'I am different. I am special. I am somebody',[12] Sizer quotes, highlighting the unique value of each student. Because 'no two students, no two teachers, no two schools, no two communities are ever precisely alike or even alike from one year to the next'[13] they should not be treated as precisely alike, asserts Sizer, and they cannot function on a basis of one best curriculum, one best pedagogy, one best learning pace or one best test. Standardization 'is as inefficient as it is often cruel' he argues, and it is profoundly discriminatory.

Yet, Sizer believes, individuals or individual issues cannot be viewed in isolation from their environment, they should be seen as part of a coherent whole. Just as students' values and goals are important, so is the need to consider the school as a whole, and the values and concerns of parents and communities. 'Schools have to have a collective culture, a "moral order", one which is in balance with individual autonomy',[14] a culture created by collaboration among teachers, students, and families of students in a particular community. Such local and collective cultures, small enough to be coherent, intentional communities of friends, or 'small democracies', as Sizer calls them, cannot be fashioned by outside agencies, but rather achieved through exploration and dialogue. Outsiders, or 'critical friends' to use Sizer's term, may influence this process, but they cannot control it. This classic argument demonstrates his total rejection of the prevailing system with its centralized structures, top-down strategies and bureaucratic, mechanistic, distant, single-minded authority.

Sizer offers a systemic educational view, involving every component and level of the system including the curriculum, instruction, learning, assessment, organizational structure, educational policy, professional development and out-of-school reality, all bound synergistically together to form a coherent whole. Embodied in it are new kinds of relationships between people, groups and institutions, all grounded in an ongoing dialogue open to changing events, needs and hopes. Integration and interrelatedness are thus dominant building blocks in Sizer's conception, which regards conventionally paired and traditionally opposing notions such as emotion and mind, intellectual and moral, challenge and comfort; educational practices and assessment tools, as being related to and embedded in one another – not as mutually exclusive. Likewise he conceives knowledge holistically, building on its transient, contextual and authentic nature, while rejecting an exclusive reliance on a static disciplinary organization.

By ridding education of its rigid boundaries, Sizer is seeking the local and the universal, the individual and the collective. This quest for balance, inherent as it is in a tolerance for uncertainty and a need to compromise, gains expression in Sizer's approach to the highly controversial issue of national standards. In his insistence that standards are grounded in values that are diverse, ambiguous, changeable and context dependent, while at the same time also widely distributed, deeply held and shared, Sizer is convinced that standards cannot be unequivocally clear or discrete, nor can they solely be decided on either by the local school or the national authorities. He believes that student 'Exhibitions'[15] can serve as a basis for establishing national standards, through a national dialogue between the individual schools with their students, teachers and parents, and the wider professional community.

Significant research activity succeeded Sizer's efforts toward school reform, resulting in an abundance of instructive and encouraging findings.[16] The studies generally demonstrate that when a school commits to Sizer's ideas, both within the classrooms themselves and throughout the school, the result is an increase in student engagement in academic work, enhanced levels of student achievement and parent, teacher and student satisfaction, a positive effect on student behaviour, and more equity of achievement among different groups of students.

In 1999, Sizer returned to Harvard as a visiting professor, while continuing to chair the CES. Since retiring from Brown in 1998, he and Nancy Faust Sizer, his wife and colleague since 1955, and co-author of his recent book (1999), have served as co-principals of Parker Charter School (1998–99) thus continuing the pattern of consistent academic activity interwoven with time spent in the schools that has typified Ted Sizer's career.

An inspirational, indefatigable scholar-activist, who consistently, and throughout his career, has interspersed an abiding relationship with the theoretical and academic world with an exceptionally challenging and influential career in the real world of schools, schooling and education, Sizer has supplied educational theory with a set of fundamental principles uniting his deeply held convictions regarding quality in education, with the insights of contemporary theorists. His hope is that we can develop a school culture capable of promising our society a meaningful education for all our children together with a climate of social equity. Thanks to his exceptional sensitivity to adolescents' needs, coupled with a forward looking, humanistic perception of the dynamic and complex nature of the world, Sizer challenges us all to draw each of our children toward 'thoughtful freedom'. His scholarly work reflects his struggle to inculcate a respect for differences and a value of diversity. It is inspired by a deep and heartfelt concern and sustained by the markedly human tone and lucid elegance of his writing.

An educator who acts by what he preaches, who is committed to, and persistently fights for, what he believes in, Sizer challenges researchers, practitioners and policy-makers, to bring powerful ideas to fruition. He demonstrates how a systemic view of schooling focusing on high academic expectations across the student body, driven by a challenging, flexible, authentic and humanistic learning environment can lie within our reach. Yet, his contribution to our educational thinking and practices is that the 'be all and end all', the heart of education and the deserving goal of our intellectual and affective efforts and attention, is the human being – especially the student. Therefore we need to know our students, believe in them, trust them and respect them, help them to grow into thoughtful, responsible, creative, caring, trustworthy people, who are sensitive to themselves and to others, and who are eager to learn and seek after wisdom. Sizer reminds us that the key to these goals lies in the thinking habits, values and behaviours that we bring to our relationships with others, be they young or old, and furthermore reminds us that the nature of our work is genuinely a deeply moral one.

Notes

1 A quote from the first two essential principles. For further reading of the best known, and often criticized idea, see *Horace's School*, p.109; *Horace's Hope*, p.87; and K. Cushman, 'Less is More: The Secret of Being Essential', *Horace*, 11, 2, 1994.

2 Sizer, *Horace's School*.

3 *Reinventing Our School: A Conversation with Ted Sizer*, a video conversation with Ted Sizer (from a series of six video conversations with leading reformers, 1994. Available: www.ed..psu.edu/insys/esd/sizer/PromPrac.html.

4 R. Hample, *The Last Little Citadel*, Boston, MA: Houghton Mifflin, 1986. A.G. Powell, E. Farrar and D.K. Cohen, *The Shopping Mall High Schools: Winners and Losers in the Educational Marketplace*, Boston, MA: Houghton Mifflin, 1985.

5 The Horace trilogy portrays Sizer's path of research, conceptualization, active involvement and a reflection on years of efforts to reform high schools. Horace Smith, a fictitious teacher, provides the lens through which Sizer reflects on contemporary school practices, their origins, assumptions and organization (*Horace's Compromise*), describes a portrait of his vision regarding an essential school (*Horace's Schools*), and reflects on the impact of his efforts (*Horace's Hope*).

6 While most of the schools are in the secondary sector as originally planned, a number of elementary schools have joined the CES since 1996.

7 'From Schoolhouse to Statehouse', National CES/ECS teleconference, 1991.

8 ATLAS stands for Authentic Teaching Learning and Assessment, a joint effort embracing Gardner's work at Harvard, Comer's work at Yale, and the work of Whitla at the Educational Development Center in Cambridge, Massachusetts; described in more detail in Cynthia J. Orrell, 'ATLAS Communities: Authentic Teaching Learning for All Students', in S. Stringfield, S. Ross and L. Smith, *Bold*

Plans for School Restructuring: The New American School Designs, Mahwah, NJ: Erlbaum, pp.53–74, 1996.

9 The nine original principles are listed in *Horace's Hope*, pp.154–5, and the list of ten appears on the CES site: http://www.essentialschools.org/aboutus/phil/ 10cps.html. A version of the nine principles edited by students may be found in, 'Empowering Students: Essential Schools' Missing Links', *Horace*, 11, 1, 1994.

10 Sizer, *Horace's Compromise: The Dilemma of the American High School*, 1984.

11 Cited in the article, 'No Two Are Quite Alike', *Educational Leadership*, 57, 1, 1999.

12 Cited from *Horace's School*, p.31.

13 Ibid.

14 Cited from, Sizer, *The Students are Watching*, p.17.

15 For details see Joseph P. McDonald, 'Dilemmas of Planning Backwards: Rescuing a Good Idea', Coalition of Essential Schools Studies on Exhibitions no. 3, *Teachers College Record*, 94, 1, 1992.

16 For details see Kathleen Cushman (ed.), 'What Research Suggests About Essential School Ideas', *Horace*, 11, 3, 1995; and, for successful achievement on standardized tests see, 'Ten by Ten: Essential Schools that Exemplify the Ten Common Principles', *Horace*, 16, 1, 1999.

Sizer's major writings

Secondary Schools at the Turn of the Century, Westport, CT: Greenwood Publishing Group, 1976.

Horace's Compromise: The Dilemma of the American High School, Boston, MA: Houghton Mifflin, 1984.

Horace's School: Redesigning the American High School, Boston, MA: Houghton Mifflin, 1992.

Horace's Hope: What Works for the American High School, Boston, MA: Houghton Mifflin, 1996

Sizer, T.R. and Sizer, Nancy Faust, *The Students are Watching: Schools and the Moral Contract*, Boston, MA: Beacon Press, 1999.

Further reading

McDonald, J.P., Rogers, B. and Sizer, T., 'Standards and School Reform: Asking the Essential Questions', Coalition of Essential Schools, or its version in *Stanford Law & Policy Review*, 4, 1993.

McQuillan, P.J. and Muncey, D.E., 'Change Takes Time – A Look at the Growth of the Coalition of Essential Schools', *The School Ethnography Project*, 10, 1992.

Sizer, T., *Places for Learning, Places for Joy: Speculations on American School Reform*, Boston, MA: Harvard University Press, 1973.

TAMAR LEVIN

ELLIOT EISNER 1933–

> In a culture in which more people watch 'Family Feud' in one
> night than attend concerts of classical music all year, the marginal
> place of the arts is understandable. Yet, one hopes that educators
> would do better. Can those of us who work in education provide
> the intellectual leadership to give our children a chance to know
> and perhaps love what only a few know and love? One of my
> passions is trying to make that happen.[1]

Summarizing the career of Elliot Eisner is a daunting task. As one of his
former students, I have been asked to introduce him at a few of his speeches.
Each time, I was instructed to 'be brief'. I quickly discovered how hard it is
to condense the achievements of someone whose contributions and
accomplishments have been so expansive and distinguished. At last count,
Elliot Eisner's *curriculum vitae* is ninety-two pages and reveals the markers
of notable achievement: Lee Jacks Professor of Education and Art at
Stanford University; five honorary degrees since earning his Ph.D. at the
University of Chicago in 1962; election to two European royal societies and
to the National Academy of Education in the United States; numerous
presidencies of scholarly organizations, from the National Art Education
Association to the American Educational Research Association; and several
awards for his work, including a Guggenheim fellowship.

He has written 285 articles and fifteen books, averaging about seven
published articles per year since 1970. With regards to this body of work, my
list of essential Eisner reading would include: *The Art of Educational
Evaluation* (a collection of essays capturing his early ideas), *The Educational
Imagination* (vital for all curriculum workers), *Cognition and Curriculum
Reconsidered* (his definitive work on mind and representation), *The
Enlightened Eye* (his major text on qualitative research), *Educating Artistic
Vision* (for all art educators) and *The Kind of Schools We Need* (a collection
of essays on school reform).

That Eisner would turn out to become such a prolific writer on
educational topics was hardly expected in his early years. When Elliot's
third-grade teacher praised his artistic talent to his mother, she enrolled him
in Saturday morning art classes at the Art Institute of Chicago. His mother
hoped he would become a commercial artist – a position in which he could
make money. He did go on to major in art (and education). However, while
in college he took a job teaching African-American boys in The American
Boys Commonwealth in the neighbourhood in which he grew up in the west
side of Chicago. This experience shifted his focus from art to art education.
From this shift, however, ideas that would ultimately influence educators
around the world began forming. Eisner recognized that schools omitting
the arts were providing an unbalanced or inequitable type of education.
Moreover, he began to realize that conceptions of cognition lacking artistic
modes of thinking were inadequate.

> In the context of schooling ... we have ideas about the
> development of mind that are getting in the way of the arts and
> their potential contribution to educational development.[2]

247

Over the course of his career, Eisner redefined the way we view education. Up to the 1970s, educational and programme evaluation was predominantly quantitative. Until Eisner, curriculum work meant focusing on behavioural objectives. It entailed searching for social-scientific laws of human behaviour. It stressed teacher-proofing curriculum. It depended on scientific and industrial metaphors for education. Before Eisner, the arts were merely affective and creative endeavours – certainly not cognitive ones. Eisner's primary legacy so far is to have freed education from the dominant scientific and technocratic modes of thinking, adding a variety of new ways to view research and evaluation, school reform and the role of art in education. Other educators worked in similar intellectual areas, but few provided the cogent and eloquent explanations that he did, speaking to both practitioners and scholars. Even fewer had the perceptiveness and imagination to tackle so many different issues in new ways.

Art education had rested on a number of premises that Eisner exposed as inadequate. He helped overthrow the ideas that children left to their own devices will spontaneously develop artistic sensibilities, that teachers should just provide students with an array of art activities and then stay out of their way, and that the arts are merely emotional and creative outlets. Eisner stressed that environment shapes artistic aptitudes and that art education has unique contributions to make to growing children. In large measure due to Eisner's advocacy, art education has become a content-oriented discipline.

In 1967, Eisner initiated the Kettering Project, providing visual art instructional materials for untrained elementary teachers.[3] The project's two key assumptions were that the most important contribution that can be made by the visual arts to a child's education is that which is inherent to art and that the curriculum should attend not only to the productive domain but to the aesthetic, critical and historical domains as well. These ideas were a precursor of what would become the dominant art approach in the 1990s – discipline-based art education (DBAE). The most powerful organization promoting DBAE is the Getty Center for Education in the Arts. Eisner has been on its advisory board since its inception in 1982 and authored its first general statement on its aims. Today, The National Art Education Association embraces DBAE's approach as an ideal for thinking about and organizing curriculum. Almost every US state embraces the DBAE model, and it is also used in Australia and the UK.

Eisner also took a cue from art criticism and devised *educational connoisseurship and criticism*, a mode of evaluation and research that focused on what actually transpires in schools and classrooms. Connoisseurship is fundamentally the art of appreciation with criticism the art of disclosure. The critic renders what he or she has learned through connoisseurship employing description, interpretation, evaluation and thematics. Description enables others to secure a vivid picture of what is discussed and to participate in it vicariously. Interpretation is the process of accounting for what one has described. It involves the meaning of an event. Evaluation is the making of value judgements about the educational import of what has been examined. Thematics provides the 'moral of the story' – it enumerates the lessons learned. Generally, educational critics examine a school's curriculum ideology (beliefs about what schools should teach, and for what ends) by focusing on the school's major dimensions (intentions, curriculum, pedagogy, school structure and evaluation). Today educational connoisseurship and criticism is used by educators worldwide for both research and evaluation. Madaus and Kellaghan cite this approach as one of five major types of qualitative research and evaluation.[4]

An offshoot of Eisner's work is the growing arts-based inquiry movement. Its adherents embrace Eisner's idea that each form of representation has the potential to influence our experience and subsequently the way in which we understand the world. Applying this insight to research, they assert that the written word cannot adequately represent all of the ways that we come to understand and interpret education. Hence, Eisner's ideas on cognition and forms of representation legitimize paintings and installation art exhibits, and other arts-based modes of knowing to promote meaning and understanding of educational contexts.[5]

> Children ... come into the world ... mindless. I know that must sound a bit strange to you. They do not come in without brains. Brains are biological; minds are cultural. Minds are a form of cultural achievement. And the kinds of minds children come to own is in large measure influenced by the kinds of opportunities they have in their lives. And the kind of opportunities ... is largely influenced by the kinds of programs and options that are made available to them in the course of their childhood.[6]

Eisner has also contributed to school reform in three major ways. First he advocated moving beyond technocratic and behaviouristic modes of thinking. For example, alongside educational objectives, Eisner proposed that educators consider 'expressive outcomes' – the consequences of curriculum activities – in their planning. Eisner pointed out that promoting lesson plans that only articulated specific, narrow outcomes do not allow either teachers or students to grow from unexpected discoveries (e.g., watching a play, inviting a range of unforeseen responses).

Second, Eisner warned against reliance on slogans or educational fads. He revitalized concern with fundamentals: What is basic in education? What is literacy? What is mind? Eisner criticized the dominant paradigms in America as those of the factory and the assembly line, which misconceived and underestimated the complexities of teaching and learning. Eisner instead promoted a biological metaphor (informed by the aesthetic theories of John Dewey, Suzanne Langer, Herbert Read and Nelson Goodman) that began with an understanding of human nature.

To summarize, this approach stressed that human beings interact with the environment largely through their senses, which are designed to selectively take in information. From such interactions, concepts form. Concept formation, which precedes language, depends upon images derived from the sensory material. When people express themselves, they convert their concepts into forms of representation, which may be linguistic, but which also may be musical or visual, for example. Each form of representation, which allows us to express some things but not others, reveals and conceals.

From this foundation, Eisner asserted that many central notions in education needed to be reconsidered. Literacy, for example, should not refer merely to reading words but rather the ability to encode and decode the content embodied in a variety of forms of representation. Rationality, which was generally conceived of as logical in nature, could be construed as 'the exercise of intelligence in the creation or perception of elements as they relate to the whole in which they participate'.[7] Hence logic is a subset of rationality. Cognition, which had been reduced to knowing in words, could now be thought of as the process through which an organism gains awareness through his or her senses. Eisner stressed that the senses are intricately tied to knowing. Moreover, he suggested that schools ought not to limit knowing to propositional language and mathematics (what is measured on SATs). Students should be allowed to learn through a variety of forms of representation and express themselves in a variety of forms.

Eisner's third main contribution was in his role as a cognitive pluralist (one who believes that mind is socially created and that knowledge can be represented in many ways). Eisner showed that the impoverished mind is one that has few symbol systems or forms of representation at its disposal. Schools, according to Eisner, ought to help children create meaning from experience, and to do so requires an education devoted to the senses, to concept formation through numerous forms of representation, to meaning-making activities, and to the imagination. Ultimately Eisner has been concerned with helping children realize their unique potential – the cultivation of 'productive idiosyncrasies'.

> It is certainly possible for everyone here to recall for a moment a horse walking down a street. Now take that horse and turn it into a horse that is blue and give it wings. It is unlikely to see blue horses with wings, but we can conceptualize to generate for ourselves possibilities that we never encounter in our daily lives. That particular ability to exercise the imagination – to convert things in recall – is a part of what I would call a 'basic' in education. In order for a culture to remain viable, for it literally to grow – unless children and adults have the ability to make that conversion from things recalled into things possible you get a static culture.[8]

Eisner's lasting contribution has been to reform how we think about art and how we think about education. From his perspective, both are essential for a full, integrated and satisfying life. Eisner strove not merely to infuse education with art, but to make art central to the mission of schools:

> The arts inform as well as stimulate, they challenge as well as satisfy. Their location is not limited to galleries, concert halls, and theatres. Their home can be found whenever humans choose to have attentive and vital intercourse with life itself. This is, perhaps, the largest lesson that the arts in education can teach, the lesson that life itself can be led as a work of art. In so doing, the maker himself or herself is remade. This remaking, this re-creation is at the heart of the process of education.[9]

Eisner is truly an educational artist whose great success and achievement is the remaking of the educational endeavour in the last third of the twentieth century.

Notes

1 Elliot Eisner, 'My Educational Passions', in D.L. Burleson (ed.), *Reflections: Personal Essays by 33 Distinguished Educators*, Bloomington, IN: Phi Delta Kappa Educational Foundations, p.137, 1991.
2 Quote taken from a speech ('Minding the Arts') given at the University of Denver, Denver, Colorado in January 1998.
3 Elliot Eisner, Teaching Art to the Young: A Curriculum Development Project in Art Education, November 1969, Stanford University.
4 G. Madaus and T. Kellaghan, 'Curriculum Evaluation and Assessment', in P. Jackson (ed.), *Handbook of Research on Curriculum*, New York: Macmillan, pp.119–54, 1992.
5 See Elliot Eisner, 'The Promise and Perils of Alternative Forms of Data Representation', *Educational Researcher*, 26, 6, August–September, 1997. Also, 'The Eisner–Gardner Debate: Should a Novel Count as a Dissertation in Education', *Research in the Teaching of English*, 30, 4, 1996.
6 Text taken from a speech ('Minding the Arts') given at the University of Denver, Denver, Colorado in January 1998.
7 Elliot Eisner, *The Enlightened Eye: Qualitative Inquiry and the Enhancement of Educational Practice*, New York: Macmillan, 51, 1991.
8 Text taken from a speech ('Minding the Arts') given at the University of Denver, Denver, Colorado in January 1998.
9 Elliot Eisner, *The Kind of Schools We Need*, Portsmouth, NH: Heinemann, p.56, 1998.

See also

In this book: Read
In *Fifty Major Thinkers on Education*: Dewey

Eisner's major writings

Educating Artistic Vision, New York: Macmillan, 1972.
'Examining Some Myths in Art Education', *Studies in Art Education*, 15, 2, pp.7–16, 1973–74.
Conflicting Conceptions of Curriculum, E.W. Eisner and E. Vallance (eds), Berkeley, CA: McCutchan Publishing Corporation, 1974.
The Educational Imagination: On the Design and Evaluation of School Programs, New York: Macmillan, 3rd edn, 1994 (prior editions 1985, 1979).
Cognition and Curriculum Reconsidered, New York: Teachers College Press, 1994 (original edition *Cognition and Curriculum: A Basis for Deciding What to Teach*, London: Longman, 1982).
'The Art and Craft of Teaching', *Educational Leadership*, 40, 4, January, pp.4–13, 1983.
The Art of Educational Evaluation: A Personal View, London: The Falmer Press, 1985.
Learning and Teaching the Ways of Knowing, Elliot W. Eisner (ed.), Eighty-fourth Yearbook of the National Society for the Study of Education, Chicago, IL: University of Chicago Press, 1985.
The Role of Discipline-based Art Education in America's Schools, Los Angeles, CA: The Getty Center for Education in the Arts, 1987.

'The Primacy of Experience and the Politics of Method', *Educational Researcher*, 17, 5, June–July, pp.15–20, 1988.

Qualitative Inquiry in Education: The Continuing Debate, Elliot W. Eisner and Alan Peshkin (eds), New York: Teachers College Press, 1990.

'Taking a Second Look: Educational Connoisseurship Revisited', *Evaluation and Education at Quarter Century*, National Society for the Study of Education Yearbook, Denis Phillips and Milbrey McLaughlin (eds), Chicago, IL: Illinois: University of Chicago Press, 1991.

The Enlightened Eye: Qualitative Inquiry and the Enhancement of Educational Practice, New York: Macmillan, 1991.

The Kind of Schools We Need, Portsmouth: Heinemann, 1998.

Further reading

'An interview with Elliot Eisner', *Educational Leadership*, 45, 4, December 1987–January 1988.

Barone, T.E., 'From the Classrooms of Stanford to the Alleys of Amsterdam: Elliot Eisner as Pedagogue', in C. Kridel, R. Bullough Jr and P. Shaker (eds), *Teachers and Mentors: Profiles of Distinguished 20th Century Professors of Education*, New York: Garland Publishing, 1996.

Jackson, P. (ed.), *Handbook of Research on Curriculum*, New York: Macmillan, 1992.

Jaeger, R. (ed.), *Complimentary Methods of Educational Research*, New York: Macmillan, 1997.

William Pinar, W., Reynolds, W., Slattery, P. and Taubman, P., *Understanding Curriculum*, New York: Peter Lang, 1995.

P. BRUCE UHRMACHER

JOHN WHITE 1934–

> Not only teachers and parents may have a responsibility to reflect on what the aims of education should be: *every* citizen has an interest in this. 'What should our society be like?' is a question he cannot avoid. It overlaps so much with the question about education that the two cannot sensibly be kept apart ... [1]

John White emerged to prominence in educational research as a member of a remarkable group of philosophers of education whom Professor Richard Peters recruited at University of London's Institute of Education during the late 1960s. Under Peters' leadership, the group revitalized British philosophy of education by bringing to bear the methods of analytic philosophy on educational problems. White has remained at the Institute throughout his career, retiring from a personal chair in 2000. He is the husband of Patricia White, another prominent member of the group that Peters brought together. Both have similar philosophical interests and their published work attests to strong mutual influence.

White's intellectual leadership in British philosophy of education is widely acknowledged. A founding member and now Honorary Vice-President of the Philosophy of Education Society of Great Britain, he has long served on the editorial board of its *Journal of Philosophy of Education*, and he has been a regular contributor since the journal's inception. He is a prolific writer whose work has ranged widely from educational issues at the edges of philosophy of mind and aesthetics to educational policy disputes in British newspapers. He has also co-authored with Peter Gordon an acclaimed book on British Idealism and its formative influence on educational policy before the First World War, *Philosophers as Educational Reformers*. His most recent work has spanned a variety of topics: education and national identity, assessment, the future of work and Howard Gardner's theory of multiple intelligence.

Despite the great breadth of his interests, a clear line of intellectual continuity is discernible in White's major writings. His abiding preoccupation has been to identify the aims of education that befit a society in which claims to ethical knowledge and authority are no longer tenable, liberal political norms have been established, and citizens must find meaningful lives in a culturally fluid and technologically complex world.

White's earliest essays are marked by the circumspect analytic style that Peters impressed on a generation of British scholars. The early essays are also exemplary specimens of that genre. His work on creativity, intelligence and indoctrination are primarily exercises in conceptual analysis, although in each case, as in Peters' work, the charting of conceptual boundaries is combined with a sharp sense of how analysis can resolve disabling confusions in educational practice. White's first book, *Towards a Compulsory Curriculum* (1973), represented a methodological departure from this early phase of British analytic philosophy of education and broached themes that would remain central to his career.

The book contains little conceptual analysis. It defends a distinctive compulsory curriculum – one that combines a range of required subjects, with some latitude for students' choices – on the basis of an ideal of personal autonomy. That ideal is in turn grounded in ethical subjectivism (i.e., nothing has intrinsic value in abstraction from the wants or choices of agents). An epistemological distinction between activities as objects of choice (i.e., between those that can be knowingly chosen without direct experience and those that cannot) enables White to defend the curriculum he favours as a signal contribution to the development of autonomy. The compulsory curriculum should focus on activities that cannot be knowingly chosen without direct experience since that is the most effective way to enlarge the scope of eligible options available to students when they eventually choose how to live as autonomous adults.

The general project of finding a philosophical rationale for the structure and content of the curriculum was central to analytic philosophy of education during this period. But *Towards a Compulsory Curriculum* diverged in one striking way from rival theories developed by Peters, P.H. Hirst and others. For although an epistemological doctrine figured in White's curricular argument as a necessary premise, the argument's ultimate foundation was in ethics: questions about the nature of human value and the good life were key to understanding education in general and the school's role in particular. Peters and Hirst had been preoccupied with the nature of knowledge and reason as the foremost philosophical issues in determining the content of education. White was beginning to chart a different course.

Autonomy, the human good, and the school's curriculum are again addressed in White's next major work, *The Aims of Education Restated*. His conception of autonomy now builds on arguments developed in John Rawls' *A Theory of Justice*, where the good is defined as what one would choose after informed reflection on available options. White argues that autonomy is necessary to individual wellbeing because without it children will either be mired in conflicts of desire or they will look to arbitrary authority to resolve the conflict for them. Authority must be arbitrary in this context because without ethical knowledge there can be no ethical expertise that merits anyone's deference. But White is also keenly aware of the problems of defining the good for *all* individuals in terms that exaggerate the value of reflection. The chief problem he recognizes is that the definition seems to obscure the fulfilment to be found by many people in relatively unreflective ways of life. This point is registered in White's argument for a curriculum that strikes a balance between 'developing enthusiasms' and encouraging reflective depth.

The book also addresses the relation between the good life and the good society more explicitly and deeply than White had previously done. An education for personal autonomy is examined in a broad setting that includes the economic and civic purposes of schooling, the need to integrate self-interest in the autonomous life with the altruism necessary to sustain the common good, lifelong learning, and community as a context for the pursuit of educational ends. In its sheer ambition and eagerness to address hard normative questions head-on, *The Aims of Education Restated* broke free of many of the constraints of the British analytic tradition under the principate of Peters. On the one hand, the book tacitly embraces the large conception of the philosopher of education's role as a source of reasoned normative judgement, a conception that had been canonical in philosophy of education before the ascendancy of analysis. On the other, White's effort to understand educational practice in the light of abstract ethico-political principles echoed recent, revolutionary developments in moral and political philosophy, where Rawls and others had shown that analytic rigour required no rejection of philosophy's ancient preoccupation with the substance (and not just the definition) of the right and the good.

Education and the Good Life revisits the leading ideas of White's earlier book, addressing them in ways that reflect the influence of some of the most notable work in moral and political philosophy during the 1980s, especially Joseph Raz's *The Morality of Freedom* and Bernard Williams' *Ethics and the Limits of Philosophy*. But the book is as much an eloquent political polemic as it is a contribution to philosophy of education. Its subtitle – *Beyond the National Curriculum* – indicates White's interest in leading public discourse on education beyond the shallow controversy surrounding the recently introduced compulsory curriculum for schools in England and Wales. That curriculum had been introduced in 1988 by a Conservative government. White regarded it as an arbitrary coercive imposition, which combined an abundance of specific prescriptions with no rationale for the prescriptions that could be derived from the principles of liberal democratic government. Thus the purpose of the book is to critique the existing national curriculum and to construct an alternative rooted in the core values of free societies.

The argument for autonomy in White's earlier writings had hinged on reasons that purported to have universal application. The alleged arbitrariness of deference to ethical authority, our susceptibility to conflicting desires that threaten to paralyse deliberation, the dependence of freedom on the understanding of options – all these considerations purported to establish the desirability of autonomy for any human being in any place at any time. But under the influence of Raz and Williams, White re-fashioned the case for autonomy to reflect a more historical, contextually sensitive sense of its educational and political importance. According to White, certain structural features of technologically advanced liberal democracies create an 'autonomy supporting environment' in which individual wellbeing and autonomy tend to converge. In traditional societies the autonomous life and the good life might well be very different from each other, but the rigidity of traditional societies belongs to an irretrievable past from which powerful trends in contemporary societies carry us ever further away.

White does not merely echo Williams' and Raz's point that an autonomous life is a sociological necessity. He is mindful that current social circumstances are sufficiently permissive regarding the unreflective life that a thoughtless adherence to existing conventional structures is still possible and widespread. His claim is rather that the ideal of autonomy inheres in existing social and political structures in the sense that the responsibilities we face when living under those structures cannot be met without the cultivation of autonomy. Autonomy is deemed necessary here not only for self-regarding reasons (i.e., a personally fulfilling life is unlikely to be achieved under these circumstances without autonomy) but also for other-regarding reasons (i.e., one will not contribute adequately to the fulfilment of others without it). Indeed, White casts doubt on any sharp distinction between self-regarding and other-regarding reasons in an education for autonomy, seeing that process as integrating self-interest and altruism to a high degree while eliciting the reflective capability that individuals need to adjudicate between competing reasons.

But if autonomous wellbeing is the cardinal educational value in free societies, the national curriculum stands indicted as a fundamentally illiberal and undemocratic initiative because it is grounded in a narrowly utilitarian scheme of values in which fitting children for jobs in a highly stratified economy is the paramount goal. White sketches the outline of an alternative curriculum, in which knowledge is selected on the basis of its contribution to the personal dispositions that constitute autonomous character. A privileged place is assigned to the arts in this curriculum because of its power to enrich our understanding of value-conflicts, a power that only art can supply in the absence of religious authority and utopian politics. That particular theme would later be developed in White's Inaugural Lecture as Chair of Philosophy of Education at the Institute of Education, *Education and Personal Well-Being in a Secular Universe*.

Beyond the National Curriculum assailed the idea that schools are a mere antechamber to the labour market. But the book does not ask how an education for autonomous wellbeing should be connected to the work which students undertake as adults. That question is taken up in *Education and the End of Work*, a provocative essay on both the future of work in post-industrial societies and the education that would prepare children for that future. White usefully distinguishes between *autonomous work*, which is activity undertaken to yield some end-product strongly and intrinsically valued by the agent, and *autonomy in work*, which refers to the range of self-direction a working role affords the agent, regardless of the value attached by the agent to the end-product. Autonomous work is the crucial concept for White, and his case for 'the end of work' is an argument for the end of heteronomous work as a practice repugnant to autonomous flourishing. Thus the education for work we need cannot be narrowly vocational. Neither can it be an exercise in long-term career planning since the fluidity of the post-industrial economy makes such planning largely redundant. The proper conception of education for work requires the introduction of children and adolescents to the range of possibilities of autonomous work, as well as its ethical, economic and technological context.

Perhaps White's enduring contribution has been to carry the normative revolution in moral and political philosophy into the discipline that Peters had transformed in the earlier, analytic transformation that occurred during the 1960s. Philosophy of education has maintained its great vitality in Britain and Ireland in large part because of that second revolution, and White continues to be among its leading exponents.

Note

1   John White, *The Aims of Education Restated*, London: Routledge & Kegan Paul, p.1, 1982.

See also

In this book: Hirst, Peters

White's major writings

Towards a Compulsory Curriculum, London: Routledge & Kegan Paul, 1973.
The Aims of Education Restated, London: Routledge & Kegan Paul, 1982.
Education and the Good Life: Beyond the National Curriculum, London: Kogan Page, 1990.
Education and Personal Well-Being in a Secular Universe, London: University of London Institute of Education, 1994.
Education and the End of Work, London: Cassell, 1997.

Further reading

Callan, Eamonn, *Autonomy and Schooling*, Montreal and Kingston, 1988.
Clayton, Matthew, 'White on Autonomy, Neutrality and Well-Being', *Journal of Philosophy of Education*, 27, pp.101–12, 1993.
Thompson, Keith and White, John, *Curriculum Development: a Dialogue between Keith Thompson and John White*, London: Pitman, 1975.

EAMONN CALLAN

LEE S. SHULMAN 1938–

> With Aristotle we declare that the ultimate test of understanding
> rests on one's ability to transform one's knowledge into teaching.
> Those who can, do. Those who understand, teach.[1]
>
> Research begins in wonder and curiosity but ends in teaching.[2]

Lee S. Shulman has spent his professional life advocating for the importance of teaching at all levels, from kindergarten through graduate school. He is best known for his theoretical and empirical work on teacher cognition, for his work on the knowledge base of teaching, including the construct of 'pedagogical content knowledge', and for promoting the scholarship of teaching in higher education. After holding professorships at Michigan State University and Stanford University, he currently serves as President of the Carnegie Foundation for the Advancement of Teaching.

Lee Shulman was born and raised in Chicago, the only son of Jewish immigrants who owned a small delicatessen. Educated at a yeshiva high school (that mixed secular with sacred studies), Shulman won a scholarship to study at the University of Chicago.

Throughout his career, Shulman has never lost sight of the importance of subject matter in discussions of teaching. Shulman's interest in the teaching of subject matter and the entailments of different disciplines grew out of his undergraduate education in the College of the University of Chicago with a concentration in philosophy, and later as a doctoral student in Chicago's department of education under mentors Benjamin Bloom and Joseph Schwab. Shulman was particularly influenced by Schwab's notion of the structures of different disciplines – the concepts, traditions and tools that disciplines use to make claims, verify knowledge, and determine the quality of contributions.[3] A literary interpretation is not the same as a scientific proof; the concept of causality in biology is not identical to notions of causality in history. This early introduction to disciplinary difference has proved to be a consistent thread throughout Shulman's career.

Shulman's first academic job was at Michigan State University, where he joined the faculty of education. One of his earliest experiences as an assistant professor involved serving as the recorder for a conference on learning by discovery, a conference attended by luminaries such as David Hawkins, Lee J. Cronbach, Jerome Kagan, Jerome Bruner, among others. Shulman edited the book that emerged from this conference, and credits the experience with first raising his awareness of the wisdom of practice.[4]

One of his best-known early contributions arose from his collaboration with a colleague in the medical school, and former college roommate, Arthur Elstein. In a widely cited study, Shulman and his colleagues studied the thinking of expert medical diagnosticians as they engaged in clinical diagnosis.[5] Two themes from this work were to resonate throughout Shulman's later work: (1) the focus on cognition under conditions of uncertainty in professional practice and, (2) the domain-specificity of expertise. Expert diagnosticians did not behave as psychologists predicted or as medical educators taught students to behave. Instead of gathering large amounts of data prior to making a hypothesis, the physicians formed multiple competing hypotheses and sought to confirm one of them. Shulman and his colleagues realized that the doctors were responding to the complexity of the task and drawing on their knowledge and experience to guide them. This study affirmed the wisdom of practitioners, even when they acted contrary to the understanding of psychologists. As Shulman described,

> The challenge is to get inside the heads of practitioners, to see the world as they see it, then to understand the manner in which experts construct their problem spaces, their definitions of the situation, thus permitting them to act as they do.[6]

Shulman's attention to, and respect for, the wisdom of practice represent a hallmark of his work. A second key finding of the research was that doctors' specializations affected their diagnostic expertise. There was no such category of an expert diagnostician 'in general'. Rather, doctors demonstrated their expertise within their areas of specialty. The theme of subject-specific expertise, in medicine and teaching, reverberates throughout Shulman's work.

Shulman believed that teaching was no less complex than medicine, and that teachers, like doctors, were actively engaged in gathering data and making decisions that informed their practice. Shulman's respect for the cognitive complexity of teaching determined the shape of the highly influential panel report for the National Institute of Education commission on future directions for educational research, entitled *Teaching as Clinical Information Processing*.[7] This report ran counter to the prevailing view of teaching as something that could be understood through checklists of discrete skills and behaviours. The NIE report represented teaching as a complex multifaceted deliberative activity – a formulation that helped spur the cognitive turn in research on teaching.[8] It was during this time that Shulman and Judith Lanier competed with Stanford University for a research centre on teaching, funded by the US Department of Education; Shulman and his colleagues won the competition and moved the Institute for Research on Teaching to Michigan State University.

While Shulman lauded the emerging research on teacher cognition, he still found the field wanting in its attention to issues of content. One of Shulman's earliest attempts to map out a more subject-specific research programme was laid out in his 1974 article 'Psychology of School Subjects: A Premature Obituary'. In this prescient essay, Shulman claimed that the time had come for educational researchers to put aside Thorndike's dreams of sweeping laws of learning that achieved generality only by ignoring the content of the subjects in the school curriculum. Instead Shulman adopted R.K. Merton's notion of theories of 'the middle range', more modest and flexible theories tailored to particular educational problems, such as how youngsters come to master fractions, how adolescents achieve historical perspective, or how teachers develop ways to engage young people's interest in literature. Shulman's approach ran counter to the prevailing ethos of his day, in which either behavioural approaches, which spurned thinking altogether, or the generic problem solving approaches that dissolved subject matter distinctions, such as Robert Gagne's instructional psychology, prevailed. Shulman called for a methodological eclecticism in educational research, urging his colleagues to take up observational and ethnographic approaches in order to understand the complexity of teaching and learning. This essay also illustrates Shulman's continuing interest in appropriate methods for the study of teaching. Coupled with the recognition of teaching's complexity came puzzles about how to study the phenomenon. How do researchers study classroom teaching in all its buzzing confusion? What lenses do they use to focus their inquiries? What is the role of the traditional disciplines in research on teaching? In an early article, 'Reconstruction of Educational Research', Shulman laid the groundwork for future considerations of appropriate methods for the study of teaching. In this early review of research on teaching, Shulman pleaded for researchers to attend to the importance of environmental factors. 'It is only through such environment-centered research that behavioral scientists can develop adequate terms to describe the educationally relevant attributes of the settings within which human learning occurs.'[9] This article foreshadowed the shift in educational psychology to more situated perspectives, as well as describing an early version of wisdom of practice studies. Throughout his career, Shulman continued to ask questions about relationships among research purposes, questions, settings, investigators, and methods in the study of education.[10]

In his chapter 'Paradigms and Research Programs in the Study of Teaching' Shulman provided a synoptic view of the field of research on teaching. In his critique, Shulman returned to the theme of subject matter differences, claiming that there was a 'missing paradigm' in the field. Amidst the hundreds of studies in research on teaching that filled the third edition of the *Handbook of Research on Teaching*, there were few studies that took seriously the demands and challenges of teaching particular pieces of content – how elementary teachers deal with the counterintuitive notion of negative numbers, or how history teachers combat children's tendency to search for the 'right answer' in historical interpretation. Shulman challenged the field to restore this missing paradigm to research on teaching.[11]

Shulman moved to Stanford University in 1982, where he was to become the Charles E. Ducommun Professor of Education. In his first years at Stanford, Shulman engaged in a longitudinal study of knowledge growth in teaching – tracking the changes in teachers' subject matter knowledge as they completed their teacher education programme and began full-time teaching. It was during this field-based, longitudinal work that Shulman and colleagues developed the concept of pedagogical content knowledge.[12] This construct bridged the divide between subject matter knowledge and generic knowledge of pedagogy. In his 1985 Presidential Address to the American Education Research Association Shulman first defined the essence of pedagogical content knowledge:

Within the category of pedagogical content knowledge I include, for the most regularly taught topics in one's subject area, the most useful form of representation of those ideas, the most powerful analogies, illustrations, examples, explanations, and demonstrations – in a word, the ways of representing and formulating the subject that make it comprehensible to others. ... Pedagogical content knowledge also includes an understanding of what makes the learning of specific topics easy or difficult: the conceptions and preconceptions that students of different ages and backgrounds bring with them to the learning of those most frequently taught topics and lessons. If those preconceptions are misconceptions, which they so often are, teachers need knowledge of the strategies most likely to be fruitful in reorganizing the understanding of learners, because those learners are unlikely to appear before them as blank slates.[13]

At the heart of this construct was the notion of a specialized body of knowledge that only teachers possessed, a category of knowledge that might distinguish between researchers in a field and those who were responsible for teaching it. While both historians and history teachers might understand the role of primary source documents in constructing historical interpretations, only history teachers might know the kinds of beliefs about text that students bring to primary source documents. While both scientists and science teachers might hold similar knowledge about photosynthesis, only elementary science teachers might be able to explicate the various misconceptions of photosynthesis held by younger children. The construct of pedagogical content knowledge challenged the belief that a good teacher can teach anything, as well as the notion that subject matter knowledge alone is sufficient for teaching.

Shulman's interest in teachers' knowledge related to his desire to make teaching into a profession. As one of the hallmarks of traditional professions is the existence of a specialized knowledge base, discussions of the knowledge base of teaching had a decidedly practical bent. Another hallmark of a profession is the ability of its members to regulate and assess themselves. Up to this time, teaching had been assessed largely by administrators using checklists that reflected a behavioural view of teaching. In 1986, Shulman and his friend and colleague Gary Sykes wrote a proposal to the Carnegie Corporation laying out an initial blueprint for a national board for teaching. A subsequent grant from Carnegie launched the Teacher Assessment Project, a research and development project at Stanford that designed performance-based assessments for teaching. Rather than relying on multiple-choice tests as proxies for teacher knowledge, Shulman and his colleagues developed assessment exercises – complex, multifaceted tasks that attempted to approximate the complexity of teaching.[14] To complement these exercises, Shulman's research team designed prototypes of field-based portfolios that teachers would complete over time in their own classrooms. This work combined traditional assessment goals (such as the ability to discriminate between different levels of performance) with a sensitivity to the myriad variations in context in which teachers worked. Shulman's Teacher Assessment Project laid the foundation for the National Board of Professional Teaching Standards, which has emerged as the largest and most successful system of voluntary certification for teachers in North America.

In 1997 Shulman left Stanford to assume the presidency of the Carnegie Foundation for the Advancement of Teaching, where he has extended his work on teaching into the world of higher education. He challenged colleges and universities to create cultures in which teaching was central, not peripheral, to the scholarly work of professors. He called upon professors to make teaching public, through teaching portfolios, artifacts, and carefully crafted cases. Shulman also elaborated and delineated the concept of a scholarship of teaching, a phrase used by his predecessor at the Carnegie Foundation, Ernest Boyer. Shulman has tried to distinguish between teaching that is scholarly, and scholarly inquiry into one's teaching. One of his first creations as President of the Carnegie Foundation was the Carnegie Academy for the Scholarship of Teaching and Learning (CASTL). This programme invites scholars to investigate their own teaching and to make the products of their investigations public. The goals of the programme are not only to improve the practice of teaching and learning of students, but to 'bring to teaching the recognition afforded to other forms of scholarly work'.[15] Shulman has also initiated a comparative study of professional education, to look at both commonalities and diversities in how students are prepared for professional practice. In his article, 'Theory, Practice, and the Education of Professionals', Shulman describes six attributes, or common-places, that characterize a profession.[16] These commonplaces include: (1) the obligation of service to others; (2) scholarly or theoretical understanding; (3) a domain of skilled practice; (4) the exercise of judgement under uncertainty; (5) the need to learn from experience; (6) a professional community to uphold standards and accumulate knowledge. Shulman goes on to wrestle with the dilemmas these commonplaces create for the preparation of professionals.

Shulman has had enormous impact on the field of education, in large part because of the grand ideas and visions that have marked his work. He made his mark as a theoretician, who honed theories by testing them against the work of practitioners and policy-makers. But Shulman is far more than a visionary; he is an actor and creator. Through his constant attention to the world outside the university, to the worlds of policy and practice, Shulman has been able to translate his ideas into concrete entities, ranging from the National Board for Professional Teaching Standards, to the CASTL programme at the Carnegie Foundation, to the pedagogical colloquium during job interviews. His visions now permeate everyday discourse about teaching, in talk about teaching portfolios, pedagogical content knowledge, and the scholarship of teaching. Shulman's genius lies in his ability to unite the worlds of thought and action, to turn his creative energies not only to research but into building institutions and structures that transport his visions of the possible into the world of practice.

Notes

1   L.S. Shulman, 'Those Who Understand: Knowledge Growth in Teaching', *Educational Research*, 15, 2, p.14, 1986.
2   L.S. Shulman, 'Disciplines of Inquiry in Education: A New Overview', in R.M. Jaeger (ed.), *Complementary Methods for Research in Education*, Washington DC: American Educational Research Association, p.6, 1997.
3   Schwab's work, or more precisely Shulman's interpretation of it, paved the way for a host of distinct research programmes by Shulman, as well as by his students and colleagues who were influenced by his approach.

4 L.S. Shulman, and E.R. Keislar (eds), *Learning by Discovery: A Critical Appraisal*, Chicago, IL: Rand McNally, 1966.
5 See A.S. Elstein, L.S. Shulman and S.A. Sprafka, *Medical Problem Solving: Analysis of Clinical Reasoning*, Chicago, IL: University of Chicago Press, 1978.
6 L.S. Shulman, 'The Wisdom of Practice: Managing Complexity in Medicine and Teaching', in D.C. Berliner and B.V. Rosenshine (eds), *Talks to Teachers: A Festschrift for N.L. Gage*, New York: Random House.
7 National Institute of Education, *Teaching as Clinical Information Processing*, Report of Panel 6, National Conference on Studies in Teaching, Washington, DC: National Institute of Education, 1975a.
8 See C. Clark and P.L. Peterson, 'Teachers' Thought Processes', *Handbook of Research on Teaching*, New York: Macmillan, pp.255–98, 3rd edn, 1986, for a discussion of early research that focused on teacher cognition.
9 L.S. Shulman, 'Reconstruction of Educational Research', *Review of Educational Research*, 40, p.376, 1970.
10 L. S. Shulman, 'Disciplines of Inquiry in Education: A New Overview', in R.M. Jaeger (ed.), *Complementary Methods for Research in Education*, Washington, DC: American Educational Research Association, pp.3–31, 1997, for a discussion of the relationships among these dimensions of research endeavours.
11 See L. S. Shulman and K. Quinlan, 'The Comparative Psychology of School Subjects', in D.C. Berliner and R.C. Calfee (eds), *Handbook of Educational Psychology*, New York: Macmillan, pp.399–422, 1996, for a mapping of recent research in this area. Far from an obituary, this chapter heralds the rebirth of a psychology of school subjects.
12 See, for example, W.C. Carlsen, 'Subject Matter Knowledge and Science Teaching: A Pragmatic Perspective', in J.E. Brophy (ed.), *Advances in Research on Teaching: Vol. 2. Teachers' Subject Matter Knowledge and Classroom Instruction*, Greenwich, CT: JAI Press, pp.115–43, 1991; P.L. Grossman, *The Making of a Teacher: Teacher Knowledge and Teacher Education*, New York: Teachers College Press, 1990; S. Gudmundsdottir, 'Values in Pedagogical Content Knowledge', *Journal of Teacher Education*, 41, 3, pp.44–52, 1990; S.M. Wilson and S.S. Wineburg, 'Peering at History Through Different Lenses: The Role of Disciplinary Perspectives in Teaching History', *Teachers College Record*, 89, pp.525–39, 1988, for descriptions of this programme of research.
13 In Shulman, Paradigms and Research Programs in the Study of Teaching', pp.9–10.
14 See S.M. Wilson and S.S. Wineburg, 'Wrinkles in Time: Using Performance Assessments to Understand the Knowledge of History Teachers', *American Educational Research Journal*, 30, pp.729–69, 1993.
15 P. Hutchings and L.S. Shulman, 'The Scholarship of Teaching', *Change*, 31, 5, p.10, 1999.
16 L.S. Shulman, 'Theory, Practice, and the Education of Professionals', *Elementary School Journal*, 98, pp.511–26, 1998.

See also

In this book: Bloom, Bruner, Cronbach, Schwab

Shulman's major writings

'Reconstruction of Educational Research', *Review of Educational Research*, 40, pp.371–96, 1970.
'The Psychology of School Subjects: A Premature Obituary?', *Journal of Research in Science Teaching*, 11, pp.319–39, 1974.
Shulman, L.S. and Elstein, A.S., 'Studies of Problem Solving, Judgment, and Decision

Making: Implications for Educational Research', in F.N. Kerlinger (ed.), *Review of Research in Education*, vol. 3, Itasca, IL: Peacock, 1976.

'Knowledge and Teaching: Foundations of the New Reform', *Harvard Educational Review*, 57, 1, pp.1–22, 1987.

'Paradigms and Research Programs in the Study of Teaching: A Contemporary Perspective', in M.C. Wittrock (ed.), *Handbook of Research on Teaching*, New York: Macmillan, 3rd edn, 1986.

Shulman, L.S. and Quinlan, K., 'The Comparative Psychology of School Subjects', in D.C. Berliner and R.C. Calfee (eds), *Handbook of Educational Psychology*, New York: Macmillan, pp.399–422, 1996.

'Theory, Practice, and the Education of Professionals', *Elementary School Journal*, 98, pp.511–26, 1998.

Further reading

Elstein, A.S., Shulman, L.S. and Sprafka, S.A., *Medical Problem Solving: An Analysis of Clinical Reasoning*, Chicago, IL: University of Chicago Press, 1978.

Hutchings, P. and Shulman, L.S., 'The Scholarship of Teaching', *Change*, 31, 5, pp.10–16.

Schwab, J.S. 'Education and the Structure of the Disciplines', in I. Westburg and N.J. Wilkof (eds), *Science, Curriculum, and Liberal Education*, Chicago, IL: University of Chicago Press, pp.229–72, 1978.

Shulman, L.S. and Keislar, E.R. (eds), *Learning by Discovery: A Critical Appraisal*, Chicago, IL: Rand McNally, 1966.

PAM GROSSMAN AND SAM WINEBURG

MICHAEL W. APPLE 1942–

> The denial of basic human rights, the destruction of the environment, the deadly conditions under which people (barely) survive, the lack of a meaningful future for the thousands of children I noted in my story, ... [this] is a reality that millions of people experience in their bodies everyday. Educational work that is not connected deeply to a powerful understanding of these realities ... is in danger of losing its soul. The lives of our children demand no less.
>
> (Michael W. Apple, *Remembering Capital*)

Michael W. Apple is a leading educational theorist and a prominent voice in current progressive/critical education.[1] Along with such critical educators as Paulo Freire, Henry A. Giroux, Peter McLaren and others, he has helped to make critical education studies a focal point of the prevailing national controversy on essentially all educational issues of significance: from teacher education to curriculum, to testing, to educational financing and governance.[2]

Apple was born on 20 August 1942 into a working-class family, with parents who were involved ardently in leftist politics. Because of his family's financial situation, he had to support himself early on and his possibilities for a college education were in doubt. While working as a union printer and truck driver, Apple studied at two small state teachers colleges. After several years and one year of college credits, he was drafted. In the army, Apple taught compass reading and first aid and credits these experiences with his formation as a teacher. Because of the enormous teacher shortage in the Paterson, New Jersey public schools and his army teaching experience, Apple was hired as a full-time substitute despite the lack of a degree, at nineteen years of age.

Because of his deep involvement in Paterson's African-American and Hispanic communities, he was usually assigned to schools with subordinated populations – often with as many as forty-six children in a classroom. Apple's activism in racial and class politics led him to become a founding member of the Paterson chapter of the Congress of Racial Equality (CORE). In turn, he became immersed in teacher politics and served for a period of time as president of a teachers union. Throughout this process, Apple identified himself politically by examining his practice as an activist and by situating himself in his family's extensive political tradition. Apple completed his bachelor's degree while teaching in Paterson and, afterward, undertook graduate studies at Columbia University during the political upheaval surrounding the Vietnam War and civil rights movement in the United States, with its attendant scope of radical literature and intellectual sustenance.

After receiving an MA in Curriculum Studies and Philosophy (1968), and a Ph.D. (1970) in Curriculum Studies from Columbia University, he took a position at the University of Wisconsin at Madison. During the interview, military tanks responded to tenacious antiwar protests on that campus and tear gas filled the building. In Apple's own words, he knew when he was interviewed that this was the place he wanted to be. Today, Apple is the John Bascom Professor of Curriculum and Instruction and Educational Policy Studies at the University of Wisconsin-Madison. His teaching focuses on curriculum theory and research and on the sociology of curriculum. Apple travels extensively in addition to dedicating time to his writing and research. He lectures and engages in grass-roots political work in the United States and abroad. Apple has held visiting professorships and been in residence in Australia, Spain, the University of Auckland in New Zealand, the Pontifical University of São Paulo in Brazil, the University of Trondheim in Norway, and UNAM (the National Autonomous University) in Mexico.

Apple scrutinizes, assesses and deconstructs educational systems in the United States (and elsewhere) in ways that are simultaneously disturbing, stimulating and inspiring. His work explores the relationship between culture and power in education, underscoring the perils and liabilities of the business/corporate-driven nature of curriculum in most school districts. He believes democratic practices must permeate the public schools in ways that typify democratic ideals for the larger society. He also examines technological literacy from a cultural and socio-economic perspective (rather than as merely a technical issue).

Ideologically, Apple is too eclectic to be reduced to a limited set of tenets or even to strict adherence to a particular school of thought. He is, nonetheless, among the more prominent exponents of the so-called Frankfurt School of critical theory. Originating at the Institute for Social Research in Frankfurt, Germany between the two world wars, this school highlights how the changing character of capitalist societies affects their relationship with citizens and institutions; the level of individual self-determination, and the new forms of domination that emerge through this process.[3] Although it was never a meticulously defined philosophy, the early Frankfurt School owes significant intellectual debts to Kant, Hegel, Marx, modernism and the core elements of contemporary scientific analysis. Theorists who bring this perspective to view are 'critical' in at least two ways: (1) they utilize the critique as process for their research; and (2) their well-established condemnation of the innately disproportionate and repressive impact of capitalism on the individual (especially on those who are subordinated or marginalized in society).

In the United States, critical scholars have broadened the scope of the early Frankfurt school. For the most part, these scholars conclude that social theory, in all its manifestations, needs to go beyond analysis and documentation and engage directly in social change. Critical educators such as Apple promote education as a process for such transformation and explore the broader contexts of schools in society (socio-economic, political, cultural, and historical). These educators pursue change as a result of integrating themselves with the self-consciousness of subordinated groups in society. Paulo Freire, perhaps the most renowned and revered critical scholar, adroitly summarizes the importance of generating 'hope' throughout this process: 'One of the tasks of the progressive educator, through a serious, correct political analysis is to unveil opportunities for hope, no matter what the obstacles may be ... when we fight as hopeless or despairing persons, our struggle will be suicidal.'[4]

Among the topics and areas embraced by critical educators are: social reproduction theory (why schools tend to reproduce the *status quo* instead of fostering upward mobility); the schools' socialization of students as consumers; the hidden curriculum of schooling (what is taught implicitly); the societal roots of oppositional or resistant behaviours on the part of students; school subcultures (peer groups, gangs, cliques); and the distinction between 'schooling' (socialization) and education (acquisition of values, perspectives, knowledge, proficiencies).

To appreciate the significance of Apple's contributions we must look at the context in which they are made. Curriculum is a perennial preoccupation in the United States; along with issues of race, the economy, language and culture, it constitutes a major part of the national discourse. The heterogeneity of this country restrains consensus on most issues of consequence. Social, political, economic, religious and ethnic backgrounds influence opinion about what is important to teach, for what reason or toward what end, and whose perspective is to be 'official' and adhered to.

Into this debate, Apple brings meaning to the notion of providing 'education for all'. Perhaps one of his greatest contributions is his authoritative and candid reasoning as he reveals the social, political and economic disproportionalities of public education in the United States and other capitalist countries. Unlike many other education theorists or writers (who often consider theory in isolation from practice, or explain local or national education issues detached from the rest of the society), Apple correlates theory, practice, schools, politics and the economy, and society. He integrates the 'global with the local',[5] to illustrate the aggregate consequences on what is essential to the process of education. Along the way, Apple looks at such issues as the imposition of conservative ideology and tactics on curriculum and textbook adoption policies; the 'why' of educational technology rather than merely the 'how to'; attempts by the for-profit private sector to ingrain their self-interests into the schools; the disproportionate distribution of selective knowledge among dominant and subordinate social groups; and the effects of all of this on educational policy and its application.

One of Apple's central concerns is the way in which (under capitalism) knowledge is produced, 'sanitized', apportioned differentially to particular groups, and (ultimately) accumulated by those in power. The following compendium, edited from several of his works (individually or with co-authors), illustrates this point:

> The curriculum is never simply a neutral assemblage of knowledge, somehow appearing in the texts and classrooms of a nation. It is always part of a selective tradition, someone's selection, some group's vision of legitimate knowledge. The decision to define some groups' knowledge as the most legitimate, as official knowledge, while other groups' knowledge hardly sees the light of day, says something extremely important about who has power in society.[6]
>
> Currently, 'public education is under a concerted attack from right wing forces that wish to substitute an ethic of private gain and an accountant's profit and loss sheet for the public good'.[7] More specifically, the 'Right'[8] prefers a market-style 'consumer-oriented' system that would, implicitly, make 'the needs of business and industry into the goals of education'.[9] Under such pressures, schools lose much of their role as agents of democracy and equality.[10] In fact, 'the idea of democracy has been altered' from a political concept to an economic one focused almost exclusively on instilling habits of consumption.[11] The result has been the 'marketization', or 'commodification' of schools and their curriculum in which the common good is marginalized[12] in favour of the self-interest of for-profit corporations (Channel One; Coca Cola; textbook companies). Knowledge has become a kind of capital that educational institutions manage and distribute to students in a manner similar to what economic institutions do with financial capital.[13] As has been observed historically, these and other values or 'social meanings became particularly school meanings, and thus now have the weight of decades of acceptance behind them'.[14] Intrinsically, then, the educational and cultural system of the United States is structured and intended for 'cultural reproduction'.[15] That is, to preserve existing social patterns and relationships of dominance and subordination, such that particular social groups disproportionately expand their allotment of cultural capital, usually procuring such gains as a result of 'cultural gifts that come naturally from their class or race or gender position'.[16]

The school's role here may not be obvious. Thus, Apple proposes that to unveil how schools contribute to cultural reproduction, one need only scrutinize how schools encourage individual success, and observe which groups or individuals actually succeed as a result of schools' efforts. As do other social-reproduction and critical theorists, Apple challenges the presupposition that public schools in the United States serve to equalize the social classes and that all children have the opportunity to advance beyond the socio-economic status into which they were born.

With regard to the involvement of private corporations and businesses in the shaping of curricula, Apple holds that this involvement is born out of self-interest rather than out of concern for students' wellbeing. Instead of supporting programmes that foster discriminating, self-directed students, corporations emphasize training students as workers and consumers. Apple points to the experiences with Channel One[17] in the classroom as an example of a corporation's desire to see youth as passive consumers.[18] 'Freedom in a democracy is no longer defined as participating in building the common good, but as living in an unfettered commercial market, in which the educational system must now be integrated into that market's mechanisms.'[19]

Along similar lines, Apple sees a disintegration of the social democratic accord on which policy was formed after the Second World War. These policies are assailed by neo-conservative intellectuals who are more interested in creating conditions for increasing international competitiveness, profits, discipline and a return to a romanticized past of 'ideal' home, family and school than in improving conditions for women and other subordinated groups or the poor and working classes.[20] Accordingly, Apple maintains that we give 'too much importance to the school as the issue, instead of being part of the larger framework of social relations that are structurally exploitative'.[21] With co-author Christopher Zenk, he contends that the blame for many social ills that public education receives is unjustified because what is positive or negative about school practice does not provoke most social, political, or economic problems.[22]

Apple believes that one of the goals of the rightist coalition is to separate national identity from origin and ethnicity. This is accomplished by dividing history from politics, prying social consciousness loose from social experience and imposing a vision of a classless, homogeneous society with a common transcendent culture in which everyone is an individual.[23] Correspondingly, all that happens to an individual is the result of his/her own choices, not of social stratification, racism, gender discrimination, or the like.[24]

Equally as insidious, this conservative coalition hides (under the guise of 'choice') its attempts to privatize education through such mechanisms as tax-credits (for parents who send their children to private schools) and school vouchers (which can be used by parents to send their children to private schools).[25] Many 'savvy' middle-class parents would send their children to private schools, further depleting already scarce resources from public education. Most poor and working-class families would not be able to make up the difference between what vouchers or tax-credits provide and the actual tuition at a private school. Public education would be primarily for students who have no other choices available to them. Despite its drastically reduced resources, public education would most probably be subjected to increasing centralized regulation of curricula and instruction and held responsible for economic and social problems. This trend can already be seen in nationally standardized textbooks, and in overtures toward national curricula and nationally standardized high-stakes tests, and calls for ongoing surveillance of teacher and student proficiencies and learning outcomes.[26]

The use of technology in schools and 'technological literacy' is another Apple focus. He warns that using computers and other technologies for education is not merely a technical matter, and that technology is not content neutral. On the contrary, educators are faced with myriad pedagogical, ethical, economic, ideological and political questions. If we pursue only the technical issues when defining the purpose of technology in education, we end up solely addressing the questions of 'how to' rather questions of 'why?' and 'at what cost?'.[27]

> New technology is not just an assemblage of machines and their accompanying software. It embodies a form of thinking that orients a person to approach the world in a particular way. Computers involve ways of thinking that under current educational conditions are primarily technical. The more the new technology transforms the classroom into its own image, the more a technical logic will replace critical political and ethical understanding. The discourse of the classroom will center on technique, and less on substance.[28]

Apple's perspective on how to approach the educational crises he identifies is multifaceted and well proportioned rather than skewed toward one or another 'party line'. He makes evident who benefits and who suffers from conservative policies and proposals and how these further stratify students by class, race and gender as they pursue the acquisition of knowledge. Yet, he does not defend the *status quo*. Instead, he maintains that many school districts' indifference, lack of flexibility and unresponsive bureaucracy in fact drive many constituents toward the political right.[29]

In the final analysis, Apple believes that the controversy in education is over the role education plays (or should play) in the development of democracy and in preparing citizens to value and negotiate inherent conflicts and uncertainties. Issues of education in the United States today revolve around 'competing social visions' in which neo-liberal/neo-conservative curricular reforms do not consider the broader context of a 'democratic education and a more democratic society'.[30] He underscores the need for political education and social justice inquiry by students in schools as antidotes to the determinism or social reproduction created by schools devoid of these discourses.[31] In defence of US public education, Apple proposes a blend of political and educational strategies, in the process of education, that he calls 'non-reformist reforms'.[32] In this approach, such issues as social equality and justice are accounted for through regular, critical interaction with the fundamentals of classroom practices and experiences, while simultaneously connecting these to 'a larger social vision and to a larger social movement'.[33] 'Those who engage in critical scholarship in education should have constant and close ties to the real world of teachers, students and parents.'[34] They need to join with those who are now striving to keep 'gains that have been made in democratizing education and to make certain that our schools and the curricular and teaching practices within them are responsive in race, gender, and class terms'.[35]

Although Apple's terminology can sound like that of a conspiracy theorist ('The Right', neo-liberals, neo-conservatives, neo-Gramscians), he demonstrates clearly that conservative reasoning is grounded on familiar deeply ingrained beliefs about the need to safeguard the 'merit-based' class-hierarchy in the United States. This broad understanding fortifies Apple's critical examination of the issues he considers pivotal: the marketing of education under the semblance of 'choice'; national standardized testing; and plans for a national curriculum.[36]

Apple's work is both substantial and significant, especially in the current educational environment in the United States and other capitalist societies. Apple brings focus to momentous issues that are not being discussed broadly and that are often unknown or unexamined by educators or the general public. A related strength of Apple's work is that it calls to task much of postmodernist and poststructuralist analysis for its failure to concern itself with the commonplace particulars of the school day. Apple does not usually offer explicit utilitarian remedies for dealing with the problems he identifies. However, a principal value of his efforts is the effective, reliable, coherent manner in which he compels us to ascertain the intensity and congruity of these problems, their implication for progressive educational policy and practice, and sources and allure of the conservative agenda.

Michael Apple's influence in education has been clearly established. His work has been quoted or reviewed by many noted philosophers, theorists and practitioners (Paulo Freire, Linda Darling-Hammond, Maxine Greene, Cameron McCarthy, Diane Ravitch, Jeannie Oakes, Peter McLaren, Henry Giroux, Paul Willis, and others). It has been discussed in myriad scholarly journals and other important professional publications. In December of 1999, *Education Week* (arguably the most prominent educational news source in the United States) selected his 1979 publication, *Ideology and Curriculum*, as one of the Books of the Century.[37] In December 1991, the *Journal of Educational Thought* declared this work to be 'required reading for all who are legally charged with the responsibility of establishing the public school curriculum, especially state legislators and school board members'.

In 1995, Apple was selected to deliver the John Dewey Lecture.[38] This presentation resulted in the publication of *Cultural Politics and Education*. Of Apple's seminal volume *Education and Power* (originally published in 1982; revised in 1995), the *Harvard Educational Review* says 'it is an important book. It is a book of questions, observations, and interpretations'. The *Library Journal* proclaims it as 'Thoughtful, carefully reasoned, and compelling'. Of *Teachers and Texts: A Political Economy of Class and Gender Relations in Education*, Giroux again exclaims that Apple 'has brought his extraordinary insight to bear on the political economy of schooling. ... This is a book that states its case clearly and with great brilliance'. Peter McLaren calls it a 'provocative treatise'.

In their commentaries of *Official Knowledge*, Paul Willis, Maxine Greene, and Paulo Freire are, perhaps, exemplary of the regard in which Apple's work is held by most of his peers. Willis said that it is 'Open. Personal.

Revealing. Also political and panoramic . . . a humanistic document for our positivistic educational times'. Greene declares earnestly to 'have read this book with enjoyment and considerable excitement'. Freire simply affirms that 'as *Official Knowledge* demonstrates, Michael Apple is among the most distinguished scholars in the world who are involved in this struggle to build a critical and democratic education'.

Notes

My grateful appreciation to Dr Xaé Reyes (University of Connecticut at Storrs) and Mr Neill Edwards for their generous gifts, to this author, of time and effort.

1 This biographical section borrows liberally from an interview conducted with Michael Apple by Carlos Torres and Raymond Morrow (published originally in 1990) which appears in the appendix to M.W. Apple, *Official Knowledge: Democratic Education in a Conservative Age*, New York: Routledge, 2nd edn, 2000.
2 C.A. Torres, *Education, Power, and Personal Biography: Dialogues with Critical Educators*, New York: Routledge, 1998.
3 H.A. Giroux, *Theory and Resistance in Education: A Pedagogy for the Opposition*, New York: Bergin & Garvey, p.7, 1983.
4 P. Freire, *Pedagogy of Hope*, New York: Continuum, p.9, 1998.
5 Michael W. Apple, *Cultural Politics and Education*, New York: Teachers College Press, Columbia University, p.115, 1996.
6 Michael W. Apple, 'The Politics of Official Knowledge: Does a National Curriculum Make Sense?', *Teachers College Record*, 95, 2, 1993, pp.222–41. Also see: Michael W. Apple, *Ideology and Curriculum*, New York: Routledge, 2nd edn, 1990; and *Official Knowledge: Democratic Education in a Conservative Age*, New York: Routledge, 1993.
7 Landon E. Beyer and Michael W. Apple (eds), *The Curriculum: Problems, Politics, and Possibilities*, Albany, NY: State University of New York Press, p.4, 2nd edn, 1998. This statement was written, originally, for the introduction to their 1988 edition of this book. Interestingly, in the ten years intervening between editions, no revision was in order as the state of affairs depicted here has only deepened.
8 A, sometimes uneasy, coalition of conservative, neo-conservative, and neo-liberal movements and groups (at various points in the political spectrum) referred to collectively as 'the Right'.
9 Michael W. Apple, *Cultural Politics and Education*, chap. 4, with Christopher Zenk, New York: Teachers College Press, Columbia University, p.99, 1996.
10 Michael W. Apple, *Education and Power*, New York: Routledge, 1995.
11 Ibid.
12 Ibid. Also see, Michael W. Apple, 'Cultural Capital and Official Knowledge', in M. Bérubé and C. Nelson (eds), *Higher Education Under Fire: Politics, Economics, and the Crisis of the Humanities*, New York: Routledge, pp.91–106, 1995.
13 Michael W. Apple, 'Cultural Capital and Official Knowledge', in M. Bérubé and C. Nelson (eds), *Higher Education Under Fire: Politics, Economics, and the Crisis of the Humanities*, New York: Routledge, pp.91–106, 1995.
14 M.W. Apple and N.R. King, 'What do Schools Teach?', in A. Molnar and J A. Zahorik (eds), *Curriculum Theory*, Washington, DC: The Association for Supervision and Curriculum Development, pp.108–26, 1977.
15 Michael W. Apple, *Education and Power*, New York: Routledge, p.21, 1982.

16 Michael W. Apple, 'Cultural Capital and Official Knowledge', in M. Bérubé and C. Nelson (eds), *Higher Education Under Fire: Politics, Economics, and the Crisis of the Humanities*, New York: Routledge, pp.91–106, 1995.

17 Channel One is a for-profit commercial and brief, light news television programme broadcast to nearly one-third of the schools in the United States every day and watched by more than 40 per cent of students in middle schools and high schools. The corporation that produces it provides schools with some electronic equipment in exchange for a guaranteed audience for its advertising segments.

18 Michael W. Apple, 'Selling our Children: Channel One and the Politics of Education', in Robert W. McChesney, Ellen Meiksins Wood and John Bellamy Foster, *Capitalism and the Information Age: The Political Economy of the Global Communication Revolution*, New York: Monthly Review Press, pp.135–49, 1998.

19 Ibid., p.146. (For more on this point, also see, Apple, *Cultural Politics and Education* and *Education and Power*.)

20 Michael W. Apple, *Official Knowledge: Democratic Education in a Conservative Age*, New York: Routledge, 1993.

21 Michael W. Apple, *Education and Power*, New York: Routledge, p.9, rev. edn 1995; 1st edn 1982.

22 Apple, thus, claims that by focusing only on such concerns as youth at risk and school 'dropouts', the 'Right' aspires to disregard these core issues by addressing the symptoms.

23 Michael W. Apple, *Education and Power*, New York: Routledge, 1995.

24 Here, Apple suggests parallels between postmodernist and poststructural emphasis of circulation of discourses that he describes as neo-Gramscian.

25 Michael W. Apple, *Cultural Politics and Education*, chap. 4, with Christopher Zenk, New York: Teachers College Press, Columbia University, p.98, 1996. Also see: Michael W. Apple, 'Cultural Capital and Official Knowledge', in M. Bérubé and C. Nelson (eds), *Higher Education under Fire: Politics, Economics, and the Crisis of the Humanities*, New York: Routledge, pp.91–106, 1995.

26 Michael W. Apple, *Cultural Politics and Education*, chap. 4, with Christopher Zenk, New York: Teachers College Press, Columbia University, p.99, 1996.

27 Michael W. Apple, *Teachers and Texts: A Political Economy of Class and Gender Relations in Education*, New York: Routledge & Kegan Paul, 1988.

28 Michael W. Apple, 'The New Technology: Is It Part of the Solution or Part of the Problem in Education?', *Computers in the Schools*, 8, 1/2/3, p.75, 1991.

29 Michael W. Apple, *Cultural Politics and Education*, New York: Teachers College Press, Columbia University, 1996.

30 Ibid., p.97.

31 Michael W. Apple, *Education and Power*, New York: Routledge, p.9, 1995.

32 Michael W. Apple, *Cultural Politics and Education*, New York: Teachers College Press, Columbia University, p.107, 1996.

33 Michael W. Apple, *Cultural Politics and Education*, New York: Teachers College Press, Columbia University, p.109, 1996.

34 Michael W. Apple, *Education and Power*, New York: Routledge, p.204, 1995.

35 Ibid.

36 Michael W. Apple, *Cultural Politics and Education*, New York: Teachers College Press, Columbia University, 1996.

37 *Education Week*, 19, 16, 15 December, p.41, 1999.

38 The John Dewey Lecture is given annual at the John Dewey Society's annual meeting (held in conjunction with the American Educational Research Association) and again at Teachers College.

See also

In this book: Darling-Hammond, Freire, Giroux, Greene
In *Fifty Major Thinkers on Education*: Kant, Hegel

Apple's major writings

Ideology and Curriculum, Boston, MA: Routledge & Kegan, 1979.
Education and Power, New York: Routledge, rev. edn 1995; 1st edn, Boston 1982.
Teachers and Texts: A Political Economy of Class and Gender Relations in Education, New York: Routledge, 1988.
Official Knowledge: Democratic Education in a Conservative Age, 2nd edn, New York: Routledge, 2000; 1st edn, 1993.
Cultural Politics and Education, The John Dewey Lecture, New York: Teachers College Press, 1996.

Further reading

Apple, M.W., *Power, Meaning, and Identity: Essays in Critical Educational Studies*, Counterpoints, vol. 109, New York: Peter Lang, 1999.
Bromley, H. and Apple, M.W., *Education/Technology/Power: Educational Computing as a Social Practice*, Albany, NY: SUNY Press, 1999.
Freire, P., *Pedagogy of the Oppressed*, new rev. 20th-anniversay edn, New York: Continuum Publishing Co., 1998.
Torres, C.A., *Education, Power, and Personal Biography: Dialogues with Critical Educators*, New York: Routledge, 1998.

CARLOS ANTONIO TORRE

HOWARD GARDNER 1943–

> Education must ultimately justify itself in terms of enhancing human understanding.[1]

Howard Gardner, among the most well-known thinkers in education in the United States at the turn of the millennium, did not seem destined to take up this role. In fact, he published six books and over 100 scholarly articles in cognitive development and neuropsychology prior to gaining much recognition from educators in the field or researchers outside the realm of arts education. Even his seventh book: *Frames of Mind: The Theory of Multiple Intelligences*[2] was not a work that focused on education. In fact, it contained only two pages directly bearing on the application of his 'MI' theory to educational practice. Yet, it is this book, now translated into more than a dozen languages, which has placed Gardner at the centre of educational theory and practice in the United States and established for him a prominent role worldwide.

An exploration of Gardner's life and work prior to *Frames of Mind*, and his intellectual pursuits thereafter, helps to explain Gardner's enormous impact.

Gardner was born in Scranton, Pennsylvania in 1943 to parents who had fled, penniless, from Nazi Germany. His parents had lost a talented first son in a childhood sledding accident at age eight, just prior to Gardner's birth. This fact, along with the horrors of the Holocaust, went undiscussed during Gardner's childhood. Nevertheless these events 'were to exert long-lasting effects on my development and my thinking'.[3] Young Gardner's exposure to activities that might engender physical harm – bicycling, and rough sports – were reined in, even as his early proclivities in music, reading and writing were eagerly nurtured. As Gardner gradually became aware of these unspoken influences, he recognized that, as the eldest surviving son in his extended family, he was expected to make his mark in this new country. And yet, even before adolescence, Gardner recognized the obstacles to doing so. He knew that other Jewish thinkers of German and Austrian origins – Einstein, Freud, Marx, Mahler – 'had lived in the intellectual centers of Europe, and had studied and competed with the leading figures of their generation [while] I had been cast into an uninteresting, intellectually stagnant, and economically depressed Pennsylvania valley'.[4]

Gardner's time in the outpost of Scranton did not last terribly long. He was sent to board at a nearby prep school, at which nurturing teachers showed him great attention. From there, it was off to Harvard University in 1961, where he has thus far spent all but two of his ensuing years.

Gardner entered Harvard planning to study history in preparation for a law career. His undergraduate years saw encounters with several of the leading thinkers of the day, but it was his tutor, Erik Erikson, the charismatic psychoanalyst and scholar of development over the lifespan, who 'probably sealed my ambition to be a scholar'.[5]

Immediately after graduation, Gardner began working for Jerome Bruner, a cognitive and educational psychologist. Bruner's influence was marked. He was 'the perfect career model'.[6] Gardner, in this volume, traces his ultimate attraction to education to Bruner's 1960 book, *The Process of Education*[7] and also to his work on Bruner's curriculum development project, 'Man: A Course of Study'. The curriculum addressed three 'mind-opening questions': 'What makes human beings human? How did they get that way? How could they be made more so?'[8] These questions echo in Gardner's own work. Gardner's investigations of human cognition address in part the first of Bruner's questions. Gardner's research on the development of symbol systems may be seen as a response to the second. And his most recent research, which seeks to examine how people operate both brilliantly and humanely, can be seen as inspired by the last.

Gardner's experimental work in human cognition was spurred by his exposure to the work of Jean Piaget during the Bruner project. Piaget's elegant experiments appealed to Gardner's keenly logical mind. At the same time, Gardner recognized that Piaget's stage theory of human development was inadequate. Central to Piaget's work was a conception of the child as an incipient scientist. But Gardner's early musical education, as well as his fascination with all other art forms, indicated that the scientist did not necessarily exemplify the highest form of human cognition. What it meant to be 'developed' needed to be informed by:

> attention to the skills and capacities of painters, writers, musicians, dancers, and other artists. Stimulated (rather than intimidated) by

the prospect of broadening the definition of cognition, I found it comfortable to deem the capacities of those in the arts as fully cognitive – no less cognitive than the skills of mathematicians and scientists, as viewed by my fellow developmentalists.[9]

Gardner entered graduate school with an interest in creativity and cognition in the arts, a line of research for which there were no real mentors within the psychology department faculty. His opportunity to pursue this work came in 1967 when the philosopher Nelson Goodman formed Harvard Project Zero, a research group that was intended to strengthen arts education. Through the remainder of his graduate education to the present day, Project Zero has been at the centre of Gardner's intellectual life. It has 'been the site where my own ideas have developed and the intellectual community in which I have felt especially at home'.[10] Since 1971, when Goodman retired, Project Zero has been under the stewardship of Gardner and his long-time colleague, David Perkins. The organization has grown into one of the leading centres for educational research in the United States. During these years, Gardner has mentored scores of young researchers, and the organization has grown from examining cognition in the arts, to investigating learning, thinking, and creativity across the range of disciplines, age groups, and educational settings.

At Project Zero, Gardner initially pursued studies of children's development in the visual arts, music and figurative language. Although he also explored the creative processes of adult artists, he was especially concerned with children's development of symbol systems as they are used in the arts. He studied these topics empirically by adapting Piagetian methods to explore the development of children's reasoning with artistic symbol systems. During the 1970s and early 1980s, this line of research yielded some forty articles and book chapters. These addressed such issues as children's sensitivity to style in drawings,[11] their use of figurative language,[12] and the development of artistry.[13]

In an effort to understand how the brain processed different symbol systems, in 1969 Project Zero invited Norman Geschwind, an eminent neurologist, to speak about his work. Geschwind's studies of symbol use and breakdown in brain-damaged patients was 'riveting'.[14] Very shortly thereafter, Gardner began conducting empirical work in neuropsychology at the Boston Veterans' Administration Hospital. Over the next two decades, he published more than sixty articles and book chapters focused largely on symbol processing in individuals, oftentimes artists who have suffered brain injury.[15]

These dual lines of empirical research converged on a single compelling point. As Gardner wrote,

the daily opportunity to work with children and with brain-damaged adults impressed me with one brute fact of human nature: People have a wide range of capacities. A person's strength in one area of performance simply does not predict any comparable strengths in other areas.[16]

By the mid 1970s, Gardner began to construct a theory of human cognition that ran counter both to Piagetian theory, with its pre-eminent scientist, and to psychometric theory, with its keystone of general intelligence or 'g'. In Gardner's model, the full possibilities of human thinking and accomplishment might be explained. The opportunity to develop this theory was realized during the early 1980s, while Gardner was a leading member in the Project on Human Potential. This project was devised and funded by the Bernard van Leer Foundation 'to assess the state of scientific knowledge concerning human potential and its realization'[17] Gardner's product for the project was his groundbreaking book, *Frames of Mind*,[18] in which he spelled out his theory of multiple intelligences.

Gardner's theory, unlike those generated by traditional psychometric methods, was not a response to the implicit question: what are the cognitive abilities underlying a good IQ test score? Instead, MI was Gardner's response to the explicit question: what are the cognitive abilities that ultimately enable human beings to perform the range of adult roles (or 'endstates') found across cultures?

To get at this question, Gardner scoured a wide range of scientific and social science literatures for candidate intelligences. He maintained that candidate intelligences should meet most, if not all, of the eight criteria that he developed: an intelligence should be found in isolation among brain-damaged individuals. It should also be seen in relative isolation in prodigies, autistic savants or other exceptional populations. An intelligence ought to have a distinct developmental trajectory (for instance, the rate of development from infancy to adult expert is not identical for music, language, or interpersonal abilities). Gardner also claimed that an intelligence should be plausible from the perspective of evolutionary biology. That is, it would be needed for survival in human ancestors and evident in other mammals. In addition, an intelligence should be encodable in symbol systems. Two additional criteria are that an intelligence should be supported not only by psychometric tests but also by evidence from experimental psychological tasks. Finally, an intelligence should demonstrate a core set of processing operations, such as pitch detection in music, or syntax in language, which are stimulated by information relevant to that intelligence.

Using these criteria, Gardner ultimately identified eight relatively autonomous intelligences: linguistic, logical-mathematical, spatial, musical, bodily-kinesthetic, interpersonal, intrapersonal, and naturalist.[19] The latter enables human beings to recognize, categorize and draw upon features of the environment. Gardner has also noted that additional intelligences may be added if they meet most of his criteria. The number of intelligences is less important than that there is a multiplicity of them and that each human being has a unique mix (or 'profile') of strengths and weaknesses in the intelligences.

While academic psychology has remained lukewarm to the theory,[20] for educators, MI holds enormous appeal. The theory has been widely embraced by teachers throughout North America, South America and Australia, and in parts of Europe and Asia. It has been applied at all levels of education, from pre-school through adult education. It has been used across academic disciplines and in vocational education, and it has found a home in classrooms serving largely typical students as well as those serving the learning disabled or gifted.

There are several reasons why MI has taken hold in education. Among these are that the theory validates educators' everyday experience: students think and learn in many different ways. It also provides educators with a conceptual framework for organizing and reflecting on curriculum, assessment and pedagogical practices. In turn, this reflection has led many educators to develop new approaches that might better meet the needs of the range of learners in their classrooms.[21]

While the educational applications of Gardner's theory are widespread, the quality of these applications has ranged wildly. Because *Frames of Mind* did not spell out how to apply the theory, teachers, administrators and numerous independent consultants brought their own ideas to this problem. While some of these appear to enable children's development and understanding of the disciplines, many others simply require that every topic be addressed in seven or eight, oftentimes, superficial ways. The unevenness of the theory's application has led simultaneously to the theory's praise[22] and damnation.[23]

While Gardner recognized the variability in MI applications, he initially felt that it was beyond his sphere, as a theorist and psychologist, to right this situation. Instead, he focused on generating compelling new ideas in the areas of educational assessment,[24] the development of disciplinary understanding,[25] and creativity.[26] However, he began to take on the task of guiding educational applications of MI in his book, *The Unschooled Mind*,[27] and more explicitly in *Intelligence Reframed*,[28] and *The Disciplined Mind*.[29]

Each of these books underscores Gardner's belief that education's central mission should be the development of understanding. '[M]y educational vision should be clear. Deep understanding should be our central goal; we should strive to inculcate understanding of what, within a cultural context, is considered true or false, beautiful or unpalatable, good or evil.'[30] These themes 'motivate individuals to learn about and understand their world ...'.[31]

Gardner asserts that understanding is marked by performances in which students take knowledge gleaned in a particular setting and apply it to an unfamiliar problem or setting. For this to happen, educators must opt for depth over breadth. Students must have extended opportunities to work on a topic.[32] Gardner maintains that providing students with opportunities to represent and explore a given topic in many ways, in part by engaging a range of intelligences, fosters understanding. Recent research undertaken at Project Zero provides some evidence for this.[33]

Gardner's views about understanding stand at odds with the contemporary American trend to harness classroom instruction to broad, extensively detailed, and state-mandated curriculum frameworks. It is nevertheless a vision that is well-grounded in the traditions of Socrates, John Dewey and John Henry Cardinal Newman. It is also consistent with an empirically based understanding of cognition and with the reality that modern educational systems reside within increasingly multiethnic and technologically driven societies.

For at least a decade, Gardner has emphasized that educators must inculcate understanding in the disciplines, which he regards as among the key inventions of humankind. Yet, as crucial as disciplinary understanding is, it has become clear to Gardner that education must aim for something more than this. The 'task for the new millennium' is to 'figure out how intelligence and morality can work together to create a world in which a great variety of people will want to live. After all, a society led by "smart" people still might blow up itself or the rest of the world.'[34] In line with this task, in 1994, Gardner and his colleagues, Mihaly Csikszentmihalyi and William Damon, established the 'Good Work Project'. The ultimate goal of the project is to identify how individuals at the cutting-edge of their professions can produce work that is both exemplary, according to professional standards, and also contributes to the good of the wider society. By infusing the findings from this project into educational settings, it may be possible to enhance the disciplinary, as well as the humanitarian, performances of ensuing generations. It is a hope, and a research project, which Gardner plans to purse for many years to come.

Notes

1 Howard Gardner, *Intelligence Reframed*, New York: Basic Books, p.178, 1999.
2 Howard Gardner, *Frames of Mind: The Theory of Multiple Intelligences*, New York: Basic Books, 1983.
3 Howard Gardner, *To Open Minds: Chinese Clues to the Dilemma of Contemporary Education*, New York: Basic Books, p.22, 1989.
4 Ibid., p.23.
5 Ibid., p.47.
6 Ibid., p.56.
7 Jerome Bruner, *The Process of Education*, Cambridge, MA: Harvard University Press, 1960.
8 Gardner, *To Open Minds*, p.50.
9 Gardner, *Intelligence Reframed*, p.28.
10 Gardner, *To Open Minds*, p.65.
11 For example, Howard Gardner, 'Children's Sensitivity to Painting Styles', *Child Development*, 41, pp.813–21, 1970. Howard Gardner, 'The Development of Sensitivity to Artistic Styles', *Journal of Aesthetics and Art Criticism*, 29, pp.515–27, 1971. Howard Gardner, 'Style Sensitivity in Children', *Human Development*, 15, pp.325–38, 1972. Howard Gardner and Judith Gardner, 'Development Trends in Sensitivity to Painting Style and Subject Matter', *Studies in Art Education*, 12, pp.11–16, 1970. Howard Gardner and Judith Gardner, 'Development Trends in Sensitivity to Form and Subject Matter in Paintings', *Studies in Art Education*, 14, pp.52–6, 1973.
12 For example, Howard Gardner, 'Metaphors and Modalities: How Children Project Polar Adjectives onto Diverse Domains', *Child Development*, 45, pp.84–91, 1974. Howard Gardner, M. Kircher, M. Ellen Winner, David Perkins, 'Children's Metaphoric Productions and Preferences', *Journal of Child Language*, 2, pp.125–41, 1975; Howard Gardner, Ellen Winner, R. Bechhofer and Dennie Wolf, 'The Development of Figurative Language', in K. Nelson (ed.), *Children's Language*, New York: Gardner Press, pp.1–38, 1978.
13 For example, Howard Gardner, 'Unfolding or Teaching: on the Optimal Training of Artistic Skills', in E. Eisner (ed.), *The Arts, Human Development, and Education*, Berkeley, CA: McCutchan Publishing Company, pp.100–10, 1976; Howard Gardner, 'Entering the World of the Arts: The Child as Artist', *Journal of Communication*, Autumn, pp.146–56, 1979; Howard Gardner, Dennie Wolf and A. Smith, 'Artistic Symbols in Early Childhood', *New York Education Quarterly*, 6, pp.13–21, 1975; Dennie Wolf and Howard Gardner, 'Beyond

Playing or Polishing: The Development of Artistry', in J. Hausman (ed.), *The Arts and the Schools*, New York: McGraw-Hill, 1980.

14 Gardner, *To Open Minds*, p.83.

15 For example, Howard Gardner, 'Artistry Following Damage to the Human Brain', in A. Ellis (ed.), *Normality and Pathology in Cognitive Functions*, London: Academic Press, pp.299–323, 1982; Howard Gardner, J. Silverman, G. Denes, C. Semenze and A. Rosenstiel, 'Sensitivity to Musical Denotation and Connotation in Organic Patients', *Cortex*, 13, pp.22–256, 1977; Howard Gardner and Ellen Winner, 'Artistry and Aphasia', in M.T. Sarno (ed.), *Acquired Aphasia*, New York: Academic Press.

16 Gardner, *Intelligence Reframed*, p.30.

17 Gardner, *Frames of Mind*, paperback edition, New York: Basic Books, p.xix, 1985.

18 Gardner, *Frames of Mind*, New York: Basic Books, 1983.

19 Gardner, *Frames of Mind*, 1983; Howard Gardner, 'Are There Additional Intelligences? The Case for Naturalist, Spiritual, and Existential Intelligences', in J. Kane (ed.), *Education, Information, and Transformation*, Upper Saddle River, NJ: Prentice Hall, pp.111–31, 1999.

20 For example, Richard Herrnstein and Charles Murray, *The Bell Curve*, New York: Free Press, 1994; Sandra Scarr, 'An Author's Frame of Mind: Review of *Frames of Mind* by Howard Gardner', *New Ideas in Psychology* 3, 1, pp.95–100, 1985.

21 Mindy Kornhaber, 'Multiple Intelligences Theory in Practice', in J. Block *et al.* (eds), *Comprehensive School Improvement Programs*, Dubuque, IA: Kendall/ Hunt, 1999.

22 For example, Richard Knox, 'Brainchild', *Boston Globe Magazine*, 5 November, 1995, pp.22–3, 38–9, 41–2, 45–8. Elaine Woo, 'Teaching that Goes Beyond IQ', *Los Angeles Times*, 20 January 1995, pp.A1, A22.

23 James Collins, 'Seven Kinds of Smart', *Time Magazine*, 19 October 1998, pp.94–6; James Traub, 'Multiple Intelligence Disorder', *The New Republic*, October, pp.27, 77–83, 1998.

24 For example, Howard Gardner, 'Assessment in Context: The Alternative to Standardized Testing', in B.R. Gifford and M.C. O'Connor (eds), *Changing Assessments: Alternative Views of Aptitude, Achievement, and Instruction*, Boston, MA: Kluwer, pp.77–120, 1991. Mara Krechevsky and Howard Gardner, 'Approaching School Intelligently: An Infusion Approach', in Deanna Kuhn (ed.), *Developmental Perspectives on Teaching and Learning Thinking Skills*, Basel: S. Karger, pp.79–94, 1990; C. Wexler-Sherman, Howard Gardner and David Feldman, 'A Pluralistic View of Early Assessment: The Project Spectrum Approach', *Theory into Practice*, 27, pp.77–83, 1988.

25 For example, Howard Gardner and Veronica Boix-Mansilla, 'Teaching for Understanding Within and Across the Disciplines', *Educational Leadership*, 51, 5, pp.14–18, 1994; Howard Gardner and Veronica Boix-Mansilla, 'Teaching for Understanding in the Disciplines – and Beyond', *Teachers College Record*, 96, 2, pp.198–218, 1994; Howard Gardner, 'Educating for Understanding', *The American School Board Journal*, 180 7, pp.20–4, 1993.

26 Howard Gardner, *Creating Minds: An Anatomy of Creativity Seen Through the Lives of Freud, Einstein, Picasso, Stravinsky, Eliot, Graham, and Gandhi*, New York: Basic Books, 1993; Howard Gardner, 'How Extraordinary was Mozart?', in J.M. Morris, *On Mozart*, Washington, DC: Woodrow Wilson Center Press, 1994; Jin Li and Howard Gardner, 'How Domains Constrain Creativity: The Case of Traditional Chinese and Western Painting', *American Behavioral Scientist*, 37, 11, pp.94–101, 1993.

27 Howard Gardner, *The Unschooled Mind: How Children Think and How Schools Should Teach*, New York: Basic Books, 1991.

28 Gardner, *Intelligence Reframed*, 1999.

29 Gardner, *The Disciplined Mind*, 1999.
30 Gardner, *The Disciplined Mind*, p.186.
31 Ibid., p.24.
32 Gardner, *The Unschooled Mind*, 1991; Gardner, *The Disciplined Mind*, 1999.
33 Kornhaber, 'Multiple Intelligences Theory in Practice', 1999; Mindy Kornhaber, Edward Fierros and Shirley Veenema, *Multiple Intelligences: Best Ideas from Practice and Project Zero*, Needham, MA: Allyn & Bacon, forthcoming.
34 Gardner, *Intelligence Reframed*, p.4.

See also

In this book: Bruner, Piaget
In *Fifty Major Thinkers on Education*: Newman

Gardner's major writings

The Quest for Mind: Jean Piaget, Claude Lévi-Strauss, and the Structuralist Movement, New York: Knopf, 1973.
The Shattered Mind, New York: Knopf, 1975.
Artful Scribbles: The Significance of Children's Drawings, New York: Basic Books, 1980.
Art, Mind, and Brain: A Cognitive Approach to Creativity, New York: Basic Books, 1982.
Frames of Mind: The Theory of Multiple Intelligences, New York: Basic Books, 1983.
The Mind's New Science: A History of the Cognitive Revolution, New York: Basic Books, 1985.
To Open Minds: Chinese Clues to the Dilemma of Contemporary Education, New York: Basic Books, 1989.
The Unschooled Mind: How Children Think and How Schools Should Teach, New York: Basic Books, 1991.
Creating Minds: An Anatomy of Creativity Seen Through the Lives of Freud, Einstein, Picasso, Stravinsky, Eliot, Graham, and Gandhi, New York: Basic Books, 1993.
Leading Minds: An Anatomy of Leadership, New York: Basic Books, 1995.
Extraordinary Minds: Portraits of Exceptional Individuals and an Examination of our Extraordinariness, New York: Basic Books, 1997.
Intelligence Reframed: Multiple Intelligences for the 21st Century, New York: Basic Books, 1999.
The Disciplined Mind: What All Students Should Understand, New York: Simon and Schuster, 1999.

Further reading

'Harvard Project Zero', *Harvard Graduate School of Education Alumni Bulletin*, 39, 1, December, Cambridge, MA: Harvard University, 1994.

MINDY L. KORNHABER

HENRY GIROUX 1943–

> Radical pedagogy needs a vision – one that celebrates not what is
> but what could be, that looks beyond the immediate to the future
> and links struggle to a new set of human possibilities.[1]

Few academics in recent educational history have succeeded like Giroux in combining stunning, inspiring polemic with rigorous academic scholarship. His compelling arguments and dazzling language, Nietzschean in its aphoristic power, hold out the possibility for radical, critical pedagogy to further equality, democracy and humanity, which he sees as currently under threat across the world.

Henry Giroux received his doctorate from Carnegie-Mellon University in 1977, writing on curriculum theory, sociology and sociology of education. He taught at Boston University from 1977–83, and then at Miami University from 1983–92, being Professor of Education and Renowned Scholar in Residence. From 1992 he has been the Waterbury Chair Professor of Secondary Education at Penn State University.

There are several key focuses in his major works, for example: equality, democracy, cultural politics, critical pedagogy, teachers as transformative intellectuals, the promotion of human dignity and the reduction of oppression in various forms. It is notable that Giroux not only returns to these focuses repeatedly throughout his work, but that he expands the field of their embrace over time, moving to a recognition of the connectedness between education and multiple other sites of cultural production and struggle. For Giroux, education has to break beyond the confines of schooling; that immediately inserts education into the public sphere and renders it intensely and inescapably political.

Giroux's early work draws heavily on the Frankfurt School, particularly Horkheimer, Adorno, Marcuse and Habermas. He critiques the dominance of the controlling and dehumanizing mentality of instrumental reason for its perpetuation of inequality in society. He argues that education is more than a site simply of cultural reproduction[2] which serves to empower the already-empowered in society and to maintain the marginalization of the disempowered. Rather, he suggests, schools should be sites of resistance, contestation, agency, cultural struggle, challenge to a cultural hegemony which stigmatizes, marginalizes, oppresses and excludes significant portions of the population. He argues against reproduction theorists such as Bowles and Gintis and Bourdieu,[2] whom he criticizes for their mechanistic views of social reproduction through education and their neglect of the possibility for intervening in, or breaking the cycle of, reproduction. He sees in these authors an overdetermination of structure at the expense of an adequate account of human agency.

Schools, in Giroux's view, should be sites of cultural production and transformation rather than reproduction; they should be sites of empowerment and emancipation of individuals and groups within a just society, enabling individual and collective autonomy to be promoted in participatory democracies that embrace a diversity and plurality of cultures and social groups. This is a view of democracy as a celebration of difference and diversity rather than as serving the agenda of an élite, powerful minority or ideology.[3] Indeed he argues that democracy involves the operation of ideology critique, and in this respect he suggests that democracy can be equated with critical democracy. Critical participatory democracy is designed to bring genuine equality to redress the 'bad times' that he witnesses everywhere – where poverty, despair, hopelessness, joblessness, stigmatization, the waste of generations of young, mediocrity in mass culture, greed, commodification, chauvinism, sexism, racism, materialism, dehumanization, militaristic ideologies of nationalism, and urban colonialism abound.[4]

Rather than being simply the lamenting Jeremiah for which Eagleton[5] criticizes several members of the Frankfurt School, Giroux is at pains to argue for the need to combine a 'language of critique' with a 'language of possibility', i.e. indicating how the 'chinks in the armour'[1]) of schools as sites of social reproduction might be penetrated and developed. Ideology critique of the illegitimate exercise of power, echoing Habermas, combines with an agenda for reform. In this enterprise Giroux's advocacy of critical pedagogy/radical pedagogy as a form of cultural politics has established his reputation worldwide. Critical pedagogy, for Giroux, is not simply a matter of classroom methodology,[6] but, as with the work of Freire, goes much wider than schools and is part of the development of an emancipated citizenry.[7] This, in turn, replaces systemic inequality with empowered students and communities.

For Giroux[8] the development of emancipatory citizenship in and through education involves: (1) a rejection of the ahistorical, transcendent notions of truth and authority, as the struggle for recognition, rights and 'voice' is here and now and has to engage the lived experiences of oppression; (2) a politicization of interpersonal relations in order to increase solidarity in a 'radical pluralism'; (3) a casting of citizenship in a language of both critique and possibility; (4) a redefinition of schools as public spheres where engagement and democracy can be cultivated in a struggle for a 'radical democratic society'. The achievement of a critical democracy engages a struggle for meaning, voice, rights, freedoms and emancipation, which, resonating with Habermas' 'ideal speech situation', engages three factors:[8] (1) the acceptance of the rights of all groups to participate in educational discourse; (2) the need to link pedagogical practices in schools with the wider society (e.g. encouraging democratic behaviour in schools as a preparation for democratic behaviour in society); (3) the need for educators to link to other progressive social groups outside school in order to create alliances and solidarity.

For Giroux, then, the task is to make the pedagogical more political and the political more pedagogical.[1] Radical pedagogy, for Giroux, is not a set of techniques but a questioning of received assumptions about the nature, content and purpose of schooling.[6] In this sense it is a form of 'cultural politics' as it questions whose cultures are represented in education and how legitimate this might be. It is interdisciplinary, questioning the fundamental categories and status of disciplines, and it has a deliberate purpose of making society more democratic, which moves from an historical and ideological critique of society and schooling *as they are* (e.g. schools in the service of economic efficiency) towards a view of schools and society *as they ought to be* (e.g. schools problematizing ways of life and developing individual autonomy within egalitarian societies). That this owes its pedigree to Marxism is recognized by Giroux.[9] Schools, curricula and pedagogical relations are contestable, they are ideologically saturated, frequently serving the existing (asymmetrical) power and relations structures in society; for Giroux, this needs to be exposed and held up to the searchlight of legitimacy.

Educators and students, Giroux suggests, need to interrogate whose curricula are represented and under-represented in schools, in whose interests these are operating, what the effects of this operation of interests are in society, and how legitimate are these curricula and pedagogic forms in schools.[7] Giroux's powerful advocacy of the rights of disempowered and oppressed groups for recognition in and through education includes extended intellectual engagement with feminism, anti-sexism, anti-racism and anti-exploitation. In this respect he does not fight shy of withering critiques of contemporary American society and educational policies which, as evidenced in the rising tide of new conservatism, he sees as a disturbing manifestation of colonialism on home ground.

Giroux[10] articulates several principles for a critical pedagogy:

- Attention needs to be paid to pedagogy as much as to traditional scholarship, (re)constructing schools as democratic public spheres.
- Ethics are of central concern in critical pedagogy, questioning educative practices that perpetuate inequality, exploitation and human suffering.
- The political implications of the celebration of difference in democratic societies must be addressed.
- A language that embraces several versions of solidarity and politics needs to be developed.
- There is no single script or grand narrative, but, rather, several scripts, several curricula, several versions of education which need to be critically interrogated, just as there are several versions and areas of exploitation and oppression in society which mediate each other.
- Cultural representations in curricula have to be regarded as discourses of power and asymmetrical relations of power.
- The curriculum is a 'cultural script' whose messages should be susceptible to critique.
- The politics of voice require an affirmation of diversity and of the rights of oppressed groups for recognition in education.

In developing a critical pedagogy, which links educational practice with the wider society, teachers and educators must act as 'transformative intellectuals'.[11] These are intellectuals who render teaching and learning political activities. Schools, for Giroux, are sites of struggle for meaning and power. Transformative intellectuals raise students' awareness of these contested issues, treating students as critical agents, questioning how – and whose – knowledge is produced and distributed in schools and in whose interests this is operating. The intention is to make students more ideologically critical with a view to their emancipation. Teachers work on, and with, the experiences that students bring to the educational encounter and enable students to interrogate and critique these experiences for their ideological messages. The intention here is to expose oppression, inequality and the construction of social identities within asymmetrical relations of power of different groups in society, with a view to transforming students' ways of looking at their lives, life situations and life chances, so that they experience empowerment and emancipation as members of diverse cultures and communities. They develop their 'voice' within participatory democracies.

Trend[12] suggests that Giroux's particular potency in his writing about education is his moral commitment to democratic practices that are inclusive, that engage all citizens in their own governance, however different the cultural experiences or backgrounds of participants might be. Giroux speaks to all different groups; change concerns the empowered and the disempowered.

The notion of 'difference' in cultural and social locations of groups and within participatory democracies is neither ideologically neutral nor innocent; it is shot through with differences of power, privileging certain discourses and silencing others. If equality in society is to be achieved then the operation of power (within education, curricula and society) needs to be exposed and transformed. This finds expression in Giroux's notion of 'border pedagogy',[6] where teachers and students interrogate and cross traditional boundaries (borders) of power, epistemology, decision-making, cultural and social representation in curricula, where existing curricular borders that are 'forged in domination' are both challenged and redefined. In border pedagogy issues of inequality, power, silencing, oppression and suffering in different institutional structures need to be challenged. Giroux,[6] for example, argues that, though whites might have a heavy political and cultural investment in ignoring differences, this masks the underlying asymmetrical relations of power, where not to be white, or male, or middle class is to be denied access to power or a voice. Indeed Giroux himself writes[13] that the opposite of equality is inequality, not simply difference.

Giroux[6] recognizes that there are several spheres of cultural production in which education must operate. There are several fractions of society to whom 'difference' and 'border pedagogy' refer, and that there is no single grand narrative in accounting for the social construction of identity and power. In this respect his later work[6] marks a distinct movement towards postmodernism and away from his earlier roots in the modernistic critical theory of the Frankfurt School. Indeed he finds in postmodernism a way of 'reclaiming power and identity for subordinate groups', it breaks the power of Eurocentric rationality,[6] whereas modernist culture, for him, negates the possibility of providing an adequate account of diversity, voice and the possibility for 'border crossings' (e.g. breaking down existing boundaries of curricula and curricular decision-making which reinforce power structures in society). Modernism's reliance on rationality allows inequality to be perpetuated; for Giroux rationality itself is not free of ideology, and value-neutrality is chimerical. One of Giroux's singular achievements is to maintain an ethical discourse that is combined with ideology critique and to locate these in a postmodernist context which avoids the frequently raised problem of relativism in postmodernism.

Giroux's alliance with postmodernism is coupled with a broadening of his embrace or field of focus. He suggests that, while schooling, to which he had largely confined himself in his earlier work, is a crucial site for developing critical citizenship, the task of education necessarily moves beyond the sole sphere of schooling.[6] To reduce education to schooling is too insular, and circumscribes the possibility of developing critical pedagogy as cultural politics within several spheres of cultural production and reproduction outside schools. Hence his sympathy to postmodernism in the watershed book of 1992 recognizes the need to adopt a multiplicity of paradigms and to operate in a variety of spheres simultaneously (and postmodernism squeezes time into a continual present[14]), if constructive alliances within and beyond education are to be formed to tackle the complexity of social life and the social theory that accompanies this.

In light of his espousal of some tenets of postmodernism, it is perhaps unsurprising that more recently one can see in his writings the enlargement of critical cultural pedagogy beyond simply that which takes place in school, to include greater attention to cultural and media issues, including popular culture and the impact of new technologies on society and education.[15] This was signalled in his earlier works of 1989 and 1992, where extended discussion is offered of particular films and artists.

Whether his move away from modernism and towards postmodernism marks an experimental departure from his intellectual roots and of the wholesale possibility for the emancipation of subordinate groups, or whether it is a more realistic recognition of the multiple and complex cultural sites in which the struggle for emancipation through education must occur, is, perhaps, an open question. Further, whether Giroux's work turns out only to be high on the 'feel good' factor, whose high-sounding prose and ideas put fire into one's belly, but whose contribution to daily practice is limited, being merely generalized and visionary (one remarks Miedama's and Wardekker's suggestion[16] that critical pedagogy was a stillborn child), remains to be seen. Nonetheless his work holds out the hope of a better life for us all. His work is profoundly humanitarian; that is as unsettling as it is optimistic. Education needs its visionaries.

Notes

1 Giroux, *Theory and Resistance in Education*, p.242.
2 Giroux, *Ideology, Culture and the Process of Schooling* and *Theory and Resistance in Education*.
3 Giroux, *Border Crossings*, p.11.
4 Giroux, *Schooling for Democracy*, p. 26; *Border Crossings*, p.4.
5 Eagleton, *Ideology*.
6 Giroux, *Border Crossings*.
7 Giroux, *Schooling for Democracy*.
8 Giroux, *Schooling for Democracy*, pp.28–33.
9 Giroux, *Schooling for Democracy*, p.13.
10 Giroux, *Border Crossings*, pp.73–82.
11 Giroux and Aronowitz, *Education Under Siege*; Giroux, *Schooling for Democracy*.
12 Trend's interview with Giroux is reported in Giroux, *Border Crossings*, p.149.
13 Giroux, *Border Crossings*, p.69.
14 Jameson, *Postmodernism, or the Cultural Logic of Late Capitalism*.
15 For example, Giroux, *Disturbing Pleasures, Fugitive Cultures, Channel Surfing* and *The Mouse that Roared*.
16 Miedama and Wardekker, 'Emergent Identity versus Consistent Identity', p.68.

See also

In this book: Apple, Freire, Habermas, Greene

Giroux's major writings

Ideology, Culture and the Process of Schooling, London: Falmer Press, 1981.
Theory and Resistance in Education, London: Heinemann, 1983.
Giroux, H. and Aronowitz, S., *Education Under Siege: The Conservative, Liberal and Radical Debate over Schooling*, London, Routledge & Kegan Paul, 1986.
Teachers as Intellectuals: Toward a Critical Pedagogy of Learning, Granby, MA: Bergin and Garvey, 1988.
Schooling for Democracy: Critical Pedagogy in the Modern Age, London: Routledge, 1989.
Schooling and the Struggle for Public Life, Granby, MA: Bergin and Garvey, 1989.
Giroux, H. and McLaren, P., *Critical Pedagogy, the State, and the Struggle for Culture*, New York: State University of New York Press, 1989.
Giroux, H., *Postmodernism, Feminism, and Cultural Politics*, New York: State University of New York Press, 1991.
Border Crossings: Cultural Workers and the Politics of Education, London: Routledge, 1992.
Disturbing Pleasures: Learning Popular Culture, London: Routledge, 1994.
Fugitive Cultures: Violence, Race and Youth, London: Routledge, 1996.
Channel Surfing: Race Talk and the Destruction of American Youth, Basingstoke: Macmillan, 1997.
The Mouse that Roared: Disney and the End of Innocence, Lanham, MD: Rowman and Littlefield, 1999.

Further reading

Eagleton, T., *Ideology*, London: Verso, 1991.
Freire, P., *Pedagogy of the Oppressed*, Harmondsworth: Penguin, 1972.
Jameson, F., *Postmodernism, or the Cultural Logic of Late Capitalism*, London: Verso, 1991.
Leistyna, P., Woodrum, A. and Sherblom, S.A. (eds), *Breaking Free*, Cambridge, MA: Harvard Educational Review.
Miedama, S. and Wardekker, W.L., 'Emergent Identity versus Consistent Identity: Possibilities for a Postmodern Repoliticization of Critical Pedagogy', in T. Popkewitz and L. Fendler (eds), *Critical Theories in Education: Changing Terrains of Knowledge and Politics*, London: Routledge, pp.67–83, 1999.

KEITH MORRISON

LINDA DARLING-HAMMOND 1951–

> This changed mission for education requires a new model for school reform, one in which policy makers shift their efforts from *designing controls* ... to *developing the capacity* for schools and teachers to be responsible for student learning and responsive to student and community needs, interests, and concerns.[1]

As a consequence of structural inequalities in access to knowledge

and resources, students from racial and ethnic 'minority' groups
... face persistent and profound barriers to educational
opportunities. Serious policy attention to these ongoing, systematic inequalities is critical for improving educational quality and
outcomes.[2]

Linda Darling-Hammond, Charles E. Ducommun Professor of Education
at Stanford University School of Education and Executive Director of the
National Commission on Teaching and America's Future is without a doubt
the most influential educational policy-maker and educational reformer in
the United States today. Her work has influenced federal legislation, state
policies, local school districts and teachers' practice, turning their attention
to the quality of teaching, coupled with serious attention to issues of equity.
She has not only become the most visible and important educational policy-
maker in the United States, but also its most important policy researcher
and activist. How these two seemingly opposite positions – policy-maker
and research/activist find themselves in one woman is, in fact, the story of
her fame and influence. But how did this happen? How were these ideas
learned and shaped in a woman so young, yet so powerfully influential in the
politics and practices of public schooling in the United States. What has
shaped her vision and the body of work that she has written in so short a
time?

To best understand her influence on public policy and practice in
education, it is important to describe her social, political and intellectual
development. As a child, the Darling family moved often so that their
children could go to better schools. Growing up in the late 1950s and 1960s
in Cleveland, Ohio, schools were encouraged to provide more student
choice, more project work, less rote learning and more active involvement of
students. The Curriculum Reform Movement of the 1960s called for
educators to pay deeper attention to the curriculum and to find ways for
students to experience what it meant to be a historian, a scientist, etc. It was
the era of 'the new math' and numerous curricular reforms attempting to
provide broader experiences for students to engage with curricular content.
As an outstanding student, Darling was the recipient of a good education
having had many thoughtful, competent teachers. Coming from a working-
class family and community where few of her friends went to college, a
guidance counsellor encouraged her to apply to Yale University as they were
accepting women and substantial numbers of 'minorities' and public school
students for the first time in their history. She was accepted and went to Yale
from 1969–73 as a member of the first class to accept women.

This was a turbulent time in the United States. There were anti-Vietnam
rallies, student demonstrations on many university campuses, calls for
greater attention to students, and less to the bureaucratizing of education.
This era was only preparation for the Civil Rights movement that was to
follow in its wake. Yale, the context of the times, and the character of the
student body was a heady education for the young Linda Darling. The
contrasts between many of the students who had gone to private schools and
those from public schools were evident. Private school males who were
wealthy, privileged and upper class were in stark contrast to female,
'minority' students who had attended public schools in less affluent areas.

Differences of race, class and access to knowledge were readily evident at Yale.

Recognizing, by her own experience, how life chances could be decided by having access to quality education and schooling, she became active in the struggles that were, by then, ubiquitous on campus. The theme, equal access to quality education for all students was to become one of the areas of her work and subsequent writing. As a student she worked hard and eventually graduated from Yale as a magna cum laude.

But it didn't end there. Having developed an interest in public school teaching, she got an alternate certificate for teaching during the summer following graduation and became a student teacher in Camden, New Jersey, a large urban, economically depressed community. Her school, like many others in urban areas, had few materials or books for students or their teachers. She was told to teach the library classification system of books by her supervisor. But observing that many of her students could neither read nor write, she brought in books by authors that would appeal to her high-school students, related the themes of the books to the students' experiences and connected to the students as adolescents struggling to understand the world and their place in it. As a teacher she was learning that if you didn't follow the rules you were insubordinate, but as a sensitive adult she was formulating a view of what it meant to be a professional who should be responsible and responsive to their clients.

Later, in the Philadelphia area, she taught students in the vocational education track and saw firsthand how segregation and tracking within the bureaucratic context of the school assured that learning for low tracked students was rarely deep – not only because of the curriculum – but because new inexperienced teachers most often got the students who needed the most help. Her own lack of experience in knowing how to teach students to read helped her develop an awareness that the *system* itself was haphazard and that the profession was designed to gain compliance from teachers precisely because there was so little knowledge available to them. Compliance rather than competence was the norm. Policies were clearly beyond the control of teachers. Feeling passionate about the wrongs of the situation and wanting to know more she entered a doctoral programme.

As a graduate student at Temple University with a major in Urban Education, Darling found a mentor in Professor Bernard Watson. In one interview he admitted her to the programme, gave her a scholarship and hired her as a research assistant. Her dissertation, for which she won an award, was an economic analysis of low income students and the degree of inequality in spending. Portions of it led to a piece of model legislation for the State of Pennsylvania. From her mentor she learned and soon internalized the idea that one could be empirical, rigorous and passionate all at the same time. As he enthusiastically stated 'her passion and commitment to teaching and her capacity to combine active engagement with the community and do stunning work is unparalleled in our field'.[3]

After working on a School Finance Reform Project for the National Urban Coalition, Darling-Hammond (now married) became a social scientist and policy researcher at the Rand Corporation, a well-known prestigious think tank. It was here through the Center for the Study of Teaching and Policy, which her colleague Arthur Wise created and led, that she began to do research, create policy and develop an alternative way of thinking about teaching. During her ten years working with Arthur Wise, she studied and wrote about teacher supply and demand, the recruitment of teachers, teacher licensing, effective teacher evaluation practices, and scores of other articles and monographs. Most importantly, she was building a corpus of work that was helping shape a different view of teacher policy – one built on the professionalization rather than the bureaucratization of teaching.

In 1989 Darling-Hammond went to Teachers College, Columbia University long known for its vision of a democratic education for students. It was here that she was to be involved in thinking about teaching and schooling – from experienced teachers who were her students, her colleagues at Teachers College and her connections to a reform oriented and activist group of educators in New York City. These years were to afford Darling-Hammond the opportunity to think, learn from and study with innovative educators who were creating small schools in New York City (see for example, Darling-Hammond and Jacqueline Ancess, 1994).[4] These schools were living examples of how to provide good education for all students in one of the most diverse and complex environments in the world.[5]

With Ann Lieberman, she created the National Center for Restructuring Education, Schools and Teaching (NCREST) at Teachers College. The organization was founded to create and understand new structures for policy development and professional development by linking together school reformers and reform organizations, documenting promising new practices and disseminating this knowledge. In the process new forms of documentation were created. The publications she wrote with her colleagues helped clarify a new view of school reform and the policies needed to support them.[6] At the same time she was connecting these local examples of professional practice to state policies that would support reformed local practice through her work as Chair of the New York State Curriculum and Assessment Council where she helped facilitate a way to think about professional rather than bureaucratic accountability. The experiences with state policy-making bodies, coupled with Darling-Hammond's immersion with small, progressive schools in New York City, her involvement in the Teachers College community and the innovative NCREST, gave her experience in, and opportunities for, thinking about the need for a strong professional infrastructure that could join teacher training, ongoing professional development in collegial settings and a system of professional accountability. The potential influence of building such a professional system was to be made possible by an invitation from the Rockefeller Foundation to create a bi-partisan Commission that would join together government, business, legislators, community, education leaders and teachers to focus on the future of teaching in the United States.

Having now produced literally scores of articles, chapters and mono-graphs where she was teaching not only her own students at Teachers College, but the public and its policy-makers about the need to create policies that support new more professional practices, Darling-Hammond directed a National Commission on Teaching and America's Future, chaired by Governor James Hunt of North Carolina and including political, business, community and education leaders from across the country. Within two years she produced a report (signed by the various representative constituencies) that was to give the country a blueprint for transforming how teachers and principals are prepared, recruited, selected and inducted, and how schools support, assess and reward their work. The report was an immediate success, capturing the inchoate yearnings of many policy-makers and practitioners for a synthesis of not only what is problematic in schools, but data and examples of what might solve these problems. Its five seemingly simple recommendations have continued to capture the attention of the education community six years later. They are:

- Get serious about standards, for both students and teachers.
- Reinvent teacher preparation and professional development.
- Fix teacher recruitment and put qualified teachers in every classroom.
- Encourage and reward teacher knowledge and skill.
- Create schools that are organized for student and teacher success.

The report has stimulated dozens of pieces of federal and state legislation, a wide array of local initiatives to improve teaching, at least two federally funded research and development initiatives and well over 1500 articles both here and abroad. At least eighteen states and nine urban school districts are working as partners with the support of the Commission and the participation of a broad constituency (including governors, state departments of education, legislative leaders and educators), to implement the ideas contained within the Commission's report.

The Commission Report was printed in 1996. In 1997, her book *The Right to Learn* was published. Whereas the Commission Report described the policy initiatives that needed to be put in place to provide quality teachers for every child, the book provided the research, practice, policies and reasons for building democratic schools. The book had been in the making for ten years and provided the needed knowledge to create 'learner and learning-centered schools'. Both these publications show the powerful effects of Darling-Hammond's reach which continues to influence a broad audience including the public, policy-makers, the research community and educators in schools both in the United States and abroad. In providing leadership for educators, researchers and policy-makers, Darling-Hammond has truly been a pioneer, a pioneer with a vision of schools and teachers who participate in the building of democratic communities inhabiting a more just and equitable society.

Her ability to apply the knowledge of the academy to the fundamental programmes of school reform through research and writing, her leadership and tireless work in helping create policies that support practices that will enable all students to succeed, make her, as the President of Claremont College said in awarding her one of her five honorary degrees, a model of the American Scholar for the twenty-first century.

Notes

1 Linda Darling-Hammond, 'Reframing the School Reform Agenda: Developing the Capacity for School Transformation', *Phi Delta Kappan*, June, p.754, 1993.
2 Linda Darling-Hammond, 'New Standards, Old Inequalities: The Current

LINDA DARLING-HAMMOND

Challenge for African-American Education', in L.A. Daniels (ed.), *The State of Black America*, New York: National Urban League, pp.109–71, 1998.
3 From an interview with Bernard Watson, March, 1996.
4 See for example, *Graduation by Portfolio at Central Park East Secondary School*, with Jackqueline A. Ancess, New York: National Center for Restructuring Education, Schools and Teaching, Teachers College, Columbia University, 1994; and *Authentic Teaching, Learning, and Assessment with New English Learners at International High School*, with Jacqueline A. Ancess, New York: National Center for Restructuring Education, Schools and Teaching, Teachers College, Columbia University, 1994.
5 See for example, Ann Lieberman, *Visit to a Small School (Trying to do Big Things)*, New York: National Center for Restructuring Education, Schools and Teaching, Teachers College, Columbia University, 1996.
6 See for example, 'Reframing the School Reform Agenda: Developing Capacity for School Transformation', *Phi Delta Kappan*, 74, 10, June, pp.753–61, 1993; 'Policy for Restructuring', in A. Lieberman (ed.), *The Work of Restructuring Schools: Building from the Ground Up*, New York: Teachers College Press, pp.157–75, 1995; 'Policies that Support Professional Development in an Era of Reform', with Milbrey W. McLaughlin, in Milbrey W. McLaughlin and Ida Oberman (eds), *Teacher Learning: New Policies, New Practices*, New York: Teachers College Press, pp.202–35, 1996.

Darling-Hammond's major writings

Darling-Hammond is a prolific writer having produced over 200 articles, monographs, chapters and journal articles to date. She has published widely in policy and research journals as well as practitioner magazines. She is also author or editor of eight books.
Beyond the Commission Reports: The Coming Crisis in Teaching, Santa Monica: CA: RAND Corporation, 1984.
What Matters Most: Teaching for America's Future, New York: National Commission on Teaching and America's Future, Teachers College, Columbia University, September, 1996.
The Right to Learn, San Francisco, CA: Jossey-Bass, Inc, 1997.
'New Standards, Old Inequalities: The Current Challenge for African-American Education', in L.A. Daniels (ed.), *The State of Black America*, New York: National Urban League, pp.109–71, 1998.

Further reading

Lieberman, A. (ed.), *The Work of Restructuring Schools: Building from the Ground Up*, New York: Teachers College Press, 1995.
McLaughlin, M.W., 'Learning from Experience: Lessons from Policy Implementation', *Educational Evaluation and Policy Analysis*, 9, 2, pp.171–8, 1987.
Meier, D., *The Power of their Ideas: Lessons from America from a Small School in Harlem*, Boston, MA: Beacon Press, 1987.

ANN LIEBERMAN

290